The Big Outside

Dave Foreman
and
Howie Wolke

Foreword by
Michael Frome

Cartography by Helen Wilson
Cover by Charles Withuhn

A NED LUDD BOOK
TUCSON, ARIZONA
1989

Published by Ned Ludd Books
PO Box 5141
Tucson, AZ 85703
Printed by Ed's Printing, Chico, California
Cover and Chapter Headings by Charles Withuhn
  and Cathy Seymoure of Signs & Graphic Designs
  Chico, California

Printed on recycled paper

ISBN 0-933285-04-3

Dedicated to
Edward Abbey 1927-1989

Perhaps only Henry David Thoreau, John Muir, Aldo Leopold and Rachel Carson have inspired lovers of "wild things and sunsets" as much as has Cactus Ed Abbey. Author of **Desert Solitaire, The Monkey Wrench Gang, The Fool's Progress,** and many other works of fiction and essays, Edward Abbey was the preeminent interpreter of wilderness to a generation of Americans, and gave the inspiration for countless heroic acts in defense of the wild.

It is with honor and with deep appreciation to Ed that we dedicate **The Big Outside** to his memory, with thanks for his friendship, inspiration and support.

His death as we went to press with this book came as a staggering loss, as though the last Redwood had been felled or the Grand Canyon dammed. We can not replace such a man, but it is our duty to do our damnedest to carry on his fight. Rest easy in the desert, Ed, we will piss on the bastards' graves.

Table of Contents

Foreword

In the beginning, when the planet was new and fresh, all of it was wilderness. It was Earth National Park. God in His wisdom, or Her wisdom, or in the wisdom of the Dolphin-God, or of many many gods in sky, rocks, trees, and water, did not call it an ecosystem, and didn't even know the word. There was no need to. All of that came later. God, as mother of life, simply set evolution in motion and watched the emergence and development of different kinds of creatures and loved them all.

The point is that the Wilderness Act of 1964 did not "create" wilderness, any more than the Yellowstone Act of 1872, or the National Park Organic Act of 1916, "created" parks. Those laws are mere human contrivances, definitions establishing boundaries -- political boundaries influenced by the goals of an economic system -- where the earth itself knows no such boundaries because it operates on a different and much older system.

Thus Congressional action to include this area or that one in the National Wilderness Preservation System doesn't really add to our storehouse of wild nature preserved. To the contrary, it *subtracts* from it. I learned this particular lesson during the four years I spent in Idaho, a state with more wilderness, classified and unclassified, than any other state outside of Alaska. The Idaho national forests in the late 1980s, the time of this writing, embrace nine-plus million acres of roadless land -- that is, *de facto* wilderness, protected as such until Congress or the forest planning process determines otherwise. If the proposal of Senator James McClure and Governor Cecil Andrus for about 1.6 million acres of wilderness were accepted, the remaining 7.4 million acres would then be open to road construction, logging, and other forms of development and disturbance. If conservation groups united behind a proposal of four million acres of wilderness and were successful, another five million would still be lost.

Humankind plainly has been chip-chip-chipping away at Earth National Park, devouring the goodies. "Places of scenic beauty do not increase," observed Lord Bryce many years ago while serving as the ambassador of Great Britain to the United

States, "but on the contrary are in danger of being reduced in number and diminished in quantity." God, alas, isn't making any more of it.

This wonderful and important book by Dave Foreman and Howie Wolke challenges human conscience and courage to rescue the few remaining fragments of original America while there is still a chance to do so. Every word between its covers counts toward that end. Dave and Howie tell where wilderness is located, where and how to rescue each and every bit of it. If I were to choose a single sentence to summarize the spirit of the book it would be this one near the opening: "There is not enough wilderness left to compromise any further."

Let us not compromise any further, not out on the land, nor in our own hearts and minds. Yes, national parks and wilderness in the national forests appear to be extensive, but all the units have been very carefully selected, not to insure protection of the choicest, most inspiring, but to be sure that anything with commercial potential is *not* set aside. Rock and ice are abundant, but very little of great forests, and even less of our wildlife heritage.

Let us not settle for any less, but rather set our sights on higher goals. I think of the redwoods to make the point. Of two million acres of these ancients that clothed the California north coast only one century ago, a small fraction has been saved, and that only after struggle, sacrifice, and bitter tears. The national park is a meagre representation. 106,000 acres, including the 1978 expansion area of 48,000 acres, mostly cutover lands -- with 200 miles of logging roads, 3,000 miles of skid trails, and thousands upon thousands of burnt stumps of what once were magnificent redwood trees.

In ten centuries another forest of giants may grace the north coast of California. I pray that civilization will endure that long. But none of us will be around the see the rebirth and bloom. For our own time, let us vow that no more standing redwoods be cut, not on public or private land. No more big trees anywhere. Leave them be. They are more meaningful as trees than as paper, pulp, or plywood. Let us learn to live within our means, rediscovering the essentials of life, so that trees and other life-forms may live, too.

Dave Foreman and Howie Wolke are blessed with the clear vision. I respect and admire Dave and Howie as models of individual empowerment. Accepting self-responsibility, as they have done, brings with it power and clarity of purpose. In the most modest but determined of ways, they call for missionaries like themselves to go forth among the people with glad tidings: We can have a better world and each of us can make the difference.

I see wilderness, the Big Outside, as sanctuary of the spirit, the heart of a moral world governed by peace and love. Thank you, Dave and Howie, for the valuable descriptive inventory that points the way.

Michael Frome
Bellingham, WA
November, 1988

THE BIG OUTSIDE

The universe of the wilderness is disappearing like a snowbank on a south-facing slope on a warm June day
Robert Marshall

This book is a descriptive inventory of the remaining large roadless areas in the United States outside of Alaska and Hawaii. Every roadless area of 100,000 acres or larger in the Western states or 50,000 acres or larger in the Eastern states is listed and described, regardless of land ownership or administrative agency. It is as objective an inventory of the Big Outside as we, the authors, are capable of compiling.

It is also an argument for the idea of Big Wilderness, for the notion that size is an important criterion for nature preserves. In other words, while protecting all remaining wildlands is important, it is absolutely crucial that we protect all remaining large tracts of wild country. We hope that by identifying the big areas that remain in an essentially roadless and undeveloped condition, we will be able to focus the attention of preservationists on them. The areas listed in this book are the most important wild areas in the United States (outside of Alaska and Hawaii). Conservation groups, activists and conservation biologists should emphasize these areas and defend them to the best of their abilities. In that sense this book is a call to arms and a guidebook for action. There is a surprising number of large roadless areas left in many parts of the country, but these areas compose a tiny fraction of the total acreage of the United States. (See *Figure 1.*) They represent the remaining natural heritage of temperate North America and are the reservoirs of native diversity and ecological integrity in the United States.

This book is also a sad, lingering look at the vanishing American Wilderness. Many of these areas are under imminent threat of destruction from roading, logging, mining, grazing and

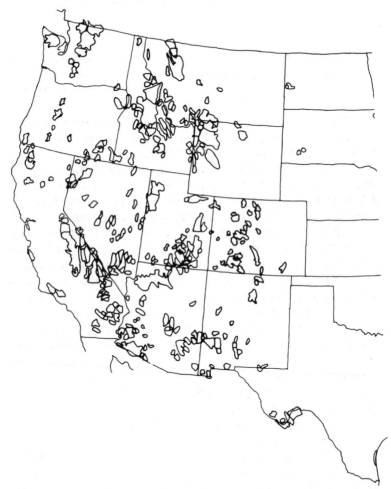

Figure 1   The largest remaining roadless areas in the United States. Every roadless area over 100,000 acres in the West and 50,000 acres in the East is shown. *Map by Dave Foreman.*

other abuses. In Chapter 3 we discuss the threats to wilderness in general, and in the inventory section of the book (Chapters 4 - 18) we tally the specific threats to each of the big roadless areas.

In the 1920s, Will Dilg, founder of the Izaak Walton league, wrote:

I am weary of civilization's madness and I yearn for the harmonious gladness of the woods and of the streams. I am tired of your piles of buildings and I ache from your iron streets. I feel jailed in your greatest cities and I long for the unharnessed freedom of the big outside.

The Big Outside is most essentially an expression of our agreement with Dilg and of our absolute, fanatical love for wilderness. We hope it will serve as a box of ammunition in the age-old struggle to defend the wild against those who "know the price of everything and the value of nothing."

It is important, however, to understand that this book is *not* a proposal. The areas and acreages listed do not constitute Wilderness proposals from us, from Earth First! or from any other group. We discuss proposals for preservation, yes, but the roadless areas inventoried herein make up just that — an inventory. This is a methodically researched account of what, by our definition, is roadless. In nearly every case we would argue for the preservation of larger areas than those listed here. Roads should be closed, vehicles banned, clearcuts rehabilitated, rivers freed of dams, cattle and sheep removed, extirpated wildlife reintroduced and *ecological wilderness* restored to larger areas. This inventory of existing large roadless areas forms the basis for visionary wilderness rehabilitation proposals which will be the subject of a future book. But before we can preserve what remains and restore what has been lost, we need a basic inventory of the large areas that retain a fundamental wildness.

During the mid-1930s, Robert Marshall, legendary hiker, Alaska explorer and founder of The Wilderness Society, conducted a personal inventory of the largest remaining roadless areas in the United States. He found 48 forested areas over 300,000 acres in size and 29 desert areas larger than 500,000 acres. (He felt the larger size was necessary in non-forested areas to give one a similar sense of solitude.) His purpose was to draw attention to the vanishing universe of the wilderness and to encourage efforts toward the preservation of the largest and most important remnants of the American heritage.

Marshall hoped *The New York Times* would publish an article about his inventory. It did not, nor did any major periodical. Marshall eventually presented his study, with an accompanying map by Althea Dobbins, in the November, 1936, issue of *The Living Wilderness,* the magazine of The Wilderness Society. There it was printed, and there it was forgotten. *Earth First!* reprinted it in September, 1982, and it is included here as Appendix C of this book.

Marshall's inventory was unprecedented, and it has not been updated until now — fifty years later. To be sure, Marshall had done a preliminary inventory of National Forest roadless areas over one million acres in size in 1927. I found a hand-written card with this inventory in the Robert Marshall papers at the University of California's Bancroft Library (Berkeley) in 1982. Even George Marshall, Bob's surviving brother, was unaware of the 1927 inventory when I wrote him about it. The information from it is presented in Appendix D.

Marshall, as head of Recreation for the US Forest Service (FS) in the late 1930s, was responsible for setting up a system for protecting the "Primitive Areas" administratively established by the Forest Service. Under Marshall's regulations, these areas would, after study, be designated "Wilderness Areas" if over 100,000 acres and as "Wild Areas" if under 100,000 acres. Marshall died suddenly in 1939 and without him to watchdog the process, the Forest Service began to pare back protection.

By the 1950s, conservation groups, led by Howard Zahniser of The Wilderness Society and David Brower of the Sierra Club, became alarmed at the Forest Service's continuing dismemberment of Marshall's system and began calling for Congressional protection of Wilderness Areas. Hubert Humphrey and John Saylor introduced the first Wilderness bills into the Senate and House, respectively, in 1956. The national campaign for the Wilderness Act required eight years to overcome entrenched opposition from loggers, miners, ranchers (their champion was Rep. Wayne Aspinall of Colorado, Chairman of the House Interior Committee) and federal agencies (the Forest Service and Park Service stridently opposed the bill). President Lyndon Johnson signed the Wilderness Act on September 3, 1964.

By the early 1960s, conservation groups lobbying for passage of the Wilderness Act had compiled rough figures of what they thought might qualify for Wilderness designation on the federal lands: Roadlessness was one of the characteristics they used. But their list was by no means comprehensive.

In 1961, the University of California Wildland Research Center conducted an independent study commissioned by the Outdoor Recreation Resources Review Commission. This survey found 64 roadless areas of 100,000 acres or larger in the National Forests and National Parks. Michael Frome points out in **Battle for the Wilderness** that the largest area found was about 2 million acres, whereas a Forest Service study in 1926 had found the largest roadless area to be 7 million acres. Moreover, the 1961 study found only 19 areas over 230,400 acres, totalling 17 million acres, where there had been 74 areas of that size or larger, totalling 55 million acres, in 1926.

The Wilderness Act instructed the National Park Service and US Fish & Wildlife Service[1] to review the lands they

---

[1]Land ownership and management in the United States is complicated, unplanned and often irrational. There may be private and state school trust land inholdings in National Parks, for example. Some BLM or Forest Service lands are "checkerboarded" with intermixed sections (square miles -- 640 acres) of state school trust, railroad or other private lands. Although this is not the place for a detailed explanation of land management in the United States, some understanding is necessary to follow the text of this book. The Federal government owns approximately one-third of the land area of the country. The federal lands include:

1) The National Forests (NF), National Grasslands and some National Recreation Areas (NRA) managed by the US Forest Service (USFS or FS) in the Department of Agriculture. These are "multiple-use" (multiple-abuse) lands generally open to commercial timber harvesting, livestock grazing, mining and energy extraction, Off-Road-Vehicles (ORVs), fuelwood collecting, hunting, etc.

2) National Parks (NP), National Monuments (NM), National Seashores, National Recreation Areas (NRA) and National Preserves

managed for possible Wilderness recommendation (they were to consider every roadless area over 5,000 acres in size). The agencies did so, often in a rather desultory fashion, and looking only at the specific lands they managed. No effort was made to look at all federal lands in a coordinated way. (Under the Act, only Congress can designate or undesignate an area as Wilderness; the agencies only make recommendations.)

The Wilderness and Wild Areas on the National Forests were immediately placed under protection of the Wilderness Act in 1964 (54 areas totalling 9.1 million acres out of the 191 million acre National Forest system). The Forest Service was instructed to present Wilderness recommendations to Congress by 1974 for the 34 remaining Primitive Areas totalling 5.5 million acres (those areas not yet designated as Wilderness or Wild by the Forest Service). Conservationists in several Western states encouraged the Forest Service to appraise additional roadless areas for Wilderness recommendation but the agency refused. When Congress in 1968 considered a bill that would add the Lincoln-Scapegoat area (not a Primitive Area) in Montana to the Wilderness System over FS objection,

---

managed by the National Park Service (NPS) in the Department of the Interior. NPS managed lands are generally not open to hunting, ORVs, livestock grazing, logging, mining or energy extraction, but there are notable exceptions.

3) National Wildlife Refuges (NWR) managed by the US Fish & Wildlife Service (FWS) in the Department of the Interior. Although ostensibly dedicated for wildlife production (unfortunately, not for habitat protection), some NWRs are open to logging, mining, energy extraction, grazing, ORVs and hunting.

4) Public lands and National Conservation Areas managed by the Bureau of Land Management (BLM) in the Department of the Interior. These are multiple-use lands like the National Forests but with even less supervision from the agency.

5) Air Force, Army, Navy and Marine Corps reservations, ranges, bases and forts under the Department of Defense.

Other large land managers include various other federal agencies, the states (including state parks, state wildlife refuges, conservation lands, school trust lands), Indian tribes (Indian reservations -- IR), The Nature Conservancy and timber companies.

(Nb -- the above abbreviations are used throughout this book.)

conservation groups throughout the West began to end-run the agency and make proposals directly to Congress.

The Forest Service undertook a "Roadless Area Review and Evaluation" (RARE) in 1971-72 to head off the citizen initiatives by supposedly considering all roadless areas on the National Forests for Wilderness Area potential. Although RARE was meant to be an objective and comprehensive inventory of what was still roadless on the National Forests (in areas of 5,000 acres or larger), it was fraught with sloppiness, inaccuracy, inconsistency and insouciance. Conservationists sued the Forest Service (*Sierra Club* v. *Butz*), but after an out of court settlement proved inadequate, conservation groups once again went to Congress (with the "Endangered American Wilderness Act" in 1976) to protest the botched job and ask Congress to directly designate a select group of areas as Wilderness without FS study. The Forest Service responded with RARE II — a far more detailed review, but nearly as disappointing as its predecessor.

Following the dismal RARE II recommendations in 1979 (only 15 million acres out of a total of 80 million roadless acres on the National Forests were proposed for Wilderness designation[2]), conservation groups again approached Congress. By this time, however, the timber industry and other opponents were bending Congress with more muscle than that flexed by conservationists. The informal solution was for each state's Congressional delegation to develop a National Forest Wilderness bill for that particular state. (This approach was unfortunate because it made Wilderness designation more of a local issue than a national decision. Powerful pressure groups with economic interests in the National Forests — mining, grazing and logging industries — and user groups like off-road-

---

[2] The Forest Service inventoried and considered 62 million acres of roadless areas in RARE II. An additional 18 million acres or so that were largely roadless and undeveloped were not included in RARE II because 1) the FS had completed "unit plans" covering these areas and had determined against Wilderness recommendation; or 2) the RARE II inventory was shabby in certain National Forests. Therefore, there were a total of 80 million acres of NF land meeting the FS's criteria as roadless in 1978.

vehicle owners are more influential on the state level.) Two bills passed in 1980, the bulk in 1984, and Montana, Michigan and Oklahoma in 1988. (President Reagan pocket vetoed the Montana bill in what fittingly served as the conservation finale to his administration.) Idaho, Nevada, North Dakota, Illinois, Puerto Rico and, because of Reagan's veto, Montana still did not have RARE II Wilderness bills passed through Congress at the close of 1988.

The Wilderness Society and Sierra Club realized in 1979 that the RARE II Final Environmental Impact Statement was inadequate and thereby open to a court challenge, but they feared the political repercussions of such a suit. Huey Johnson, the scrappy Secretary of Resources for California, did not fear political repercussions and sued the Forest Service to prevent development in a select list of roadless areas in California (*California* v. *Block*). The Federal District Court agreed with Johnson and prohibited the Forest Service from destroying the wilderness values of the cited roadless areas without an adequate environmental impact statement. Earth First! and the Oregon Natural Resources Council successfully sued the Forest Service on identical grounds in 1983 to halt the Bald Mountain timber access road in Oregon's North Kalmiopsis roadless area. This suit effectively extended the *California* v. *Block* decision to all RARE II areas.

The timber industry also realized in 1979 that RARE II was vulnerable in court. Due to their pressure on members of Congress, a central feature of the proposed RARE II bills became "release language." Most FS roadless areas not designated as Wilderness in a state bill (the overwhelming majority of the roadless acreage) are "released" by Congress, which means that they are available for logging, roading and other multiple-use ("multiple-abuse"), and that such activity is not subject to judicial review based on inadequate consideration of Wilderness by the agency (i.e., *California* v. *Block* is nullified, and conservation groups cannot further sue to stop development in such roadless areas based on the inadequacy of the FS's RARE II final environmental impact statement). Furthermore, this release language directs the Forest Service not to consider released roadless areas for possible Wilderness recommendation until the next round of

Forest Plans in the late 1990s. This is the standard "soft"
release language which was developed by the Sierra Club as a
compromise. The timber industry proposed more draconian
language — "hard" release — which would *mandate*
development of released roadless areas and prohibit the Forest
Service from *ever* considering such areas for Wilderness recommendation. In essence, then, it would be fair to label the
RARE II bills passed so far as "nonwilderness bills" instead of
as "Wilderness bills" because more de facto wilderness acreage
has been opened for development instead of protected as
Wilderness. The RARE II process constitutes a net loss of wild
country, not a means to protect it.

The 1964 Wilderness Act left the Bureau of Land
Management (BLM), the largest land manager in the US, out of
the Wilderness System. In 1976 this was rectified when
Congress passed an "Organic Act" (Federal Lands Policy and
Management Act — FLPMA) for BLM. In it, BLM was
mandated to perform a roadless area review, select Wilderness
Study Areas (WSAs), study them and make Wilderness
recommendations to Congress by 1991. That review, still in
process, has been at best a mixed bag in terms of accuracy —
much like the RAREs of its sibling agency.

With few exceptions, there has been no effort to inventory
roadless areas on Indian reservations, military reservations,
other federal lands, state lands or private lands. There have,
though, been several efforts to safeguard wilderness values on
such lands. Marshall, as Director of Forestry for the Bureau of
Indian Affairs, was instrumental in establishing a Roadless
Area system on reservations in 1937, but most of those areas had
been declassified by the 1960s. Some reservations do, however,
have Tribal Wilderness Areas. California, New York and
Michigan have Wilderness Systems for their state parks.
Pennsylvania has a Wild Areas System for its state forests.

Despite all this, Bob Marshall's 1936 inventory stands
alone as an effort to document the large wild areas of our
country, irrespective of ownership or management.

Until now.

For the past seven years, Howie Wolke and I have been
compiling an inventory of the big roadless areas left in the

United States. This book is the first comprehensive account of that ongoing study.

It is instructive to compare Marshall's fifty-year-old inventory with ours to document what has been lost. In doing so, it is important to recognize that Marshall had even less accurate information to use in assembling his inventory than we have had for ours. As he pointed out in *The Living Wilderness*, ". . . this is only a preliminary study, we realize there will be a number of mistakes. This is especially true of the desert areas. . .." Moreover, Marshall was conservative in determining what was roadless, and he excluded a half-mile-wide buffer zone along boundary roads and on either side of cherrystemmed (intruding) roads in calculating his acreages.

Marshall overlooked a number of areas: Cabeza Prieta in Arizona, Saline Range in California, Black Rock Desert in Nevada, Black Range in New Mexico and Everglades in Florida. He artificially divided two very large areas: Central Idaho (the Selway-Bitterroot from the Idaho Primitive Area — now the River of No Return Wilderness— along the Salmon River) and California's High Sierra (southern Yosemite National Park from the main body of the range to the south). And a number of acreages are listed as smaller than what they must have actually been in 1936: Gila (New Mexico), High Uintas (Utah), Salmon-Trinity Alps (California), Gros Ventre (Wyoming) and Eagle Cap (Oregon).[3]

In some cases roadless areas may actually be larger today than they were in 1936 due to homesteaders or others giving up their efforts to make a buck on a disagreeable piece of country. Many rural areas today are less populated than they were 50 years ago, as marginal areas have been abandoned. Moreover, wildlife protection laws and scientific game management have increased populations of some species after populations bottomed out early in this century due to market hunting and

---

[3] Analyzing Marshall's inventory is difficult because none of his maps or other documentation still exist, to the best of our knowledge. The Robert Marshall Papers in the University of California's Bancroft Library in Berkeley do not have this material and his brothers, George and James Marshall, when asked, did not know where it might be. All that is available is reprinted in Appendix C.

other unrestrained forms of exploitation. While, overall, native diversity and wildness have suffered immeasurably in these 50 years, lovers of the wild can be encouraged by the recovery of wilderness in specific locations.

Nonetheless, in looking at Marshall's 1936 study, one is struck by what we have lost. Fifty years ago, the largest roadless area in the United States was the Escalante-Glen Canyon region along the Colorado River in southern Utah — nearly 9 million acres (14,000 square miles) in one piece! The Owyhee Canyonlands where Idaho, Oregon and Nevada come together had over 4 million acres unbroken by a road; the Grand Canyon 4 million; Desolation Canyon on the Green River in Utah 2.5 million; the North Cascades, as yet undivided by the "North Cascades Scenic Highway," nearly 3 million. Even more illustrative of what we have lost in two generations is Marshall's 1927 inventory — Central Idaho had over 7.5 million acres; the North Cascades nearly 3.5 million; Mt. Rainier 1.3 million; the Gila 1.3 million; the mountains above Santa Barbara, California, 1 million. All of these acreages represent intact single roadless areas.

Keep these figures in mind as you read our inventory, which is correct to the mid-1980s.[4]

In conducting our inventory we looked simply at the land. The Forest Service in RARE and RARE II stopped at National Forest boundaries, sometimes subdividing intact roadless areas when they overlapped into several National Forests and always ignoring the continuation of biological roadless areas after they left FS jurisdiction. The Park Service in conducting its mandated Wilderness review did not look at the wildland contiguous to but outside of the National Parks. No one has looked at military lands, Indian reservations, state lands or private lands in a comprehensive fashion. In other words, no

---

[4] In certain cases, we will cross-reference our roadless areas with Marshall's 1927 and 1936 inventories in italics. For example *RM27: 1,327,360* under New Mexico's Gila indicates Marshall found that roadless acreage there in his 1927 inventory. *RM36* refers to his 1936 inventory. An asterisk on the acreage means that other roadless areas inventoried in this book were part of Marshall's single roadless area at that time.

one has looked at the land, at the wilderness in a manner unfettered by artificial boundaries. Other roadless inventories have looked at administrative designations, not at the true roadless area.

A telling example is the High Sierra roadless area in California. At 2,800,000 acres, it is the second largest roadless area in the 48 contiguous states. But no one heretofore knew it was the second largest roadless area because no one had ever calculated its size. Why? Because it embraces three National Parks, seven National Forest Wilderness Areas, undesignated roadless areas in three National Forests, a dozen Bureau of Land Management roadless areas, and scattered tracts of Forest Service, BLM, NPS and private land. Similarly, many large roadless areas in the West include state, private, military or Indian land, as well as that administered by one or more federal agencies.

The inventory in this book outlines intact areas which are essentially roadless and undeveloped, irrespective of land ownership or administrative agency. To identify the large primitive areas remaining in the United States, we have used roadlessness as our major cri-terion. Although the presence or absence of roads is not the only factor determining whether an area is wilderness or possesses a significant degree of ecological integrity and native diversity, it is a key one.

Napoleon's army may have marched on its stomach, but the army of wilderness destruction travels by road and motorized vehicle. Roads are used for logging; dam building; oil & gas exploration; overgrazing "management"; powerline construction and maintenance; mineral exploration and extraction; and ski area, recreational and subdivision development. Trappers, poachers, slob hunters, prospectors, seismographic crews, archaeological site vandals and other vanguards of the industrial spoliation of the wild use roads. Roads provide freebooters with access to key areas of wildlife habitat and to the core of wild areas. Roads cause erosion, disrupt wildlife migration and create an "edge effect" that allows common weedy species of plants and animals to invade pristine areas providing refuge to sensitive and rare native species. Many creatures are killed by vehicles on roads.

Without roads, without mechanized access, native species are more secure from harassment and habitat destruction, and fewer people with fewer "tools" are able to abuse the land.

Yet, some roads rest relatively lightly on the terrain. If they were closed to motorized vehicles, they would be irrelevant. In looking at a large wild area from the air, a dirt road cutting across it can be very small indeed. These roads impact the wild insofar as they provide access for the commercial and recreational destruction of natural values. The presence of roads should not disqualify an area from Wilderness designation. By closing a road and prohibiting motorized vehicles, its impact can be removed.

Nevertheless, we have chosen "roadlessness" as the key characteristic for easily identifying the most pristine large areas in the United States. We have done so because the presence of roads nearly always indicates the presence of other impacts on the natural integrity of an area. Also, roadlessness has traditionally been, since Aldo Leopold's 1921 Gila Wilderness proposal, the primary factor for Wilderness consideration.[5]

The first step in identifying a roadless area is to define a "road." Roads, of course, cover a wide spectrum from the one-time passage of four tires to a four-lane, divided interstate highway. In 1972, the Southwest Region of the Forest Service (New Mexico and Arizona) defined "road" for the first RARE process as a parallel set of tire tracks that remain visible into the next season. In other words, if an irresponsible hunter drove a jeep across a wet meadow during the fall Elk season and the tracks were visible the next summer, that was a "road" and the area was disqualified from Wilderness consideration. It is

---

[5] However, just because an area is roadless does not mean that it is entirely "wild" in an ecological sense. For example, many roadless areas included in this inventory have been severely overgrazed for many decades, resulting in drastic declines in native diversity. In addition, barbed wire fences, small impoundments, acid rain, poaching and other problems abound in many of our remaining wild areas. In essence, the American wilderness of the 1980s, grand though it is, is wilderness with an asterisk. The acreage in this inventory overstates the true wilderness of modern America.

instructive to note that in 1977, using a more realistic definition of "road" in RARE II, the Forest Service found three times the roadless acreage on Southwestern National Forests.

While acknowledging that the determination of what is and is not a "road" is a somewhat arbitrary process, for the purposes of this inventory we have essentially followed the general criteria used by the Forest Service in RARE II and by BLM in their Wilderness Review. (It would be more accurate to say the criteria the Forest Service and BLM were *supposed to objectively use*.) This definition of a "road" is succinctly spelled out in the 1976 BLM "Organic Act" House Report:

The word "roadless" refers to the absence of roads which have been improved and maintained by mechanical means to insure relatively regular and continuous use. A way maintained solely by the passage of vehicles does not constitute a road.

In many cases, a road penetrates, but does not cross, an otherwise roadless area. Such roads are referred to as "cherrystem" roads in the wilderness business. We draw the boundaries of the roadless areas in this book along the edges of both cherrystem and boundary roads. Where it is feasible to do so, such cherrystems are indicated on the location maps or mentioned in the text.

We have generally used major pipelines and powerlines to disqualify lands from this inventory. (In the few exceptions, their presence is noted.) Reservoirs, recent clearcuts, large vegetative manipulation projects (chainings and seedings), and dense networks of jeep trails have also served to eliminate areas from this inventory. Solitary jeep trails, "ways" and other unconstructed routes, or constructed roads that have not been maintained, have not been considered as "roads" in this inventory.

Our determination in each case is unavoidably arbitrary since it is based on personal judgment and, in some cases, scanty information and a lack of direct observation (we have obviously not been able to inspect every one of these areas, although we can't think of anything we'd rather do). In some cases, specific roadless areas discussed in this book could be considerably expanded if marginal dirt roads were not considered to be real roads; in other cases, what we have called a single roadless area is crossed by a vehicle route that is on the borderline of being a "road." Such cases are noted in the descriptions for each area. (Future editions of this book will have more accurate information, including our further personal inspection, on which to base judgments for such areas.) Like Marshall, we must leave the reader with the caveat that this inventory is not exact, that there are undoubtedly mistakes herein. The maps included are not precise; they are used to indicate the general location of individual roadless areas and the relationship of groups of roadless areas. Our acreage figures are rounded off to indicate this lack of absolute certainty in our figures; in some cases acreage figures are estimates.

Another question to be asked is "Why is size important for wilderness?" Howie Wolke discusses this in Chapter 2. Size is obviously not the only standard to determine the importance of a wilderness. Some areas, like the Pajarito Mountains in Arizona, Salmo-Priest in Washington and Idaho, Big Thicket in Texas, Joyce Kilmer-Slickrock in North Carolina, and Middle Santiam in Oregon are internationally significant for the native biological diversity they contain, but all are too small to be included in this inventory.

Our minimum acreage is not entirely arbitrary. 100,000 acres was the dividing line Bob Marshall devised between Wilderness Areas and Wild Areas in 1937. We simply had to select some least common denominator on which to base our inventory. This is an inventory of *large roadless areas*. We think that identifying roadless areas in excess of 100,000 acres in the West and 50,000 acres in the East is the best general means to identify areas in the lower 48 states that retain significant degrees of ecological integrity and wildness, and that hold the possibility of serving as the cores for wilderness restoration.[6]

---

[6] Also important are clusters of large roadless areas. There are sundry locations in the United States where minor dirt roads or other developments separate two or several large roadless areas. Because groups of wild areas function as a single habitat for populations of species, and offer greater diversity, such clusters are generally more important than a single large roadless area (unless, of course, it is very

Because so few areas in the East met the 100,000 acre floor, we decided to also include areas between 50,000 and 100,000 acres east of the Rocky Mountains. Furthermore, areas in the more humid East generally have a greater ecological resiliency than do areas in the West.

Only the 48 coterminous states are included in this inventory. Alaska is excluded because roadless areas there are on a different scale, and because motorboats, snowmobiles, airplanes and all-terrain vehicles (ATVs) provide access to permanently inhabited communities far from a constructed road. Hawaii is excluded because we were unable to compile information on roadless areas there. We hope to include Hawaii in future editions of this book and would welcome information on roadless areas of 50,000 acres or larger in the island state. Thus, when we refer to the United States in this book, we are usually meaning only the 48 coterminous states.

Since this is an inventory of large ecologically important areas, we considered listing areas by Ecoregion (Northern Rocky Mountains, Great Basin, etc.) instead of by state. We finally decided to organize the inventory by state because the protection or destruction of these areas is fundamentally through the political process which is based on states. Moreover, we decided that most readers would be better able to grasp the location of inventoried roadless areas if they were oriented by state. In a future edition of this book, though, we hope to do an analysis of the Big Outside by Ecoregion or even by the 106 Kuchler Potential Natural Vegetation types.[7]

---

large -- a solitary 500,000 acre roadless area is more important than a complex of five 100,000 acre roadless areas, but the complex of five is more important than a single 100,000 acre area in similar habitat). We have indicated the relationship between roadless areas in our discussion. The maps also graphically portray such roadless area complexes. We particularly call the attention of conservationists to these clusters, since they generally are more valuable as cores for wilderness restoration than are isolated single roadless areas.

[7] Let it be pointed out here, however, that of the 24 Ecoregions defined by R. G. Bailey, 7 do not have any large roadless areas remaining and 6 others are very weakly represented in our inventory. Furthermore, 22 states out of 48 (Nebraska, Kansas, Oklahoma, Louisiana, Arkansas, Missouri, Iowa, Wisconsin, Illinois, Indiana, Ohio, Kentucky,

Within each state we have further divided the inventory
by region to aid the reader in locating individual areas and in
comprehending their relationship to one another.   This
regional breakdown within states is arbitrary and somewhat
inconsistent — for some states we have used bioregional
divisions, for others we have simply used geographic divisions
(i.e., northwest, southwest).

The format for the inventory portion of this book is as
follows:

√ An introductory discussion for each state or region
including the history of the state's Big Outside, an ecological
description, specific and general threats, recent preservation
efforts and the conservation groups involved there.

√ The name and acreage for each roadless area with a
breakdown of the roadless acreage by ownership or
administrative agency.

√ A description of the terrain, flora and fauna of the area,
with historical tidbits thrown in.

√ A status report on the area — what is protected, what is
proposed for preservation, what threatens it.

A listing of all 365 roadless areas in order of acreage is in
Appendix A. A listing in order of acreage within each state is
in Appendix B.

In the inventory we mention conservation groups involved in
protecting these areas. Addresses for these groups are given in
Appendix E.   In certain cases we may criticize some
organizations in this book. That is because conservation groups
have sometimes been timid and compromising. It is the task of
conservationists to advocate protection of wilderness and
native diversity. Period. It is not our job to devise pragmatic,
compromised solutions. *There is not enough wilderness left to
compromise any further.* We must fight for every acre. We
should not give up one inch.   Where we are critical of
conservation groups in this book, it is to encourage them to see

Mississippi, Alabama, South Carolina, Maryland, Delaware, New Jersey,
Pennsylvania, Connecticut, Rhode Island and Massachusetts) do not
have any roadless areas of 50,000 acres or larger left within their
boundaries.   Two, Virginia and West Virginia, are questionably
represented.

the integrity of these larger areas. It is an extraordinary responsibility to acquiesce in the destruction of a wilderness. It is not a decision to be made lightly. Nonetheless, we applaud the efforts of all conservation groups and active individuals, whatever approach they take, from lobbying to monkey-wrenching, to protect these areas. We encourage the readers of this book to contact those groups covering the areas in which they are interested and offer their support.

Finally, a word about style. Throughout this book we have capitalized the proper names of species. Therefore, "Gray Wolf" or "Big Sagebrush," being distinct species, are capitalized; "wolf" or "sagebrush," being generic terms, are not. We capitalize "Wilderness" when it refers to formal, Congressionally designated Wilderness; we leave "wilderness" uncapitalized when it refers to de facto or undesignated wilderness. We capitalize "National Park," "National Forest," "National Wildlife Refuge" whether they refer to a specific unit (e.g., Grand Canyon National Park) or simply to a generalized area or concept. Capitalization denotes a form of respect, and formal species' names or preservation systems deserve, we believe, that respect. It goes without saying that we therefore capitalize "Earth."

Note: Howie Wolke wrote Chapter 2 and generally compiled and wrote the inventory for Idaho, Montana and Wyoming. Dave Foreman generally wrote and compiled the rest of the book. Each of us reviewed and edited the other's work and added supplemental information. When "we" is used, it refers to both authors; when "I" is used, it refers to the individual author responsible for that section.

⤳ Big Wilderness ⟿
is Ecological Wilderness

Merely a few centuries ago, the land we now call the United States of America was a wilderness paradise, vibrant and diverse, cyclical yet stable, pure and unpolluted. Within its mountains, deserts, prairies, tundras and forests lived a diversity and abundance of life that staggers the imagination. It was home to an estimated 60 million Bison, billions of Passenger Pigeons, 100,000 or so Grizzlies ranging from the Pacific Coast nearly to the Mississippi, and Gray Wolves, Mountain Lions, Elk, Bighorn, Prairie Chicken, Eskimo Curlew, anadromous salmon and other wild animals in nearly unbelievable profusion.

So great was the pre-Columbian American wilderness that the fragmented remnants which we today call "wild" pale in comparison. The most diverse temperate forest on Earth blanketed the eastern third of the country, gradually becoming interspersed with the lush Tallgrass Prairies of the Mississippi Valley. To the west, the Mid- and Shortgrass Prairies supported a post-Pleistocene megafauna second only to that of Africa's Serengeti. And the rugged front of the high Rockies rising above the grassland sea was the fortress of a rich wilderness of soaring peaks, towering conifers, glacial lakes, deep canyons, broad river valleys, and thriving populations of Elk, Bison, Bighorn, Mountain Goat, Mule and Whitetail Deer, Black Bear and Grizzly Bear, Mountain Lion, Gray Wolf, Lynx, Bobcat, Wolverine, Beaver, River Otter, Fisher, Bald and Golden Eagle, Peregrine Falcon, Pileated Woodpecker, Whooping Crane, Trumpeter Swan and many more species.

The Great Basin was an unblemished world of bunchgrass, sagebrush and Pronghorn, broken by conifer-clad island mountain ranges. The mighty Colorado River formed a 2,000-

mile-long oasis, gouging precipitous canyons through some of the world's most spectacular and colorful sedimentary rocks. And in the Northwest, an unbroken forest of coniferous giants — unlike any other on Earth — guarded the rugged peaks of the Coast Range, the Olympics and the Cascades.

In pre-Columbian America, those humans whom we now call Indians hunted Bison, Elk, deer and bear, foraged for roots and berries, set fire to forests and prairies to improve the hunting, and, in some places, grew crops. But the wilderness was huge and diverse, and all life — including human — was subservient to the overwhelming forces of nature.

Today, the American wilderness is under attack and vanishing rapidly. Most of America's wild places are on public lands managed by various federal and state agencies. But rather than protecting these sacred bastions of natural diversity, public agencies most often promote their destruction. For example, with unguarded arrogance, the US Forest Service (FS) brags that it has been eliminating between one and two million acres of wild, unroaded country each year, and that the devastation will continue well into the next century. That agency plans to construct a minimum of 100,000 miles of new roads in inventoried Roadless Areas alone! There are already about 375,000 miles of constructed roads in our National Forests, not including state, county, and federal rights of way. Road construction in the National Forests proceeds at the rate of about 10,000 miles per year.

Similarly, the Bureau of Land Management (BLM) is allowing exploiters to destroy wilderness at nearly the same rate; the National Park Service is too often wedded to industrial tourism at the expense of preservation; and the US Fish and Wildlife Service (and most state wildlife agencies) frequently can't differentiate between a game farm and a natural ecosystem. (For example, in order to provide motorized access for hunters to herds of Desert Bighorn Sheep, the agency recently bladed roads into the heart of its wildest unit, the Cabeza Prieta National Wildlife Refuge in Arizona's Sonoran Desert.) On the public lands as a whole, wilderness is disappearing at the rate of *at least* two million acres a year. That is an area roughly equivalent in size to Yellowstone National Park!

Today, perhaps 700-800 Grizzlies survive south of Canada. Only 30 or so Florida Panthers remain in the wild, and the few scattered reports of Cougar elsewhere in the East suggest that no viable populations remain. The Tallgrass Prairie no longer exists except as tiny relict museum patches surrounded by crops and suburbs, or as heavily grazed and fenced cow pastures. The Passenger Pigeon is extinct. So are the Carolina Parakeet, Heath Hen, Great Auk, Eastern Elk and Sea Mink. Ivory-billed Woodpeckers are probably extinct on the North American Continent, though ornithologists think that several survive in Cuba. The Red Wolf was extinct from the wild; a small population has been reintroduced to Alligator National Wildlife Refuge in coastal North Carolina. The Black-footed Ferret and California Condor survive only in captivity. (With several of these extirpated species, occasional reported sightings do lend a small degree of hope that a few last individuals survive in the wild, but even if the sightings are valid, the remaining individuals do not constitute viable breeding populations.)

Only a few remnants of the Eastern Deciduous Forest survive relatively intact. The Great Plains are barren of Elk, Gray Wolves, Grizzlies, Bison and wildness. The Rockies are laced with roads, clearcuts, ski resorts, condominiums and mines. The Great Basin is a huge overgrazed cow pasture of sagebrush, dirt and exotic plants — Cheatgrass, Crested Wheatgrass, Halogeton and Russian Thistle (tumbleweed). Except for a few scattered stands, the great Pacific conifers have been milled into two-by-fours for condominiums, hot tubs, homes, offices and picnic tables. Real wilderness in chunks big enough to support all native species, all native predator-prey relationships, all natural perturbations (such as fire, insect outbreaks, drought, flood) — no longer exists in the United States outside of Alaska. That's the sad truth of the 1980s.

In the American West, several areas are perhaps large enough and natural enough in and of themselves to *almost* be considered real wilderness. They are few and far between, and include the River of No Return and Selway-Bitterroot Wildernesses of central Idaho and extreme western Montana, the Bob Marshall complex of northwestern Montana, the South Absaroka complex of northwestern Wyoming, and the Cabeza

Prieta and Organ Pipe Cactus country of southern Arizona. But on the whole, wilderness in America survives only as small scattered remnants, biologically impoverished to varying extents, geographically isolated, frequently polluted by exotic species; yet still sublime, diverse, eminently salvageable. The surviving wildlands provide our last hope in a world of ecological despair; our only chance to balance humanity's insane destruction of the natural world with sane ecological policy.

Today, approximately 10% of the land area of the contiguous 48 states is still "wild" — that is, in a wilderness condition as defined by America's only federal Wilderness law. Section 2(c) of the 1964 Wilderness Act defines wilderness as an area "untrammeled by man . . . retaining its primeval character and influence . . . which generally appears to have been affected primarily by the forces of nature, with the imprint of man's work substantially unnoticeable . . . [and which] has at least 5,000 acres of land. . . ."

To put this in perspective, 5,000 acres equals about eight square miles. That's not very large. At an average walking pace in gentle terrain, one could cross a 5,000-acre square in about an hour. Today, most of America's remnant wildlands are wild only relative to the industrial wasteland surrounding them. Even most of today's ostensible big wildernesses — areas of 100,000 acres or more (50,000 in the East) — are far too small to be considered wilderness in the real, biological sense of the term. One hundred thousand acres is about 156 square miles, or the equivalent of a 12 mile by 13 mile rectangular block of country. That is not nearly large enough — unless adjacent to other wildlands — to harbor a complete representation of native flora and fauna, including top trophic level carnivores, such as wolves, Mountain Lions and Grizzlies. To illustrate the smallness of even our biggest wildernesses, there is no place in the contiguous 48 states farther than 21 air miles from a constructed road. The farthest point from a road, outside Alaska, is along the Thorofare River in Wyoming's Teton Wilderness, part of the 2 million acre South Absaroka wilderness complex. Even in the huge Bob Marshall and River of No Return Wildernesses, there is no place more than 18 air miles from a road.

Nonetheless, all remaining wildlands, however small and incomplete, are important and should be protected. Despite their indigence, they still provide habitat for a multitude of species that cannot tolerate logging, mining, roads, agriculture, and other forms of industrial development. They still provide reservoirs of genetic diversity, and they still provide the opportunity for species to evolve under a wide range of ecological conditions. In addition, they still provide opportunities for human creativity and enlightenment.

From a biological standpoint, big means diverse. Not only is it likely that a big chunk of wilderness will include more kinds of habitats — and thus, more species — than will a small wilderness, but we're learning too, that even in comparable habitats, bigger is better with regard to native diversity. Scientists studying the new discipline of Island Biogeography are learning that in most any given biological region, large blocks of habitat can support more species than can smaller blocks. Small blocks of natural habitat that are isolated from other parcels of wild country are particularly vulnerable to species extinctions, while big wildernesses, particularly if adjacent to or connected via corridors with other wild areas, are best able to support the full array of indigenous species in a given region. Protecting *natural diversity*, then, must be the major goal of the wilderness movement. In the highest sense of the term, natural diversity means that all indigenous species must be free to evolve under natural conditions, in as many different natural habitats as possible. It also means that land managers and citizen activists must pay particular attention to wilderness-dependent species such as Grizzly, Mountain Goat and Wolverine, and species of late seral stages such as Marten, Fisher, Spotted Owl, Prairie Chicken and Red-cockaded Woodpecker. These species, nowadays, are rare, especially when compared with early successional species and those that readily adapt to civilization, such as Whitetail Deer and Song Sparrow.

Maintaining natural diversity means that Grizzlies and Gray Wolves should be allowed to thrive and evolve in the Southern Rockies and on the Shortgrass Prairie, that Elk should be allowed to thrive and evolve on the prairies and in the eastern hardwoods, that Bison should no longer be restricted to Yellowstone Park and a few other tiny enclaves, and that kangaroo rats should be allowed to evolve free from human assault and harassment in big chunks of wild country where cows and sheep haven't devoured the native bunchgrasses.

Managing for natural diversity in a holistic sense is the biocentric antithesis of anthropocentric over-manipulation. Managing in accordance with the concept of natural diversity means all native species of a particular bioregion (and on a larger scale, of the biosphere), including top trophic level predators and omnivores, must be allowed and encouraged to thrive under natural conditions. Thus, all management — passive or active — should be designed to promote the goal of maximum *natural* diversity. This does not necessarily mean that each acre — or even each square mile — should be managed to maximize the number of species within it. Nor does it mean that it is sound policy for bureaucrats to create artificial mosaics of different communities, as the Forest Service now does by interspersing clearcuts with standing forest. Such manipulations tend to benefit "weed species" that are adapted to disturbed areas and that are abundant elsewhere. Exotics also benefit from such misguided manipulations. Again, it is wilderness-dependent and late-successional species that usually are in short supply. They benefit from wilderness and suffer from artificial manipulation and habitat fragmentation.

To promote maximum *natural* diversity for the biosphere, humans must protect big wilderness wherever it survives. As I've mentioned, large wild areas naturally include more different kinds of habitats and more species, than do smaller ones. Thus, large wildernesses are inherently more valuable than are small ones. Furthermore, big wilderness offers a buffer not only against the effects of industrial civilization, but against periodic natural catastrophes as well. Forest fires, insect infestations, volcanoes, floods, earthquakes, and even ice ages fuel the fires of evolution, but only if ample undisturbed areas exist to serve as refugia, and only if there remain corridors of natural habitat to provide for migration, recolonization and gene flow. It is sad to note that in the conterminous United States there is no individual wild area nearly large enough to incorporate a shifting mosaic of habitats controlled by natural disturbances.

Nonetheless, the preservation of big wilderness provides us with at least a measure of insurance against the continued biological and genetic impoverishment of this magnificent planet, and these last vestiges of natural diversity can become the building blocks for a wilderness system that resembles the primordial wonderland that once spanned the continent.

Big wilderness also provides refuge for those of us desperate to periodically escape the industrial juggernaut; the preservation of all big wilderness can thus ameliorate the deterioration, due to human overcrowding, of National Parks and other popular wild areas. Furthermore, big wilderness is self-protecting. Its core is buffered against the ill effects of civilization by its outskirts. It is important that we protect all remaining wild country, but it is *absolutely critical* that we protect all remaining big wilderness.

Unfortunately, timber companies, mining companies, real estate and ski area developers, some cattlemen, and at least four huge federal bureaucracies (especially the Forest Service and the BLM) are working diligently to make certain that wilderness in America — big or small — is not protected. Thus far, they are winning. The developers have powerful allies in Congress, unfair laws and regulations that are inherently biased against the preservation of natural diversity, and the deadweight momentum of intransigent bureaucracy in their favor. Moreover, as Dave points out in the next chapter, humans have been destroying wilderness since well before modern agriculture, industry and bureaucracy. Today's destruction, then, can also be viewed as an illogical but predictable extension of a very old trend. And, until now, the modern wilderness despoilers have had another important advantage — the political demarcation of American lands.

The history of America's public lands is complex and sordid. Today's resulting ownership patterns and administrative boundaries make little biological, ecological or economic sense. For example, in many Western mountains, the Forest Service administers the high forests, meadows and peaks. These habitats are primary summer ranges for various migratory or wide-ranging mammals such as Elk, Bighorn and

Grizzly, and various migratory birds such as Mountain Chickadee and Townsend's Solitaire. But the low elevation habitats that are critical winter ranges for Elk, Bighorn, Mule Deer and other species including Mountain Chickadee and Townsend's Solitaire, often fall under BLM, state or private jurisdiction, or a mixture of all three. Furthermore, National Forest boundaries often follow hydrographic divides along the crests of rugged mountain ranges. Such administrative divisions as these often effectively subdivide coherent wildland units so that the organic whole — the cohesive undivided wilderness — loses its true identity and appears to be much smaller than it really is. There are scores of examples of this throughout America's public lands. In addition, National Park boundaries frequently bisect ecological systems by artificially following lines of latitude and longitude. Scattered sections (a section is a square mile: 640 acres) of state land, or of private or corporate lands so resulting from 19th century railroad grants, lie imbedded within the boundaries of National Forests and other public lands. Privately owned wildlands, controlled by developers, timber companies, miners, ranchers and others, contain enormous ecological wealth, but are being severely degraded. This also impoverishes adjacent public wildlands. Generally speaking, land ownership patterns in the US make development easy, preservation difficult.

Too often, wilderness advocates allow themselves to be constrained by artificial bureaucratic and administrative boundaries. They accept agency boundaries as the limits of what might be protected rather than defining and defending an entire unroaded wildland entity, regardless of the artificial political boundaries lying within. As the last big wildernesses edge toward oblivion, it is imperative that eco-activists develop and advance proposals for wildland ecosystem protection that utterly disregard political and bureaucratic boundaries and jurisdictions. The biological whole is the overriding entity to which politics must become subservient.

Let us advocate wilderness as if wilderness mattered. Aldo Leopold once said that "the first rule for intelligent tinkering is to save all the parts." On a micro scale, that's true for genes. On a macro scale, it's true for wilderness. But first we must begin to *recognize* all the parts. This inventory is an attempt to do just that. We hope it will be a step toward the recognition of wilderness as an organic whole — not as a political subdivision — and toward the preservation of *all* that remains wild. The destruction of wild country must stop. Period. No qualifier. Already there is too little wilderness remaining, and even our remaining big wilderness is too small.

The Destruction of Wilderness

To ask the question, "Why do we destroy wilderness?" is to grapple with the fundamental problem of our species. The profound questions with which philosophers have danced since the Athenian Academy, "What is Beauty? What is Truth? Who are we? Where are we going? What is the purpose of life? What is the Nature of Man?" are subsumed by that of human destruction of the wild. It is the keystone to understanding our alienation from Nature, which is the central problem of Civilization.

Analyzing why we destroy wilderness requires us to step back 10,000 years to the nascency of agriculture, that brought with it the city, bureaucracy, patriarchy, war and empire. It was agriculture that severed our kind from the natural world and prompted our devastation of native diversity. (Some, like Paul Martin of the University of Arizona, argue persuasively that this devastation began earlier, as small bands of skilled hunters first entered Australia, Oceania, Siberia, Madagascar, North and South America at the close of the last Ice Age and caused the extinction of dozens of genera of large mammals and birds that were not experienced in evading so skilled a predator.)

Before agriculture was midwifed in the Middle East, humans were in the wilderness. We had no concept of "wilderness" because everything was wilderness and we were *a part of* it. But with irrigation ditches, crop surpluses and permanent villages, we became *apart from* the natural world and substituted our fields, habitations, temples and storehouses. Between the wilderness that created us and the civilization created by us, grew an ever widening rift.

Fortunately, we do not need to delve further into this complex question here. The topic of this chapter is far simpler: *How* are we destroying wilderness in the United States of

America in the late twentieth century? As we discuss this, we will also uncover *who* is destroying wilderness.*

The ways in which we are destroying the last American wilderness are interrelated and synergistic in their effects, but can be broken down into the following categories:

√ Road-building
√ Logging
√ Grazing
√ Mining
√ Energy extraction
√ Dams and other water developments
√ Pipeline and powerline corridors
√ Slob hunting
√ Wildlife "management"
√ Eradication of species
√ Introduction of exotics
√ Wildfire suppression
√ Off-road-vehicles (ORVs)
√ Industrial tourism
√ Wilderness recreation
√ Outside impacts

We will briefly discuss each of these in this chapter. The inventory section of the book will relate each to threats toward specific large roadless areas. Since space limits us to only touching the surface of the factors threatening the Big Outside, references for further reading are given in the Bibliography.

Road-building

The army of wilderness destruction travels by road. With few exceptions, each of the items on the above laundry list requires roads or motorized vehicles to exploit the wild. Chapter 2 demonstrated just how pervasive the road network is

---

*Although in fairness, we must recognize that all of us are destroying wilderness because of the alienation of our society from nature; because of human arrogance; and because of the gross overpopulation of our species combined with the wasteful lifestyle of modern humans that converts thirty percent of Earth's photosynthetic production to human purposes.

in the United States — that there are few areas ten miles or more from a road.

The National Forest System contains a large share of the Big Outside in the lower 48 states, but it also boasts 375,000 miles of road — the largest road network managed by any single entity in the world. The United States Forest Service employs the second highest number of road engineers of any agency in the world (over 1,000). During the next half century, the FS plans to build an additional 350,000 - 580,000 miles of road — mostly for logging. At least 100,000 miles of that will be in currently roadless areas. This road construction costs the American taxpayer half a billion dollars a year. Reducing — better yet, eliminating — the bloated FS road-building budget in the Congressional appropriations process is one of the best ways to defend wilderness. Simply writing one's members of Congress and demanding that the FS road budget be cut or eliminated is one of the more effective single acts any of us can perform.

The Bureau of Land Management is also beefing up its road network — for the benefit of graziers, energy companies and motorized recreationists. Many BLM areas could be classified and protected vast wilderness preserves if one or two dirt roads were closed.

The wilderness of our best-known National Parks has been rent by "scenic motorways." The Going-to-the-Sun road in Glacier, Tioga Pass road in Yosemite, Skyline Drive in Shenandoah, Newfound Gap road in Great Smoky Mountains, Trail Ridge road in Rocky Mountain, and Island in the Sky road in Canyonlands are prime examples. A battle is now raging in Capitol Reef National Park in Utah as local boosters persevere in their effort to pave the Burr Trail.

The impacts of roads on wilderness were summarized in Chapter 1.

Logging

As the pioneers encountered the frontier in their march from the Atlantic seaboard to the Mississippi River, their first step in civilizing the land was to "open it up": The oppressive forest, harboring savages, wild beasts and godlessness, and shutting out sunlight and progress, had to be cleared. While much of this ancient forest was simply burned, some of it fed the growing timber industry, which quickly became dominated by larger and larger companies as the timber frontier moved from New England to the Upper Midwest to the Pacific Northwest. In the view of the timbermen, the forests were endless and they were perfectly justified in ransacking an area, leaving it raw and bleeding, and moving further west. In the late 1880s and '90s public outcry over this rapaciousness led to the protection of Adirondack State Park in New York and the establishment of forest reserves in the West to protect watersheds.

John Muir hoped the forest reserves would be off-limits to logging, but under the leadership of Gifford Pinchot, they became the National Forests and were dedicated to "wise use." Pinchot established his prescripts quickly: 1) The first principle of conservation is development; and 2) There are only two things in the world — people and natural resources.

The early-day Forest Service hoped to sell its timber to private companies, but these companies still had plenty of old growth on their millions of acres of private lands and were not interested. Not until after World War II did the marketing of NF timber attract interest as the stocks on corporate lands became depleted. In the last 40 years, the annual cut on the National Forests has steadily increased, until today the Forest Service brags that it is logging (i.e., destroying) a million acres of wilderness a year.

It is important to keep in mind that "harvesting" 10-12 billion board feet of timber a year from the National Forests (about a fifth of the nation's total timber production) not only exceeds sustained yield (the amount of timber harvested is more than that grown) but that most timber sales in remaining roadless areas on the National Forests are *below cost sales*. It costs the Forest Service (thus the taxpayer) more to offer and prepare these sales for cutting than timber companies pay for them. The Office of Management and Budget reported that, in 1985, Forest Service below cost sales cost the taxpayer $600 million. Moreover, this figure does not include the associated costs of destroyed watersheds, devastated wildlife habitat, loss of recreation, herbicide pollution of air and water, decreased native diversity, concentration of wealth in fewer hands, and bureaucratic growth in the FS to administer the program.

The situation is getting even worse. According to a recent study by The Wilderness Society, proposed Forest Plans nationwide call for an increase in logging of 25% over the next decade. Virtually every unprotected large, forested roadless area on the National Forests is threatened with logging and associated road-building. Except for the small amounts of old growth forest in designated Wilderness Areas, the Forest Service plans to convert the remaining old growth to intensively managed tree farms during the next 50 years. (Unfortunately, the FS is not always successful in this: Many clearcuts have not regenerated, even with expensive replanting, fertilizing and herbiciding. Hundreds of Forest Service clearcuts remain butchered, bleeding wastelands decades after clearcutting.)

Grazing

The livestock industry has probably done more basic ecological damage to the Western United States than has any other single agent. The Gray Wolf and Grizzly have been exterminated throughout most of the West for stockmen (Grizzlies are still being killed around Yellowstone National Park and the Rocky Mountain Front for sheep ranchers; the new Gray Wolf pack in Glacier NP has been largely wiped out to protect cattle; and ranchers are the leading opponents of wolf reintroduction in Yellowstone and the Southwest). The Mountain Lion, Bobcat, Black Bear, Coyote, Golden Eagle and Raven have been relentlessly shot, trapped and poisoned by and for ranchers until lion and Bobcat populations are fractions of their former numbers. Elk, Bighorn, Pronghorn and Bison populations have been tragically reduced through the impacts of livestock grazing. Streams and riparian vegetation have been degraded almost to the point of no return throughout much of the West. The grazing of cattle and sheep has dramatically altered native vegetation communities and has led to the introduction of non-native grasses palatable only to domestic livestock. Sheet and gully erosion from overgrazing have swept away most of the topsoil in the West. In non-timbered areas, most "developments" on public lands — roads, fences, juniper chainings, windmills, pipelines, stock tanks and the like — benefit only a few ranchers.

Vast areas of the Great Basin and Southwest could be designated as Wilderness were it not for the livestock industry. Throughout the rural West, public lands ranchers are the most vocal and militant lobby against environmental protection or Wilderness designation. Sadly, designation of an area as Wilderness or National Wildlife Refuge does not restrict commercial livestock grazing. Even some National Parks are legally grazed. Of course, nearly all National Forest, BLM and state lands in the West are grazed by domestic livestock.

To make this situation more outrageous, all this is done to produce only 2% of the nation's red meat; 98% of US beef production is on private lands, mostly in the Eastern states. The ranchers using the public lands are *welfare ranchers*. In 1988 they paid only $1.50 per AUM (Animal Unit Month — the average amount of forage a cow and her calf eat during a month), which is less than one-fourth of the cost of grazing leases on private lands. Additionally, BLM and Forest Service range specialists perform many services for their welfare charges, and fences, roads, stock ponds and other improvements for increased grazing are often built at taxpayer expense. All in all, the Forest Service and BLM lose about $100 million a year with their grazing programs — and this does not count the costs of environmental degradation, which run into the hundreds of millions of dollars annually. The 22,000 ranchers with BLM or FS grazing leases are among the most accomplished welfare chiselers in the nation (perhaps only military contractors are more facile at living on the public dole).

Mining

Although mining has affected a smaller acreage than have logging or grazing, where it has occurred, its impact has been momentous, as a glance at the Santa Rita open pit copper mine in New Mexico or uranium tailings around Moab, Utah, will attest. Besides the scarification of the land and attendant air, water and soil pollution, mining requires a network of roads, powerlines, pipelines and other infrastructure, which drive away wildlife and dispel wildness. Geological processes are such that minerals tend to be most concentrated in rugged terrain, which is not only more vulnerable to damage but is also more likely to be wild and roadless than is gentler country.

Mining on the National Forests and BLM lands is sanctioned by the 1872 Mining Act, an antique from the days of the early gold rushes in the Wild West. This law allows any individual or corporation to claim minerals on federal lands. Such claims are staked by only a small filing fee and maintained by only $100 worth of work a year, and can be taken to patent (passed into private ownership) if a reasonable mineral production is made. Like logging and grazing, mining on the public lands is a gigantic rip-off. Most National Parks and Wildlife Refuges are closed to new claims, as were Wilderness Areas after 1984 (previous claims — those filed prior to 1984 for Wilderness Areas; prior to designation for Parks and Refuges — can be mined in all of these areas, however). The FS and BLM are limited in restricting or regulating mining on their lands, although they have more authority than they exercise.

There are essentially two types of miners operating today: the so-called "small miner" and the mining corporation. Small miners are typically ne'er-do-wells with a bulldozer and a fanatical conviction that they're going to make a big strike that they can sell to a large corporation for millions. These pitiful pieces of human flotsam live in backwater towns near their diggings, or commute on weekends from Phoenix, Los Angeles and other cities to the backcountry. Although these little guys have made virtually no large strikes, they seem to be everywhere in the West and can be enormously destructive to wild country as they prospect. They are also likely to poach, trap or pursue other unsavory habits. They are vocal and potentially violent opponents of Wilderness designation and other "lockups."

Medium to large corporations do the real mining. They have professional geologists, use sophisticated methods to locate potential ore bodies, and carry large exploration budgets. Although financially and institutionally better able to practice mining and reclamation in a less environmentally destructive manner than small miners, they are not inclined to do so unless forced. Mining companies have considerable political clout in the Western states, and they and their lobbying association, the American Mining Congress, are powerful opponents of Wilderness and National Park designations, arguing that all the public lands must remain available for more sophisticated prospecting techniques which will be developed in the future so they can patriotically produce the strategic minerals America needs to hold the worldwide godless communist conspiracy at bay (no exaggeration!).

A national effort to replace the 1872 Mining Law with a lease and royalty system, having environmental safeguards, failed in the late 1970s due to pressure from both types of miners. National conservation groups are again considering such a campaign. It is long overdue. Even more overdue is a ban on mining in all remaining wild (roadless) areas.

Energy Extraction

Unlike hard-rock mining, energy extraction (oil & gas, coal, tar sands, geothermal) on the public lands by private companies is governed by leasing. Leasing, in contrast to claiming, returns fees to the federal treasury, and does not transfer ownership of the land from the federal government. It is based on several laws more recent than the 1872 Mining Law. Although the Secretary of the Interior has considerable discretion in leasing, the federal government (especially under the Reaganauts) has been enthusiastic to lease as much of its land as possible to the few giant corporations (Exxon, Mobile, Shell, Chevron, Union, Getty, etc.) that dominate all facets of the industry.

Exploration for oil & gas begins with seismographic crews, who use explosives or "thumper trucks" to produce vibrations in the ground. Subterranean echoes are then read on monitors to determine where potentially favorable geological formations exist. Because each of several competing companies carefully guards its information, sometimes a dozen different seismo crews go over the same terrain. Their blasting disturbs wildlife, and thousands of miles of road have been bladed through Western wildlands for thumper trucks.

After a favorable formation is found and an exploration lease obtained, exploratory drilling begins. Roads are built into wild areas, drilling pads are cleared, and outsized drilling rigs are set up for several weeks or months. The roughnecks who work on such crews are often ORVers, poachers, pot hunters and other unenlightened users of the wild. Even if a strike is not made (a dry hole), exploration roads frequently become part of the permanent road system of the National Forest or BLM District, and provide access to wild country for the motor-bound public.

If a strike is made, more wells are drilled, roads built, pipelines constructed and pumping stations installed until dozens of square miles of public land become an industrial complex, and Elk, bear and other critters are displaced. Such is the scenario for hundreds of thousands of acres of roadless country in the so-called Overthrust Belt of, the Central and Northern Rockies.

Geothermal leasing, exploration and extraction generally follow the same pattern as that for oil & gas. Coal (usually strip mined) is a leasable mineral on the public lands. It is a threat to wilderness primarily in Utah (as are tar sands).

Dams and Other Water Developments

Some of the most remarkable wildlands and rivers in the United States have been flooded by dams and their reservoirs. Glen Canyon, Hetch Hetchy and much of Hells Canyon have been drowned beneath stagnant reservoir water. Only all-out national campaigns by conservationists have prevented dams in the Grand Canyon, Dinosaur National Monument, the Gila Wilderness and the remainder of Hells Canyon. Dams on the Columbia River have decimated salmon runs in the wildernesses of the Northwest and Central Idaho. Upstream dams on the Colorado, Green and Rio Grande have severely affected wildlands downsteam.

These dams have been built by the Army Corps of Engineers, Bureau of Reclamation and Bonneville Power Administration for electric power generation, flood control, irrigation and "recreation."

The era of giant dam building in the United States is coming to a close and only a few large roadless areas are threatened by future construction. A new threat, however, is that of "small hydro" — the construction of small dams and powerplants to produce electricity from thousands of small rivers and streams which are often in the wilder corners of the National Forests. As encouraged by the Public Utilities Regulatory Power Act

(PURPA), the Federal Energy Regulatory Commission (FERC) can issue permits to private individuals for such projects. Applications threaten dozens of areas inventoried in this book — mostly on the West Coast.

The best tool for protecting free-flowing rivers and streams is designation as part of the National Wild & Scenic Rivers System or a state river protection system. The national system was established by the 1968 National Wild & Scenic Rivers Act; many state systems have since been established as well. Although Wild & Scenic River designation has been inadequately utilized during the past twenty years, conservationists are gearing up a major new national campaign. Inclusion in the system generally places only a quarter-mile wide zone on each side of the river under protection, but it does protect a river from dams and other development that would modify its free-flowing character.

Powerline and Pipeline Corridors

Associated with the extraction of energy sources is the construction of pipelines, powerlines, coal-fired power plants and so forth. Powerlines and pipelines slice across the backcountry and divide many units of the Big Outside from one another. Irrigation canals, aqueducts and powerlines from hydropower and water storage dams cut across many remote sections of the country, dividing large roadless areas from one another. More lines are projected, and new transmission corridors will be proposed through large roadless areas.

Slob Hunting

Both authors of this book are hunters. We are proud to be hunters and we recognize that hunters have been among the most effective wilderness and wildlife conservationists. This does not negate, however, the impact of the slob hunter (and of poor public policy catering to slob hunters) on wildlife and wildlands. The popular conception of the hunter as a fat, drunken bumpkin or urban good ol' boy cruising the backwoods in a jeep, armed with little natural history or appreciation of nature but plenty of ammunition, is all too true. Slob hunters fall into several categories:

1) The market hunter. A booming black market exists for body parts of Black Bears (gall bladders, paws), Elk antlers and teeth, Grizzly claws and skins, etc. for practicioners of oriental medicine, collectors and other sexually-deficient odd-balls. Big bucks can be made both by individuals and well-organized rings. Over-worked game wardens catch only a handful of these dangerous criminals.

Apologists for hunting claim that no species has become extinct because of hunting. In reality, market hunting and "game hogging" for American Alligator, Bison, Gray Wolf, Elk, Bighorn, Passenger Pigeon, Wild Turkey and numerous species of waterfowl and shorebirds played as major a role as did habitat destruction in extirpating or drastically reducing these species.

2) The road hunter. This is the stereotypical hunter. He wants to drive his jeep, trail bike or ATV to where he'll shoot his freezer meat or anything else that moves. He opposes Wilderness because he can't drive in it. He doesn't like predators because they're eating *his* deer, Elk or Moose. The Arizona Wildlife Federation, for example, generally opposes Wilderness designations because it largely represents this type of hunter. On the other hand, the Idaho Wildlife Federation supports more Wilderness than does the Sierra Club because it's made up of *real* hunters — men and women who know that wilderness provides hunting at its best.

3) The "gut hunter." These fellows shoot at any game they see, regardless of the distance. Firing countless rounds at an Elk or deer several hundred yards away, gut hunters miss more often than not. Too often, however, they succeed in gut shooting a critter which then wanders off to die in agony.

4) The poacher. These people also need roads. They shoot without respect, and outside the law.

5) The trophy hunter. Some trophy hunters are conservationists and support protection of the land. Others, such as many in the Foundation for North American Wild Sheep, want to eliminate predators and have road access everywhere. Trophy Bighorn Sheep hunters are usually wealthy, and are leading opponents of Wilderness designation for areas in the California Desert and in Arizona National Wildlife Refuges.

Other sleazy trophy hunters concentrate on Mountain Lion, Grizzly and other top level predators.

6) The trapper. Trapping is legal and encouraged by fish & game departments in most states. Not only is it cruel, but it is usually done from road or ATV. Trapping targets Bobcat, Lynx, Marten, Mink, Fisher, River Otter and other predators with low reproductive rates. Trapping upsets the normal predator-prey balance. Trapping caused the near-extermination of Beaver from much of the United States, and trapping today continues to keep Beaver populations at an unnatural low. (Trapping by Native Americans in Canada and Alaska is arguably another matter.)

7) The "put-and-take" fisherman. While flyfishing for native, naturally reproducing fish is one of life's higher callings, many fishermen just want to catch their limit (or exceed it if no game warden is about). They are a powerful lobby which has created a fish farming orientation among state wildlife agencies. Non-native, hatchery-reared fish which compete with natives have been introduced throughout the United States. Put-and-take fishermen have caused the introduction of trout to many high country lakes and tarns in Wilderness Areas that did not naturally contain fish. This has upset delicate aquatic ecosystems. Lake and riverine fauna has been more transformed than any other in the United States. Put-and-take fishermen have been as much to blame for this as have polluters and dam-builders.

Slob hunters of all flavors oppose Wilderness designations, create roads, kill excessive numbers of wildlife, and help turn the backcountry into a game farm.

Wildlife "Management"

The US Fish & Wildlife Service and state game & fish departments are partially composed of outstanding professionals who love wildlife and wilderness. They are disciples of Aldo Leopold, who founded the science of wildlife management and argued for the "land ethic." Unfortunately, many wildlife agencies are controlled by political appointees who represent slob hunters or welfare ranchers, and are staffed by arrogant bureaucrats who believe in running game farms on the public lands for their constituency — road hunters and put-and-take

fishermen. This kind of wildlife manager supports clearcutting, vegetative manipulation, predator control and roads because these often favor weed species like deer or provide hunter
access. This kind of wildlife manager stocks lakes and rivers
with exotic fish or hatchery-reared fish because such stocking
sells licenses and brings more money to the department. This
kind of manager promotes hunting of top level carnivores such
as Mountain Lion and Grizzly because politically powerful
ranchers and trophy hunters demand it. This kind of wildlife
manager releases non-native birds like pheasant and Chukar
because quail and grouse don't provide enough hunting. In
bizarre cases, such as occurred with the New Mexico Game &
Fish Department in the early 1970s, exotic species such as Oryx,
Barbary Sheep and Iranian Ibex have been released on the
public lands to create huntable populations for which high
license fees are charged.

Of course, we must understand that any bureaucracy promotes programs that create work for itself. Not until wildlife
managers realize that their job is not to maximize the production of deer, pheasant, trout or other "desirable" game species,
but to maintain wildness and native diversity, will the profes-
sion live up to the standards Aldo Leopold established for it.

Eradication of Species

With rare exceptions, every ecosystem in temperate North
America has lost key species. In the East, Cougar, Grey Wolf
and Elk have virtually disappeared. In the heartland, Bison,
once 60 million strong, are gone. In the West, Grizzly and Gray
Wolf have been largely extirpated. Along the northern border,
Wolverine, Woodland Caribou, Lynx and Fisher are ghosts,
lingering only in the wildest places. In the Southwest, the
tropical cats (Jaguar, Ocelot, Jaguarundi) are shadows seldom
seen. Bighorn Sheep, Black Bear and Wild Turkey have been
severely reduced in number wherever they once ranged. Riparian systems have had their native fish and invertebrate faunas
so altered that exotics now dominate. Without the sensitive,
wilderness-dependent species, wilderness is a hollow shell.
Without the top carnivores, the dynamic balance no longer
exists. What will become of the deer without the wolf to

whittle its swift legs? Is the mountain still alive without the bear?

Extirpation of native species is perhaps the most insidious tool of wilderness destruction. For conservationists, it is not enough to merely protect the land from the bulldozer and chainsaw. We must return the rightful inhabitants to their homes. As Lois Crisler wrote, "Wilderness without wildlife is just scenery."

Introduction of Exotics

As native species have disappeared, as the balance has been upset, exotic, weedy species have invaded, thereby changing whole ecosystems. Fragmented ecosystems, with smaller cores and greater area in "edge" conditions, are highly vulnerable to invasion by such species. Many of these exotics were deliberately introduced by unthinking people. Most of the grasses in California are exotics. The salt cedar (tamarisk), from the Middle East, crowds out cottonwood and willow in the Colorado and Rio Grande drainages. House Sparrows, Rock Doves, Starlings and Chukars have taken over the air and fields in many places. Spotted Knapweed chokes out native grasses in the Northern Rockies of Idaho and Montana. Alfred Crosby, in his brilliant and ground-breaking **Biological Imperialism** argues that we have created "Neo-Europes" in temperate areas around the world. The deliberate and criminal introduction of Crested Wheatgrass by the BLM in the Great Basin is probably the major current attack on the Big Outside from this angle.

Suppression of Wildfire

Naturally occurring wildfire (generally started by lightning) is an important component of most ecosystems in the lower 48 states. Periodic fire is necessary to cause certain seeds to sprout, recycle nutrients, maintain prairies, thin out vegetation and accomplish other ecosystem services. The suppression of wildfire (the "Smokey the Bear Syndrome") has degraded wildernesses throughout the country. The fires that raged through the Pacific Coast forests in 1987 and across Yellowstone in 1988 were simply inevitable natural events which accomplished much ecological good. The Forest Service and Park

Service have begun to acknowledge the valuable role of fire in wilderness ecosystems and have, in some cases, established "let burn" policies for natural fire in Wilderness Areas. Unfortunately, when commercial timberlands or private property outside the Wilderness are threatened, full-scale fire control, including bulldozers and slurry bombers, is unleashed. Fighting a forest or grass fire is nearly always more destructive than letting it burn.

Off-Road-Vehicles (ORVs)

Twenty years ago the problem of ORVs scarcely existed. Jeeps, four-wheel-drive pickups, dirt bikes and snowmobiles were rare. Motorized tricycles and other all-terrain-vehicles (ATVs) were not invented. Today, however, millions of these infernal machines are piloted by pimply-faced boys trying to exorcise the demons of their puberty, or by weak, soft men and women wanting to "get into the backcountry" to hunt, fish, trap, poach, treasure hunt, prospect or camp. ORVs destroy vegetation, disrupt wildlife, erode the land, foul streams and air, and provide access to pristine areas for people who do not respect such places. Barry Goldwater may be correct in calling ORVs "the Japanese revenge."

The disturbing question is, "Why do land managers allow ORVs?" Both the BLM and Forest Service have full power to restrict or prohibit off-road travel. Presidents Nixon and Carter each issued Executive Orders giving federal agencies explicit authority to control ORVs. The vast majority of the over 300 million acres of National Forest and BLM land in the lower 48, however, is open to ORVs — not just on jeep routes or dirt bike trails, but *cross-country*. ORVs carve thousands of miles of new low-standard roads into roadless areas of the public lands every year. At the very least, vehicles should be restricted to designated roads with all cross-country travel absolutely banned.

Why is this not done? Two reasons come to mind. First, many FS and BLM employees and managers are pudgy and out of shape. They use ORVs in the backcountry themselves, and therefore identify with other recreational ORVers. Second, ORVers are well organized and vocal. They scream bloody murder when they are restricted in any way from exercising their "constitutional rights" to drive wherever they wish. Although the public dislikes ORVs and their use on the public lands, this rude minority gets its way.

Four-wheelers, dirt bikers and other motorized recreationists present the strongest opposition to protection of the California Desert. They represent a large anti-Wilderness constituency in other areas as well. Snowmobilers are a similar stumbling block to protection of wildlands in the northern states and Rockies.

Industrial Tourism

Outdoor recreation has become a big business. Large corporations, land developers, and small businessmen operating in National Parks (concessionaires) and "gateway" towns (including local chambers of commerce) have exploitative attitudes towards wildlands that rival those of loggers or miners. National Park administrators rank their "success" by the number of visitors they host (as indicated by Yellowstone NP's declaration that they plan to heavily advertise to get visitation up again after the adverse publicity of the 1988 fires). A large number of outdoor recreationists loathe "roughing it" and demand full hookups (electricity, water, sewage) for their travel trailers or motor homes — Recreation Vehicles (RVs).

RV campgrounds, condominiums, second home subdivisions, resorts, golf courses, ski areas, tennis clubs, recreational reservoirs, marinas, scenic highways, visitor centers, motels and access roads serve these industrial tourists ("tourons"). In doing so, they usurp prime winter habitat for Elk and Bighorn, cause (indirectly) the death of Grizzly (in Yellowstone and Glacier), create air pollution and traffic jams in remote areas, replace native vegetation with exotics, destroy wild rivers and streams, overfish and overhunt (thereby encouraging the game farming mentality), and bring far too many inexperienced people into delicate ecosystems.

Large roadless areas are threatened by ski area development in California and Colorado; ambitious wilderness recovery plans are being torpedoed by condos and recreation subdivisions in New England; the survival of the Grizzly in Yellowstone is jeopardized by RV campgrounds; and water skiers zip over the drowned Glen Canyon. In every section of the country, wilderness and wildlife are trampled underfoot by various manifestations of industrial tourism.

The National Park Service has many fine employees (as do the Forest Service and BLM), people who value the wild and answer a calling to protect it. Unfortunately, some of the top administrators have lost touch with the wild nature their Parks were established to preserve, and have become, in many cases, leading threats to the Parks. Developments such as Fishing Bridge and Grant Village, and arrogant mismanagement of Grizzlies have disrupted the ecological integrity of Yellowstone National Park. The tacky urban center of Yosemite Valley is a national disgrace. Commercial outfitters dictate policies on river running in Grand Canyon and other Parks and lock out private boaters. Corporations offering "scenic overflights" are given free access to skies over Parks by Park Superintendents who enjoy buzzing around in helicopters, too. Concentrating on scenic views and visitor services, Park Superintendents have allowed development in sensitive ecosystems. The primary constituency of the Parks is not the residents — wildlife — but local chambers of commerce, concessionaires and the motorized tourist. Indeed, concessionaires (often subsidiaries of multi-national corporations) have largely usurped management of popular Parks from the Park Service, and run them to maximize their profits.

Unless the National Park Service can get back on track with a philosophy of ecosystem management, and kick out the concessionaires, the National Park ideal which the United States gave the world will become a cruel hoax.

Wilderness Recreation

One would think that those who take the time to hike, float or horsepack into Wilderness Areas would seek to protect the pristine quality of the land. Most do, but a minority, often locals on horseback but sometimes urban backpackers, shows no respect to the Wilderness. Fire rings without number, semi-burned aluminum foil, toilet paper "flowers," hacked green trees, empty Coors beer cans, discarded fishing line, soap in streams and lakes, horse tethering in campsites or hobbling around lakes — all are the calling cards of wilderness slobs. In extreme cases, commercial hunting guides and packers establish semi-permanent Wilderness camps which resemble small towns. Some outfitters have even packed in prostitutes to service hunters in places such as Wyoming's Teton Wilderness Area.

Wilderness recreationists who fail to practice sensitive backcountry ethics should be fined and banned for specific periods from entering Wilderness Areas. Commercial outfitters should be carefully supervised, and have their permits yanked for trashing Wildernesses. The FS, BLM, FWS and NPS need to hire more (and qualified!) Wilderness Rangers to enforce proper backcountry use.

Chapter 2 discussed the principles of Island Biogeography and the need for large ecological preserves. Let us simply repeat here that by chopping large ecosystems into smaller pieces, not only do these pieces become extremely vulnerable to disruption, but they can no longer support the full array of native animals and vegetation that they once supported as larger areas. None of the remaining roadless areas in the United States is large enough to stand alone. None is large enough to maintain the minimum viable populations of top trophic level, wide-ranging carnivores. Identifying the remnants of the Big Outside in the lower 48 states is the first step toward restoring healthy wilderness ecosystems.

In 1956, conservationists accepted a compromise on the Colorado River Storage Act which cancelled a huge dam on the Green and Yampa Rivers in Dinosaur National Monument in favor of one on the Colorado River at Glen Canyon. Except for a few pioneer river runners like Ken Sleight and Katie Lee, no one objected. The conservationists who made that compromise knew the canyons of Dinosaur but they didn't know Glen Canyon. David Brower has said that that compromise was the greatest mistake he ever made. It was the tragedy of "the place no one knew." The damming of Glen Canyon cut the heart out of the largest roadless area in the United States.

Other great roadless areas have similarly been destroyed because they were unknown. The southern Nevada desert, described by Bob Marshall as the finest desert wilderness he ever visited, also was neglected. It became an atomic bomb testing range. In too many other cases, conservationists have not fought for areas, large and small, because they were known merely as blank spots on maps.

It is the purpose of this book to prevent that from happening again. With its publication, the largest roadless areas left in the United States have been delineated and described. May we never again lose the place no one knew!

WASHINGTON

BELLINGHAM

EVERETT

SEATTLE

YAKIMA

WALLA
WALLA

1. Olympic Mountains
2. Mt. Baker
3. Pasayten
4. Glacier Peak
5. Alpine Lakes
6. Mt. Rainier
7. Cougar Lakes
8. Goat Rocks
9. Mt. Adams
10. Wenaha-Tucannon

Washington

Upon first glance at any map showing Wilderness Areas and National Parks, the state of Washington appears to be particularly favored. Of the 48 coterminous states, it has the largest percentage of its land area in such protective classifications. Moreover, Washington is the only state with three roadless areas of a million acres or more primarily within its boundaries.

Unfortunately, an ecological appraisal of Washington's Parks and Wildernesses shatters this pleasant illusion. Olympic, North Cascades and Mt. Rainier National Parks; and Mt. Baker, Pasayten, Glacier Peak, Alpine Lakes, William O. Douglas and other Wilderness Areas are mostly higher-elevation rocks and ice. The alpine areas of Washington above timberline are well protected. The ecologically productive, diverse and fragile old growth forests are not.

On the Olympic Peninsula and the west slope of the Cascades, old growth coniferous rainforest achieves a magnificence unsurpassed in the world. East of the Cascade crest, the forests are more arid, less diverse and have smaller trees, but are ecologically crucial nonetheless. These forests — the western rainforest and the drier east slope Ponderosa Pine, Lodgepole Pine and Douglas-fir forests — are where the battle for Washington's Big Outside is joined.

There are forests protected in the Parks and designated Wilderness Areas. But they are isolated island patches of what was once continuous temperate rainforest for nearly two thousand miles along the Pacific Coast. Each of the remaining large roadless areas in Washington represents a core of alpine wilderness fringed with disjunct old growth fingers in the valleys isolated from the forests edging the next core highland. In most cases the protected forests around each alpine core are not even well connected — the lower ends of the valleys where the forests would connect with each other have been clearcut and intensively roaded.

Until this decade, Washington's wildlands on the Canadian border were joined to a chain of wilderness stretching to the arctic sea. With timber practices and overhunting even worse in British Columbia today than in the United States, that connection has also been severed.

This isolation and fragmentation of old growth habitats is devastating to sensitive species, from Grizzly Bear to Redbacked Vole. Unless conservation groups from the Audubon Society to Earth First!, using every tool at their disposal, can halt the destruction of the unprotected forests linking the preserved units, the fabric of native diversity will unravel in Washington, and that state will have a scenic but ecologically sterile system of National Parks and Wilderness Areas.

Politically, Washington is liberal compared to other Western states. Although the timber industry is powerful, conservationists are also influential. In the past, however, preservation of Wilderness has focused on prime recreational areas — the scenic lakes and peaks of timberline regions — at the expense of the most ecologically significant areas — old growth forests. Hiking, backpacking, kayaking, mountain climbing and cross-country skiing are compatible uses of National Parks and Wilderness Areas, but they are not — or should not be — the purpose for such areas. The fundamental reason for designating National Parks and Wilderness Areas is to preserve reservoirs of native diversity, reserves for continuing evolution. Such areas are not mere scenery or outdoor exercise yards. They are the repository of three and a half billion years of organic evolution on Earth. Within a few decades, we will destroy that continuum of life, unless we act now.

Washington is one of the places where we have the best chance to save the shards of wildness that remain.

To the east of the Cascades, a rainshadow falls, creating what once was a fascinating semi-desert region — the Palouse Grasslands — in southeastern Washington. That area of rolling hills has been transformed into wheat fields. North of the Palouse the richly forested mountains of the Kettle Range and Selkirks combine Cascade and Northern Rocky Mountain char-

Mt. Baker, Washington. Photo by George Wuerthner.

acteristics. A few Grizzly Bear and possibly Woodland Caribou remain, but no roadless areas of more than 100,000 acres. Clearcut logging and road-building have fractured the wild. Visionary wilderness restoration is essential here in Washington's northeast quadrant, but the immediate task at hand is saving the smaller pieces of old growth habitat that still exist. South of the Palouse, the Blue Mountains ride the Washington-Oregon border. This area of interior forest has one big roadless area.

The 1984 Washington Wilderness Act designated 1,021,933 out of 2,128,464 RARE II inventoried acres (Washington conservation groups proposed 2,655,355 National Forest acres for Wilderness), giving the state a total of 2,591,818 acres in the Wilderness System. 1,723,189 acres in Olympic, Mt. Rainier and North Cascades National Parks were designated as Wilderness by a bill passed by Congress and signed by President Reagan late in 1988.

Olympic Mountains 1,060,000 acres

Olympic National Park Wilderness Area and roadless	823,100
Designated Buckhorn Wilderness Area Olympic NF)	45,257
Designated The Brothers Wilderness Area (Olympic NF)	17,226
Designated Mt. Skokamish Wilderness Area (Olympic NF)	15,700
Designated Colonel Bob Wilderness Area (Olympic NF)	12,200
Designated Wonder Mountain Wilderness Area (Olympic NF)	2,320
Additional Olympic National Forest roadless	87,000
Clearwater River state roadless	57,450

Description: Olympic National Park and surrounding National Forest and state lands on the Olympic Peninsula in western Washington. The deeply carved glacial mountains of the Olympics (Mt. Olympus is 7,965') drop down to 400' elevations in the big, gentle valleys of the Hoh, Queets and Quinault Rivers. These lower elevation valleys are filled with the crowning temperate rainforest on Earth: Douglas-fir, Western Red Cedar, Sitka Spruce and Western Hemlock reach nearly 300 feet in height and over 8 feet in diameter. Grand Fir, Pacific Silver Fir and Big-leaf Maple are also widespread. Up to 140 inches of precipitation a year fall here, allowing many epiphytic mosses, lichens and ferns to grow. Olympic Rockmat is an imperiled plant in the area; there are 10 endemic plants including Flett's Violet and Piper's Bellflower. Mountain Lion (possibly the densest population in the USA), Roosevelt Elk (14,000 in several herds), Olympic Marmot, Black-tailed Deer and Black Bear are native. The Mountain Goat was introduced in the 1920s and the herd has grown to over 1,000 individuals. Many small lakes, 60 glaciers (three are more than two miles long) and large areas of alpine tundra make this one of the most glacially-influenced areas in the country.

The peerless old growth forest of the Olympics was nearly lost in the 1930s when it was under Forest Service management and slated for "truck trails" and logging, and again, during World War II after it was a National Park, when large timber companies, seeking profit under the guise of patriotism, demanded entry to convert its perfect spruce into airplanes for the war effort against fascism. Each time, conservation groups, led by The Wilderness Society, rallied to protect the wilderness forests.

Status: The area surrounding the roadless area has been devastated by industrial logging. The roadless but unprotected NF areas are scheduled to be roaded and clearcut (both old growth and roadless acreage on the Olympic NF will be halved in the next decade). The Northern Spotted Owl is particularly imperiled here since clearcutting and metropolitan development have severed this population from those in the Cascades. Because of the isolation of the Olympic wilderness from other wildlands due to logging, some biologists predict the Park will lose 50% of its large carnivores over the next century. Restoration of surrounding lower elevation areas should be a high priority in order to develop habitat for such sensitive species.

A major battle is occurring over the logging of state land which is prime Spotted Owl habitat in the Hoh and Clearwater valleys adjacent to the Park. Late in 1988 the Washington Department of Natural Resources began clearcutting some of the largest cedars remaining on Earth. Trees up to 16' in diameter were felled. An observer of the carnage reported, "This tree was thousands of years old. When it hit the ground it shattered, sending a swarm of bats into the sky." This area should be immediately added to the National Park.

Olympic National Park is a prime site for reintroduction of the Gray Wolf, but local stockmen around the Park defeated a reintroduction proposal several years ago. Widespread support for wolf reintroduction is needed to prod the Park Service into acting with courage. The introduced Mountain Goats (not historically present) are damaging the delicate alpine areas. They will supposedly be removed from the the core of the Park but allowed to remain in the adjacent Olympic NF (presumably to mollify trophy hunters). This is no solution since they will repopulate the Park from their FS refuge.

The Elwha River historically boasted excellent salmon runs. Now-unneeded hydroelectric dams (one is in the Park) destroyed those runs. Washington Earth First! and other conservationists are campaigning to remove the dams and restore the Elwha River and its salmon — there is a good chance that the dam in the Park will be removed.

Nearly all of this roadless area in the Park was designated as Wilderness late in 1988.
RM36: 1,200,000 RM27: 1,440,640

Mt. Baker 742,000 (also in Canada)

Designated Mt. Baker Wilderness Area (Mt. Baker-Snoqualmie NF)	116,100
North Cascades National Park Wilderness Area and roadless	271,400
Ross Lake National Recreation Area roadless	29,100
Designated Noisy-Diobsud Wilderness Area (Mt. Baker-Snoqualmie NF)	14,300
Additional Mt. Baker-Snoqualmie NF roadless	144,800
British Columbia roadless	166,000

Description: Northwestern Washington east of Bellingham, centered on the 10,750' volcanic cone of Mt. Baker in the North Cascades, divided from the Glacier Peak area by the North Cascades Highway, and from the Pasayten area by Ross

"Lake." This spectacular landscape of ice and fire, including Mt. Shuksan at 9,127', drops to 1,600' along Ross "Lake." These archetypical alpine mountains have over 300 glaciers, large rushing streams, hanging valleys, lakes in cirques, pinnacles, massifs, ridges and cols. The area's heavy precipitation — over 100" on the west side, including 500" of snow — has produced outstanding old growth forests of Douglas-fir, cedar, fir, spruce, Western White Pine and Mountain Hemlock below the alpine zone. Mountain Goat (native in the Cascades, unlike the Olympics), Wolverine, Fisher, Black Bear, Cougar, salmon, Peregrine Falcon, Bald Eagle and Spotted Owl are key wilderness-dependent species. A small Grizzly Bear population remains and transient Gray Wolves are reported. There are more than 50 sensitive, Threatened or Endangered plants in the North Cascades Ecosystem.

Status: Clearcutting and roads are planned for the unprotected NF areas. There has already been severe erosion from clearcuts along the Nooksack River, the main timber harvest drainage in the Mt. Baker area outside roadless areas. The west slope is especially sensitive to acid rain, which is beginning to damage lakes and forests here.

Most of the roadless area in North Cascades NP was designated as Wilderness late in 1988.

This was part of a three million acre roadless area in the US until Ross Dam and the North Cascades "Scenic" Highway cut it off from the Pasayten and Glacier Peak areas in the early 1960s. These intrusions should be removed and a single three million acre Wilderness established. The creation of North Cascades National Park was a campaign fought over several decades. Washington Earth First! has developed a detailed, carefully-researched proposal for a 8.5 million acre North Cascades Ecological Preserve in Washington and British Columbia.

The portion of the roadless area in British Columbia is also under assault. The timber beasts are in control of BC and the clearcutting is even worse than in the United States. The BC portion is cut into four small areas and one large irregular unit penetrated by many roaded and logged cherrystems, all connected by roadless corridors to the roadless area in Washington. Most of this adjacent roadless country in BC will not last long (indeed, the northern half is connected to the rest by a narrow roadless "wasp waist"). The area in the Skagit Valley Recreation Area may be a happy exception. The ongoing destruction of wild country in southern Canada is cutting wildlands in Washington, Idaho and Montana off from the great wilderness stretching north to the Arctic and will make it difficult for Grizzly, Wolverine, Caribou, Wolf, Lynx and other wildlife to travel down into the States. In effect, the North Cascades in Washington are being transformed into a habitat island and will suffer losses of wilderness-dependent species as a result.

RM36: 2,800,000* RM27: 3,435,520*

Pasayten 1,191,000 acres (also in Canada)

Designated Pasayten Wilderness Area	
(Mt. Baker-Snoqualmie & Okanogan NFs)	529,607
Additional Okanogan National Forest roadless	215,000
North Cascades Scenic Highway corridor roadless	39,730
Ross Lake National Recreation Area Wilderness	
Area and roadless	26,350
State and private roadless to east	25,000
British Columbia roadless	355,000

Description: North-central Washington west of Oroville; the North Cascades along the border with British Columbia. Jack Mountain at 8,928' is the high point; elevations drop to 1,600' on the shore of Ross "Lake" on the west side and 1,200' near Chopaka Lake on the east side. An ecological west-east transect from lower elevation wet forest (Douglas-fir, cedar, spruce, fir, hemlock) to jagged mountains of rock and ice down into dry Lodgepole Pine forest and sagebrush makes this an extremely diverse area. Subalpine Larch and Whitebark Pine are trees of the higher elevations. White-tailed Ptarmigan, Wolverine, Mountain Lion, Fisher, Mountain Goat, Lynx, Moose (one of the few populations in Washington) and a few Grizzly Bear inhabit the area.

Status: As elsewhere in the Northwest, the Forest Service is eager to log the unprotected portions of this area. They especially want to connect the Touts-Coulee road on the southeast border of the Pasayten Wilderness with other roads and cut the Lodgepole Pine in the Long Swamp area. This would cut off 84,000 acres from the roadless area at one fell swoop.

The Pasayten country should be reconnected with the Glacier Peak Wilderness by closing the North Cascades "Scenic Highway." Grizzly Bear populations should be augmented and the Gray Wolf reintroduced.

The western portion of the British Columbia area includes part of Manning Provincial Park, and a long unprotected finger to the northwest (up to Hope) that is being steadily chewed away by chainsaws and bulldozers. The eastern portion, less cut up by corridors but also under attack, includes Cathedral Park. See Mt. Baker for a discussion of the Canadian situation.

The portion of this roadless area in the Ross Lake NRA was designated as Wilderness late in 1988.

RM36: 2,800,000* RM27: 3,435,520*

Glacier Peak 1,607,000 acres

Designated Glacier Peak Wilderness Area (Mt. Baker-Snoqualmie & Wenatchee NFs)	576,600
Designated Lake Chelan-Sawtooth Wilderness Area (Okanogan & Wenatchee NFs)	152,835
Designated Henry M. Jackson Wilderness Area (Mt. Baker-Snoqualmie & Wenatchee NFs)	102,024
North Cascades National Park Wilderness Area and roadless	222,500
North Cascades Scenic Highway corridor roadless	38,780
Lake Chelan National Recreation Area Wilderness Area and roadless	59,000
Additional Mt. Baker-Snoqualmie, Wenatchee & Okanogan NFs roadless	455,000

Description: Northwestern Washington east of Everett. This internationally-significant alpine wilderness is centered on Glacier Peak, a 10,541' glacier-clad volcanic cone, and includes rushing rivers and streams (the headwaters of the Entiat, Suiattle and Sauk Rivers), many lakes, well over 100 glaciers, deep old growth forests, and rolling alpine country. Western White Pine, Douglas-fir, Grand & Silver Fir, Mountain & Western Hemlock, Engelmann & Sitka Spruce, Alaska & Western Red Cedar constitute a temperate forest with few peers. Wildlife includes Mountain Goat, Black-tailed Deer, Wolverine, Marten, Fisher, Hoary Marmot, a few Grizzly Bear, grouse (Ruffed, Spruce & Blue), White-tailed Ptarmigan, Cutthroat Trout, Steelhead, and Chinook Salmon. Elevations drop to 1,100' on Lake Chelan. The Lake Chelan-Sawtooth Wilderness is on the east side of Lake Chelan while the main bulk of the roadless complex is west of the lake. Rattlesnakes are common on dry slopes in the eastern portion.

Status: The nearly half-million acres of unprotected National Forests of this area are among the most threatened wildlands in America. The Wenatchee National Forest is mounting a full scale assault of logging and roading on the hundreds of thousands of acres of Lodgepole Pine/Ponderosa Pine/Douglas-fir forests on the east slope of the Cascades. All other NF roadless areas around the protected units are under similar attack.

The National Park Service is not fighting expanded development in the Park-surrounded town of Stehekin at the upper end of Lake Chelan. Ongoing development in this private enclave will adversely affect adjacent roadless areas. Virtually all of the NPS managed portion of this roadless area was designated as Wilderness late in 1988, however.

The Glacier Peak roadless area is penetrated by numerous cherrystem roads, as are most of the large roadless areas in Washington. Indeed, the Lake Chelan-Stehekin exclusion almost cuts the roadless area in half. Only four miles of roadless high country in North Cascades NP separates the terminus of the Stehekin road from the Mineral Park road on the western side of the divide. These intrusions reduce the effective size of the roadless area since the core is closer to roads than would be the case in an equally large area that was not burdened with such cherrystems. These penetrating roads considerably increase the amount of developed "edge" around the roadless area and cause greater stress for wildlife. Conservationists should not only fight to protect all of the currently roadless area here, but also to close or push back as far as possible these penetrating roads in order to restore the integrity of the greater wilderness ecosystem.

Until the early 1960s, Glacier Peak was connected with the Pasayten and Mt. Baker regions in a huge North Cascades roadless area of over three million acres, but the ill-conceived North Cascades "Scenic Highway" and Ross Dam and reservoir split this wildland into thirds. The highway should be closed, the reservoir drained, and the areas reunited in an unbroken Wilderness of three million acres — the highway is closed by snow half of the year as it is.

    RM36: 2,800,000* RM27: 3,435,520*

Alpine Lakes <u>464,000 acres</u>·

Designated Alpine Lakes Wilderness Area	
(Mt. Baker-Snoqualmie & Wenatchee NFs)	*391,558*
Additional Mt. Baker-Snoqualmie	
& Wenatchee NFs roadless	*72,000*

Description: Western Washington, east of Seattle; in the central Cascades south of Stevens Pass from the Glacier Peak roadless area. This popular region of lakes, tarns and stunning alpine scenery is home to Marten, Pika and Spotted Owl. Exotic Rainbow Trout are stocked. Old growth cedar and Douglas-fir fill the deep, glacial valleys. Lovely alpine meadows, Mountain Hemlock forests and rock scree dominate the high country. Ecologically, it is similar to other North Cascades areas.

Status: The FS proposes building a major bridge across the Middle Fork Snoqualmie River to gain access for road-building and clearcutting in the old growth and regenerated second growth of the Pratt River valley, which was left out of the Wilderness. This drainage was railroad logged 60 years ago, but is roadless and in relatively good shape today. Conservationists should rally to defend this entire roadless area. The Alpine Lakes are the most sensitive area in Washington to acid rain and are already suffering.

    South of the roadless area, the state Department of Natural Resources, Weyerhaeuser and Burlington Northern are massacring their lands, thereby cutting off Spotted Owl and other old growth dependent populations from their counterparts to the south. The Wenatchee NF is chipping away at the Teanaway area with logging and gold mining. ORVs from the town of Wenatchee are also a threat.

    RM36: 550,000

Mt. Rainier 233,000 acres

Mt. Rainier National Park Wilderness Area and roadless	*195,000*
Designated Clearwater Wilderness Area (Mt. Baker-Snoqualmie NF)	*14,300*
Designated Glacier View Wilderness Area (Gifford Pinchot NF)	*3,050*
Additional Mt. Baker-Snoqualmie & Gifford Pinchot NFs roadless	*20,680*

Description: Southwestern Washington southeast of Seattle. The icefields and glaciers of 14,410' high Mt. Rainier drop down into thousand-year-old forests of huge Western Hemlock and Western Red Cedar. Snow accumulation is extremely heavy (Emmons Glacier is the largest in the nation outside of Alaska). Deer, Black Bear, Elk, Mountain Goat and Bobcat are noteworthy inhabitants. Ice caves, steaming fumaroles, 27 species of trees, over 100 species of moss, and many beautiful waterfalls distinguish this area. Willi Unsoeld, conservationist, educator and first American to climb Mt. Everest, died in an avalanche on Mt. Rainier, a mountain he loved and had climbed many times. May all of us be that fortunate in the place death chooses to embrace us.

Status: The Greater Mt. Rainier Ecosystem exists in name only. The core of this once-great area, Mt. Rainier National Park, is largely cut off from lower elevation wildlands in the Cascades by habitat fragmentation and clearcut logging (the Mt. Baker-Snoqualmie NF is currently trashing the northern border of the area). Nonetheless, Mt. Rainier, Cougar Lakes, Goat Rocks, Mt. Adams and several smaller roadless areas form a complex that is severed only by single roads. These areas are, of course, largely rocks and ice.

Excessive tourism is a problem in the Park, as is acid rain. An overabundance of climbers has created a human waste problem on Mt. Rainier's glaciers, where a fall into a crevasse can be a vile experience.

Most of the roadless area in the Park was designated as Wilderness in 1988.

RM27: 1,356,800*

Cougar Lakes <u>219,000 acres</u>

Designated *William O. Douglas Wilderness Area*	
(Gifford Pinchot & Wenatchee NFs)	164,969
Mt. Rainier National Park Wilderness Area and	
roadless	19,800
Additional Wenatchee & Gifford Pinchot NFs	
roadless	34,000

Description: Southwestern Washington northwest of Yakima and east of Mt. Rainier in the central Cascades. The Cougar Lakes country is the old stomping grounds of William O. Douglas. Elevations range from 3,200' in the valley bottoms to 7,779' on Mt. Aix. Mule and Black-tailed Deer, Elk, Black Bear, Lynx, Mountain Goat, Wolverine, Fisher, Cougar, Cascade Red Fox and grouse dwell here. Scattered peaks, sharp ridges, the large, flat Tumac Plateau and hundreds of small lakes adorn this area which is along the divide of the Cascades. Forests are similar to those of other Cascades areas, although there are relatively few trees.

Status: Clearcutting and roads are currently chewing up the unprotected area. The Mt. Rainier NP portion was largely designated Wilderness in 1988.

RM27: 1,356,800*

Goat Rocks <u>196,000 acres</u>

Designated *Goat Rocks Wilderness Area*	
(Gifford Pinchot & Wenatchee NFs)	109,235
Yakima Indian Reservation roadless	75,000
Additional Wenatchee & Gifford Pinchot NFs	
roadless	11,400

Description: Southwestern Washington southwest of Yakima. The Goat Rocks are an "alpine wonderland" according to the US Forest Service. Visitors may find mist-shrouded rocky crags, a glacier; Mountain Goats, Elk; good trout fishing in the lakes and streams; Blue, Ruffed, and Spruce Grouse; and excellent views of Mt. Rainier, Mt. Adams and Mt. St. Helens. Elevation drops from 8,201' to 3,000'. The 1981 eruption of Mt.

St. Helens gave this area a good dusting of ash. Western Larch, Whitebark Pine and Noble Fir complement the more prevalent Douglas-fir, cedar and spruce.

Status: The Forest Service has chainsaws and bulldozers poised to deforest and road the unprotected portion. The status of the Yakima reservation is uncertain.

RM36: 370,000

Mt. Adams 103,000 acres

Designated Mt. Adams Wilderness Area (Gifford Pinchot NF)	36,721
Designated Mt. Adams Wilderness Area (Yakima Indian Reservation)	10,055
Additional Yakima Indian Reservation roadless	28,000
Additional Gifford Pinchot NF roadless	28,120

Description: Southwestern Washington southwest of Yakima. This roadless area encompasses the volcanic cone and slopes of 12,307' Mt. Adams, second highest in Washington. Glaciers, rushing streams, gentle terrain, large meadows and marshes, Black Bear, grouse, Elk and Black-tailed Deer grace this varied area. The lower elevations support a rich variety of trees combining both west slope old growth and drier interior forests.

Status: Roads and clearcuts are the future for the unprotected NF areas. The status of the Yakima lands is uncertain, except for the 10,000 acres of the Mt. Adams Wilderness Area on the reservation (to the best of our knowledge this is the only unit of the National Wilderness Preservation System on Indian reservation lands).

Wenaha-Tucannon 200,000 acres (also in Oregon)

Designated Wenaha-Tucannon Wilderness Area (Umatilla NF, WA)	111,048
Designated Wenaha-Tucannon Wilderness Area (Umatilla NF, OR)	66,375
Additional Umatilla NF roadless (WA & OR)	22,100

Description: Extreme southeastern Washington and north-eastern Oregon, east of Walla Walla in the Blue Mountains. Extremely steep canyons bisect this glacially carved plateau of deep basalts. Oregon Butte is 6,401'; the low point along the Wenaha River is under 2,000'. Interior dry forest of Ponderosa Pine covers much of the area. Other lower elevation trees include Douglas-fir, Western Larch, Grand Fir and Engelmann Spruce; trees above 4,000' include Lodgepole Pine, Subalpine Fir, Grand Fir, spruce and larch. Lush grasslands are made up of Bluebunch Wheatgrass and Idaho Fescue. Wildlife includes Elk, Mule Deer, White-tail Deer, Mountain Lion, Marten, Black Bear, Goshawk, Bald and Golden Eagle, and Barred Owl (the Barred Owl is extending its range west and is a direct competitor with the declining, old growth-dependent Spotted Owl). Spawning runs of Chinook Salmon and Steelhead are still good but have declined as a result of dams on the Columbia River. Native Rainbow Trout thrive in the watercourses; there is no hatchery stocking in the area.

Status: Logging threatens the undesignated portion.

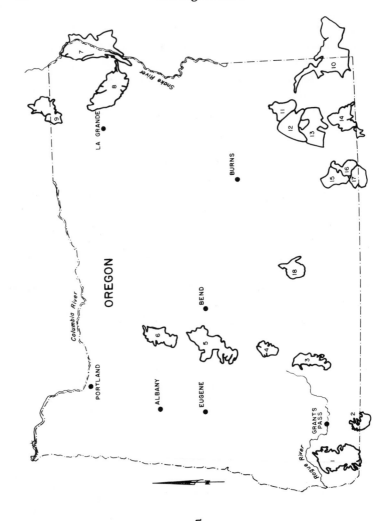

1. Kalmiopsis
2. Red Buttes
3. Sky Lakes
4. Mt. Thielsen
5. Three Sisters
6. Mt. Jefferson
7. Hells Canyon
8. Eagle Cap
9. Wenaha-Tucannon
10. Owyhee Canyons
11. Myotis
12. Sheepshead Mts
13. Alvord Desert
14. Trout Creek Mts
15. Basque Hills
16. Catlow Rim
17. Hawksie-Walksie
18. Diablo Mountain

Oregon

One hundred and forty years ago, when their wagons came to a welcome halt after traversing half the continent on the Oregon Trail, the pioneers were greeted by the grandest coniferous forest on Earth. Stretching from the Big Sur coast south of San Francisco Bay to Glacier Bay in Alaska, over two dozen species of pine, cedar, spruce, fir, hemlock and other conifers grew; some to heights of 300 feet and ages of a thousand or more years. These were not just large individual trees, however. They were bound together as a *forest*, were a single, interlocked entity — a community. The web of mycorrhizal fungi in the Pacific Northwest forest floor, Red-backed Voles, Northern Flying Squirrels and Northern Spotted Owls tied the trees together into a whole far greater than the sum of individual trees. This *old growth* forest, watered by the fog and plentiful rain of the Pacific Ocean, created — with the sodden reservoir of water trapped in fallen trees, thick duff and moss — its own climate beneath the overstory. The coastal forest was a graceful interpenetration between land and sea, with salmon and Steelhead as much members of the community as Black Bear and Pacific Salamander, with the Marbled Murrelet, an ocean bird, nesting in the crowns of the tallest trees, with seals and sea lions hauling themselves out where the ancient forest came down to the sea.

This forest flowed east to the crest of the Cascades, which split Oregon on a north-south line. Douglas-fir, hemlock, spruce, cedar and fir exchanged dominance in the forest with distance from the sea, proximity to watercourses, elevation, and elapsed time since previous catastrophic events such as forest fires. Nevertheless, it was a forest from the Pacific Ocean to the heights of the Cascades such as we shall never see again for a thousand years.

The wealth of this forest, its awesome grandeur and silence, its powerful, constant recycling of life, should have been a humbling experience, drawing the Oregonians into a new relationship with the land. Instead, it was merely an inducement to greed.

During the next century, the best of these forests passed into the ownership of large logging companies, as the timber frontier moved from the North Woods to the Pacific Northwest. By the end of World War II, most of the old growth forests on corporate land had been sacked, and the timber industry turned its eyes toward the remaining giants — on the National Forests. The Forest Service, long eager to open its holdings to the timber industry, readily complied with industry wishes. Tens of thousands of miles of road were bulldozed on the National Forests, clearcuts appeared like mange through the Coast Range and the lower elevations of the Cascades, streams turned thick with silt, and profits from the dismemberment of the titans flowed into the pockets of timber company stockholders.

The ancient forests of Oregon and Washington, west of the Cascade crest, contained 19 million acres of pure old growth before logging on an industrial scale began in the 1860-1865 era. This figure allows for the fact that all forests here were not old growth because of fire and disease outbreaks. Of that original 19 million acres, The Wilderness Society has inventoried only 950,000 acres in the two states protected in Wilderness Areas or National Parks, and a mere 1.3 million acres of quality old growth left unprotected on National Forest lands. Old growth experts in Oregon estimate that only 2% of Oregon's original old growth is "saved" while 3% remains. Even these minuscule figures are misleading because many of the ancient forest tracts are surrounded by a sea of clearcuts and naked, eroding land. Such areas have already lost their integrity as a forest: they are isolated island habitats open to windthrow, catastrophic fire, and invasion by alien species along their edges; and are unable to sustain their natural fauna of Wolverine, Fisher, River Otter, Pileated Woodpecker, Spotted Owl. . . .

Only a precious few old growth areas in western Oregon are of such a size that they can be preserved as real old growth, can be secure as a forest and not simply as a collection of large trees in an open-air museum. But even as the Forest Service's own researchers tell the agency that an old growth forest isn't a farm of big trees that can be cut down and regrown, that an old growth forest is an interdependent, functioning cycle that maintains its own climate and life-support system, the Forest Service is destroying the last large ancient forest ecosystems in Oregon, California, Washington and Alaska. (British Columbia, sadly, is doing the same.)

We have not simply turned trees into lumber. We have destroyed a complex, stable, ancient community. In the space of a century we have wrought a holocaust in the wilderness. And we continue.

On the east slope of the Cascades, the forest becomes drier, emphasizing Ponderosa Pine. Farther east, Oregon becomes another world as the Cascade rainshadow falls for hundreds of miles. The forests of northeastern Oregon in the Blue and Wallowa Mountains are more akin to those of the Northern Rocky Mountains than to the coastal rainforests. In southeastern Oregon, the Great Basin lays claim to the land with sagebrush steppe, creating a cold desert resistant to being "civilized."

Logging and road-building assault the large roadless areas of northeastern Oregon as they do the coastal and Cascade forests. On the 2.2 million acre Wallowa-Whitman NF, FS engineers have built 10,000 miles of road, and clearcutting has encroached even to timberline. The FS is also swiftly destroying the scattered forests which exist in Hells Canyon National Recreation Area. Furthermore, disruption of the natural fire cycle which created the unique, open, park-like stands of ancient Ponderosa Pine, has led to further degradation. Here, additionally, sheep and cattle damage the National Forests. Forest Service policies have destroyed habitat for Elk, Pine Marten, Spotted Frog, Goshawk and Great Grey Owl.

The high desert of southeastern Oregon, managed by the BLM, is cow country. The blading of roads, digging of stock tanks, stringing of barbed wire, extermination of Gray Wolf, control of Mountain Lion and Coyote, and transformation of sagebrush steppe into artificial pastures of exotic Crested Wheatgrass — all has been done for the benefit of a few big ranches. And more is yet to come.

Cascades Old Growth Forest, Oregon.
Photo by George Wuerthner.

The BLM has proposed one million acres of Wilderness out of 2,648,749 acres of WSAs. Oregon conservation groups, led by the Oregon Natural Resources Council (ONRC), in a remarkably daring and far-sighted proposal, have recommended closing minor dirt roads and combining roadless areas to create several large Wilderness Areas. They propose in excess of 5 million acres of Wilderness in the Oregon High Desert.

In no other state can one man take the credit for destroying wilderness as single-handedly as can Sen. Mark Hatfield in Oregon. It is Hatfield, with his brick-wall arrogance, it is Hatfield, handmaiden to the timber industry, it is Hatfield, the dovish, liberal Republican, who has insured that the Forest Service will not be constrained from its chosen task of liquidating the last Oregon old growth. At every step of the political process, Mark Hatfield has used his legislative mastery and power to block protection of Wilderness with trees in it, to thwart restrictions on Forest Service roading and logging, to deny consideration of old growth as anything more than a collection of dying trees that must be harvested.

Hatfield crushed Oregon Congressman Jim Weaver in 1978 as Weaver tried to gain Wilderness designation for the North Kalmiopsis Roadless Area, the largest, most intact, diverse and healthy tract of old growth left in Oregon. Hatfield encouraged the Forest Service in RARE II to make forested Roadless Areas available for clearcutting. Hatfield designed the 1984 Oregon Wilderness bill to protect only 853,062 out of 4 million roadless acres on the Oregon National Forests — and nearly all of that rock and ice, except for a few museum pieces of ancient forest. It has been Mark Hatfield who has defended the bloated road-building budget of the Forest Service as conservationists have tried to pare it back. And Mark Hatfield is the manipulator of the legislative process who has inserted rider after rider in appropriations bills to prevent legal challenges by conservationists to Forest Service timber sales.[*]

---

[*] This is not to pretend that Hatfield has done his dirty work without assistance. Much of it has been done with the support of a supposedly conservation-oriented Democratic Congressman from Oregon -- Les AuCoin. AuCoin, regularly supported for re-election by the Sierra Club

If Oregon didn't have a gutsy state-wide wilderness group like ONRC, if hundreds of Earth First!ers hadn't blockaded bulldozers and chainsaws with their own bodies, Hatfield and the Forest Service would be even more effective in their service to the timber industry. But, at this writing as 1988 becomes 1989, efforts to save the North Kalmiopsis by tree-sitters, legislation and lawsuits appear to have failed. Like the Nazis after *Kristallnacht*, the Forest Service stands before a helpless community.

When comes the time for Oregon to remember Mark Hatfield, a stump, a giant, bronzed stump, will suffice.

Western Oregon

The Coast Range and Cascades parallel each other through Oregon and Northern California with the Willamette and Sacramento Valleys, respectively, dividing them. Along the state border, the Siskiyou Mountains bridge the gap between the two ranges, creating an area of astonishing diversity. Some areas in western Oregon receive more than 100" of precipitation a year. Several National Forests share these ranges.

Kalmiopsis 408,000 acres (also in California)

Designated Kalmiopsis Wilderness Area	
(Siskiyou NF)	*168,900*
Additional Siskiyou NF roadless (OR)	*235,000*
Six Rivers NF roadless (CA)	*4,000*

Description: Extreme southwestern Oregon west of Grants Pass and extreme northeastern California north of Crescent City. Elevations drop from 4,903' to 240' in this rugged area of ridges divided by deep river canyons. The many streams form the headwaters of the Chetco and Smith Rivers and of tributaries to the Rogue. The Illinois Wild & Scenic River flows

---

(but not by the Oregon League of Conservation Voters), has led the fight for an increased Forest Service road-building budget in the House, and in 1984 he knifed Weaver in the back during negotiations between the larger House-passed Oregon Wilderness bill and Hatfield's inadequate measure.

through the area and offers an extremely challenging float trip.

The Kalmiopsis holds the most diverse coniferous forest on Earth (28 conifer species) and may be the center of conifer evolution. The Coast Redwood reaches its northern limit and Alaska Cedar and Pacific Silver Fir are at their southern extremes here. The Forest Service calls this the most interesting botanical area in the Northwest (but that doesn't restrain them from using chainsaws to make it less interesting). Only the Southern Appalachians surpass the Kalmiopsis for botanical diversity in the US. There are 92 distinct plant communities and over 100 rare and sensitive plants here. Most of the area under Wilderness protection has serpentine soils which cause stunted tree growth (*Kalmiopsis leachiana* — a rare heath — grows here). The area north of Bald Mountain (outside the Wilderness Area boundary) has dense old growth forests in Silver, Indigo, Lawson and Shasta Costa Creeks, harboring possibly the largest Spotted Owl population in the Northwest and the largest area of virgin forest on the coast. Brewer Spruce, Port-Orford-Cedar and Sadler Oak are rare plants which are common in this area. Black Bear, Bigfoot, Cougar, Pine Marten, Wolverine, Mountain Beaver (a rare rodent not closely related to the Beaver), Northern Spotted Owl and Pacific Salamander are among the forest denizens. The area is also noted for vicious yellow jackets, rattlesnakes, ticks and Poison Oak. See David Rains Wallace's **The Klamath Knot** (Sierra Club Books, 1983) for details on this fascinating region.

Status: One of the most important and threatened roadless areas in America, the 150,000 acre North Kalmiopsis is slated for clearcutting and roading by the Forest Service over the next several years. Senator Mark Hatfield, pitbull of the timber industry, kept this area from being designated as part of the Kalmiopsis Wilderness in the late 1970s. A famous Earth First! blockade (44 arrests) and law suit (*EF!, ONRC, et al* v. *Block*) stopped Forest Service destruction in 1983, but the battle has been renewed, with several dozen Earth First!ers arrested in 1987-88. The Forest Service is using the 1987 Silver Fire, which burned through here, as an excuse to road and log the area (supposedly to rehabilitate it). In reality, the fire did relatively little damage and was overall beneficial. Less than

10% burned like in Smokey the Bear posters, and that was recovering nicely by 1988. Logging after a forest fire is like raping
a burn victim.

The Kalmiopsis is the centerpiece of a 750,000 acre
Siskiyou National Park proposal (including the Rogue River
Wilderness) advocated by the Oregon Natural Resources Council; this Park proposal should be expanded to the south to include the Smith River-Siskiyou country in California for a 2
million acre National Park protecting matchless old growth
forest and wild rivers. The prime area in Oregon for
reintroduction of Grizzly Bear and Gray Wolf is the Kalmiopsis.

RM36: 830,000

Red Buttes 104,000 acres (also in California)
See California for description and status.

Sky Lakes 166,000 acres

Designated Sky Lake Wilderness Area	
(Rogue River & Winema NFs)	*116,300*
Crater Lake National Park roadless	*23,100*
Additional Rogue River & Winema NFs roadless	*26,800*

Description: Southwestern Oregon, northwest of Klamath
Falls; south of Crater Lake National Park along the southern
Cascade crest to Mt. McLoughlin — at 9,495', the high point.
Elevations drop to 3,800' on the Middle Fork of the Rogue
River. Over 200 pools of water, from ponds to 40 acre lakes,
display the lushness of the area. Common trees include Shasta
Red Fir, Pacific Yew, White Fir, Mountain Hemlock and Sub-
alpine Fir. Elk, deer and Pronghorn live here.

Status: The NPS and conservationists propose the Crater
Lake NP area for Wilderness. Unprotected FS areas will eventually fall to the chainsaw. Pelican Butte, on the southeastern
portion of the roadless area and at the western edge of Upper
Klamath Lake, is particularly threatened by FS roading and
logging. It has the highest concentration of Spotted Owls on
the east side of Oregon's Cascades, and is also important habitat for Bald Eagles. Chamber of commerce boosters and other

fast-buck artists in Klamath Falls have long proposed a down-hill ski area on Pelican Butte, too.

Mount Thielsen 105,000 acres

Designated Mount Thielsen Wilderness Area	
(Umpqua, Deschutes & Winema NFs)	*55,100*
Additional Umpqua, Deschutes & Winema	
NFs roadless	*50,000*

Description: Southwestern Oregon, east of Roseburg and north of Crater Lake National Park along the Cascade crest. Mount Thielsen reaches 9,182'; the low point is 4,300'. The Pacific Crest National Scenic Trail traverses the length of the area, attaining the high point of the Oregon portion of the trail: 7,650'. The area offers spectacular vistas west to the Oregon Coast Range, and east all the way to Steens Mountain. Mt. Thielsen is a stately landmark of rugged basalt with a distinctively pointed cap, or volcanic plug. The east side is characterized by U shaped glacial valleys punctuated by flats with large marshes, while the west side is heavily forested with a young, fire-shaped ecosystem.

Status: Threats include snowmobiles and logging outside the Wilderness. The non-wilderness portions are under a federal "recreation area" designation which was applied mainly to allow snowmobile use, which is prohibited in Wilderness.

RM36: 640,000

Three Sisters 424,000 acres

Designated Three Sisters Wilderness Area	
(Deschutes & Willamette NFs)	*285,202*
Waldo Lake Wilderness Area (Willamette NF)	*39,200*
Additional Deschutes & Willamette NF roadless	*100,000*

Description: Western Oregon, along the Cascade crest east of Eugene. The snowcapped stratovolcano (individual conically shaped, very young volcanos) Three Sisters (10,358' on South Sister — the third highest point in Oregon) and other volcanic cones drop down to lower elevation (2,000' is low point) old growth forest of Douglas-fir in French Pete Creek on the west side and to Ponderosa Pine forests on the drier east side of the Cascades. Trees also include Silver Fir, Subalpine Fir, Mountain Hemlock, Western Hemlock and Lodgepole Pine. The area includes a large area above treeline, many lakes (Mink Lake covers 360 acres), waterfalls, lava fields, obsidian cliffs, and the north and west shores of Waldo Lake. Collier Glacier between North and Middle Sisters is the largest in Oregon. Roosevelt Elk, Mule Deer, Black-tailed Deer, Black Bear, Marten, Mink, Wolverine and grouse are natives. Snow depths reach 20'. This is the only truly representative area of the western Cascade forest/volcano ecosystem.

Status: This was the site of a major conservation battle in the 1960s and '70s to protect the ancient forests of French Pete Creek. Unprotected roadless areas, including old growth lower elevation forests, are under severe threat of clearcutting and roading by the Forest Service. A major campaign is needed to protect the undesignated 100,000 acres of the Three Sisters. Fisher, Grizzly, Gray Wolf and Lynx should be reintroduced.

Waldo Lake, the purest large body of water in the world (purer than lab grade distilled water), is threatened by ski areas, logging, human waste, motor oil waste and other human impacts. Waldo Lake is generally surrounded by Wilderness and adjacent roadless lands, but has motorized access at two spots and associated development. Only complete and total protection will save this exceptional lake.

Mount Jefferson 191,000 acres

Designated Mount Jefferson Wilderness Area	
(Willamette & Deschutes NFs)	107,008
Warm Springs Indian Reservation Whitewater	
River Roadless Area	65,300
Additional Willamette & Deschutes NFs roadless	18,400

Description: Western Oregon, east of Corvallis and Albany along the Cascade crest. Mount Jefferson at 10,497' is the second highest peak in Oregon and is flanked with glaciers. Three Fingered Jack is another prominent peak. Both are popular climbs. The low point is 2,400'. Rock outcrops, talus slopes, alpine meadows, spectacular wildflowers and over 150 lakes add to the beauty of the area. 75" of precipitation falls annually. Roosevelt Elk, Black Bear, Mountain Lion and deer are present. 62% of the area is timbered, with Douglas-fir, cedar, fir, spruce and Ponderosa Pine being the most common trees.

Status: Unprotected NF portions are under threat of clearcutting and roading. Status of the Indian Reservation area is uncertain.

Northeastern Oregon

Northeastern Oregon, with Hells Canyon and the Blue and Wallowa Mountains, is ecologically more like Idaho than it is like western Oregon. The large roadless areas left are in Hells Canyon National Recreation Area (managed by the FS), and the Wallowa-Whitman and Umatilla NFs.

Hells Canyon 591,000 acres (also in Idaho)	
Designated Hells Canyon Wilderness Area _(FS, OR)_	130,095
Designated Hells Canyon Wilderness Area _(FS, ID)_	83,800
Designated Hells Canyon Wilderness Area _(BLM, ID)_	1,038
Additional Hells Canyon NRA, BLM and private _roadless (OR)_	160,000
Additional Hells Canyon NRA & private _roadless (ID)_	204,000
Snake Wild & Scenic River roadless (OR)	6,000
Snake Wild & Scenic River roadless (ID)	6,000

Description: Extreme northeastern Oregon east of Enterprise, and west-central Idaho west of Riggins. Hells Canyon on the Snake River is the deepest canyon in North America (over 8,000' deep in places) according to folks in Idaho and Oregon. (Californians claim the title for Kings Canyon, but the Northwesterners argue persuasively that Hells Canyon was formed by erosion — water flow — instead of faulting, and that it is a distinct, two-sided abyss cut in a wide plateau, not a mountain "gorge.") The Idaho portion consists of high peaks with lakes (Seven Devils Mts); the Oregon portion involves grassy benches and timbered ridges; the Snake River roars between. Very large and powerful rapids on the Snake River make it one of the "big water" runs of North America. Elevations drop from 9,393' (He Devil Mountain in Idaho) to 800' along the Snake. Black Bear, Mountain Lion, Elk, Mountain Goat, Bighorn Sheep, White Sturgeon and Peregrine Falcon populate the area. The last authenticated Grizzly in Oregon was killed here in 1937, although there are an increasing number of possible Grizzly sightings. Vegetation ranges from mixed conifer forest (Douglas-fir, Ponderosa Pine, Western Larch, Pacific Yew and Subalpine Fir) down to sagebrush grassland.

Hells Canyon was the site of major conservation battles in the 1960s and '70s over additional dams on the Snake River. 67 miles of the Snake is now a National Wild & Scenic River and Hells Canyon is a National Recreation Area, which is supposedly better protected than run-of-the-mill National Forest land. It's nice to win one now and then.

Status: A major battle is raging today over protection of the undesignated wildlands in Hells Canyon NRA (it seems we didn't entirely win back in the '70s). The Forest Service proposes major clearcutting and roading in the area, and loggers have threatened violence against "obstructionist" conservationists (eco-terrorism?). Oregon Senator Bob Packwood proposed additional Wilderness but backed off after such threats. The FS proposes 100 million board feet of logging in 1989, which conservationists say is not only destructive but blatantly illegal. They have filed one lawsuit and are planning two more. National conservation groups need to make this campaign a priority.

Motors on boats on the Snake River should be prohibited. A major RV park is proposed in the Scenic River corridor at Pittsburg Landing in one of the most archaeologically sensitive areas in the West. It should be stopped dead in its tracks. An additional 34 miles of the Snake was studied and recommended for Scenic River protection but this designation has not been forthcoming.

Minor roads should be closed and past logging abuses rehabilitated to join Hells Canyon with the Eagle Cap Wilderness to the west in order to establish a 1,500,000 acre Wilderness; Grizzlies and Gray Wolves should be reintroduced.

Cattle and sheep grazing is permitted in the Wilderness; it should be eliminated.

RM27: 1,203,840

Eagle Cap <u>452,000 acres</u>
Designated Eagle Cap Wilderness Area
  (Wallowa-Whitman NF)   *359,976*
Additional Wallowa-Whitman NF roadless   *92,000*

Description: East of La Grande and west of Hells Canyon in northeastern Oregon. The craggy Wallowa Mountain Range features exposed granite, limestone and marble; four major rivers (Minam, Imnaha, Wallowa and Lostine); over 50 lakes (including Legore Lake at 8,800' — the highest in Oregon). The high point is Sacajawea at 9,839'; 31 other peaks exceed 8,000'; the low point is 2,800'. Mixed conifer forests (Douglas-fir, Engelmann Spruce, Subalpine & Grand Fir, Whitebark & Limber Pine) drop into Ponderosa Pine. The contiguous roadless lands are lower-elevation, more biologically productive forests compared to the "rocks and ice" in the designated Wilderness. The Mountain Goat has been introduced. Mountain Lion, Black Bear, Elk, Fisher (reintroduced in 1961), Beaver, Mule Deer and the very rare Wolverine are among the native mammals. The entire population of the Wallowa Gray-crowned Rosy Finch (a subspecies) nests here. Other birds include the Great Gray Owl, Goshawk and Pileated Woodpecker. Now a popular backpacking and rock-climbing area, it is the former range of Chief Joseph and the Nez Perce. Eagle Cap is the largest protected Wilderness in Oregon and the Minam River is the only fully protected major or intermediate drainage in the state.

Status: Logging and roading threaten the portion outside of the Wilderness. The FS plans logging all the way to timberline along the southern boundary. The Eagle Cap should be combined with Hells Canyon for a one and a half million acre Wilderness. Of the formerly large herd of Bighorn Sheep (including "Spot" — the largest recorded ram in the US), 75% have died of a disease transmitted from domestic sheep. Grazing has been suspended by the FS but there is great pressure to put the "hooved locusts" (as John Muir called them) back in.

Wenaha-Tucannon 200,000 acres (also in Washington)
See Washington for description and status.

Southeastern Oregon

In surprising contrast to the deep forests of western Oregon, southeastern Oregon is part of the Great Basin Desert that covers most of Nevada. Some of the least-visited areas in the United States are tucked away in this high lonesome. The western three-quarters of the Oregon High Desert, including Steens Mountain and the Alvord Desert, is part of the geographic Great Basin with no outlet to the sea. The eastern quarter takes in the Owyhee Canyons which are part of the Snake River basin. Except for several large National Wildlife Refuges, BLM manages the public lands here. Some salute the Oregon High Desert as the last bastion of the "real" cowboy. Others kick the cow shit.

Owyhee Canyons 619,000 acres (also in Idaho)
See Idaho for description and status.

Myotis (Saddle Butte) 190,000 acres

BLM WSA 3-111	*86,300*
Additional BLM , private and state roadless to south	*67,000*
State & private roadless to northwest	*37,000*

Description: Southeastern Oregon north of Burns Junction. This apparently flat, but diverse area of lava flow, sagebrush steppe, spring-fed sinks and dry lake beds is on the divide between the Owyhee drainage and the Great Basin. Bluebunch Wheatgrass, Big Sagebrush and the exotic invader, Cheatgrass, are the dominant plants, although Shadscale and Indian Ricegrass are present in the southeast. Lava tubes and caves provide important habitat for several species of bats, including the rare Long-eared Myotis, and for mosses and ferns — unusual in this arid landscape. This is the northern limit of the Kit Fox and some of Oregon's best winter range for Pronghorn. Other inhabitants include Mule Deer, Bobcat, Yellow-bellied Marmot and an Oregon state endangered plant *Padiocactus simpson robustar*. "Wild" horses roam the area.

Status: Threats include construction of additional developments for livestock grazing. Jeep trails and a few grazing developments are the main blemishes in the roadless area, although a vehicle route which BLM uses as the southern boundary of their WSA may in fact qualify as a "road," thereby dropping 67,000 acres from this area. Nonetheless, the central portion is quite pristine.

ONRC (Oregon Natural Resources Council) proposes a 172,100 acre Wilderness on BLM land. BLM opposes Wilderness designation for this area. A dirt county road separates this area from the scenic Lower Owyhee Canyons — this road should be closed and a single 400,000 acre Wilderness established. 37,000 acres to the northeast, including Saddle Butte in this roadless area, were transferred from BLM to the state as a result of a recent land exchange. The state should be encouraged to protect their portion as Wilderness.

Sheepshead Mountains 232,000 acres

BLM WSAs 2-72 & 3-114	*231,467*
Private roadless	*500*

Description: Southeastern Oregon northwest of Burns Junction and north of the Alvord Desert. Rolling sagebrush and grass covered hills are cut by a lava flow, steep draws and canyons, ridgelines and escarpments to form this complex area. Ephemeral lakes create good waterfowl habitat in moist years. Elevations generally range from 4,000' to over 5,000', with Mickey Butte reaching 6,294' and nearby Mickey Basin dropping to 3,912'. Intermittent creeks include Heath, Wildcat, Mickey, Bone, Palomino and Antelope. Vegetative communities are Big Sagebrush/Bluebunch Wheatgrass, Shadscale/Indian Ricegrass, Low Sagebrush/Bunchgrass, Silver Sage, Great Basin Wildrye, playa margin, saline meadows, and Winter-fat, with numerous grass, forb and shrub species represented. Three potential Endangered/Threatened plants, Weak Milk-vetch, Davis' Pepper Cress and Lemmon's Onion, are present. Pronghorn, Sage Grouse, Mule Deer, Bobcat, Kit

Fox, Black-tailed Jackrabbit, Sage Sparrow and Long-eared Owl reside in the area. Raptors, including American Kestrel, Golden Eagle and Prairie Falcon, nest on the cliffs. There is potential for reintroduction of Bighorn Sheep. The Sheepsheads afford excellent views of Steens Mountain and the Alvord Desert.

Status: BLM divided this area into several WSAs based on a network of jeep trails and range developments. ONRC proposes a 245,100 acre Wilderness; although BLM considered designating the entire area as Wilderness and closing the intervening vehicle routes, they are proposing only 105,720 acres in three of the WSAs for Wilderness and the closure the routes between them. Minor dirt roads separate the Sheepshead complex from the Alvord Desert complex to the south; at the very least the Sheepsheads and Alvord Desert should be combined for a single Wilderness of 750,000 acres. Preferably, however, this area should be part of a 3 million acre Oregon Desert National Wilderness Park (see Alvord Desert for details).

The main threats are welfare ranching (several range "improvement" projects are planned —including ripping out native plant communities and replacing them with exotic Crested Wheatgrass) and ORVs.

Alvord Desert 361,000 acres

BLM WSAs 2-74 & 2-73a & h	*294,110*
Additional BLM roadless	*22,000*
Mixed private, state, BLM roadless	*45,000*

Description: Southeastern Oregon southwest of Burns Junction. The huge Alvord Playa (dry lake bed) is one of the few places where the curvature of Earth can be easily perceived, and is also one of the starkest desert areas in the nation (portions receive only 5" of precipitation a year). Hot springs (up to 210° F), sand dunes, canyons and cliffs vary the landscape. Massive Steens Mountain abruptly rises up west of this unit. The most extensive plant community is a combination of Big Sagebrush/Bunchgrass and Shadscale/Budsage. Greasewood/Saltgrass and Great Basin Wildrye are other important communities. Solitary Milk-vetch and Davis' Pepper Cress are candidates for federal Endangered status. The area provides important winter range for Pronghorn and Bighorn Sheep. Other noteworthy denizens include Snowy Plover (Threatened in Oregon), American Avocet, Sage Thrasher, Prairie Falcon, Golden Eagle and Bobcat. Ord Kangaroo Rat, Dark Kangaroo Mouse, Merriam Shrew, Collared Lizard, Great Basin Spadefoot Toad and several other species reach the northern limits of their ranges here.

Status: Some vehicle ways cut through this area, although a 160,000 acre core is pristine. BLM divided the area into three WSAs based on jeep trails. A few range developments are on the periphery. Threats include geothermal development, ORVs, a 500 KV powerline and continued overgrazing.

BLM proposes a scant 84,950 acres for Wilderness; the Oregon Natural Resources Council proposes a 322,900 acre Alvord Desert Wilderness.

The Alvord Desert is the center of a huge, essentially uninhabited northern Great Basin Desert wilderness crossed only by minor dirt roads. A 3 million acre Oregon Desert National Wilderness Park (including some land in Nevada) should be established here, consisting of the Alvord Desert, the Sheepshead Mts to the north, Trout Creek Mts to the south, Steens Mountain to the west, and the Pueblo Mts/Beatys Butte/Basque Hills/Catlow Rim/Hawksie-Walksie/Sheldon country to the southwest. Gray Wolf should be reintroduced and livestock grazing eliminated.

Trout Creek Mountains 212,000 acres (also in Nevada)

BLM WSAs 3-156 et al (OR)	*173,515*
Additional BLM, private roadless (OR)	*16,000*
BLM WSA 2-859 (NV)	*13,200*
Additional BLM roadless (NV)	*9,000*

Description: Southeastern Oregon and northwestern Nevada west of McDermitt, NV. The Trout Creek Mountains are an uplifted, tilted block with a steep southeastern escarpment. South of the escarpment is a collapsed volcanic dome, McDermitt Caldera. Many semi-parallel canyons flow from the south to the northwest. Elevations rise from 6,500' to 8,500'.

Vegetation consists primarily of grass and sagebrush, with several other shrubs common, including snowbrush, wild rose, Squaw Currant and snowberry. Mountain mahogany and Aspen grow along the streams and form extensive stands in the higher elevations; willow is also common in riparian zones. Five plants are on the Oregon state rare/endangered list and one, Bristle-flowered Collomia, is a candidate for federal Endangered listing. This is one of the most diverse and productive wildlife habitats in southeastern Oregon. Species include Beaver, Pronghorn, Mule Deer, Bobcat, Mountain Lion, Sage Grouse, Whitehorse Cutthroat Trout, Lahontan Redside Shiner and possibly the Endangered Lahontan Cutthroat Trout. Bighorn Sheep may be reintroduced.

Status: Continued overgrazing and related developments are the major threat. ORVs use the jeep trails in the area.

BLM divided the Trout Creeks into five WSAs based on jeep trails between them. ONRC proposes a single 252,000 acre Wilderness by closing jeep trails and minor dirt roads, and BLM recommends closing some jeep trails to form a single Wilderness of 136,540 acres. This area is separated from the Alvord Desert country, to the north, by a gravel road. It should be part of a 3 million acre Oregon Desert National Wilderness Park.

Basque Hills 159,000 acres

BLM WSA 2-84	*141,730*
Checkerboard BLM, private roadless	*17,000*

Description: Southeastern Oregon south of Blitzen. The Basque Hills are in the middle of nowhere. Nowhere, by the way, is a virtually uninhabited area, far from paved roads, in the Oregon High Desert consisting of several large roadless areas broken only by minor dirt roads. The Basque Hills are a range of gently rolling hills, rims and buttes; the roadless area also includes a large flat area to the west. A wide diversity of native grasses remains due to a lack of water for domestic livestock. Vegetative communities in this austere landscape are Big Sagebrush/Bluebunch Wheatgrass, Big Sagebrush/ Greasewood, Indian Ricegrass/Needlegrass, and Winter-fat; contrasting with bare playa and playa margin. A newly discovered plant, Crosby's Buckwheat, is a candidate for federal

Endangered listing. Raptors nesting along Coyote Rim and
other rims include Golden Eagle, Prairie Falcon, Red-tailed
Hawk, American Kestrel, Raven and Great-horned Owl. The
Basque Hills are a major wintering area for Pronghorn; other
critters include Brewer's Sparrow, Horned Lark, Western Rattlesnake, Canyon Mouse and Bushy-tailed Woodrat.

Status: A 500 KV powerline may be constructed through the
area. Phony wildlife improvement projects ("brush removal")
and livestock developments, including Crested Wheatgrass
seedings, also threaten it. Ranchers and pickup truck hunters
use a few jeep trails and cherrystemmed dirt roads in the area.

The Basque Hills are part of an important complex of roadless areas that includes Catlow Rim, Hawksie-Walksie,
Beatys Butte and the Pueblo Mountains and which are separated only by poor dirt roads; all should be part of a 3 million
acre Oregon Desert National Wilderness Park (see Alvord
Desert). ONRC proposes 137,200 acres for Wilderness; BLM
opposes Wilderness.

RM36: 980,000*

Catlow Rim (Rincon) <u>104,000 acres</u>
BLM WSA 2-82   *104,085*

Description: Southeastern Oregon west of Fields. Catlow
Rim rises nearly 2,000' above the valley floor and hosts one of
the highest raptor concentrations in Oregon on its west-facing
cliffs. The rim, reaching 6,350' on Square Mountain in the
north, is broken by canyons and springs. In the southern portion
of the unit, Lone Mountain rises to 6,903' in elevation and has
rock outcroppings of rhyodacitic rock forming pinnacles, columns
and natural bridges. The tables are ringed with rimrock. The
lowest elevation is 4,450' in Catlow Valley. Vegetation is primarily the Big Sagebrush/Bunchgrass community with numerous grass species. Low Sagebrush and Black Sagebrush communities also occur. A small area of Western Juniper and mountain
mahogany is found on Lone Mountain. Over 2,000 Pronghorn
sometimes winter in the southeastern portion of the area. Sage
Grouse and other birds and mammals typical of the sagebrush
steppe are present. Bighorn Sheep may be reintroduced. There
are a couple of important archaeological sites— Catlow Cave

(a well-known Paleo-Indian site) and an area with a concentration of rock art.

Status: The primary threat is the construction of "improvements" for the welfare ranchers in the area, including pipelines, fences, stock tanks and Crested Wheatgrass seedings —all at taxpayer expense, all so more cattle can destroy the vegetation and wildlife of the area. ONRC proposes a 113,100 acre Wilderness. BLM proposes a mere 20,500 acres. It should be part of a 3 million acre Oregon Desert National Wilderness Park (see Alvord Desert).

RM36: 980,000*

Hawksie-Walksie 144,000 acres (also in Nevada)

Sheldon National Wildlife Refuge roadless	
(Big Table, NV)	*71,000*
BLM WSA 1-146 (Hawk Mt, OR)	*73,340*

Description: Extreme northwestern Nevada and southeastern Oregon west of Denio, NV. This high sagebrush steppe on the basaltic mesa of Big Spring Table includes a major wintering area for the Oregon-Nevada Interstate Pronghorn herd. Other wildlife includes Coyote, Mountain Lion, Mule Deer, Bobcat, Peregrine Falcon and nesting Prairie Falcon. Numerous Sage Grouse strutting grounds are present. "Wild" horses roam here as well. Bunchgrasses and other grasses are in fairly good condition, making this an important area for preservation. There are scattered Western Juniper and one stand of mountain mahogany. Big Spring Butte is the high point on the Refuge at 6,547', while Hawk Mountain in Oregon reaches 7,234'. Hawksie-Walksie itself is a dry lake basin which fills with water in the spring, attracting waterfowl. It is the low point at 5,600'. This is a cold desert with precipitation varying from 5" to 15" annually, mostly in snow and winter rain, a very short frost-free period, and wide summer temperature swings of 50 degrees between night and day.

Status: Threats include Crested Wheatgrass seedings, increased livestock use, and "improvements" to allow the "slow elk" to "more effectively utilize the resource."

Conservationists propose a 76,900 acre BLM Hawksie-Walksie Wilderness and 92,000 acres of Wilderness on the

Refuge by closing minor dirt roads (169,000 acres total). The FWS proposes 65,500 for Wilderness; BLM proposes 69,640 for a total agency proposal of 135,000 acres. This area is separated from the Catlow Rim and Basque Hills roadless areas by minor dirt roads, and should be part of a 3 million acre Oregon Desert National Wilderness Park.

RM36: 980,000*

Diablo Mountain 142,000 acres

BLM WSA 1-58	114,930
Summer Lake State Wildlife Management Area roadless	8,000
Private roadless (Summer Dry Lake)	19,000

Description: South-central Oregon north of Lakeview. Encompassing Summer Lake playa (4,146') and adjacent salt flats and sand dunes, this area rises 1,800' above the desert to the east. Rimrock sets off Diablo Mountain. A vegetative transition from salt desert shrub (Black Greasewood, Spiny Hopsage, Shadscale, Budsage, Horsebrush, Desert Saltgrass and many wildflowers) to sagebrush communities occurs here. Bighorn Sheep may be reintroduced. Other wildlife includes Pronghorn, Mule Deer and other species typical of the Great Basin.

Status: Threats include geothermal development, ORVs and continued overgrazing. ONRC proposes a 194,000 acre Wilderness by closing a dirt road dividing this roadless area from roadless country to the east. BLM proposes 51,160 acres as Wilderness.

RM36: 540,000

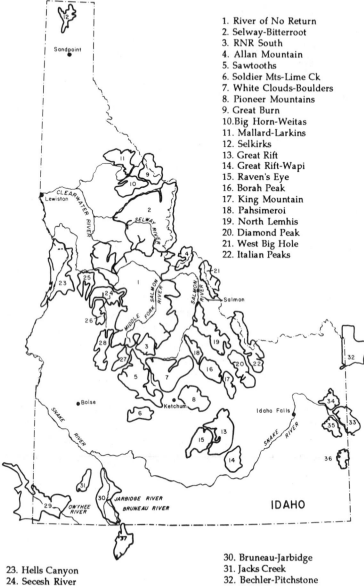

1. River of No Return
2. Selway-Bitterroot
3. RNR South
4. Allan Mountain
5. Sawtooths
6. Soldier Mts-Lime Ck
7. White Clouds-Boulders
8. Pioneer Mountains
9. Great Burn
10. Big Horn-Weitas
11. Mallard-Larkins
12. Selkirks
13. Great Rift
14. Great Rift-Wapi
15. Raven's Eye
16. Borah Peak
17. King Mountain
18. Pahsimeroi
19. North Lemhis
20. Diamond Peak
21. West Big Hole
22. Italian Peaks

23. Hells Canyon
24. Secesh River
25. French Ck-Patrick Butte
26. Needles
27. Red Mountain
28. Peace Rock
29. Owyhee Canyons

30. Bruneau-Jarbidge
31. Jacks Creek
32. Bechler-Pitchstone
33. Palisades
34. Garns Mountain
35. Bear Creek
36. Stump Creek
37. Jarbidge

Idaho

Idaho is the Wilderness State, not the Potato State. True, Idaho spud growers dominate parts of southern and southeastern Idaho, but north, east and west of the spuds is a diverse wilderness that can only be described in superlatives. For example, as a percentage of its land base, Idaho has more wilderness (designated and de facto) than any other of the contiguous states. Outside of Alaska, the nation's largest designated Wilderness Area (or wildland unit of any kind) is almost wholly within Idaho — the Frank Church-River of No Return Wilderness. The two longest true wilderness rivers in the contiguous states, the Salmon and Selway, are also in Idaho. Idaho has the highest percentage of its land in forest of the western states, in spite of its splendid wild deserts. And Idaho's National Forests include more unprotected de facto wilderness than any other state: about nine and half million vulnerable acres. Despite the spuds, Idaho is above all else a land of untamed mountains, forests, rivers, canyons and deserts.

The natural bioregions of Idaho are defined by three major areas: 1) The arid and semi-arid plains and deserts of the south, including the Snake River Plain; 2) The eastern fringe mountains, part of the Greater Yellowstone Wildland complex; and 3) Wild central and northern Idaho — an unbelievable expanse of mountains, forests, rivers and canyons.

Within the arid south are the volcanic wilds of the Great Rift-Craters of the Moon country, and in the far southwest the remote Owyhee canyons, deserts and mountains. Within these areas are huge chunks of desert wilderness, equal in rugged wild grandeur to any of the nation's better-known desert wildlands to the south. Nonetheless, it is the mountainous wilds of central and northern Idaho which really define this state. Particularly in this region, Idaho still presents the opportunity to protect big, ecologically complete wilderness within all or most of its native ecosystems.

The native ecosystems of much of the Snake River Plain and the upper Snake River Valley, though, have been obliterated and replaced with agriculture. Much of this part of southern Idaho was once a fertile intermountain grassland, rich in Bison, Elk, Pronghorn, Sandhill Crane, Long-billed Curlew, Bald Eagle, Trumpeter Swan and numerous other species now either regionally extinct or reduced to fragmented remnant populations.

In the mountains of central and northern Idaho, however, viable populations of most of the native species survive. Even Gray Wolves and Grizzlies are hanging on (not as viable populations but as scattered individuals) in parts of this region, and the mountains of central Idaho are one of the great strongholds of the Mountain Lion. A remnant population of Woodland Caribou has recently been augmented with reintroductions in the far north. This Endangered subspecies of Caribou once ranged south nearly to the Salmon River, and they, like Grizzlies and Gray Wolves, should be reintroduced to the Selway-Bitterroot Wilderness and adjacent wildlands of the Clearwater and Panhandle National Forests. Concurrently, various roads should be closed: The closure of one dirt road — the Magruder Corridor — would unite the River of No Return (RNR) and Selway-Bitterroot Wildernesses into a single 5 million acre unit; to the north, the closure of a few lightly-used dirt logging roads on the Clearwater and Panhandle National Forests would mean a Wilderness unit of roughly a million acres. With these road closures, the core of Idaho would consist of million-acre or nearly million-acre Wildernesses all the way from the desert lava flows near Craters of the Moon National Monument to the wet northern panhandle. Indeed, although today's Idaho wilderness is immense by modern standards, the potential for ecologically whole multimillion acre future Wildernesses is staggering!

The standard things threaten Idaho wilderness. Forest Service sponsored logging and road-building top the list, but hardrock mining runs a close second, especially in various areas around and within the fringes of the RNR. ORVs, subdivisions, hobby trapping and other threats can't be ignored either. In

Selway-Bitterroot Wilderness, Idaho.
Photo by Howie Wolke.

the Great Rift and Owyhee country, entrenched welfare ranching is the primary threat, as well as the main roadblock for eventual Wilderness designation.

Today, Idaho is one of the three remaining Western states (Montana and Nevada are the others) for which Congress hasn't enacted post-RARE II Wilderness legislation. Unfortunately, Idaho's political leaders are second to none in their anti-wilderness vehemence. Senator Jim McClure, ranking Republican on the Energy and Natural Resources Committee, is perhaps the major Wilderness foe in Congress. The state's other Senator, Steve Symms, would be equally dangerous if he weren't so inept. Even Democratic Governor Cecil Andrus has joined ranks with the McClure crew by proposing protection for less than two million acres of the state's nine and a half million acres of vulnerable forest wildlands. The horrible Andrus-McClure bill (proposed in 1988) would have released over 7 million acres of the state's vulnerable forest wildlands to Forest Service developers! Worse, it included various special provisions which would have had far reaching and disastrous ramifications for future Wilderness designations throughout America. Fortunately, it was so bad that conservation groups were able to stop it dead in its tracks in Congress. Thus, thanks to the anti-Wilderness extremism of McClure and Andrus, Idaho will continue without post-RARE II Wilderness legislation for at least the immediate future. For the time being, then, proposed National Forest Land (Mis)Management Plans (now being finalized by the FS, and being challenged by conservation groups in court) hold the keys to Idaho's uncertain wilderness future, unless, of course, Andrus and McClure attempt again to legislate habitat destruction. Unless these yahoos and their cohorts can be thwarted in their drive to continue to open millions of now wild acres to Forest Service and BLM sponsored "multiple use" (multiple abuse!), Idaho may indeed become the Potato State.

Central Idaho

Central Idaho is, quite simply, the wild heart of the largest complex of temperate zone wildlands remaining in North America and perhaps anywhere on Earth. Lacking the name recognition of the Greater Yellowstone, although dwarf-

ing it in sheer size, the Central Idaho Wildland Complex includes both designated and de facto wildernesses in the Big Hole and Bitterroot drainages of far western Montana, and in the Hells Canyon and Wallowa Mountains region of eastern Oregon. The complex extends from the Great Rift in the south through the Mallard-Larkins roadless area in the northern Panhandle of Idaho. Nowhere in the temperate world is there a more stupendous and diverse concentration of wildlands than here: from desert to tundra; from open park-like stands of Ponderosa Pine to moist conifer forests rife with disjunct Pacific rainforest species; from mile-deep (and deeper) river canyons to rolling plateaus of forest and meadow.

At the core of the Central Idaho Wildland Complex is a geologic formation known as the Idaho Batholith. A huge 70-80 million year-old granite intrusion, roughly 60 miles wide by over 200 miles long along a north-south axis, the batholith constitutes a gigantic, often mountainous upland, dissected by the Salmon, Selway, Clearwater and St. Joe river systems, and partially smoothed, gouged and accentuated by Pleistocene glaciers. To the geologist, central Idaho is the batholith. To the ecologist and the Wilderness activist, the batholith defines the true Central Idaho Wildland Ecosystem, the core of the sprawling wildland complex.

River of No Return 3,156,000 acres (also in Montana)

Designated River of No Return Wilderness Area (Bitterroot, Boise, Challis, Nezperce, Payette & Salmon NFs)	2,200,000
Designated Gospel Hump Wilderness Area (Nezperce NF)	206,000
Additional Bitterroot, Boise, Challis, Nezperce, Payette & Salmon NFs roadless to RNR	675,000
Additional Nezperce NF roadless to Gospel Hump	75,000

Description: Central Idaho and extreme western Montana between Salmon and McCall. This is the largest designated Wilderness and the largest roadless area in the lower 48 states. It is extremely diverse, ranging from semi-arid grass and brushlands at 2,000' along the lower Main Salmon River to alpine summits over 10,000' in the Bighorn Crags. In general, the Wilderness is distinguished by extensive coniferous forest, scattered meadows, and open grassy slopes breaking into steep rugged canyons. The RNR is probably the largest temperate climate wilderness in the world and it forms the core of what is probably the largest complex of temperate zone wildlands on Earth.

Known for its large population of Mountain Lions, the RNR's wildlife also includes Marten, Fisher, Lynx, Bobcat, Coyote, Red Fox, Mule & Whitetail Deer, Elk, Moose, Mountain Goat, Bighorn Sheep, Black Bear, Wolverine and numerous raptors. A population of Boreal Owls was recently found deep in the RNR, well south of what had been thought their exclusively Canadian geographic range. A small number of individual Gray Wolves move through the area. Expansive areas of big game winter range are entirely within the Wilderness. The major forest type is Douglas-fir, especially in the southern half of the Wilderness. Other important tree species are Ponderosa Pine, Lodgepole Pine, Engelmann Spruce and Subalpine Fir, with some Western Red-cedar, Western Larch, Grand Fir and Alpine Larch in the northern part of the Wilderness. *Penstemon lemhiensis* (Scrophulariaceae), which is now vulnerable to extinction, probably survives in the proposed Bluejoint (Montana) addition.

The canyons of the Middle Fork and main Salmon are very popular for float trips, and are among the deepest and most spectacular canyons on Earth. They are renowned for Chinook Salmon and Steelhead fisheries.

Status: Timbering threatens the contiguous roadless areas, particularly on the Salmon, Payette and Nezperce NFs. Hardrock mining is occurring in cherrystem exclusions in the RNR Wilderness and is proposed with road construction inside the actual Wilderness near Big Creek. Mining threats are extensive around the entire periphery of the RNR and in the "Special Mining Management Zone" in the designated Wilderness on the Salmon NF. A young but rapidly-spreading infestation of Spotted Knapweed (native to Eurasia) threatens to choke out natural grasslands in the Salmon River canyon. Grandfathered use of numerous airstrips and of jetboats on the Main Salmon River should be phased out. ("Grandfathered use" refers to legislation — grandfather clauses — which allows previously existing, but otherwise incompatible, use to continue in an area after it is designated as Wilderness.) The Wilderness Area is poorly administered by the FS, which divides management responsibility between different National Forest and Ranger Districts.

Closure of the dirt Magruder Corridor road (northern boundary) and addition of adjacent roadless lands would unite the RNR and the Selway-Bitterroot Wilderness into a single Wilderness of nearly 5 million acres. Except for the Salmon River Breaks link between the RNR and Gospel Hump, the Idaho Wildlands Defense Coalition has proposed zero additions to the RNR in their state-wide Wilderness proposal. They should be encouraged to propose the addition of all contiguous roadless lands to the Wilderness. Reintroduction of Grizzly Bear and Gray Wolf would create a more biologically complete central Idaho Wilderness ecosystem.

RM36: 4,800,000* RM27: 7,668,480*

Selway-Bitterroot 1,813,000 acres (also in Montana)

Designated Selway-Bitterroot Wilderness Area
  (Bitterroot, Clearwater, Nezperce & Lolo NFs) 1,338,000
Additional Bitterroot, Lolo, Nezperce &
  Clearwater NFs roadless 475,000

Description: Central Idaho and western Montana southwest of Missoula, MT. Except along the classically rugged and glacially-carved crest of the Bitterroots, most of the Wilderness is characterized by high ridges dropping off to deep canyons clothed in a dense mantle of coniferous forest. This tremendously diverse area also includes low valleys with old growth stands of Western Red-cedar, Grand Fir, Douglas-fir, Western Larch; forested ridges and rugged granite peaks; extensive subalpine spruce-fir forests; and a plethora of subalpine lakes, bogs and marshes. Rattlesnakes sun themselves on warm slopes at lower elevations. A few Grizzlies and Gray Wolves roam the Selway-Bitterroot. Elk, Moose, Mountain Goat, Black Bear, Wolverine, Pileated Woodpecker, Great Grey Owl and other species characteristic of the Northern Rockies thrive in healthy numbers. The proposed Sheephead-

Watchtower addition, along with the nearby proposed Blue-joint addition to the RNR, is habitat for a genetically pure population of Rocky Mountain Bighorn Sheep. This population has never been augmented with genetic material from else-where, which makes this population rare for the species.

Status: Much of the area outside the Wilderness is severely threatened by timber sales, including the potential Elk Summit addition which has the densest Moose population in Idaho. This huge area is separated from the 3+ million acre River of No Return Wilderness only by the dirt and gravel Magruder Corridor road to the south. Shutting down this road would unite the S-B and RNR into a single 5 million acre Wilderness.

As in the RNR, Gray Wolf and Grizzly Bear should be reintroduced (or augmented) in order to assure viable popula-tions. This is former habitat for the Woodland Caribou which should also be reintroduced.

It is interesting to note that in 1963, prior to the enactment of the 1964 Wilderness Act, the Forest Service de-classified nearly 500,000 acres from the Selway-Bitterroot Primitive Area in order to open wild forestlands to loggers. Although the Central Idaho Wilderness bill of 1980 reinstated about 100,000 acres to the Wilderness, the "protected" Selway-Bitterroot Wilderness is still smaller than it was when Bob Marshall se-cured administrative protection for it in 1936. (Marshall's pro-tection came in the nick of time — a competing plan within the Forest Service during the mid-'30s for "truck trail" construction would have chopped up the entire Selway-Bitterroot to the extent that the largest remaining roadless area would have been less than 100,000 acres!)

RM36: 4,800,000* RM27: 7,668,480*

River of No Return South 150,000 acres

Designated River of No Return Wilderness Area	
(Challis NF)	*40,000*
Additional Challis NF roadless	*110,000*

Description: Central Idaho north of Stanley. The southern lobe of the RNR is separated from the main RNR by a dirt road loop. Alpine peaks here reach 10,000', and clear subalpine lakes adorn the upper Loon Creek drainage. Roaring streams, deep canyons and lakes pervade the area. This is an important link between the main RNR and the Sawtooth complex to the south.

Status: The area outside the Wilderness is threatened by timbering and hardrock mining. It was proposed for "Reserved Status" by the Idaho Wildlife Federation but not proposed for protection by the Idaho Conservation League. Earth First! is the only group supporting additional Wilderness here.

RM27: 7,668,480*

Allan Mountain 158,000 acres (also in Montana)
See Montana for description and status.

Sawtooths 700,000 acres

Designated Sawtooth Wilderness Area (Boise, Sawtooth & Challis NFs)	*217,088*
Additional Boise, Sawtooth & Challis NFs roadless	*483,000*

Description: Central Idaho northwest of Ketchum. This rich area is nationally known for rugged peaks, alpine lakes and stunning scenery. Extensive conifer forests of spruce, fir, Douglas-fir, Ponderosa Pine and Lodgepole Pine clothe the land. The designated Wilderness is heavily used by recreationists, but the use of adjacent roadless areas is light. Mountain Goat, Black Bear, Lynx, Marten, Wolverine, Elk and deer inhabit the area. The headwaters of the South Fork Payette, and South & Middle Forks of the Boise rivers have important fisheries. Elevations rise from about 4,000' to nearly 11,000'; the area includes most of two major mountain ranges — the Sawtooths, and the lower, less rugged, and more heavily vegetated Smokey Mountains (which contain numerous geothermal features).

Status: The existing Wilderness is a textbook "Wilderness on the Rocks." Nearly all of the important wildlife habitat is in the adjacent but unprotected roadless country which includes the Smokey Mountains. The FS only recommended 150,000 acres for Wilderness in RARE II and parts of the area are threatened by timber sales. In a classic demonstration of "sensitive" Forest

Service management, ORV use is being permitted in areas where studies of the rare and elusive Wolverine are ongoing.
RM36: 820,000 RM27: 1,130,240

Soldier Mountains-Lime Creek 139,000 acres

Sawtooth NF roadless	*100,000*
BLM and private roadless	*10,000*
Boise NF roadless	*29,000*

Description: South-central Idaho northwest of Fairfield. The Soldiers are a sub-range of the Boise Mountains and separated from them by the South Fork of the Boise River. This roadless area is immediately south of the greater Sawtooth-Smokey Mountains roadless area. Smokey Dome at 10,095' is the high point. This part of the Idaho Batholith rises above the "Camas Prairie" to the south. The steep drainages, high ridges and peaks of this area provide winter and summer habitat for deer and Elk. Vegetation ranges from big, open grassy slopes to scattered stands of Aspen, Douglas-fir, Lodgepole Pine and other conifers.

Status: The FS inventoried only 14,000 acres of this area in RARE II, and recommended it for non-Wilderness. Conservationists called for 90,000 acres as "Further Planning." A few cherrystem roads intrude from the east and should be closed. Threats to this overlooked area include logging, mining and ORVs.

White Clouds-Boulders 550,000 acres

Sawtooth & Challis NFs roadless (some private)	*480,000*
BLM roadless	*70,000*

Description: Central Idaho north of Ketchum. This is the largest completely unprotected component of the vast Central Idaho Wilderness Complex and the largest unprotected FS roadless area in the contiguous United States. It includes classically rugged glaciated alpine/subalpine mountains and basins, and rolling sagebrush and grasslands hills. Mountain Goat, Bighorn Sheep, Elk, Black Bear, Pronghorn and Fisher (and perhaps a few wolves) survive here. Ocean-going Chinook Salmon and Steelhead find spawning grounds in streams on the east side. Elevations range from 6,000' to Castle Peak at 11,820'. The spectacular alpine core is a popular recreation area, and as such has developed a strong constituency for protection.

Status: The FS is studying only 283,750 acres for possible Wilderness designation (this acreage is almost entirely alpine or subalpine; the best wildlife habitat is outside of the FS study area). ORV use and mining are serious threats, especially outside the Sawtooth National Recreation Area. Overgrazing is a problem on BLM lands along the eastern flank. A few unnecessary low grade roads could be closed and rehabilitated to increase the roadless acreage to nearly 700,000 acres.

Pioneer Mountains 250,000 acres	
Challis and Sawtooth NFs roadless	*230,000*
BLM roadless	*20,000*

Description: South-central Idaho east of Ketchum. Idaho's second highest mountain range has rugged glacial canyons, tarns, dense coniferous forests, meadows, and abundant wildlife including Mule Deer, Elk, Mountain Goat and Black Bear. Elevations range from 6,000' to 12,078' atop Hyndman Peak. With picture-perfect glaciated mountain terrain, this is a popular area for hiking, fishing and hunting.

Status: The FS recommended only 106,000 acres in the western half of the range for Wilderness in RARE II. Local wilderness support is strong. Some marginal timber sales and ORV use threaten the area.

Northern Idaho

For our purposes, Northern Idaho includes the wet "Panhandle" (bordering Canada) represented here by the Selkirks, and the northern end of the Idaho Batholith, represented by the Great Burn, Mallard-Larkins and Bighorn-Weitas areas. These three areas constitute the northernmost extension of the great Central Idaho Wildlands Complex.

Great Burn 295,000 acres (also in Montana)	
Lolo and Clearwater NFs roadless	*295,000*

Description: Northern Idaho and northwestern Montana west of Missoula, MT. This northern portion of the Bitterroot Mountains was burned in the Great Fire of August 20-22, 1910. Deep valley pockets of old growth cedar and hemlock escaped the fire. High subalpine cirques, meadows, impressive stands of Mountain Hemlock and crystal-clear lakes are along the crest. Precipitation is heavy. Forested ridges are in various stages of ecological succession. One of the largest Elk herds in the Northern Rockies lives here, there is a good population of Mountain Goat, and Grizzly Bear and Gray Wolf have been sighted. Kelly and Cayuse Creeks, on the Idaho side, are blue ribbon trout streams. These streams and their tributaries also provide good habitat for Harlequin Duck. This is one of the largest and wildest unprotected roadless areas in the country.

Status: The FS recommended only 178,000 acres for Wilderness in RARE II and now has extensive plans for logging, including along tributaries of Kelly Creek. The Montana slope of the area has become a major focus of anti-Wilderness welfare loggers. Any Wilderness bill that releases parts of the Great Burn should be vigorously resisted!

RM27: 7,668,480*

Big Horn-Weitas 240,000 acres

Clearwater NF roadless	*240,000*

Description: Northern Idaho east of Moscow. High ridges, steep canyons, pellucid streams, montane & subalpine forests characterize the area. Elevations generally are between 3,000 - 6,000'. Cayuse Creek is a blue ribbon trout stream. Sightings of Gray Wolf have been reported. Along with the Mallard-Larkins, Meadow Creek and the Great Burn, this area is a major component of the northernmost wild areas of the Central Idaho-Western Montana Wilderness Complex.

Status: The FS recommended this area for non-wilderness in RARE II, and the entire area is threatened by timber sales. A number of cherrystem dirt roads intrude into the area. They should be closed and rehabilitated. The closure of a few additional dirt logging roads would allow the combination of the

Bighorn-Weitas with the Mallard-Larkins, Great Burn and
Meadow Creek areas for a roadless area of 900,000 acres!
   RM27: 7,668,480*

Mallard-Larkins 285,000 acres

Clearwater, Idaho Panhandle NFs roadless	*268,000*
Private roadless	*17,000*

Description: Northern Idaho.east of Moscow. On the west
slope of the northern Bitterroot Range (sometimes known as the
St. Joe Mountains), this area of subalpine and montane forest
straddles the high divide between the Clearwater and St. Joe
river drainages. The upper St. Joe River is designated Wild &
Scenic. Features of this area include glacial cirques, U-shaped
canyons, three subalpine lake basins, extensive Lodgepole Pine
forests, and pockets of old growth Western Red-cedar, Western
Hemlock and Western White Pine in the valleys. Cutthroat
and Rainbow Trout are abundant. Elk, Mule & Whitetail Deer,
Black Bear and Moose are common. Prime Gray Wolf habitat
makes this an ideal reintroduction site. The Mountain Goat
herd is very productive and is used for transplants to other
areas. Pileated Woodpeckers thrive in the old growth.
Northern Bog Lemming (*Synaptomys borealis*) may inhabit the
area. The Idaho Fish & Game Department rates the Mallard-
Larkins as *the* most important unprotected roadless area in the
state for wildlife. The area is popular for hunting, fishing and
backpacking.
   Status: The FS recommended 156,000 acres for Wilderness in
RARE II. Below cost (welfare) timber sales threaten much of
the area. Burlington-Northern "owns" 17,000 acres of land
here, largely in the Canyon Creek area. This critical Elk
habitat is the focus of an Idaho Fish & Game proposed land
exchange. All Idaho conservation groups, plus Fish & Game,
support Wilderness for all or most of the area. On the east, the
Meadow Creek roadless area, under 100,000 acres, along the
northern Bitterroot Divide is a vital link between the Mallard-Larkins and Great Burn roadless areas. The FS wants to
log this area, too.
   RM27: 7,668,480*

Selkirks 155,000 acres

Idaho Panhandle NF roadless	*115,000*
Priest State Forest & private roadless	*40,000*

Description: Extreme northern Idaho west of Bonners Ferry. This rugged, glaciated mountain range receives high precipitation. The crest consists of subalpine cirques, lakes and rugged alpine peaks draped in perennial snowfields. Long Canyon, an 18 mile-long glacial valley and the last remaining unlogged wild canyon emanating from the Selkirk Crest, is filled with outstanding intermediate and old growth forests of Western Red Cedar, Western Hemlock, Western Larch, Douglas-fir, Grand Fir and Western White Pine. Long Canyon is extremely important habitat for old growth dependent species. Spruce-fir forest is at the higher elevations. The only remnant bands of Woodland Caribou in the lower 48 states are in the Selkirks; they are being supplemented with caribou from British Columbia as part of the National Woodland Caribou Recovery effort. The Selkirks also contain rich Grizzly Bear habitat that has supported a small population of Grizzly up to the present day. Other species include Moose, Whitetail Deer, Mountain Goat, Northern Bog Lemming, Northern Goshawk and Harlequin Duck. Along with the Mallard-Larkins, this is the easternmost extension of habitat for the Pacific Giant Salamander (*Dicamptodon ensatus*).

Status: The FS inventoried 105,000 acres in RARE II and recommended only the crest for Wilderness (22,875 acres). Logging is proposed for Long Canyon. The west slope of the range is the Priest State Forest and a narrow area along the western crest is managed as a roadless area by the state to complement the FS high altitude rock & ice Wilderness proposal. Much of the lower slope of the state forest has been logged. Long Canyon is *the* critical component of the area.

South-Central Idaho

Here is a superb group of volcanic high desert wildlands, lying just south of the mountainous Idaho Batholith.

Great Rift-Craters of the Moon 463,000 acres

Designated Craters of the Moon National	
Monument Wilderness Area	43,243
BLM Great Rift Wilderness Study Area	290,000
Additional BLM & state roadless	130,000

Description: South-central Idaho southwest of Arco. Geologically recent basaltic lava flows constitute the core of this area and are flanked by high desert sagebrush steppe and desert grassland. Isolated "kipukas" — areas within the lava flow but not covered by lava — have received little or no domestic grazing and are rare examples of virgin northern desert scrub grassland. Some plant communities here are unique. Mule Deer, Pronghorn (mostly around the lava flow fringes), Bobcat, Coyote, Whitetail Jackrabbit, Prairie Falcon and rattlesnakes make this their home. This area, in the shadow of the Pioneer and Lost River Mountains directly to the north and northeast, is an outstanding example of recent geological activity (between 2,000 and 15,000 years old). Elevations are generally between 5,000 - 6,000'.

Status: BLM has recommended 268,000 acres for Wilderness, but the proposal excludes virtually all of the roadless desert rangelands around the lava flow. Major additions on the east and west sides of the flow would protect important wildlife habitat, especially for Pronghorn.

Great Rift-Wapi 164,000 acres

BLM Wilderness Study Area	84,000
Additional BLM, state and private roadless	80,000

Description: Southern Idaho west of American Falls. Like the Craters of the Moon Flow to the north, the Wapi Lava Flow is a huge area of recent volcanism slowly developing plant and animal communities via primary succession in the basaltic substrate. The Crystal Ice Caves are along the north edge of the unit. The area remains extremely wild, and has isolated kipukas.

Status: BLM has recommended just 73,000 acres for Wilderness. Their proposal includes only the lava flow proper and excludes virtually all the high quality wildlife habitat around the fringes, particularly on the west side.

Raven's Eye 263,000 acres

BLM roadless	263,000

Description: Southern Idaho southeast of Carey. A diverse area of young basaltic lava flows and expansive high desert grasslands and shrub-steppe. Excellent Pronghorn habitat, this little-known area provides substantially better wildlife habitat than the two Great Rift units to the east and southeast. It is an excellent example of the Columbia Plateau geologic province, with flora and fauna characteristic of the northern Great Basin.

Status: BLM proposes new cattle and sheep allotments, intensive grazing systems and very little forage allocated to wildlife. They have subdivided the area along a series of primitive jeep trails into six roadless areas, three of which are Wilderness Study Areas totaling 121,433 acres. This area is virtually unknown and needs a constituency. The jeep trails should be closed and rehabilitated.

East-Central Idaho

This is the eastern portion of the Central Idaho Wildland Complex, extending across the border into southwestern Montana.

Borah Peak 179,000 acres

Challis NF roadless	141,000
BLM roadless	38,000

Description: Central Idaho northeast of Ketchum. The central Lost River Range has nine summits over 12,000' including Idaho's highest, 12,665' Borah Peak. Stark peaks rise above desert basins on the east and west making the topography and general character of the land very similar to that of the Great Basin, with some elements of the Northern Rockies. Twenty lakes and the only real glacier in Idaho (on the northeast face of Borah Peak); Pronghorn, Mule Deer, Bighorn Sheep and Elk are features of this area.

Status: The FS currently recommends 116,000 acres for Wilderness; 25,000 acres of adjacent BLM land are a Wilderness Study Area. There is virtually no timber in the area. Mining and ORVs are the major threats.

King Mountain 109,000 acres

Challis NF roadless	*95,000*
BLM roadless	*14,000*

Description: Central Idaho north of Arco. The southern Lost River Range. This unusual semi-desert range includes excellent Bighorn Sheep habitat, and unique plant communities on the east slope. Caves, natural bridges, and archaeological sites including pictographs abound.

Status: The FS recommended the entire NF area for further planning in RARE II but now proposes at least one timber sale within the area.

Pahsimeroi 130,000 acres

Challis NF roadless	*100,000*
BLM roadless	*30,000*

Description: Central Idaho east of Challis. This is the northern part of Idaho's highest mountain range, the Lost Rivers. Flanked by arid desert valleys, the area ranges from desert sagebrush/grasslands at 5,000' to alpine zones reaching 11,085' on Grouse Creek Mountain. Gigantic cliffs and rugged valleys distinguish this extremely pristine, little-known and - used area. Deer, Elk, Bighorn Sheep and Pronghorn inhabit the area.

Status: The FS recommended 55,000 acres for study in RARE II. Although it is a high, arid area, planned timber sales in small pockets of slow growing timber threaten it. Such proposed sales lend credence to charges that, as an agency, the Forest Service is collectively insane. The BLM portion is completely unprotected.

North Lemhis 410,000 acres

Salmon and Challis NFs roadless	*360,000*

BLM and state roadless	50,000

Description: East-central Idaho south of Salmon. Rugged peaks, glacial canyons, lush meadows, coniferous forests, sub-alpine lakes, alpine tundra plateaus, and steep, rocky slopes rise above the arid Pahsimeroi and Lemhi valleys. It is important habitat for Black Bear, Mountain Lion, Mountain Goat, Elk, Mule Deer, Bighorn Sheep, Lynx, Marten, Golden Eagle and other Northern Rockies species. Sightings of Rocky Mountain Gray Wolf have been reported. Hiking, hunting and fishing are growing in popularity here. The Lemhis, like the Lost Rivers, are biologically and geologically a combination of the Great Basin desert ranges and the Northern Rockies, with an emphasis on the latter.

Status: The FS recommended 280,000 acres for Wilderness in RARE II but is now opposing *any* Wilderness in the Lemhis. Timber sales threaten some of the lower canyons. An old dirt road for mining exploration could easily be closed, thus uniting the entire Lemhi Range into a single roadless unit of nearly 650,000 acres.

Diamond Peak (South Lemhis) 230,000 acres

Challis & Targhee NFs roadless	185,000
BLM, state and private roadless	45,000

Description: East-central Idaho northeast of Idaho Falls. The South Lemhi Mountains rise abruptly from the arid Birch Creek and Little Lost River valleys as a striking escarpment roughly 40 miles in length. This area is not as well watered as the northern part of the range and there are few perennial streams. Components include open grassland with pockets and stringers of Douglas-fir and Lodgepole Pine, steep slopes, rugged peaks, giant limestone cliffs, and glacial cirques at the crest. Diamond Peak is the third highest in Idaho at 12,197'. Some mountain grasslands have never been grazed by livestock. Wildlife is diverse: Pronghorn, Black Bear, Cougar, Mountain Goat, Mule Deer, Bighorn Sheep (recently reintroduced), Elk and nesting raptors. This area receives very little use.

Status: A RARE II further planning area, the entire area is threatened by oil & gas exploration and development. Much of it is already under lease or lease application. It is also threatened by FS plans to open up virgin grasslands to domestic livestock grazing. The Idaho Congressional delegation opposes Wilderness in the Lemhis.

West Big Hole 210,000 acres (also in Montana)
See Montana for description and status.

Italian Peaks 360,000 acres (also in Montana)

Salmon, Targhee & Beaverhead NFs roadless	*300,000*
BLM roadless	*45,000*
State and private roadless	*15,000*

Description: Idaho-Montana border southwest of Dillon, MT. This large area runs along the Continental Divide and includes arid to semi-arid sagebrush grassland, coniferous forest, alpine peaks, a very high and rugged crest with the highest point in the Beaverhead Range, Eighteen Mile Peak at 11,141', and large areas of Quaking Aspen. It is excellent habitat for Pronghorn, Elk, Mule Deer, Black Bear and Golden Eagle.

Status: Conservation groups have recommended only part of the southern half of this large area for Wilderness (100,000 acres) and the FS recommended only 56,000 acres in RARE II. The area should be treated as a single unit, not piecemeal due to state and agency boundaries. The Idaho BLM portion particularly needs to be treated as a coherent part of this larger area. Threats include oil & gas, ORVs, and, to a lesser extent, logging.

West-Central Idaho
This is the western and southwestern edge of the Idaho Batholith, and the rugged Hells Canyon of the Snake River country.

Hells Canyon 591,000 acres (also in Oregon)
See Oregon for description and status.

Secesh River 273,000 acres
Payette NF roadless   *266,000*

Private roadless	7,000

Description: Western Idaho northeast of McCall. Adjacent to the western boundary of the River of No Return Wilderness and part of the Payette Crest complex, the Secesh River and a major portion of the lower South Fork of the Salmon River are within this area of high ridges, cirques, lakes, large subalpine meadows, and extensive stands of Ponderosa Pine and other conifers. It is valuable habitat for Bighorn Sheep, Mountain Goat, Cougar, Black Bear, Elk, Mule Deer, and perhaps a few Gray Wolves. Soils are extremely erosive, as they are throughout the South Fork of the Salmon. The Secesh River is a prime salmon and Steelhead fishery.

Status: This area was only partially inventoried and then subdivided into two widely separated areas by the FS in RARE II. The FS now supports Wilderness for less than half of the area. Timbering plans would destroy the Secesh River watershed.

French Creek-Patrick Butte 175,000 acres

Payette NF roadless	172,000
Private roadless	3,000

Description: Western Idaho northeast of McCall. Features include steep river breaks, high ridges, glacial cirques, over 50 lakes, subalpine meadows, unusual rock formations and dense coniferous forests. French Creek is a major tributary of the Salmon River. The area provides important habitat for Elk, Bighorn Sheep and other species. This area, the Secesh, and the Needles roadless areas constitute the Payette Crest, a large complex of completely unprotected wild country along the western edge of the fragile Idaho Batholith.

Status: The FS subdivided this area into two units in RARE II and recommended both for non-wilderness. Timber sales threaten important Elk calving areas.

Needles 173,000 acres

Payette NF roadless	170,000
Private roadless	3,000

Description: Western Idaho northeast of McCall, part of the Payette Crest complex. The South Fork of the Salmon River, for which it is a critical watershed, forms the eastern boundary. Steep river breaks, high ridges, lakes and coniferous forests offer habitat for Bighorn Sheep, Mountain Goat, Cougar and Black Bear. High, glacially carved terrain includes the pinnacles of The Needles on the roadless area's southern boundary.

Status: The FS plans to log the southern part of the area. Logging on the highly erosive soils of the Idaho Batholith in the 1960s caused extensive damage to the South Fork of the Salmon River salmon and Steelhead fishery. The watershed is slowly recovering but is threatened anew by FS logging plans.

Red Mountain 100,000 acres
Boise & Challis NFs roadless   *100,000*

Description: Central Idaho northeast of Boise. Located between the greater Sawtooth Wilderness complex and the RNR Wilderness, the Red Mountain area forms an important watershed for the South Fork of the Payette River, replete with high granite ridges, deep stream valleys, coniferous forests and large meadows. Red Mountain reaches 8,733' and the area drops to about 4,000' on the South Fork of the Payette. Like other areas in the Idaho Batholith, soils are very unstable. Good habitat for Elk, Mountain Goat, Wolverine and Black Bear is provided here.

Status: Not included in RARE II due to a completed land use plan, major parts of the area are now threatened by timber sales proposed for the mid-1980s. Much of the roadless area originally identified in RARE I has already been destroyed by timber sales and road-building.

Peace Rock 196,000 acres
Boise NF roadless   *196,000*

Description: West-central Idaho northeast of Boise, in the western part of the Idaho Batholith, just southwest of the River of No Return Wilderness. Rugged granite ridges, streams,

V-shaped canyons, hot springs, winter range for Elk and Mule Deer, extensive stands of Ponderosa Pine, Douglas-fir, Sub-alpine Fir, Lodgepole Pine and other conifers characterize this area. Elevation varies from just over 3,000' to nearly 9,000'. The largest unprotected roadless area on the Boise NF, it forms an important watershed for the Payette River.

Status: This area wasn't in RARE II due to a completed land use plan. Its proximity to Boise makes it an increasingly popular recreation area — for ORVs as well as hikers, hunters and fishers. Major timber sales are planned and some logging may have already reduced the size of this area.

Southwestern Idaho

Southwestern Idaho is part of a high desert bioregion which includes extreme southeastern Oregon and northern Nevada. The biota represents both the volcanic Columbia Plateau, and the Basin and Range Province, most of which lies to the south in arid Nevada.

Owyhee Canyons 619,000 acres (also in Oregon)	
BLM roadless with intermixed state & private (ID)	333,000
BLM roadless with intermixed state & private (OR)	286,000

Description: Extreme southwestern Idaho south of Boise and extreme southeastern Oregon. Rising from its headwaters in the high desert of Nevada, Idaho and Oregon, the Owyhee River and its tributaries cut a stunning complex of deep, steep walled canyons through the basaltic plateaus of the area, making this one of the finest wilderness and wild river complexes in the nation, and offering challenging white-water boating, solitary hiking and hot springs. Mule Deer, Mountain Lion, River Otter, Beaver, Pronghorn, Red Band Trout, Golden Eagle, Bald Eagle, Prairie Falcon, Sage Grouse, Mountain Quail and many other mammals, birds and fish find homes here. This is important habitat for the California Bighorn (*Ovis canadensis californiana*), an increasingly rare subspecies listed as "sensitive" by Idaho wildlife officials. The upper Owyhee

River system is a rich reproductive area for waterfowl, and 18 species of ducks and four of geese occur as residents or migrants. Salmon spawned in the Owyhee until downstream dams were built. The plateaus are a mosaic of low sagebrush species, Big Sagebrush, bunchgrasses and Antelope Bitterbrush. Eight species of sensitive, Threatened or Endangered plants occur in the area. Scattered stands of juniper dot the northern portion of the area.

Status: Unfortunately, vehicle "ways" penetrate this area on the flat sagebrush steppe mesas above the canyons and there are numerous "range improvements" — all for the benefit of a few welfare ranchers. Moreover, cattle have caused the deterioration of the native bunchgrasses and allowed them to be replaced by exotic and noxious Cheatgrass, and have decimated riparian habitats, nearly eliminating willow, cottonwood and Aspen, except in tributary canyons.

Determining what is actually a "road" in this area is not easy, but the 619,000 acre figure represents our best judgment. Surrounding this canyon and mesa wilderness are hundreds of thousands of acres of the same kind of landscape in several additional roadless areas separated by minor dirt roads.

Threats to the Owyhee come from the welfare ranchers in the area, whose political clout is grossly out of proportion to their number. They are opposed to any wilderness designation and want more roads and government funded developments (including the seeding of areas with exotic Crested Wheatgrass after scraping away the sagebrush) for their overgrazing. Small hydro projects are also a possibility, as are mining and powerline construction. A major gas pipeline with pumping stations forms the southeastern boundary of the roadless area.

BLM is proposing a 172,100 acre Wilderness. The Committee for Idaho's High Desert (CIHD) and other conservation groups have recommended a far more visionary Wilderness of 1,189,337 acres in Idaho, Oregon and Nevada by closing several minor dirt roads. The Owyhee country should be on the top of the agenda for national conservation groups. Areas with minor intrusions for the promotion of ranching in this dry country should be rehabilitated and livestock grazing prohibited. A Wilderness National Park of 8 to 10 million acres should be es-

tablished, including the Bruneau-Jarbidge and Jacks Creek
river systems as well as the Owyhee River.
RM36: 4,130,000

Bruneau-Jarbidge Rivers <u>350,000 acres</u>
BLM with intermixed state & private roadless   *350,000*

Description: Southwestern Idaho south of Mountain Home.
The Bruneau and Jarbidge Rivers rise in the high country of
Nevada's Humboldt National Forest and Jarbidge Wilderness,
and flow north into Idaho cutting 800' deep canyons for 100
miles through the basaltic plateaus of Idaho's high desert.
The free-flowing Bruneau River is a blue ribbon trout stream;
before the downstream dams on the Columbia and Snake were
built, it had sturgeon and salmon. It is also a nationally-recog-
nized technical white-water run. Wildlife includes deer,
Bighorn, Mountain Lion, Bobcat, River Otter, Golden Eagle,
Red-tailed Hawk, Great Blue Heron and rattlesnake. See
Owyhee Canyons for general description.

Status: See Owyhee Canyons for general status. Grazing
and mining are the primary threats, although geothermal development could dry up the delightful hot springs along the
rivers. BLM has proposed three tiny Wildernesses totaling
43,100 acres (canyons only, no benchland included); CIHD and
its allies recommend 450,000 acres by closing minor dirt roads.
RM36: 650,000

Jacks Creek <u>100,000 acres</u>
BLM and intermixed state and private roadless   *100,000*

Description: Southwestern Idaho south of Boise, west of the
Bruneau-Jarbidge canyons and northeast of the Owyhee
canyons. Similar country to the Owyhee and Bruneau-Jarbidge,
it encompasses an awe-inspiring canyon along Big Jacks Creek.
Virgin high desert grassland on the mesas makes this area ex-
traordinarily important ecologically, in particular for
California Bighorn Sheep. It is separated from several hundred thousand acres of similar wild canyon and mesa country by
minor dirt roads used for ranching. See Owyhee for general
description.

Status: A major battle is brewing here over conservationists' efforts to protect the never-cowed grasslands of this area and the adjacent Little Jacks country. BLM and welfare ranchers in the area propose to make accessible the relict grassland communities by building a water pipeline along a dirt road separating the roadless areas so that cattle can have water and graze the area. This must be stopped.

BLM proposes 49,900 acres Wilderness; CIHD calls for a 265,000 acre Wilderness by closing several minor dirt roads and joining Little Jacks with Big Jacks. This should be part of a large Owyhee Canyons National Park.

Jarbidge 189,000 acres (also in Nevada)
See Nevada for description and status.

Eastern Idaho

These areas along the Wyoming border are part of the Greater Yellowstone Wildlands Complex, and lie adjacent to a number of other Big Outside units in Yellowstone and Grand Teton National Parks, and the Bridger-Teton National Forest.

Bechler-Pitchstone 468,000 acres (also in Wyoming)
See Wyoming for description and status.

Palisades 240,000 acres (also in Wyoming)
See Wyoming for description and status.

Garns Mountain 115,000 acres
Targhee NF roadless   *115,000*

Description: Eastern Idaho east of Idaho Falls. This sedimentary range lies across the Pierre's Hole valley from the Teton Range in Wyoming, and is actually a northwestern extension of the Snake River Range (a narrow highway separates it from the Palisades roadless area). Characteristics are stream canyons, coniferous forests interspersed with lush meadows and Quaking Aspen, steep to rolling terrain, 5,100' to 9,000' elevations, and Mule Deer, Elk, Moose and Black Bear. It is known locally as the "Big Hole" Mountains.

Status: Recommended for non-wilderness by the FS in RARE II, it is threatened by oil & gas development (entire area) and timber sales (northern end).

Bear Creek 107,000 acres
Caribou and Targhee NFs roadless   107,000

Description: Southeastern Idaho southeast of Idaho Falls along the Wyoming border. Rugged ridges and steep stream valleys provide excellent wildlife habitat, especially for Elk, due to a vegetative mosaic of coniferous forest interspersed with meadows. Douglas-fir, Lodgepole Pine, Engelmann Spruce, Subalpine Fir and Aspen are common tree species.

Status: The entire area is part of the so-called "Overthrust Belt" and is severely threatened by oil & gas development. Timber sales are a lesser, but real threat. It was recommended for "non-wilderness" in RARE II.

Stump Creek 103,000 acres
Caribou NF roadless   103,000

Description: Southeastern Idaho. This area consists of ridges, open valleys, meadows, stands of Quaking Aspen and scattered patches of coniferous forest. It includes excellent summer range and calving areas for Elk. Moose, Mule Deer and Black Bear also inhabit the area. Soils are particularly erodible. It is interesting to note that historically, caribou never occurred in the Caribou National Forest.

Status: The entire area is severely threatened by oil & gas development. There is little commercial timber. The Caribou City roadless area just to the north comprised over 100,000 acres prior to RARE II but oil & gas exploration and logging have reduced its size. Like nearly all roadless lands in the "Overthrust Belt," it was recommended for non-Wilderness in RARE II.

Montana

Montana is a land of soaring mountains and rolling prairies. Here, the Rocky Mountains rise abruptly above the western edge of the Great Plains in a seemingly endless series of individual ranges. Montana is big, wild and diverse, and within the perimeter of our fourth largest state lie major portions of three of the nation's great wildland complexes: the Central Idaho-Western Montana (which includes the River of No Return and Selway-Bitterroot Wildernesses); Greater Yellowstone; and the Northern Continental Divide (which includes Glacier National Park and the Bob Marshall Wilderness region).

Montana can easily be divided into two major bioregions, the Great Plains and the Rocky Mountains. The ironic nature of this state, though, is the duality of landforms within the two bioregions. Rising above the high plains of central and eastern Montana are a number of isolated "island ranges" such as the Big Snowies and the Crazies. And separating many of the major mountain ranges of the state's western third are a series of north-south trending valleys dominated by sagebrush, grass or both. This diversity of intermingled habitats and climates adds immeasurably to the natural diversity of this awesome and beautiful land.

As with most of the West, big wilderness survives almost exclusively in the high, rugged, spectacular and cold mountain ranges, which characterize the state's western third. Once again, humanity's penchant for populating the protected valleys, and humanity's prejudice against preserving valleys and plains have resulted in an alarming lack of representation of these gentler habitats among the state's protected public lands. True, Montanans can boast about the wild beauty of Glacier National Park, the Bob Marshall and Selway-Bitterroot

19. Gallatin Range
20. North Madison Range
21. South Madison Range
22. Cascade Mts
23. Snowcrest Range
24. Crazy Mountains
25. Little Bighorn
26. Big Snowy Mts
27. Tenderfoot-Deep Ck

MONTANA

1. Bob Marshall
2. Mission Mountains
3. North Glacier
4. South Glacier
5. Cabinet Mountains
6. Great Burn
7. Selway-Bitterroot
8. Allan Mountain
9. Stony Mountain
10. Anaconda-Pintlar/Sapphires
11. River of No Return
12. West Pioneer Mts
13. East Pioneer Mts.
14. West Big Hole
15. Italian Peaks
16. Tobacco Root Mts
17. Absaroka-Beartooth
18. Deep Lake

Wilderness Areas, and the unmatched trout fishing of the Big Hole River. But until restoration efforts reclaim the big wilderness on the plains and in the valleys, Montana Wilderness will remain half-a-loaf, at best.

Montana's plains and valleys once harbored wildlife in unbelievable abundance. Central and eastern Montana was arguably the richest and most productive prairie ecosystem in North America. Of course today, the Grizzly, Elk, Gray Wolf and Black-footed Ferret are gone; the grasses are overgrazed and fenced in; and although much of eastern Montana still is an open and powerful land of big sky and waving grass, it's a tame land.

The Grizzly and wolf are even gone from most of the state's western mountains; so is the Woodland Caribou, once an important inhabitant of the state's heavily forested northwest. The Trumpeter Swan survives only in the vicinity of Red Rocks Lake. Many other species, even in the state's mountain ranges, are endangered and severely depleted. The Northern Bog Lemming and Harlequin Duck are two such imperiled creatures. Even while there is growing sentiment for some kind of large prairie nature reserve in eastern Montana (possibly in the Missouri River Breaks country), habitat destruction on the state's National Forests in western and central Montana continues at a shocking rate. Once again, FS logging and roading are the chief culprits. Which brings us to Montana politics.

Unlike most states in the Rockies, prior to the '88 elections Montana politics had generally been dominated by Democrats, particularly in the state's mountainous western third. Its former senior Senator, Democrat John Melcher, opposed nearly all sizable Wilderness proposals. Montana's other Senator, Max Baucus, and western district Congressman Pat Williams — both of whom purport to be sympathetic to environmental protection — have never had the courage to cross Melcher and his deranged views. But now, Melcher is gone. In 1988, his bid for re-election was thwarted by right wing anti-Wilderness Republican Conrad Burns. Eastern district Rep. Ron Marlenee, once the delegation's lone Republican, is an anti-Wilderness extremist of the Wallop-McClure-Hatfield mold. It is already obvious that he and Burns share the same anti-Wilderness idiot-ology.

Along with Idaho and Nevada, Montana continues to lack a post-RARE II Wilderness bill, and like most Western states, there's precious little BLM, National Park or National Wildlife Refuge Wilderness. In 1988, Melcher, Baucus and Williams agreed on a bad bill which would have protected only 1.4 out of 6.2 million roadless National Forest acres in the state. The bill would have formally released over 4 million acres of wild country to multiple abuse — although many of those lands are already being logged and roaded with little effective opposition from environmental groups. Ironically, Marlenee may have done Wilderness lovers a favor by helping to convince President Reagan to pocket veto the awful bill (too much Wilderness for the two Rons). This was the first time a Wilderness bill had been vetoed because of containing too much Wilderness. (Reagan vetoed a Florida Wilderness bill early in his administration because of a spending provision. That provision was removed during the next session of Congress and Reagan signed the bill.)

Now, Conrad Burns promises to develop an even more truncated bill than the Melcher-Baucus-Williams proposal. Although the newly formed Alliance for the Wild Rockies will attempt to elevate the Montana and Idaho wilderness struggle to a well-deserved national status, the legislative future of Montana wilderness remains questionable.

Thus, in lieu of a bill, proposed Forest Service Land Mismanagement Plans gain added importance. The past support by conservation groups for a Wilderness alternative of only 2.4 million acres has proven to be ill-advised. Simply put, Montana's remaining National Forest wildlands will continue to be destroyed by the Forest Service and the loggers unless Wilderness advocates can develop stronger support for the protection of all remaining wildlands in the state. Although isolated pockets of pro-logging, anti-Wilderness greed and ignorance exist, pro-Wilderness hotbeds such as Missoula and Bozeman, as well as Wilderness support elsewhere in the state, make Montana ripe for escalated ecodefense efforts. The politicians and the Forest Service will, no doubt, meet increased physical resistance to the destruction of wildlands under the Big Sky.

Upper White River, Bob Marshall Wilderness, Montana. Photo by Howie Wolke.

Northern Continental Divide

The Northern Continental Divide Ecosystem (NCDE), al-
though smaller than its two big sister wildland complexes in
the Rockies, the Central Idaho and Greater Yellowstone, is the
healthiest big mountain ecosystem in America south of Canada.
(See the description below of the Bob Marshall area.) The Bob
Marshall and Glacier National Park highlight the NCDE, but
also included are lands along the Rocky Mountain Front where
the Great Plains meet the Rockies, the rugged Mission Moun-
tains, and the Whitefish Range. Although Forest Service-
sponsored logging and roading have liquidated big wilderness
in the Whitefish Range, this well-watered, Grizzly-rich area
(adjacent to the western edge of Glacier Park's north unit)
should be a top priority for conservationist efforts to restore at
least one unit of big wilderness.

Bob Marshall 2,485,000 acres	
Designated Bob Marshall Wilderness Area	
(Flathead, Lewis & Clark NFs)	*1,009,356*
Designated Great Bear Wilderness Area	
(Flathead NF)	*286,700*
Designated Scapegoat Wilderness Area	
(Helena, Lewis & Clark, Lolo NFs)	*239,296*
Additional Helena, Flathead, Lolo,	
Lewis & Clark NFs roadless	*890,000*
State, private, BLM roadless	*60,000*

Description: Northwestern Montana northeast of Missoula.
The "Bob" is the most ecologically complete mountain Wilderness in the country, and is a key component of the Northern
Continental Divide Ecosystem. Rugged peaks, big river valleys
(North and South Forks of the Sun, and Middle and South Forks
of the Flathead), lakes, large meadows and extensive conifer-
ous forests characterize this area. The Chinese Wall along the
Continental Divide is a well-known landmark. The Rocky
Mountain Front Range on the east is relatively dry and open
while the Continental Divide, Flathead and Swan Ranges
receive more precipitation and have dense timber. A healthy
Grizzly population ranges down onto the Great Plains from the

Rocky Mountain Front (the only place this still occurs). Every species of mammal indigenous to the Northern Rockies (including a few Gray Wolves) still lives in the Bob Marshall/Glacier National Park bioregion, except for Plains Bison which formerly roamed the adjacent high plains and lower slopes of the Rocky Mountain Front, and Woodland Caribou which historically roamed the western side of Glacier National Park and the Whitefish Range along the US/Canadian border. The Bob is noted for huge herds of Elk, Bighorn and Mountain Goat. It borders Glacier National Park, an International Biosphere Reserve, on the north.

Status: The Rocky Mountain Front (outside the small portion with Wilderness protection) is severely threatened by oil & gas exploration. Conservationists are engaged in a major battle as they try to add this area to the Wilderness. The Front is more critical for wildlife than the areas already protected as Wilderness. Ironically, the Front's Deep Creek roadless area received a perfect Wilderness Attribute Rating from the FS in RARE II, despite agency opposition to Wilderness for that area. Other potential additions on the south and west of the designated Wildernesses are threatened by timbering. The Flathead National Forest allows ORV use in Grizzly habitat; subdivision of adjacent private lands also threatens Grizzly, and ranchers on the plains adjacent to the Front want carte blanche to blow away Grizzlies and Gray Wolves to protect their sheep and cattle. Public support for adding large acreages to the Wilderness is high.

Mission Mountains (176,000 acres)

Designated Mission Mountain Wilderness Area (Flathead NF)	73,877
Mission Mts. Tribal Wilderness Area (Flathead Reservation)	89,000
Private, and additional Indian, FS roadless	13,000

Description: Northwestern Montana north of Missoula. This distinct range, just west of the Bob Marshall complex, has over 200 high lakes, jagged peaks, and dense, Pacific Northwest-type forests of larch, Douglas-fir, Western Red Cedar, spruce, fir, Lodgepole and Ponderosa Pine. Elevations range from 3,500' to 9,820' atop McDonald Peak. A dense population of Grizzly lives in the Missions along with Mountain Goat, Black Bear, deer, Wolverine, Lynx and other species of the Northern Rockies.

Status: Because of checkerboard ownership, the lower slopes of the Missions on the east side have been extensively logged and are not included in this roadless area; however, the Tribal Wilderness extends all the way down the west slope to the Flathead Valley. Additional timber sales on the Swan Valley (east) side further threaten to sever the Missions even more from the rest of the NCDE.

RM36: 310,000

North Glacier 660,000 acres (also in Canada)

Glacier National Park roadless	*545,000*
Blackfoot Indian Reservation roadless (MT)	*30,000*
British Columbia roadless	*25,000*
Waterton Lakes National Park roadless (Alberta)	*60,000*

Description: Northwestern Montana northeast of Kalispell. This is unparalleled rugged glaciated mountain country along the Continental Divide. The spectacular scenery of glacial lakes, glaciers, cirques, peaks, waterfalls, flower-strewn meadows, and thick diverse coniferous forest is world renowned. The west slope is very moist with over 100" annual precipitation in places and lush old growth forests of cedar, larch and Douglas-fir in the valleys; the east slope is much drier with Shortgrass Prairie grading into Aspen, Lodgepole Pine, and spruce-fir forest. Along the west slope lower valleys draining into the North Fork of the Flathead, are a number of large, spectacular, fjord-like glacial lakes. Wildlife includes Grizzly and Black Bear, Gray Wolf (the only active wolf pack in the West is here), Moose, Elk, Mule & Whitetail Deer, Bighorn Sheep, Mountain Goat, Lynx, Marten, Wolverine, Bald Eagle and over 200 other bird species. Mt. Cleveland, the highest point in the Park, is 10,466'.

Status: The Park Service has recommended most of this area for Wilderness designation, but improvements are needed in their proposal. The Cabin Creek Coal Mine in Canada is a threat to the North Fork of the Flathead, and pollution from the Columbia Falls smelter reaches the Park. Trapping and hunting in adjacent Canada also threaten the newly established wolf pack. Moreover, the US Department of Agriculture has set up a $40,000 program to kill the wolves at the insistence of local welfare ranchers, as the US Fish & Wildlife Service tries to protect them. Oil & gas drilling, and subdivisions threaten the North Fork of the Flathead.

To the north of Glacier Park, only one road crosses Canada's Great Divide between the US border and Canadian Route 3. That logging road, still considered by us as this area's northern boundary, has recently been closed. North to Route 3, roads and clearcuts have penetrated every major drainage beneath the divide, up to about 5,000' (although the crest itself and a few spur ridges remain roadless to Route 3). With additional closures and rehabilitation, another 200,000 acres could easily be added to this unit (over 100,000 acres of mostly rocks and ice are roadless along this stretch of the Continental Divide today).

South Glacier (430,000 acres)

Glacier National Park roadless	*415,000*
Blackfoot Indian Reservation roadless	*15,000*

Description: Just south of the Going to the Sun Road from North Glacier (see for description) and north of US 2 from the huge Bob Marshall complex. Like the north unit of the Park, here is more unparalleled glaciated mountain terrain along the Continental Divide. The high basins along the divide are only slightly less well-watered than those to the north, and old growth Pacific Northwest-type forests thrive in scattered lowland pockets here, too. There is nice Aspen high prairie parkland in the eastern foothills. Triple Divide Peak (8,011') divides the headwaters of river systems draining three of the continent's major watersheds: Hudson Bay, Pacific Ocean, and Gulf of Mexico. Mt. Stimson, at 10,142', is the highest point.

Status: Same as for North Glacier. Subdivisions outside the Park threaten wildlife.

Northwestern Montana

Cabinet Mountains 134,000 acres

Designated Cabinet Mountains Wilderness	
(Kootenai and Kaniksu NFs)	94,272
Additional Kootenai & Kaniksu NFs roadless	40,000

Description: Extreme northwestern Montana southwest of Libby. Parts of the Cabinets receive over 100 inches of precipitation annually, resulting in thick lowland forests of Western Red Cedar, Douglas-fir, Western White Pine, Western Hemlock and other conifers. Rugged peaks and glacial cirques rise above the forests, lakes and subalpine meadows. The high point is 8,712' Snowshoe Peak. Wildlife is abundant and typical of the Northern Rockies. There may be as few as a dozen Grizzlies left here; the Great Bear is in serious trouble in northwest Montana. The Rough-skinned Newt (*Taricha granulosa*) may occur here.

Status: Most of the designated Wilderness is "rock & ice" and high subalpine basins. In RARE II the FS recommended 15,600 acres, including a few remnant unlogged valleys of old growth timber, but the remaining roadless lands, including old growth, are slated to be clearcut. *Much of the designated Wilderness is under imminent threat of large-scale hardrock mining for silver.* Conservation groups have not been able to thwart this major mining assault on the National Wilderness Preservation System. The FS and some locals are opposing a plan to augment the tiny Grizzly population.

Great Burn 295,000 acres (also in Idaho)
See Idaho for description and status.

Western and Southwestern Montana

Most of these wildlands, excluding the Tobacco Roots, are adjacent to the big wilds of central Idaho which lie to the west. Thus, most of these areas can be considered to be part of the vast Central Idaho-Western Montana Wildlands Complex.

Selway-Bitterroot 1,813,000 acres (also in Idaho)

See Idaho for description and status.

Allan Mountain 158,000 acres (also in Idaho)

Bitterroot and Salmon NFs roadless   *158,000*

Description: Idaho-Montana border northwest of Salmon, Idaho. This area of high forested ridges, subalpine meadows and steep canyons forms a major portion of the Salmon River-Bitterroot River Divide, and is the closest major roadless area east of the Selway-Bitterroot and River of No Return Wildernesses. Wildlife includes Black Bear, Lynx, Marten and other species of the Northern Rockies. Big Ponderosa Pines thrive in some of the remaining roadless drainages. The roadless area is now defined by a sea of clearcuts around its perimeter.

Status: The entire area was recommended for non-wilderness by the FS in RARE II and is severely threatened by logging plans. A small roadless core would survive for the next decade, according to the proposed Bitterroot and Salmon Forest Plans. This area is in dire need of a constituency, since it's not even proposed for Wilderness by Montana or Idaho "conservation" groups!

Stony Mountain 110,000 acres

Bitterroot and Deerlodge NFs roadless   *110,000*

Description: West-central Montana between Hamilton and Anaconda. This central part of the Sapphire Range (see Anaconda-Pintlar/Sapphires below) is an important watershed for the Bitterroot River to the west and for Rock Creek — a blue ribbon trout fishery — to the east.

Status: Recommended by the FS for non-wilderness, the entire area is severely threatened by logging. A cherrystem road and logging operation invading the wilderness from the Bitterroot Valley should be closed and the area included in a 115,000 acre Stony Mountain Wilderness. Like the Sapphires roadless area, the lower elevation slopes here have been heavily logged and are not included in this roadless area.

Anaconda-Pintlar/Sapphires (391,000 acres)

Designated Anaconda-Pintlar Wilderness Area	
(Beaverhead, Bitterroot, Deerlodge NFs)	157,874
Sapphires Roadless Area (Bitterroot &	
Deerlodge NFs)	116,500
Additional Beaverhead, Bitterroot, Deerlodge	
NFs roadless to Anaconda-Pintlar	117,000

Description: Western Montana between Anaconda and Hamilton, south of the Stony Mountain roadless area. A three-mile-wide roadless corridor in the Upper Moose Creek drainage unites these two mountain ranges. The A-P country consists of rugged peaks (to over 10,000') along the Continental Divide, drained by the Big Hole and Bitterroot Rivers. There are over a dozen species of conifers on the north slope; the south slope's major tree species is Lodgepole Pine. Numerous lakes and U-shaped canyons reveal the past presence of glaciers. The Sapphires are relatively low, rolling mountains with most of the summits under 9,000'; and forested with spruce, fir, Western Larch and Douglas-fir. Excellent Moose habitat and Elk summer range are present. Other wildlife includes Mountain Goat, Black Bear, Mountain Lion, Wolverine and Lynx.

Status: This was recently a much larger roadless area but Forest Service logging has devastated the lower slopes since the 1960s. Logging continues to destroy unprotected portions. 98,000 acres of the Sapphires are a Congressional Wilderness Study Area, thanks to the late Senator Lee Metcalf. The FS recommended only 18,000 acres of additions to the Anaconda-Pintlar Wilderness in RARE II, and Montana "conservation" groups support only 45,000 acres.

River of No Return 3,156,000 acres (also in Idaho)
See Idaho for description and status.

West Pioneer Mountains (243,000 acres)

Beaverhead NF roadless	243,000

Description: Southwestern Montana southwest of Butte. These rolling, wooded hills, rising to over 9,000', encompass an important watershed for the Big Hole River. One of Montana's largest and healthiest herds of Elk live here. Arctic Grayling inhabit some of the lakes. The high slopes support the world's oldest Whitebark Pines. The peaks aren't spectacular from the perspective of recreationists, but this predominantly forested area is very wild and includes prime habitat for Moose, deer, Mountain Lion, Black Bear, Lynx, Marten and Wolverine.

Status: The 151,000 acre core is a Congressional Wilderness Study Area. The rest was released by the Forest Service prior to RARE II via a unit plan and is already being logged in places, including at least three 1987 clearcuts that can be seen from the Big Hole Valley. The FS hopes to cut the entire area, but local opposition is strong. The FS is proceeding here with illegal timber sales in a display of arrogance that is unusually blatant — even for them. One Congressional proposal would open the entire area to ORVs.

East Pioneers 110,000 acres
Beaverhead NF roadless   *110,000*

Description: Southwestern Montana southwest of Butte. This area boasts glaciated peaks rising to 11,000', numerous subalpine lakes, abundant Elk and Moose, and Black Bear, Marten and Mountain Lion. It is separated from the West Pioneers by a narrow dirt road along the Wise River.

Status: The FS recommended 94,000 acres for Wilderness in RARE II; the rest was released by the Beaverhead Unit Plan. Hard rock mining has disturbed much of the mountain range outside the roadless area. The Wise River road should be closed and the East and West Pioneers united into a single 400,000 acre Wilderness.

West Big Hole 210,000 acres (also in Idaho)
Salmon and Beaverhead NFs roadless   *195,000*
BLM roadless   *15,000*

Description: Idaho-Montana border east of Salmon, Idaho. The Beaverheads, a sub-range of the Bitterroots, rise abruptly nearly 7,000' above the Salmon River. Rugged peaks, semi-arid foothills (Idaho side), glacial valleys and lakes, and thick forests (Montana side) are prevalent. Elevation ranges from 4,500' to nearly 11,000'. The east slope drains into a world famous blue ribbon trout fishery, the Big Hole River. Wildlife includes Black Bear, Mountain Goat, deer, Elk, Lynx and Marten. Marshy glacial valleys on the east slope constitute some of the best Moose habitat in Montana.

Status: In RARE II the FS recommended it for non-wilderness, but there is much support for protection in Montana. The area would be greatly enhanced by closing four cherrystem roads on the Montana side. Threats include ORVs on the Idaho side. Logging is an *immediate* threat on the Montana side, despite local opposition to logging in the Big Hole drainage.

Italian Peaks 360,000 acres (also in Idaho)
See Idaho for description and status.

Tobacco Root Mountains 104,000 acres

Beaverhead NF roadless	*98,000*
Private roadless	*6,000*

Description: Southwestern Montana west of Bozeman. This isolated alpine range — with a dense concentration of 10,000' peaks, glacial lakes and cirques — forms a prominent southwestern Montana landmark and the watershed for the Madison and Jefferson Rivers. Wildlife is typical of the Northern Rockies.

Status: This range is highly mineralized and there has been much small scale mining in the past. Mining roads form numerous cherrystems into the roadless core of the range. Wilderness recovery is needed along the periphery and private land within the roadless area should be acquired. The FS recommended 40,000 acres for Further Planning in RARE II. The Church Universal Triumphant (CUT) has recently bought land along the lower slopes, which they plan to log.

Yellowstone Region

These rich wildlands of south-central and southwest Montana are a major component of the Greater Yellowstone Ecosystem (see Wyoming for description).

Absaroka-Beartooth   1,154,000 acres (also in Wyoming)

Designated Absaroka-Beartooth Wilderness Area (Custer, Gallatin NFs, MT)	920,310
Designated Absaroka-Beartooth Wilderness Area (Shoshone NF, WY)	23,750
Yellowstone National Park roadless (WY, MT)	90,000
Additional Gallatin, Custer and Shoshone NFs roadless (MT, WY)	120,000

Description: South-central Montana south of Big Timber and northwestern Wyoming. This very large area consists of two major mountain ranges: on the east the Beartooths are rugged, glaciated, granitic, and predominantly above treeline with huge alpine plateaus; the Absarokas on the west are more heavily forested, with rugged peaks along the crest. The Black Canyon of the Yellowstone River is in the southwest portion and the Wyoming High Lakes area in the southeast. This diverse area has semi-arid grasslands at 5,000', with elevations up to the highest point in Montana, 12,799' Granite Peak. It is a key part of the Greater Yellowstone Ecosystem with habitat for Grizzly and Black Bear, Bighorn Sheep, Elk, Moose, Mountain Lion, Pronghorn, Bison, Lynx and Marten.

Status: The Grizzly is in trouble here as it is throughout the Yellowstone area. Hardrock mining is the major threat to this area, especially along the northeast face of the Beartooths outside of the designated Wilderness. Major additions are needed in both Montana (west slope of Absarokas and northeast face of Beartooths) and Wyoming (remaining part of High Lakes).

Deep Lake   135,000 acres (also in Wyoming)
See Wyoming for description and status.

Gallatin Range 525,000 acres (also in Wyoming)
See Wyoming for description and status.

North Madison Range 140,000 acres

Designated Lee Metcalf Wilderness Area (Spanish Peaks unit — Beaverhead, Gallatin NFs)	*76,406*
Designated BLM Lee Metcalf Wilderness (Beartrap Canyon unit)	*6,000*
Beaverhead and Gallatin NF roadless with intermixed Burlington Northern lands	*51,500*
Additional private and BLM roadless	*6,000*

Description: Southwestern Montana southwest of Bozeman. This jumbled region of alpine peaks drops into semi-arid Beartrap Canyon on the northwest along the Madison River and into Gallatin Canyon on the east. This important component of the Greater Yellowstone Ecosystem is crucial Grizzly habitat. Extensive stands of Lodgepole Pine grow beneath craggy peaks and subalpine lakes. Elevations range from 4,500' along the Madison to 11,015' atop Gallatin Peak. This is an extremely popular recreation area and is the former home of imprisoned Mountain Men Don & Dan Nichols.

Status: The Lee Metcalf Wilderness Act (a Montana Wilderness bill), one of the worst Wilderness bills to be passed, severed Beartrap Canyon from the main Spanish Peaks area by excluding the rich Cowboys Heaven country from the Wilderness, even though the entire area was and still is one contiguous roadless unit. The same bill allowed this North Madison area to be cut from the South Madisons by roading and logging in the Jacks Creek drainage west of the Big Sky Resort (the area was a 515,000+ acre roadless area before this). Logging, especially on Burlington Northern lands, threatens the northern part of the North Madisons. Sen. Lee Metcalf was arguably the greatest champion of Wilderness ever to serve in the Senate. After Metcalf's untimely death, Montana Sen. John Melcher ramrodded a dreadful Wilderness bill through Congress. Naming the area to be designated Wilderness after the highly-respected Lee Metcalf was a calculated Melcher ploy to pass the bill —

whose main purpose was to release wildlands in the Madison Range for development.

South Madison Range 375,000 acres

Designated Lee Metcalf Wilderness (Taylor-Hilgard unit — Gallatin and Beaverhead NFs)	*141,000*
Designated Lee Metcalf Wilderness (Monument unit — Gallatin and Beaverhead NFs)	*32,891*
Cabin Creek Wildlife Management Area roadless	*38,000*
Yellowstone National Park roadless	*16,000*
Gallatin & Beaverhead NFs roadless with Burlington Northern checkerboard lands	*134,000*
Private and BLM roadless	*13,000*

Description: Southwestern Montana south of Bozeman at the northwest corner of Yellowstone Park. This area encompasses glaciated peaks, high lakes, deep canyons, meadows, Lodgepole Pine and spruce-fir forests, and exceptional habitat for Elk, Moose, Bighorn and Grizzly. Hilgard Peak is 11,316'. It is a major recreation area and borders the western edge of Yellowstone National Park.

Status: The South Madison was recently part of a larger roadless area but has been severed from the North Madison by roading and logging in the Jacks Creek drainage. Logging continues to threaten the Burlington Northern lands. ORVs are trashing the Cabin Creek Wildlife Management area (their continued use was guaranteed by the abysmal Lee Metcalf Wilderness bill — a disservice to this great Senator). The proposed "Ski Yellowstone" resort threatens important Grizzly habitat in the southern part of the area. This is one of the most important and endangered wildlife areas in the Greater Yellowstone Ecosystem.

Cascade Mountain 127,000 acres

Beaverhead NF roadless	*110,000*
Red Rock Lakes National Wildlife Refuge roadless	*2,500*
State roadless	*12,000*
BLM roadless	*2,500*

Description: Southwestern Montana west of West Yellow-stone. The major remaining roadless area in the Gravelly Range, this is an area of high, rolling grasslands broken by patches of Aspen and conifer. The high point is 9,400'. It offers excellent big game habitat, and good winter range for deer and Elk. It is directly north of Red Rocks Lake NWR and is an extension of the Greater Yellowstone Ecosystem.

Status: Same as for Snowcrest Range below. ORVs are a major threat.

Snowcrest Range 130,000 acres

Beaverhead NF roadless	*97,000*
State roadless	*14,000*
BLM roadless	*9,000*
Private roadless	*10,000*

Description: Southwestern Montana southeast of Dillon. The Snowcrest — a large block of wild country with very few cherrystem intrusions — is one of the least known ranges in Montana. The NF portion is the core. This is a precipitous range with a crest well over 10,000' in elevation. Vegetation consists of grasslands, and conifers and Aspen interspersed on rocky ridges, which creates excellent big game habitat, particularly for Elk and Mule Deer. The non-Forest Service lands at lower elevations offer good winter range.

Status: This area was not included in RARE II because the previous Beaverhead NF unit plan recommended it for non-wilderness. Earth First! is the only conservation group to recommend it for Wilderness protection.

Central Montana

Except for the Little Bighorn's Montana extension, these wild areas are island mountain ranges rising above the once-wild and rich Shortgrass Prairie of central Montana.

Crazy Mountains 140,000 acres

Gallatin, Lewis & Clark NFs roadless	*88,000*
Intermingled private roadless	*52,000*

Description: South-central Montana north of Livingston. The Crazies rise abruptly from the Great Plains and form a spectacular escarpment of 10,000 - 11,000' high peaks and ridges. This glaciated terrain is drained entirely by the Yellowstone River. It has abundant lakes. Shortgrass Prairie at lower elevations grades into coniferous forest, then alpine tundra, rock and snowfields. Wildlife includes Elk, Black Bear, Pronghorn, Mule & Whitetail Deer. Mountain Goat have been introduced.

Status: The Forest Service has recommended non-wilderness. Almost the entire area is in checkerboarded private and FS ownership due to 19th century railroad grants. The private landowners are many. Conservationists have proposed various land exchange schemes to rectify this problem. This range is threatened by logging, mining and oil & gas.

Little Bighorn 155,000 acres (also in Wyoming)
See Wyoming for description and status.

Big Snowy Mountains 105,000 acres
Lewis & Clark NF roadless	*98,000*
BLM roadless	*7,000*

Description: Central Montana, south of Lewistown. The isolated Big Snowies are an island of high timbered ridges (up to nearly 9,000') — replete with Ponderosa Pine, spruce & fir, lakes and clear streams — rising above a sea of Shortgrass Prairie. Deer and Black Bear are numerous.

Status: Virtually the entire FS portion is a Congressionally designated Wilderness Study Area, but is now proposed for non-wilderness by Montana politicos and the FS. Logging has therefore become a major threat.

Tenderfoot-Deep Creek 105,000 acres
Lewis & Clark NF roadless	*95,000*
Private roadless	*10,000*

Description: Central Montana southeast of Great Falls, the Little Belt Mountains rise from the rolling prairies of central

Montana. Forested ridges under 9,000' and spectacular lime-stone river canyons characterize this westernmost roadless area in the Little Belts. Ponderosa Pine and Douglas-fir are common tree species. The Smith River Canyon along the western fringe of the area is a popular float trip. Mule & Whitetail Deer, Black Bear and Elk inhabit this bit of Montana canyon country.

Status: Recommended for non-wilderness by the Forest Service, but proposed for protection by conservationists, threats to Tenderfoot-Deep Creek include logging and mining.

Wyoming

Wyoming is a high-altitude land where sky-scraping snowy mountains meet high plains and wind-ripped desert basins. This is a land of open space, wild mountains and a grandeur unmatched anywhere else in the contiguous 48 states. Indeed, former Wyoming Congressman Teno Roncalio once referred to Wyoming as "the Alaska of the lower 48 states."

The bioregions of the state include: 1) the northern extension of the Southern Rocky Mountains, most of which lie to the south in Colorado. This region includes the Laramie, Medicine Bow and Sierra Madre ranges of southeastern Wyoming; 2) the Great Plains of eastern and central Wyoming; 3) the Red Desert and adjacent arid lands of west-central and southwestern Wyoming; 4) the Bighorn Basin (Desert) of north-central Wyoming; 5) the Bighorn Mountains and adjacent foothills which lie just east of the Bighorn Basin; and 6) the Greater Yellowstone Highlands of the Middle Rocky Mountains Province with the ranges of western and northwestern Wyoming, overlapping into the adjacent states of Idaho and Montana. This last region includes Yellowstone and Grand Teton National Parks, and the Bridger-Teton, Targhee and Shoshone National Forests which hold some of the largest and wildest tracts in the contiguous 48 states.

Unfortunately, much of Wyoming's former richness and grandeur has already been lost. Big wilderness survives only in the high mountains of regions 5 & 6 (see above). Wyoming's prairies and deserts have been laced with roads, gouged for metals and uranium, ripped apart for fossil fuels and overgrazed by livestock. Here, vigorous wilderness restoration efforts are essential. Bison, Gray Wolf, Elk, Black-footed Ferret, Swift Fox, Wyoming Toad and multitudes of other creatures large and small are either extinct or nearly extinct from Wyoming rangelands.

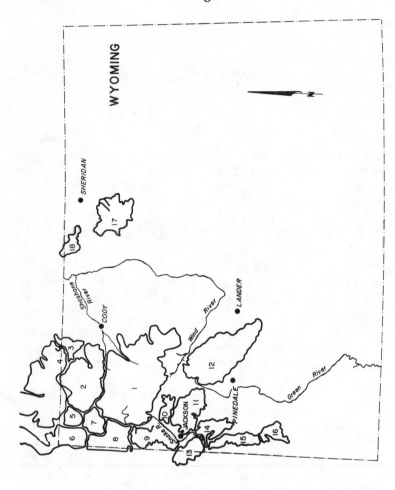

WYOMING

1. South Absaroka
2. North Absaroka
3. Deep Lake
4. Absaroka-Beartooth
5. Washburn Range
6. Gallatin Range
7. Central Plateau
8. Bechler-Pitchstone
9. Teton Range
10. Mt. Leidy
11. Gros Ventre
12. Wind River Range
13. Palisades
14. Grayback Ridge
15. Salt River Range
16. Commissary Ridge
17. Cloud Peak
18. Little Bighorn

It is important to note that southwestern Wyoming's Red Desert offers an impressive opportunity to restore ecologically viable big wilderness where today there remain no roadless tracts exceeding 100,000 acres. The closure of some dirt roads, coupled with reintroductions (including Bison) and protective management, could easily result in a million acre high desert grassland Wilderness in this vast, open, uninhabited region.

Even in the wild mountains of the west, wolves no longer roam and the Grizzly survives only in diminished numbers and precariously. New Forest Service roads and clearcuts continue to penetrate formerly wild country. Periodic "energy booms" lure seismic crews, oil riggers, road bladers, and ultimately more loggers, ORVers and other yahoos into the high country, diminishing Wyoming's wilderness further, and pushing more species closer to the brink of extinction.

The politics of Wyoming are conservative and Republican. Today, its Congressional delegation consists of three Republicans: Senators Malcolm Wallop and Alan Simpson, and Rep. Richard (Dick) Cheney. Wallop and Simpson are two of the most anti-Wilderness and generally anti-environmental Senators in the nation. Although Wallop is generally considered ineffective, Simpson is competent and therefore dangerous. On the environment, Cheney isn't much better than the Senators. These three men dictated the dismal 1984 Wyoming Wilderness Act which protected only 883,359 acres out of 4,162,878 acres that were inventoried in RARE II. Even worse than the acreage figure, much of the "protected" acreage consisted primarily of high altitude rock and ice. The Popo Agie (Wind River Range) and Cloud Peak (Bighorn Mountains) Wildernesses are classic examples of "Wilderness on the Rocks." The bill released about two and a half million acres — mostly of high quality, low- to mid-elevation habitat — to the abusive practices of the Forest Service. Moreover, were it not for now-retired Congressman John Seiberling of Ohio, the bill would have been even worse. For the most part, the bill's boundaries closely followed the Forest Service's horrible RARE II recommendations. As a result, throughout Wyoming's high and dry forests, Forest Service-sponsored habitat destruction continues, nearly unabated.

Willow Creek drainage, Grayback roadless area, Wyoming.
Photo by Howie Wolke.

Furthermore, Simpson, Wallop and Cheney have prevented Wilderness bills for Yellowstone and Grand Teton National Parks from progressing (although the Park Service completed Wilderness recommendations in 1972), and they are blocking the Park Service from reintroducing the Gray Wolf to Yellowstone. They also are to blame for allowing the notorious Fishing Bridge development to remain in prime Grizzly habitat in Yellowstone. Proposals to protect the state's extremely threatened BLM wildlands have never been seriously considered by Congress. Ironically, most public opinion polls indicate that Wyoming's population is far more sympathetic to Wilderness and environmental protection in general than is the Congressional delegation. Therefore, it's up to Wilderness activists to resist the onslaught of Forest Service and BLM-sponsored development, to continue to educate and organize, and to expose these Three Stooges of environmental folly for the corporate-bureaucratic dupes that they are.

Yellowstone Region

This is the core of the Greater Yellowstone Ecosystem (GYE), including Yellowstone National Park and immediately adjacent wildlands in northwestern Wyoming, southern Montana and extreme eastern Idaho. Yellowstone is an International Biosphere Reserve, and the Greater Yellowstone Ecosystem is, in many ways, the epitome of wildness and natural diversity. The GYE is arguably the most significant — and threatened — wildland complex in the temperate world.

South Absaroka 2,190,000 acres	
Yellowstone National Park roadless	*483,000*
Designated Washakie Wilderness Area *(Shoshone NF)*	*703,981*
Designated Teton Wilderness Area *(Bridger-Teton NF)*	*585,468*
Additional Shoshone & Bridger-Teton *NFs roadless*	*347,000*
Wind River Indian Reservation roadless	*60,000*
State & private roadless	*10,000*

Description: Northwestern Wyoming between Moran Junction and Cody. One of the largest and wildest areas in the lower 48 states, the South Absaroka includes the farthest point from a road in the US outside of Alaska (near the Thorofare River in the Teton Wilderness Area). This diverse area has giant Elk herds, Grizzly and Black Bear, Bison (occasionally), Moose, Mule & Whitetail Deer, Bighorn Sheep, Pronghorn, Cougar, Lynx, Marten, Bald & Golden Eagle, Trumpeter Swan, Common Loon, Sandhill Crane; huge meadows; extensive spruce-fir and Lodgepole Pine forests; and Douglas-fir, Aspen and sagebrush at lower elevations. Yellowstone Lake is the northwestern corner of this vast area and is included in the roadless acreage.   The Absarokas include rugged glacial canyons, extensive plateaus with well-developed alpine tundra, craggy peaks, small glaciers, geysers and hot springs. White-tailed Ptarmigan are locally common on the Absaroka tundra. West of the main Absaroka range is an extensive area of low mountains, rolling hills and gentle plateaus clothed in a rich mosaic of forest, meadow and riparian habitats. Big river valleys, rare in the Wilderness System, include the Upper Yellowstone, Snake and Thorofare. The upper Snake and Yellowstone drainages are the major stronghold in Wyoming for River Otter and Osprey. In many ways the South Absaroka is the wild heart of Greater Yellowstone. Elevations range from 5,500' to 13,140' atop Franc's Peak.

Status: Hardrock mining is a threat in the Kirwin (upper Wood River) area on the east side outside the designated Wilderness. NF lands outside of Wilderness are threatened by logging, particularly the 30,000 acre DuNoir Special Management Area which is temporarily protected by Congress. Here, FS clearcutting plans would devastate a major Elk calving and migration route, occupied Grizzly habitat, and important habitat for Trumpeter Swan and Moose. The DuNoir would be a splendid addition to the Washakie Wilderness. Oil & gas development threatens the east slope of the Absarokas. The 1984 Wyoming Wilderness Act released about 300,000 acres of roadless country here. The new Grant Village Resort in Yellowstone and poor bear management policies in general threaten the Grizzly. The NPS recommends 367,200 acres of Yellowstone NP (excluding most of Yellowstone Lake) in this area for Wilderness.

North Absaroka 950,000 acres

Designated North Absaroka Wilderness Area	
(Shoshone NF)	*350,488*
Yellowstone National Park roadless	*430,000*
Additional Shoshone NF roadless	*170,000*

Description: Northwestern Wyoming west of Cody. The most densely populated Grizzly habitat in the Greater Yellowstone Ecosystem is here. This area ranges from semi-desert foothills and sagebrush hills to moist subalpine forest and alpine tundra. The Absaroka crest has volcanic plateaus and rugged peaks, while there are broad alluvial valleys along Pelican Creek and the Lamar River in Yellowstone Park. Extensive Lodgepole Pine forests, spruce-fir along the east slope of the Absarokas, and Douglas-fir at lower elevations adorn the land. Lakes and thermal features, the Grand Canyon of the Yellowstone, and the Mirror Plateau are among the area's spectacles. The little-known Preble's Shrew (*Sorex preblei*) has been identified at the Lamar Ranger Station in Yellowstone. The North Absaroka area may be the southernmost habitat in the Rockies for Fisher, and is certainly the major wilderness stronghold for native Bison in the US. Other wildlife includes Grizzly & Black Bear, Moose, Elk, Mule & Whitetail Deer, Bighorn Sheep, Lynx, Marten and Cougar. Much of the Lamar drainage burned during the dry summer of 1988. This will provide a superb opportunity to study the natural process of secondary ecological succession in an extensive area of Rocky Mountain forest habitat.

Status: All the NF roadless lands outside the Wilderness have been released by Congress. Threats to these areas include oil & gas development along the east slope of the Absarokas, timbering in Grizzly habitat, snowmobiles, and hardrock mining in Sunlight and Sulfur Creek drainages. The Park Service proposes 418,600 acres of their land in this roadless area for Wilderness.

Deep Lake 135,000 acres (also in Montana)

Shoshone and Custer NFs roadless	132,000
BLM and private roadless	3,000

Description: Northwestern Wyoming and southern Montana northwest of Cody. The southern end of the Beartooth Plateau has spectacular geological features including Deep Lake and Clarks Fork River Canyon. Peat beds on the plateau are underlain by permafrost. The plateau is mostly alpine and subalpine but drops steeply down to semi-arid benches above the Clarks Fork and the Bighorn Basin Desert to the east. Elevation varies from 4,500' to 11,000'. Wildlife includes Grizzly, Moose, Elk and Mule Deer. Mountain Goat have been introduced. The rare Pallid Bat (*Antrozous pallidus*) may occur at the lowest elevations. The Montana portion is known as the Line Creek Plateau.

Status: ORV use has caused localized erosion damage. Chief opposition to Wilderness designation is from a small number of snowmobilers in Cody, WY. The entire area is released, although the FS recommended the Clarks Fork Canyon for National Wild & Scenic River designation, but Congress hasn't acted. Water development interests continue to propose a major dam here. A proposal to drill for oil & gas on the fragile tundra of the Line Creek Plateau should be defeated.

Absaroka-Beartooth   1,154,000   acres   (also in Montana)

See Montana for description and status.

Washburn Range 125,000 acres

Yellowstone National Park roadless	125,000

Description: Northwestern Wyoming inside the Mammoth, Tower, Norris and Canyon road loop in Yellowstone NP. The area consists of rolling hills to steep mountains, volcanic plateaus, coniferous forests of Lodgepole Pine and Douglas-fir, and expansive grassy meadows. Elevations vary from 6,000' to 9,900' atop Dunraven Peak. Tower Creek and Lava Creek are the main drainages forming deep and rugged canyons. Elk find important summer range here. Bison, Moose, Bighorn Sheep, Mule Deer, Grizzly and Black Bear also inhabit the area.

Status: The Park Service recommends 122,000 acres of this area for Wilderness. The Norris to Mammoth or Canyon to Tower roads should be closed in order to give the Grizzly more unbroken habitat.

Gallatin Range 525,000 acres (also in Montana)

Yellowstone National Park roadless (WY & MT)	*325,000*
Gallatin National Forest roadless (MT)	*150,000*
Intermingled state & private roadless in Gallatin NF (MT)	*50,000*

Description: Extreme northwestern Wyoming and southwestern Montana west of Gardiner, MT. An integral part of the Greater Yellowstone Ecosystem, the Gallatin Range is important habitat for Grizzly, Elk, Bighorn Sheep, Wolverine and other wilderness dependent species. The area is characterized by 10,000' high peaks, large subalpine basins, and long stream valleys. In the Park, the Gardiner River valley, with grass, sagebrush, Aspen and conifers, is crucial wildlife habitat. Northward, the peaks constitute the rugged backdrop for the Yellowstone and Gallatin River valleys. Big game hunting, backpacking and horsepacking are becoming more popular.

Status: The Park Service has recommended 304,800 acres for Wilderness, but has failed to recommend that a telephone line corridor along the eastern fringe be relocated along the road so that the entire area can be protected. Because of checkerboard land ownership — a legacy of 19th century railroad land grants — logging by Burlington Northern threatens much of the northern half of the area. However, 150,000 acres, including intermixed private and state land, are a Congressional Wilderness Study Area thanks to the late Sen. Lee Metcalf. Off-road-vehicles continue to degrade the Gallatin NF portion of the area.

Central Plateau 185,000 acres

Yellowstone National Park roadless	*185,000*

Description: Northwestern Wyoming, the central core of Yellowstone surrounded by the Fishing Bridge, Old Faithful, Madison, Canyon, West Thumb and Norris developments. A high, cold plateau of broad grassy valleys, vast Lodgepole Pine forests, clear streams, thermal features and small lakes distinguishes this area. This is an especially important Grizzly and Bison area. Other wildlife includes Moose, Elk, Mule Deer, Lynx, Marten and Bald Eagle. Few trails invade this very primitive area. The well known Hayden Valley is in this area. John and Frank Craighead did much of their landmark Grizzly Bear studies during the late '50s and early '60s here.

Status: The Park Service recommends 181,500 acres for Wilderness.

Bechler-Pitchstone 468,000 acres (also in Idaho)	
Yellowstone National Park roadless (WY & ID)	*440,300*
John D. Rockefeller Parkway NRA roadless (WY)	*11,000*
Designated Winegar Hole Wilderness Area	
(Targhee NF,WY)	*14,000*
Additional Targhee NF roadless (WY & ID)	*3,000*

Description: Northwestern Wyoming and extreme eastern Idaho west of Old Faithful. This area includes the remote and unusual Pitchstone Plateau in the southwestern corner of Yellowstone NP. It also includes the Bechler River, big waterfalls, roaring streams, glacial canyons and extensive Lodgepole Pine forests. This area averages 40-50" of annual precipitation, which is very high for the Central Rockies. Shoshone Lake is the largest entirely wilderness lake in the lower 48 states. Geyser Basins, hot springs and mud pots are among the area's thermal features. The Pitchstone Plateau's waters are naturally radioactive. Elevation is generally between 6,000 and 8,500'. Wildlife includes Grizzly & Black Bear, Elk, Moose, Mule Deer, Lynx, Common Loon, Trumpeter Swan and Bald Eagle. The extensive marshy habitat in Winegar Hole is unusual in the Rockies.

Status: The NPS proposes 415,900 acres in Yellowstone for Wilderness. Closure of a portion of the narrow, dirt Grassy Lake Road would unite this part of Yellowstone with the roadless Tetons to the south, forming a Wilderness unit of about 700,000 acres.

Teton Range 334,000 acres

Grand Teton National Park roadless	145,000
Designated Jedediah Smith Wilderness Area	
(Targhee NF)	116,535
Additional Targhee & Bridger-Teton NFs roadless	60,000
John D. Rockefeller Parkway NRA roadless	12,000

Description: Northwestern Wyoming north of Jackson and south of Yellowstone NP. The stunning fault block escarpment of the Grand Tetons rises an abrupt 7,000' above Jackson Hole. These peaks, cirques, glaciers, rugged U-shaped canyons, streams and lakes are world-famous scenery. The steep east face consists of Precambrian granitic rocks, the more gentle west slope (the Jedediah Smith Wilderness and other FS lands) consists predominantly of overlying sediments above the granitic core. Low elevation coniferous forests and lush sub-alpine meadows are the main vegetation types. The Tetons are an internationally popular climbing area. Grand Teton Peak is 13,770'. Grizzly Bears utilize the north half of the range; other wildlife includes Moose, Elk and Black Bear.

Status: The Jedediah Smith Wilderness is being severely degraded by excessive sheep grazing and by poaching. A few timber sales threaten the lower west slope. The NPS has recommended 115,807 acres in Grand Teton NP for Wilderness. Jackson Lake is not included in the roadless acreage here because its level has been artificially raised by Jackson Lake Dam. The dam should be removed and the lake returned to its natural level.

Mt. Leidy 112,000 acres

Bridger-Teton NF roadless	110,000
Grand Teton National Park roadless	2,000

Description: Northwestern Wyoming northeast of Jackson. The Mt. Leidy highlands are a major unprotected part of the

Greater Yellowstone Ecosystem, linking the Gros Ventre Wilderness to the south with the Teton Wilderness of the vast South Absaroka complex to the north. It provides excellent habitat for Elk, Mule Deer, Moose, Black Bear, Mountain Lion and many smaller creatures. There are important wintering areas along the southern boundary for Bighorn Sheep. Grizzlies occasionally wander into the area from the north. Extensive coniferous forests, Aspen groves, open meadows, steep ridges and a few prominent peaks comprise a varied landscape. Elevations range from 7,000' along the Gros Ventre River to 10,337' on Grouse Mountain.

Status: This area is critical to reestablishing the traditional north-south Jackson Hole Elk herd migration and to expanding Grizzly habitat to help insure the survival of the Grizzly in the Greater Yellowstone Ecosystem. There is good local support for protecting the area. On much of the east and north, the roadless area is defined by the adjacent sea of logging roads and clearcuts. FS plans for additional extensive logging and road-building have been postponed but not canceled. Oil & gas exploration is a serious threat as well, with the FS and BLM supporting construction of a Sohare Creek access road and drilling project deep within the roadless area. Much of the Mt. Leidy highlands adjacent to this roadless area that have been heavily logged and roaded should be managed as a wilderness recovery area. This would establish an important link for wildlife between the Gros Ventre and Teton Wildernesses.

Gros Ventre 455,000 acres

Designated Gros Ventre Wilderness Area	
(Bridger-Teton NF)	*287,000*
Shoal Creek Wilderness Study Area (B-T NF)	*30,000*
Additional Bridger-Teton NF roadless	*133,000*
Jackson Hole National Elk Refuge roadless	*5,000*

Description: Western Wyoming east of Jackson. The Gros Ventre is an imposing mountain range rising from sagebrush-grassland foothills at 6,000' to alpine tundra and rocky peaks. Doubletop Peak is 11,682'. Long stream valleys, lakes, cirques,

limestone peaks, coniferous forests of Engelmann Spruce, Subalpine Fir and Lodgepole Pine characterize the area. There are
lots of rich subalpine meadows, too. Douglas-fir and Aspen are
at lower elevations. The extremely abundant wildlife includes
Elk, Moose, Mule Deer, Bighorn Sheep, Black Bear, Cougar,
Golden and Bald Eagle. This is an important summer range,
calving and migratory area for a major portion of the Jackson
Hole Elk herd. The area is used for big game hunting, fishing,
hiking and trail riding. Some of the best wildlife habitat in
the Gros Ventre is on the eastern flank of the range, draining
into the Green River. Much of the Gros Ventre's Green River
slope was excluded from the Wilderness by Congress. The Green
River drainage of the Gros Ventre includes populations of
Colorado Cutthroat Trout (*Salmo clarki pleuriticus*), a rare
subspecies which is becoming Endangered due to clearcutting,
livestock grazing and hybridization.

Status: Unprotected areas are extremely threatened by
logging, especially on the east slope draining into the Green
River. Oil & gas development is a threat in some areas,
including Little Granite Creek where Texaco has proposed a
well inside the designated Wilderness. Major big game
wintering areas were excluded from the Wilderness; they
should be added.

Western Wyoming

*The southern extension of the Greater Yellowstone Ecosys-
tem includes the rugged Wind Rivers and the rapidly diminishing wilds of the so-called "Overthrust Belt" along
Wyoming's western border south of Jackson Hole.*

Wind River Range 1,171,000 acres

Designated Bridger Wilderness Area	
(Bridger-Teton NF)	*428,169*
Designated Fitzpatrick Wilderness Area	
(Shoshone NF)	*198,525*
Designated Popo Agie Wilderness Area	
(Shoshone NF)	*101,991*
Wind River Indian Reservation roadless	*190,000*
BLM Scab Creek Primitive Area	*7,000*

Additional Shoshone & Bridger-Teton	
NFs roadless	230,000
Additional BLM roadless	10,000
Private roadless	5,000

Description: Western Wyoming west of Lander. This nationally famous glaciated mountain range features granite peaks, cirques, alpine and subalpine lakes galore, clear streams, vast alpine rock and tundra fields, and the largest glaciers in the Rocky Mountains south of Canada. It is a major destination for mountain climbing, fishing, hiking and trail riding. Elevations range from sagebrush plains at 6,000' to Wyoming's highest point, 13,804' Gannett Peak. The Continental Divide forms the crest of the range. The headwaters of the Green River form west of the divide; east of the divide, the Wind River is an important tributary of the Yellowstone-Missouri River system. Wildlife includes a large and productive herd of Bighorn Sheep, as well as Elk, Mule Deer, Black Bear, Mountain Lion, Moose, Pronghorn, Yellow-bellied Marmot and Black-crowned Rosy Finch.

Status: The addition of low- and mid-elevation FS and BLM lands mainly to the Bridger and Popo Agie Wildernesses would help complete the protected area ecologically. Timber sales threaten potential additions to the Bridger Wilderness, and ORV abuse has already degraded the Seven Lakes area on the northwestern end of the Bridger. Overgrazing by sheep and cattle, and overuse by recreationists (especially horse packers and rock climbers) are localized problems. The BLM has recommended the Scab Creek Primitive Area (7,600 acres) for Wilderness and most of the Indian roadless lands are managed as a Tribal Roadless Area.

Palisades 240,000 acres (also in Idaho)

Targhee & Bridger-Teton NFs roadless	240,000

Description: Wyoming-Idaho border west of Jackson, the Snake River Range. Features include steep, heavily vegetated sedimentary mountains with deep stream canyons, scattered coniferous forests, extensive lush meadows and mountain shrublands, and habitat for Black Bear, Moose, Mule Deer and

Bighorn Sheep. Mountain Goat has been introduced. Elevations range from 5,500' to 10,000'. Excellent big game hunting and crosscountry skiing attract visitors. Although not as "scenic" in the popular sense as the adjacent Grand Tetons, the Palisades are a vital chunk of productive habitat crucial to the survival of the Greater Yellowstone Ecosystem.

Status: The Wyoming side is a Congressional Wilderness Study Area; the Idaho portion is a FS Further Planning area, but oil & gas leases have already been given for extensive areas. ORV use on the Idaho side, logging on the Wyoming side, and domestic sheep grazing are additional threats to this area.

Grayback Ridge 225,000 acres
Bridger-Teton NF roadless   225,000

Description: Western Wyoming south of Jackson. This northern end of the Wyoming Range, locally known as the "Hoback Mountains," includes superb U-shaped valleys, waterfalls, high ridges, peaks, cirques; and a diverse vegetative mosaic of coniferous forests interspersed with Aspen, lush montane and subalpine meadows, and sagebrush on lower elevation southerly exposures. Some of the best Aspen stands in any Wyoming roadless area are here. Wildlife includes "trophy-sized" Mule Deer as well as Elk, Moose, Black Bear, Lynx, Badger, Sandhill Crane, Bald Eagle and native Cutthroat Trout. Elevations range from 6,000' to 10,862' Hoback Peak. Grayback Ridge is a prominent 18 mile long escarpment rising to 9,700' along the west side of the Willow Creek drainage. Major uses are trail riding and big game hunting.

Status: The entire area has been released by Congress. The Forest Service is proposing roadless management for the Willow Creek core but has extensive logging plans for most of the rest of the area. Part of the so-called "Overthrust Belt," nearly the entire area is under oil & gas lease and is extremely threatened by associated roading and development. The FS often uses oil & gas exploration roads to gain access to slow-growing high altitude stands of timber. Grayback Ridge and the nearby Salt River Range (see below) are the "forgotten gems" of western Wyoming, and need an active constituency very badly.

RM36: 560,000

Salt River Range <u>250,000 acres</u>

Bridger-Teton NF roadless	*245,000*
Private roadless	*5,000*

Description: Western Wyoming east of Afton. An extremely rugged north-south range of folded and faulted sedimentary rocks, glacial cirques, lakes, U-shaped canyons, waterfalls, lush subalpine meadows, coniferous forests, and scattered Aspen groves, it has very steep, unstable slopes, and is part of the Overthrust Belt. Elevations rise from 6,000' to nearly 11,000'. It offers excellent habitat for Mule Deer and Elk; also extant are Moose, Black Bear, Mountain Lion and Lynx. The steep western slope drains to the Salt River, the east slope to the Greys River, which is characterized by long drainages, forested benches and lush meadows. The major recreation use is hunting.

Status: This is a little known area, except locally in the Star Valley where there appears to be little support for its preservation. On the Greys River side, most of the lower slope adjacent to the roadless area has been logged except for Corral and Crow Creeks. Timber sales and oil & gas exploration threaten the entire area, except for parts of the crest and the west slope where steep terrain will limit development. The entire area was released by the so-called Wyoming Wilderness Act.

Commissary Ridge <u>190,000 acres</u>

Bridger-Teton NF roadless	*170,000*
BLM roadless	*20,000*

Description: Western Wyoming north of Kemmerer. This southernmost extension of the Bridger-Teton NF rises above the arid Green River basin. It is a mostly montane and subalpine wilderness of steep, folded sedimentary ridges, extensive spruce-fir and Lodgepole Pine forests, numerous meadows, streams, a few lakes (including Lake Alice — a major recreational attraction), and large populations of Elk and Mule Deer. Other wildlife includes Moose, Black Bear, Pronghorn and Cougar. Major uses are hunting and fishing. An unhybridized population of Utah Cutthroat Trout (*Salmo clarki utah*), an increasingly rare subspecies, can be found in Lake Alice and nearby streams within this area.

Status: This is one of the most immediately and completely threatened roadless areas in the country. The entire area is covered with oil & gas leases and is a focal point of energy company interest. Timber sales are a major threat and are already reducing the size of the area. ORV abuse has also degraded the area. It is near the huge La Barge oil & gas field where Exxon operates a sour gas plant.

North-Central Wyoming

The rugged Bighorn Mountains rise above the high plains to the east and the arid Bighorn Basin to the west.

Cloud Peak 443,000 acres

Designated Cloud Peak Wilderness Area	
(Bighorn NF)	*195,500*
Additional Bighorn NF roadless	*224,000*
BLM roadless	*13,000*
State roadless	*5,000*
Private roadless	*5,000*

Description: North-central Wyoming west of Buffalo. The central core of the Bighorn Mountains is a land of precipitous peaks, lakes, cirques, U-shaped canyons, extensive high alpine terrain, and coniferous forests at lower elevations. The typical wildlife of the Central Rockies lives here, including Mule Deer, Elk, Black Bear and Mountain Lion. Elevations range from 5,000' to 13,175' atop Cloud Peak. It is a popular recreation area.

Status: Most of the Cloud Peak Wilderness Area is above treeline. Nearly all of the lower elevation lands are threatened by FS timber and road-building plans even though these are some of the most unproductive timberlands in the nation. The Bighorn Forest Plan is now under appeal by conservation groups (filed in 1987). Other threats include mining, ORVs and overuse by recreationists in the Wilderness. The entire 224,000

acres of roadless NF lands were released by Congress, thanks to
Wyoming anti-Wilderness Senator Malcolm Wallop.

Little Bighorn 155,000 acres (also in Montana)	
Bighorn NF roadless (WY)	*135,000*
Crow Indian Reservation roadless (MT)	*15,000*
State & private roadless	*5,000*

Description: Northern Wyoming and southern Montana
west of Sheridan, WY. The northern end of the Bighorn Range
is a little known area of subalpine basins, meadows, forests,
with steep canyons and river breaks dropping to the Great
Plains on the east. Wildlife includes Mountain Lion, Black
Bear, Pronghorn, Mule Deer and Elk. The primary human use is
by hunters and fishermen.

Status: The entire area was released by Congress and is
threatened by water development schemes, timber sales and
road construction.

California

What a land of contrasts is California! It has the highest mountain in the 48 states and the lowest point; the largest trees on Earth and the driest, hottest, most barren desert in the United States. Perhaps the most surprising contrast, however, is that while California has the largest human population of any state, it also has the most land in the National Wilderness Preservation System (nearly six million acres) and the greatest number of roadless areas over 100,000 acres (not counting Alaska).

Natural California begins with the Coast Range flanking the Pacific Ocean. A misty forest of giant, ancient trees (over 20 species of conifers) envelops the Coast Range in the north, San Francisco Bay punches its way through the mountains in their center, and vegetation reflecting steadily drier habitats dominates south into Mexico. Inside the Coast Range is the great Central Valley, formed by the Sacramento and San Joaquin Rivers. Once it was a haven for Tule Elk, Pronghorn, Grizzly and waterfowl in mosquito-like profusion, now it is an agricultural factory. East of the Central Valley, the Cascades in northern and the Sierra Nevada in central California rear up in a stupendous mountain wall, with dark forests on the west slope, an expanse of rock and ice on the crest, and sagebrush dropping down the arid east side into the Great Basin. South and east of the Sierra, east of Los Angeles and the Coast Range, the California Desert combines three ecological deserts — the Great Basin, Mojave and Colorado (Sonoran).

Except for the Central Valley, all of these regions still have big wilderness.

This is not to say all is well with California's wilderness. Its wildlife populations have been more devastated than those of any other Western state — the Golden Bear exists only on the state flag (once California had the largest population of Grizzlies as well as the biggest bears outside of coastal Alaska);

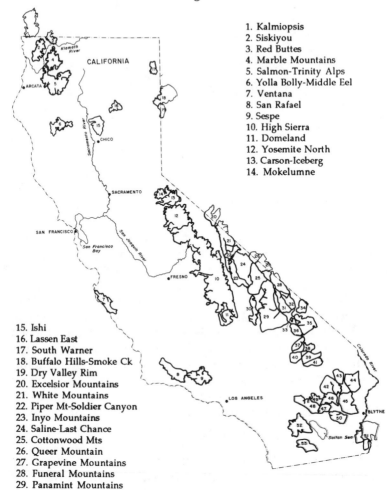

1. Kalmiopsis
2. Siskiyou
3. Red Buttes
4. Marble Mountains
5. Salmon-Trinity Alps
6. Yolla Bolly-Middle Eel
7. Ventana
8. San Rafael
9. Sespe
10. High Sierra
11. Domeland
12. Yosemite North
13. Carson-Iceberg
14. Mokelumne

15. Ishi
16. Lassen East
17. South Warner
18. Buffalo Hills-Smoke Ck
19. Dry Valley Rim
20. Excelsior Mountains
21. White Mountains
22. Piper Mt-Soldier Canyon
23. Inyo Mountains
24. Saline-Last Chance
25. Cottonwood Mts
26. Queer Mountain
27. Grapevine Mountains
28. Funeral Mountains
29. Panamint Mountains
30. Argus Range
31. Amargosa Range
32. Greenwater Range
33. Ibex Hills
34. Nopah Range
35. Kingston Range
36. Avawatz
37. Soda Mountain
38. Old Dad Mountain
39. Kelso Dunes
40. Cady Mountains
41. Granite Mountains
42. Sheep Hole
43. Old Woman Mts

44. Turtle Mountains
45. Palen-McCoy
46. Coxcomb
47. Eagle Mountains
48. Hexie-Li'l San Berdo Mts
49. Pinto Mountains
50. Chuckwalla Mts
51. Lower Colorado River
52. Santa Rosa Mts
53. Vallecito Mountains

Tule Elk and Pronghorn are virtually gone; Bighorn Sheep are but a reminder of their former populations. Moreover, no state in the West has been more thoroughly invaded by exotics, from grasses to Eucalyptus. No state has sucked more from its rivers. The peerless Redwood Forest, once stretching from the Big Sur to the Oregon border, remains in tiny museum pieces (96% has been cut in the last hundred years and another 2% faces the chainsaw today). The distraught denizens of Los Angeles, San Bernardino and San Diego relieve their frustration from living and working in such impossible cities by ripping up the desert with knobby tires, and pity the poor creature — Desert Tortoise or Creosote Bush — that gets in their way.

But because of the population and urbanity of California, the traditional land barons of the West — ranchers, timbermen, miners— are relatively less powerful here. California is also the home of the Sierra Club and has more members of conservation groups than do all of the other Western states combined. This has resulted in a greater percentage of California being preserved. In RARE II, the FS identified 6.5 million acres as roadless; conservationists asked for 6 million; and, in 1984, Congress established 1,779,432 acres of new NF Wilderness and postponed a decision on another 1.7 million acres. The same bill designated as Wilderness much of Yosemite, Kings Canyon and Sequoia National Parks. (Wilderness Areas had been previously established in Joshua Tree, Lava Beds and Pinnacles NMs; Pt. Reyes National Seashore; and Lassen Volcanic NP. Death Valley NM is the only California unit of the NPS still awaiting Wilderness designation.)

The BLM Organic Act (FLPMA) in 1976 singled out most of BLM's acreage in California (12 million acres) as a special unit: The California Desert Conservation Area (CDCA). BLM was instructed to prepare a management plan and accelerate the Wilderness review. That review, mediocre under the Carter Administration, was corrupted further by the Reaganauts. Conservationists turned to Sen. Alan Cranston, who introduced the largest, and arguably the strongest, Wilderness bill ever in the lower 48 states — The California Desert Protection Act.

The CDPA, or Cranston bill, would establish a new National Park, the 1.5 million acre Mojave NP; enlarge Death Valley National Monument by 1.3 million acres to a total of 3.4

Sierra Old Growth Forest, California.
Photo by Dave Foreman.

million acres and redesignate it as a National Park; enlarge
Joshua Tree National Monument by 245,000 acres to 795,000
acres and redesignate it a National Park; designate 4.3 million
acres in the three Parks as Wilderness; and designate 81 BLM
Wilderness Areas with an acreage of 4.5 million acres. In all,
8.8 million acres of Wilderness would be established. (BLM
lands outside the CDCA are not involved in the Cranston Bill.)

Make no mistake, though, this bill is not visionary. It
leaves unnecessary roads open in the Parks and on BLM land;
gives dirt bikers and jeepers millions of acres to pulverize; and
continues grazing and mining, even in the Parks. Far better is
the 16 million acre California Desert National Wilderness
Park proposal of Earth First!.

Moderate though it is, the Cranston Bill is under heavy
fire from the whole panoply of desert abusers. There is hope,
nevertheless, that it may see progress in Congress after it is
reintroduced in 1989. Conservationists across the country need
to voice their support for protecting the California Desert. Although the figures for the Cranston bill will quickly become
outdated, we have included them in our discussion for individual areas because they offer some kind of baseline.

At the other end of the state, conservationists, from Earth
First! to the California Wilderness Coalition, are valiantly
fighting big timber companies and the Forest Service to protect
the remaining old growth forests. Additionally, small hydro
projects are proposed for streams in many of the big roadless
areas and Friends of the River is working against those projects.
Of course, California's wilderness is sometimes crowded with
backpackers, as hacked green trees at timberline lakes and
wide, eroding trails attest. Sprawling cities encroach more and
more on wildlife habitat, and the air turns brown.

California may no longer be paradise, but it ain't all a
parking lot either.

Northern Coast Range

Northwestern California is a land of richly forested mountains, where fog strokes the Earth like a lover, and pellucid
rivers carry snow to the sea. Over 100" of precipitation falls in
places. The eastern side of the northern Coast Range drops into
the Sacramento Valley. Because the cloud-catching crest of the

range forms a rainshadow, the forest is transformed into Digger
Pine and chaparral. The Big Outside here is largely managed
by the US Forest Service.

Kalmiopsis 408,000 acres (also in Oregon)
See Oregon for description and status.

Siskiyou 249,000 acres

Designated Siskiyou Wilderness Area (Klamath,	
Six Rivers and Siskiyou NFs)	*153,000*
Additional Six Rivers, Klamath and Siskiyou	
NF roadless	*96,000*

Description: Extreme northwestern California east of Crescent City between the Smith and Klamath Rivers in the
Siskiyou Mountains. High precipitation and steep terrain with
narrow ridges and sheer granite faces make the Siskiyous
highly vulnerable to damage from road-building and logging.
Elevations drop from 7,309' on Preston Peak to 600'. There are
some open valleys and a few lakes. Because much of the area
escaped Pleistocene glaciation, vegetation is extremely diverse, with over 20 species of conifers including Grand Fir, Port-
Orford-Cedar, Knobcone Pine, Whitebark Pine, Yew, Noble Fir
and the rare Weeping Spruce; and the world's largest concentration of lily species. Perhaps the finest Wilderness-pro-
tected old growth Pacific forest is located in the Siskiyou
Wilderness Area. Wildlife includes Black Bear, Black-tailed
Deer, River Otter, Fisher, Wolverine, Bigfoot, Mountain
Beaver, Pacific Salamander, Pileated Woodpecker, Spotted
Owl, Goshawk and Osprey. Portions of the headwaters for the
Klamath, Smith and Illinois rivers are located here. The Upper South Fork of the Smith is a National Wild River. Summer
runs of Steelhead and salmon are unhindered by human-caused
obstructions. Sacred sites for the Yurok and Karok tribes are
protected in the Wilderness but some are located in the non-
Wilderness corridor for the proposed G-O Road.
    Status: The 1984 California Wilderness Act left a corridor
for the controversial G-O (Gasquet-Orleans) Road and excluded
significant old growth forest in Blue Creek and Dillon Creek

from the designated Wilderness Area. This remains an important battleground for ancient forests. The G-O Road was halted in 1983 by a landmark federal court decision based on First Amendment protection of the religious rights of Native American groups that use the high country. In 1988, the Supreme Court overturned the decision protecting Native American religious rights in the Siskiyous and remanded the case to a lower court. If the FS is permitted to go ahead with the G-O Road, a bitter battle will ensue. No G-O!

Red Buttes 104,000 acres (also in Oregon)

Designated Red Buttes Wilderness Area (Rogue River NF, CA)	16,150
Designated Red Buttes Wilderness Area (Rogue River & Siskiyou NFs, OR)	3,750
Additional Klamath, Siskiyou & Rogue River NFs roadless (CA)	49,000
Additional Rogue River NF roadless (OR)	31,800
Oregon Caves NM and BLM roadless (OR)	3,500

Description: Southwestern Oregon and northwestern California south of Medford on the Siskiyou Mountains divide between the Klamath and Rogue River watersheds. This diverse Siskiyous old growth forest includes giant cedar groves, while landforms feature glacially sculptured peaks, lakes, marshes and permanent snowfields. Elevations drop from 6,739' (Red Buttes) to 2,500'. Uncommon plants include Siskiyou Bitterroot, Weeping Spruce, Huckleberry Oak and Sadler's Oak, making this area important botanically. Black Bear, Bobcat, deer and other wildlife abound. The headwaters of the Applegate River and part of the Illinois River drainage lie in this area.

Status: The undesignated area is under imminent threat of logging and roading.

Marble Mountains 320,000 acres

Designated Marble Mountain Wilderness Area (Klamath NF)	241,744
Additional Klamath NF, BLM, private roadless	78,000

Description: Northwestern California west of Yreka and east of the Klamath River. This alpine region in the Klamath Mountains has deep, timber-choked canyons and nearly 100 lakes. The old growth forest contains 21 coniferous species (Doug-fir, Incense Cedar, Silver/Noble/ Grand/Shasta Red/White/Red Fir, Knobcone/ Digger/ Sugar/ Foxtail/ Jeffrey/Ponderosa/Whitebark/Western White/ Lodgepole Pine, Western Juniper, Weeping Spruce, Yew and Mountain Hemlock). Red and White Fir predominate above 5,000'. A total of 535 plant species have been identified, 17 of them being endemic to the Marbles and Siskiyous. Marble Mountain is crystallized limestone — marble. Elevations drop from 8,299' on Boulder Peak to 800' where Wooley Creek meets the Salmon River. Wooley Creek supports Steelhead and King Salmon runs. Wildlife includes Wolverine, Black Bear, Black-tailed Deer, Bigfoot; and it is a potential Grizzly reintroduction site. A large expanse of the southwestern part of the Wilderness is trailless except along Wooley Creek (part of which is a primitive route), making it arguably the wildest place in northern California.

Status: As with everywhere else in the northcoast region of California, the unprotected parts of this area, including portions along the Pacific Crest Trail, are under full-scale assault from logging and road-building. Conservationists should fight to get these vital forested additions out of the clutches of the timber beasts and into the Wilderness. The 1984 California Wilderness Act made some minor additions to the Marbles, but not the vital Crapo Creek area to the southwest which almost links the Marbles to the Salmon-Trinity Alps.

The Wilderness Area is plagued with excessive cattle, which not only ruin the experience of hikers, but trample and overgraze meadows, eliminating rare wildflowers, and infesting watercourses with giardia. The overgrazing in the Marbles is also a major stumbling block to reintroduction of Grizzly. It is time to get the cows out of the Marbles.

RM36: 440,000

Salmon-Trinity Alps <u>620,000 acres</u>

Designated Trinity Alps Wilderness Area (Klamath, Shasta-Trinity & Six Rivers NFs, BLM)   500,000

Additional Klamath, Shasta-Trinity & Six
  Rivers NFs, BLM and Hoopa Valley IR roadless   120,000

Description: Northwestern California east of Arcata and north of the Trinity River. This large, high area in the southern Klamath Mountains features ice-sculpted peaks, small glaciers, glacial lakes, waterfalls, fine wildflower displays, large sub-alpine meadows, deep U-shaped valleys and old growth forests of Red Fir. Elevations range from below 1,500' to 9,002' on Thompson Peak. Big Leaf Maple, Vine Maple, oak and Dogwood show bright fall colors. This large wilderness consists of three regions: the "White Trinities" high country in the center named for its light-colored granite; the "Red Trinities" to the east with red, gray and brown peaks; and the "Green Trinities" to the west with lower elevation forest. Twelve feet of snow accumulates in places during some winters. Salmon and Steelhead swim the many streams, including the South Fork of the Salmon River, Stuart Fork River, North Fork Trinity River and New River. Wolverine, many Black Bear and perhaps a remnant population of Bigfoot live here.

Status: Protection of most of this fine wilderness was the major victory in the 1984 California Wilderness Act, but vital lower elevation areas remain outside of protection and under threat of logging. A particularly important part denied protection was Orleans Mt. This northwestern extension links the Alps to the Marble Mountain area via Crapo Creek. Conservationists should make a priority of protecting this linkage so that these two large northern California wildernesses will not be further isolated and fragmented. Two dirt roads were cherrystemmed deep into the area; they should be closed and rehabilitated.

Yolla Bolly-Middle Eel 260,000 acres
Designated Yolla Bolly-Middle Eel Wilderness
  Area (Mendocino & Shasta-Trinity NFs, BLM)   153,404
Additional Mendocino, Six Rivers & Shasta-Trinity
  NFs, BLM, Round Valley IR, private roadless   107,000

Description: Central part of the Coast Range in northwestern California, west of Red Bluff. The headwaters of the Middle Eel River (still partly covered by old growth coniferous forest) lie between the North and South Yolla Bolly Mountains. Elevations drop from 8,000' to 800'. The lush forests include Douglas-fir, White and Red Fir, Ponderosa and Sugar Pine, Incense Cedar, Western Juniper, Western Hemlock and Black Cottonwood. Chamise and manzanita cover the lower elevations. This is one of the best wildlife strongholds in California, according to the California Wilderness Coalition, with 13 wilderness-associated species including Wolverine, Mountain Beaver, Mink, River Otter, Mountain Lion, Ringtail, Golden Eagle, Marten and Fisher; 150 bird species; and 80% of California's summer Steelhead. Black Bear and Black-tailed Deer are abundant. Much of the area is lower in elevation than other mountain wildernesses in California, so it is especially important ecologically.

Status: Unprotected areas are under threat of logging and roading; they should be added to the Wilderness Area. BLM has recommended against Wilderness for their 640 acre WSA (30-501) contiguous to the eastern border of the designated Wilderness Area, and the 2,391 acre Big Butte WSA (50-211) contiguous to the west — BLM plans to road and log this western WSA (but conservationists, including Northcoast Earth First!, are resisting).

The eastern WSA is part of a 35,000 acre roadless area of checkerboard BLM, FS and private land that encompasses lower elevation oak foothill country. The western WSA is part of a 30,000 acre roadless area of BLM, private, FS and Round Valley Indian land. Both areas should be major priorities for federal acquisition and addition to the Wilderness. There is no other roadless area in northern California which covers such a complete transition from semi-arid Central Valley foothills over the Coast Range and down into the coastal rainforest. Logging on the west and grazing on the east could sunder this totality unless conservationists can successfully act.

South Coast Range

Where San Francisco Bay breaks through the Coast Range, the Central Valley finds an outlet to the Pacific Ocean. South of the Bay, the Coast Range again forms the western wall of the continent. Mists and Coast Redwood predominate at first.

But as the mountains tramp south, their vegetation becomes drier and less forested until it becomes dominated by coast chaparral. The Los Padres NF manages most of the Big Outside of the South Coast Range.

Ventana 230,000 acres

Designated Ventana Wilderness Area	
(Los Padres NF)	164,144
Additional Los Padres NF and Hunter-Liggett	
Military Reservation roadless	20,000
Private and state roadless	46,000

Description: West-central California south of Monterey. In the coastal Santa Lucia Mountains east of Highway 1 along the Big Sur, topography is characterized by sharp-crested ridges dividing V-shaped valleys. Elevations range from 400' to 5,000'. Waterfalls, hot springs and deep pools are common along the plunging streams. Precipitation varies from over 100" to under 30"; summer fog fills the coastal valleys. Frequent fire has shaped this chaparral and oak woodland. Virgin stands of Coast Redwood line Big and Little Sur Rivers. Bristlecone (Santa Lucia) Fir is an endemic conifer. Other trees include California Madrone (up to 125' tall), Tanoak, Coast Live Oak, Coulter Pine, Ponderosa Pine, Douglas-fir and California Bay Laurel. Wildlife includes Mountain Lion (one of the densest populations on the continent), Mule Deer, Gray Fox, Ringtail, Red-shouldered Hawk, Prairie Falcon, Mountain Plover, Spotted Owl, Golden Eagle, Peregrine Falcon, native Rainbow Trout and Steelhead. Feral boar compete with some of these natives to the detriment of the natives. This is the landscape that inspired poet Robinson Jeffers.

Status: Largely protected; contiguous roadless lands should be added to the Wilderness. The dirt Arroyo Seco-Indians Road cuts this larger roadless area off from a second unit of the Ventana Wilderness which has a significant amount of roadless NF land around it. The road should be closed, adjacent wild private and state land added and a unified Wilderness of at least 300,000 acres protected.

San Rafael 381,000 acres

Designated San Rafael Wilderness Area	
(Los Padres NF)	151,040
Designated Dick Smith Wilderness Area	
(Los Padres NF)	64,700
Additional Los Padres NF roadless	159,000
Private roadless	6,000

Description: The mountainous backdrop to coastal Santa Barbara in southern California. Elevations decrease from 6,800' on Big Pine Mountain to under 1,000'. These rugged mountains cut by sheer canyons were a crucial part of the California Condor's habitat. The two Wilderness Areas are separated by a fire road which is closed to all non-Forest Service vehicles but which is used illegally by ORVs. Other roadless areas are separated only by jeep trails and dirt bike routes. In this area of frequent fire, vegetation is mostly chaparral, with riparian zones along the streams, and pines (Knobcone/ Jeffrey/Ponderosa/Coulter) and Big Cone Douglas-fir in higher elevations. Of particular interest are the southernmost stand of Sargent Cypress and exquisite Chumash cave paintings. Wildlife includes Black Bear, Mountain Lion and Peregrine Falcon. The San Rafael was the first Forest Service Primitive Area to be designated Wilderness under the Wilderness Act (1968).

Status: Unprotected areas are under pressure from ORVs and oil & gas leasing. This is a potential Grizzly reintroduction site. The California Condor should also be reintroduced, concurrent with the banning of lead shot and 1080 predicide within the condor's range.

RM27: 1,097,600*

Sespe 335,000 acres

Sespe-Frazier roadless area (Los Padres NF)	320,700
Private roadless	14,000

Description: Southern California north of Ventura. This rugged area of mountains and canyons rises up from the Santa Clara River Valley at under 1,000' to nearly 7,500' on Pine Mountain. Coastal chaparral grades into conifer forest (Knobcone/Jeffrey/ Ponderosa/ Coulter Pines, and Big Cone

Douglas-fir). The many permanent streams cut sheer canyons, including the almost impassable Sespe Gorge. Wildlife includes Black Bear, Mountain Lion, Bobcat, Mt. Pinos Chipmunk, Mt. Pinos Blue Grouse, Spotted Owl, Peregrine Falcon and Rubber Boa. This was the last refuge for the highly Endangered California Condor (all of the condors are now behind bars for a captive breeding program). Hot springs and Chumash cave paintings attract hikers. The Sespe is the second largest completely unprotected National Forest roadless area (only Idaho's Boulder-White Clouds is larger).

Status: This is one of the more threatened wild areas in California. ORVs are assaulting it on all sides. Demands for oil & gas leasing are pressing. Two dams have been proposed — Oat Mountain and Topa-Topa. The California Condors protected this area as long as they flew free (because they are an Endangered species), but now that they are incarcerated, the area is largely unprotected. This should also be one of the priority sites for reintroduction of the Grizzly into California. The FS in their final Los Padres Forest Plan recommended 197,047 acres for Wilderness; the local Congressman is calling for a piddling 133,000 acre Wilderness, which would leave more than half of the area open to oil & gas extraction, ORVs and mining.

RM27: 1,097,600*

Sierra Nevada

Perhaps no other mountain range in the United States has been so glorified, loved and fought for as the Sierra Nevada. With good reason. Bare granite domes, crystal lakes, rushing streams, waterfalls, Giant Sequoias, dark old growth forests, glacier-carved valleys, friendly Black Bears . . . for nearly 400 miles the Sierra Nevada forms the backbone of California. "Climb the mountains and get their good tidings," wrote John Muir. He was writing of the Sierra Nevada.

High Sierra 2,800,000 acres

Designated Yosemite National Park Wilderness Area (southern portion)	*304,000*
Designated Ansel Adams Wilderness Area (Sierra & Inyo NFs)	*228,669*

Designated John Muir Wilderness Area *(Sierra & Inyo NFs)*	580,675
Designated Dinkey Lakes Wilderness Area *(Sierra NF)*	30,000
Designated Sequoia-Kings Canyon National *Park Wilderness Area*	736,980
Designated Monarch Wilderness Area *(Sequoia & Sierra NFs)*	45,000
Designated Jennie Lakes Wilderness Area *(Sequoia NF)*	10,500
Designated Golden Trout Wilderness Area *(Inyo & Sequoia NFs)*	303,287
Designated South Sierra Wilderness Area *(Inyo & Sequoia NFs)*	63,000
Additional National Forest roadless	406,000
Additional National Park roadless	14,000
BLM roadless	78,000

Description: East-central California east of Fresno. Say "Wilderness," and most people will think of John Muir's "Range of Light" — the High Sierra. Although within an easy day's drive of the metastasizing population centers of California, the Sierra contains the second largest roadless area remaining in the United States outside of Alaska. From Mt. Whitney, at 14,495' the highest point in the 48 states, to the Giant Sequoias (several groves), this is a wilderness writ in superlatives. Vegetation ranges from the oak/chaparral of the west slope foothills (lowest elevations of 2,300'); through forests of Red Fir, Lodgepole, Jeffrey and Ponderosa Pine; to great expanses of tundra, granite domes and small glaciers; down the east slope into pinyon/juniper woodland and finally the sagebrush desert of the Great Basin. Deep canyons of the San Joaquin, Kings, Kern and other rivers cut down through the mountains. Awesome (in its proper meaning) Kings Canyon is the deepest gorge in North America, Californians aver (Idaho and Oregon chauvinists claim this distinction for Hells Canyon). Countless lakes, waterfalls and lush meadows spice the scene. Some basins are trailless. Snow is possible during any month in the high country. Wolverine, Bighorn Sheep, Black Bear and Mountain Lion still roam this backcountry of the most populous state. Nowhere else in the US is there a straight line of 150 miles that is roadless — from Bald Mountain north to Tioga Pass, no road crosses the Sierra.

Status: While most of this area is protected, parts of it suffer from extreme overuse by wilderness recreationists. Portions of the roadless area outside of the protected Wilderness and Parks are under siege from timber harvest and ORVs (particularly the Monache Meadow area next to the South Sierra Wilderness). A major dam project on Dinkey Creek has been dropped by its promoters but other dam proposals are still being discussed. More ski area destruction is also proposed on the east side near Mammoth Mountain. A significant victory in the 1984 California Wilderness Bill was protection for the "missing link" San Joaquin headwaters between Yosemite and the John Muir Wilderness, thereby preventing another trans-Sierra highway. The Dinkey Lakes Wilderness is separated from the John Muir Wilderness by a jeep trail which should be closed to vehicles. Despite the length of the Wilderness backbone, numerous cherrystem intrusions penetrate from both east and west. They should be closed and restored to wilderness.

Yosemite Valley, which is surrounded by the northern part of this roadless area, is an appalling indictment of NPS mismanagement. Monumental traffic jams (20,000 cars one Memorial Day Weekend), trashy tourist developments, lowing herds of visitors and the resultant air pollution have transformed what was once the most glorious mountain valley in America into a slum. To the south, the Central Valley gathers the airborne waste of millions of acres of factory farms and the exhaust of valley cities and drives the whole noxious, roiling mass into Sequoia and Kings Canyon, creating some of the most turbid air in the world, and choking the great trees. Even Muir's High Sierra is not immune to the by-products of the world's greatest standard of living.

RM27: 2,906,240

Domeland 212,000 acres

Designated Domeland Wilderness Area	
(Sequoia NF)	*94,695*
Additional Sequoia NF roadless	*64,000*
BLM WSAs 10-29/32	*37,004*

Private and additional BLM roadless	*16,000*

Description: East-central California east of Kernville. This southern extension of the Sierra crest includes many granite domes; elevations rise from 2,800' to 9,977' on Sirretta Peak. The northern part is a large basin surrounded by rock formations with scattered forests of Jeffrey Pine, mixed conifer, rolling sagebrush country and wet meadows. The southern part is semi-arid with rock outcrops and domes. The South Fork of the Kern River runs through the entire area north to south. A minor dirt road separates this little used area from the South Sierra Wilderness in the High Sierra roadless area.

Status: The Sirretta Peak-Little Trout Creek area outside the Wilderness is threatened by logging. BLM has recommended against Wilderness for their contiguous lands but the Cranston bill would designate 36,300 BLM acres as Wilderness.

Yosemite North 744,000 acres

Yosemite National Park Wilderness Area and additional NP roadless (northern portion)	*402,000*
Designated Emigrant Wilderness Area (Stanislaus NF)	*112,191*
Designated Hoover Wilderness Area (Inyo & Toiyabe NFs)	*48,601*
Hall Natural Area (Inyo NF)	*5,209*
Additional Inyo, Stanislaus, Toiyabe NFs, and BLM roadless	*176,000*

Description: East-central California east of Sonora. The Sierra Nevada in the northern half of Yosemite National Park includes the unparalleled Grand Canyon of the Tuolumne. Mt. Conness at 12,590' is the high point; the low point is about 3,800' along Hetch Hetchy Reservoir. The Tioga Pass road separates Yosemite North from the main High Sierra roadless area to the south. Numerous Black Bear are infamous for their ability to fetch "bear-bagged" packs. Largely a high plateau of exposed granite and innumerable lakes, the land varies from lava-capped alpine peaks down to broiling oak savannah in the western foothills. Many deep, granite-walled canyons drain the high country. This roadless area surrounds Hetch

Hetchy where John Muir battled the City of San Francisco to prevent construction of a dam in Yosemite National Park early this century. Probably not coincidentally, Muir died shortly after Congress approved the dam. This battle was one of the seminal events of the American conservation movement. See High Sierra roadless area for general ecological description.

Status: While largely protected, the undesignated NF areas are under the typical threats of logging and ORVs that most NF areas in California face.

Carson-Iceberg 279,000 acres

Designated Carson-Iceberg Wilderness Area	
(Toiyabe NF)	160,000
Additional Stanislaus and Toiyabe NFs roadless	99,000
BLM and private roadless	20,000

Description: East-central California east of Jackson. In the High Sierra between Sonora and Ebbetts Passes, just north of the Yosemite North area, geology combines black basaltic rock with white and gray granite to form a dozen peaks over 10,000'. The high point is 11,462' Sonora Peak. Scattered forests consist of Sugar, Jeffrey, Lodgepole and Western White Pine, and Red and White Fir. Several long valleys with meadows are filled each summer with stunning wildflowers. The headwaters of the East Fork Carson, Stanislaus and Mokelumne Rivers are given birth here. The Endangered Pauite Cutthroat and Threatened Lahontan Cutthroat are present in isolated creeks. Other trout species and Rocky Mountain Whitefish inhabit additional streams. River Otter and Mink fish the streams. Wolverine have been sighted in the area.

Status: 10,000 acres outside the protected area in Pacific Valley are being studied for a downhill ski resort. The rest of the unprotected area is under threat by logging, dam construction and ORVs. BLM is proposing 550 contiguous acres for Wilderness designation; conservationists should propose 10,000 acres of BLM land for addition to the Carson-Iceberg Wilderness Area.

Mokelumne 164,000

Designated Mokelumne Wilderness Area (El-

dorado, Stanislaus & Toiyabe National Forests)	*104,461*
Additional NF roadless	*60,000*

Description: East-central California east of Sacramento in the High Sierra, south of Lake Tahoe between Ebbetts and Carson Passes and north of the Carson-Iceberg area. Elevations drop from 10,830' on Round Top to 4,000' at Salt Springs Reservoir. Popular for cross-country skiing in winter, Mokelumne's spectacular wildflower displays attract recreationists in summer. Headwaters of the Mokelumne and West Fork Carson rivers spring here. The Mokelumne River Canyon is extremely rugged. Shallow valleys with many small lakes and scattered timber characterize the area.

Status: A jeep trail divides part of the designated Wilderness from the rest. It should be closed. Standard threats of logging and ORVs apply to undesignated portions.

Ishi 225,000 acres

Designated Ishi Wilderness Area (Lassen NF *& BLM)*	*41,840*
Tehama State Wildlife Area, private and *additional Lassen NF roadless*	*183,000*

Description: Northeastern California between Chico and Lassen National Park. The largest wild remnant of the California valley and foothills survives here. The high point is 4,488' and the low point is under 400'. Fine oak (and Poison-oak!) and Digger Pine forest cover the ridges; oak savannah and chaparral cloak the slopes; oaks and annual grasses clothe the foothills. Deer, Mill and Antelope Creeks have cut deep canyons lined with California Sycamore riparian forest. Scattered Ponderosa Pine and Douglas-fir grow at higher elevations. Black Bear, the Tehama Mule Deer herd, Mountain Lion, Bobcat, Peregrine Falcon, Golden Eagle and a "wild" horse herd are among Ishi's animals. Mill Creek has Steelhead and Chinook Salmon runs. Lava rimrock and many shallow caves make Ishi geologically fascinating. This was the home of Ishi, the last wild Indian in the United States.

Status: The unprotected area is threatened by small hydroelectric projects, continued welfare ranching, excessive "game management" and ORVs. There is a minor threat of logging on the unprotected NF lands. The State Game Refuge has jeep trails cutting through it. The lower part of the foothills and upper valley are private lands used for ranching. A powerline (but no road) crosses the west end. Protection of the roadless private lands should be a high priority for California conservationists. The Nature Conservancy manages the Dye Creek Ranch west of the Tehama State Wildlife Area in this roadless area. Perhaps they could explore ways of maintaining the wild character of other private lands in the Ishi.

Lassen East 100,000 acres

Designated Lassen Volcanic National Park	
Wilderness Area (eastern portion) and roadless	68,000
Designated Caribou Wilderness Area (Lassen NF)	20,625
Additional Lassen NF roadless	12,000

Description: Northeastern California east of Redding and west of Susanville in the southern Cascades. This high, gentle plateau east of Lassen Peak is dotted with lakes and volcanic cones. Bumpass Mountain at 8,763' is the high point. The fascinating recent volcanic landscape includes Snag Lake (formed by a lava flow in the 1880s), the Cinder Cones, hot springs, geysers, mud pots and other thermal features. Aspen and old growth Red Fir, White Fir and Lodgepole Pine grow throughout this high country. Black Bear, Black-tailed Deer, Wolverine, Marten, Fisher, Osprey and mosquitoes live here. Bufflehead Ducks breed on the lakes.

Status: The unprotected Lassen NF area is threatened by timber sales.

Great Basin

The eastern border of California slips into what should properly be Nevada. East from the crest of the Sierra and the Cascades, a rainshadow falls, creating a high, cool desert of sagebrush steppe in the north that southward gradually warms, culminating in the blistering hot Mojave Desert around Death Valley. The Modoc, Inyo and Toiyabe NFs, BLM, and Death Valley National Monument manage these areas.

South Warner 100,000 acres

Designated South Warner Wilderness Area	
(Modoc NF)	70,385
Additional Modoc NF roadless	16,500
BLM WSA 20-708	4,500
Private roadless	8,500

Description: Extreme northeastern California east of Alturas. The Cascades meet the Great Basin in the Warners. To the west of the undulating crest of this classic fault-block range, the snow-capped cone of Shasta rises, while dry lakes, sagebrush steppe, and basin and range stretch into Nevada to the east. Elevations climb from 4,600' to 9,892' on Eagle Peak. The vegetation is an unusual blend with Big Sagebrush climbing from the foothills (with Idaho Fescue, Bluebunch Wheatgrass and Squirrel-tail) to the highest peaks, while extensive Aspen forests and isolated groves deck the basins and slopes, and line the streams. Pinyon and juniper are common at lower elevations; they are replaced as the elevation increases by Jeffrey and Ponderosa Pine (including some very large individuals), Lodgepole Pine, White Fir, and thick forests of Whitebark Pine along the crest. Mules Ear and lupine join sagebrush in the meadows. Several glacial lakes, cirques, rushing streams, wet meadows and colorful rock formations are features of this relatively well-watered Great Basin range. Wildlife includes Mule Deer, Pronghorn, Beaver, Mountain Lion, Badger, Mink, Osprey, Pileated Woodpecker, California Quail, Goshawk, Golden Eagle and Peregrine Falcon. California Bighorn Sheep were reintroduced in 1980, but the herd was wiped out in early 1988 by a disease spread by domestic sheep, which graze much of the Modoc NF.

Status: Overgrazing by cattle and sheep is occurring in the Wilderness and adjacent lands. The Modoc NF refuses to restrict grazing by woollies despite the incompatibility of wild and domestic sheep and despite the presence of prime Bighorn habitat in the Warners. Although the Wilderness is generally lightly used, slob campers (particularly horsepackers) are damaging the Patterson Lake area. ORVs are an increasing problem outside the Wilderness and logging is a potential threat. The closure of minor dirt roads (scarcely more than jeep trails) on the NF could add around 20,000 acres to what is currently roadless. BLM is recommending only 1,187 acres of their WSA for addition to the Wilderness.

Buffalo Hills-Smoke Ck 387,000 acres (also in NV)
See Nevada for description and status.

Dry Valley Rim 100,000 acres (also in Nevada)
See Nevada for description and status.

Excelsior Mountains 232,000 acres (also in Nevada)
See Nevada for description and status.

White Mountains 358,000 acres (also in Nevada)

Inyo National Forest roadless (California)	277,000
Inyo NF roadless (Nevada)	26,000
BLM WSAs CDCA 102 & 103	20,369
Additional BLM roadless (CA)	17,000
Additional BLM and private roadless (NV)	18,000

Description: Central California-Nevada border northeast of Bishop. Across the Owens Valley from the Sierra Nevada, the White Mountains, highest range in the Great Basin, leap up 10,000' (White Mt. Peak at 14,246' is the second highest point in California; Boundary Peak at 13,140' is the highest point in Nevada). The lower slopes support a sagebrush community which merges into a pinyon/juniper forest. One of the best examples of Bristlecone Pine forest grows in the high country, and alpine vegetation occurs along the rarefied crest. Additional trees include Aspen, Limber Pine, Jeffrey Pine and Water Birch. There are four sensitive plant species in the area. Wildlife includes Inyo Shrew, Pika, Nuttall Cottontail, Yellow-bellied Marmot, Gray Fox, Ringtail, Pine Marten, Wolverine, Mountain Lion, Pronghorn and Bighorn Sheep. Tule Elk, native to the Sacramento Valley but extirpated there, were transplanted to the Owens Valley and some range into the White Mountains. No fish are native to the Whites, but several trout species have been introduced, including the Endangered Paiute Cutthroat.

Status: Several jeep trails intrude into this wild area and ORVs are the major threat to it (the FS divided this roadless area into three separate RARE II areas based on jeep trails). Cattle grazing continues to degrade the fragile meadows, riparian areas and other habitats in the area. Mining is a minor threat on the periphery of the area.

This is perhaps the most important area, after the Sespe-Frazier, left out of the 1984 California Wilderness Act. The FS proposes 120,000 acres for Wilderness, the Sierra Club 275,000 (California only), and California Earth First! 435,000. Friends of Nevada Wilderness proposes an 8,900 acre Boundary Peak Wilderness for the FS roadless area in Nevada.

Piper Mountain-Soldier Canyon 124,000 acres

BLM WSA CDCA 115 (Piper Mt)	69,282
Additional BLM roadless	13,000
Inyo NF roadless (Soldier Canyon RARE II)	38,400
Additional BLM roadless to west (non-CDCA)	3,500

Description: East-central California east of Big Pine, between the Westgard Pass and Devils Gate roads. This is a complicated roadless area consisting of the northern end of the Eureka Valley on the east, rising to the eastern ridge of the Inyo Mountains (7,703' Piper Peak), dropping into Deep Spring Valley, rising again over the main ridge of the Inyos to 9,000', and dropping into the Owens Valley on the west. The low point is 3,400' in the Eureka Valley, where a Shadscale community, including the Pale Kangaroo Mouse, exists. The northernmost Joshua Tree forest in California is in the Inyos, and higher are Singleleaf Pinyon and White Fir. Desert Bighorn and a large Mule Deer herd are present. The rare Black Toad lives in Deep Spring Valley. Other sensitive wildlife species includes Golden Eagle and Prairie Falcon (with at least one eyrie). Rock art is found throughout the area.

Status: Opposition to Wilderness designation comes from miners, ranchers and, unfortunately, from local Indians who want to gather pinyon nuts with pickup trucks. This last is not a real issue, since areas accessible by truck are not included in the Wilderness proposal.

The FS and BLM oppose any Wilderness in the area. The Cranston bill would designate 81,880 acres of Wilderness (7,040 acres would be added to Death Valley National Park). None of the Inyo NF land would be included. Conservation groups should encourage Cranston to add the NF lands for a 125,000 acre Wilderness Area.

Inyo Mountains 327,000 acres

Inyo National Forest roadless	*138,100*
BLM WSAs 10-56/55/60 & CDCA 120/122 and	
additional roadless	*189,000*

Description: East-central California east of Independence. This high (up to 11,123') but very dry mountain range east of the Owens Valley and Sierra Nevada, drops down to 1,000' above sea level on the Saline Valley salt lake. A rough dirt road in Saline Valley separates it from the big Saline and Cottonwood roadless areas. The crest affords views of the Owens Valley and Sierra Crest to the west and the Saline country to the east. Vegetation is Bristlecone Pine down through pinyon/juniper to Great Basin desert scrub. Golden Eagle, Prairie Falcon, Mule Deer and Bighorn Sheep find refuge here. The Endangered Inyo Slender Salamander lives in the running water of deep canyons coming off the Inyo crest. Some canyons have waterfalls and hanging gardens of Maidenhair Fern. Rare endemic plants grow on the limestone formations.

Status: Dirt roads from the north and south on the crest largely divide the FS portion of the roadless area in half (although there is a roadless connection of a couple of miles); the southern portion (on BLM land) has a network of rough jeep trails, and small scale mines on the periphery; several dirt roads penetrate to the eastern base of the mountains.

The Cranston bill would designate 55,440 acres of current BLM land as Wilderness in an expanded Death Valley NP, and 210,660 acres as BLM and FS Wilderness. Conservationists and Sen. Cranston have bent over backwards to appease two-bit miners and the Inyo County Commissioners by excluding possible mining areas and leaving jeep trails open.

The Saline Valley road should be closed and a two million acre Wilderness established in this region. While mainstream conservationists may feel politically unable to propose this, they should feel comfortable proposing that at least half a million acres be designated as Wilderness in the Inyos through the closure of jeep trails and dirt roads.

Saline-Last Chance 631,000 acres

Saline-Eureka-Last Chance BLM WSA CDCA 117	*486,300*
Death Valley National Monument Last Chance	
* Range roadless*	*106,500*
Additional BLM roadless	*36,600*
Inyo NF roadless	*1,500*

Description: East-central California east of Independence. This exquisite area containing the northern part of Death Valley National Monument comprises the Eureka Dunes (the highest in North America — 800'), the untracked Saline Range and the Last Chance Range. It is one of the largest and most diverse desert roadless area left in the nation. The high elevation is 8,674' on Dry Mountain. Oddities include Joshua Trees, and the Racetrack, a playa where the wind pushes rocks across slick mud thereby leaving their tracks. The volcanic, blocky Saline Range is one of the most remote and pristine areas in the United States (its highest peak was not climbed until 1973). Saline Valley has warm springs, a dry lake and a heavily vegetated salt marsh. The Last Chance Range is spectacular with its abrupt, varicolored rocky face rising up from the stunning Eureka Dunes. Desert Bighorn Sheep, Mule Deer, Desert Tortoise, Panamint Alligator Lizard and raptors dwell here. Numerous rock art sites remain intact. See Panamint Mountains for a brief overview of plant communities (pinyon/juniper to salt flat).

Status: Most of this area is included in Sen. Alan Cranston's Desert Wilderness bill as an addition to Death Valley National Park (upgraded from Monument) and as Wilderness within the Park (including most of the BLM lands).

The poor dirt road to the Devil's Racetrack and its even rougher continuation to Saline Valley should be closed. This lightly-used road is all that separates this large roadless area from the nearly equally large Cottonwood roadless area to the south. Simply by closing this road, a 1,150,000 acre desert

Wilderness could be created. By also closing the Saline Valley road, a 2 million acre Wilderness including the Inyos could be established.

The main opposition to protection is from ORVers, small miners and car-bound nudists who fear having to walk a mile to the Saline Valley Hot Springs. A KGRA (Known Geothermal Resource Area) is around the warm springs and the US Geological Survey (USGS) has offered leases, but there have been no takers. There are threats from mining, as well as irregular trespass occupancy by various weirdos around the warm springs (the Manson Gang hung out here).

Cottonwood Mts-Panamint Dunes 524,000 acres

Death Valley National Monument
Cottonwood Mts roadless	*410,300*
Panamint Dunes BLM WSA CDCA 127	*113,440*

Description: East-central California east of Lone Pine. This superb desert expanse encompasses sand dunes in Mesquite Flat in DVNM, the mile-and-a-half high Cottonwood Mountains, Darwin Plateau and, on BLM land, the Panamint Dunes. Elevations range from below sea level in Mesquite Flat to 8,953' on Cottonwood Mountain. The 250' tall Panamint Dunes are "star" dunes, which are unusual in California. The dunes support a rare plant and two rare arthropods. Joshua Trees fill the higher country. Desert Bighorn Sheep, Mule Deer, Desert Tortoise, Panamint Alligator Lizard, Prairie Falcon and Golden Eagle are other denizens of this desert fastness. See Panamint Mountains for a brief overview of plant communities (pinyon-juniper to salt flat and sand dunes).

Status: Most of this area is included in Sen. Cranston's Desert Wilderness bill. The BLM roadless area would be added to the new Death Valley National Park and most of the area would be designated as Wilderness. However, many jeep routes would remain open. These should be closed as should the poor dirt road to the Devil's Racetrack which splits this area from the Saline-Last Chance area to the north.

Feral burros are a particular problem to many of the roadless areas in Death Valley NM, competing with Bighorn herds, and destroying valuable spring areas. The BLM area has some mining claims, and ORV bozos want to trash the dunes.

Queer Mountain 155,000 acres (also in Nevada)

Death Valley National Monument roadless (CA)	*23,200*
BLM WSA CDCA 119 (CA)	*50,200*
BLM WSA 5-354 (NV)	*81,550*

Description: Southern California-Nevada border in the northern end of Death Valley NM northwest of Beatty, Nevada. Queer Mountain is separated from the large Saline and Cottonwood roadless areas by a little-used gravel road and from the Grapevine Mountain roadless area by the narrow paved Scottys Castle road. This low mountain range has many canyons, small valleys, peaks and bajadas. The high point is 7,925'. The northern part of Death Valley itself is in BLM land. BLM has established an ACEC (Area of Critical Environmental Concern) at Sand Spring to protect rare plants. The fine lower Mojave Desert vegetation here consists of the Saltbush/Greasewood community, with a dense stand of Joshua Trees in the northern tip, and pinyon/juniper higher. Mule Deer, raptors and "wild" horses are among the larger animals.

Status: There are a few decaying mining camps on the periphery. Although no historic production has occurred, 129 mining claims were filed in the California BLM area between October, 1983, and February, 1984. Livestock grazing is present on the BLM land.

The Cranston bill would add 49,560 acres (California only) to DVNP as Wilderness. The California BLM recommended 32,900 acres for Wilderness. BLM has recommended no Wilderness for the Nevada WSA, where there are threats from gold mining and ORVs.

Grapevine Mts 246,000 acres (also in Nevada)

Death Valley NM roadless (CA & NV)	*177,000*
BLM roadless (NV)	*69,000*

Description: Southern California-Nevada border south of Scottys Castle in Death Valley NM and adjacent BLM land in Nevada west of Beatty. These impressive mountains have

steep-walled canyons and colorful rock. The low point is below
sea level in Death Valley, the high point is 8,740', which then
drops 4,500' to the east on sweeping bajadas. Numerous peaks in
the Nevada portion exceed 7,000'. The Saltbush/Greasewood
plant community with some Joshua Trees phases into
pinyon/juniper forest. A few hundred Limber Pines encircle the
upper slopes of Grapevine Peak. One Endangered plant
(Rocklady — *Maurandya petrophilia*) is present as well as six
other rare or endemic plants. Desert Tortoise, Mule Deer,
Bighorn Sheep, Mountain Lion, Bobcat and feral burros are present.

Status: The NPS has proposed the DVNM portion for
Wilderness. BLM has recommended no Wilderness for the
Nevada WSA. The Titus Canyon road in DVNM should be
closed to vehicles and 75,000 acres added for a combined
Wilderness of 325,000 acres.

Funeral Mountains 287,000 acres (also in Nevada)

Death Valley National Monument roadless (CA)	*199,000*
BLM WSA CDCA 143 (CA)	*65,000*
BLM roadless (NV)	*23,000*

Description: The range east of Furnace Creek in Death
Valley NM on the southern California-Nevada border. Pyramid Peak at 6,703' is the high point; the low point is below sea
level. The Funerals are thrust fault blocks of ancient limestone
with abundant fossils. The limestone supports many rare and
endemic species, and thick populations of several cactus
species. There is a good population of Bighorn. The pinkish
Panamint Rattlesnake is present. Raptors breed on the higher
ridges. The Amargosa River flows through part of this area,
supporting an important riparian habitat zone. The Chloride
City ghost town is on the northern border of the roadless area.
Archaeological sites include stone hunting blinds.

Status: NPS proposes two Wilderness Areas, divided by
the brutal Echo Canyon jeep trail: 99,200 acres and 51,500 acres.
The route should be closed to vehicles. Under the Cranston bill
(applies to California only), 34,510 acres would be BLM
Wilderness and 25,800 acres of the BLM land would be added to

DVNP as Wilderness. California BLM has proposed a 13,709 acre Wilderness. Nevada BLM proposes zip.

Panamint Mountains 1,166,000 acres

Death Valley National Monument roadless	*600,000*
Owlshead Mountains BLM WSA CDCA 156	*136,100*
Additional BLM WSAs and roadless (CDCA)	*212,000*
Fort Irwin and China Lake Naval Weapons	
* Center (military) roadless*	*218,000*

Description: East-central California northeast of Ridge-crest. The Panamints occupy the southern end of Death Valley National Monument, and range in elevation from 11,049' atop Telescope Peak to below sea level on the floor of Death Valley, giving them the second greatest vertical relief for any roadless area in the lower 48 (the High Sierra roadless area has the greatest). Vegetation ranges from Bristlecone Pine and Limber Pine above 10,000', down through pinyon/juniper/mountain mahogany/Cliffrose, to Big Sagebrush/ Blackbrush, to Shad-scale, to Creosote Bush/Burro Bush, to the Alkali Sink Community of willow, salt bush, mesquite and Pickleweed, to salt crystals. Some of the canyons support riparian vegetation, and three of the canyons on BLM land have perennial streams. The Endangered Panamint Daisy grows here. The Death Valley floor is one of the driest places in the world, averaging only 2" of precipitation per year while the high country receives up to 15". The highest temperatures in the United States are recorded here (134° is the record). Portions of this immense area receive very little visitation. Desert Bighorn Sheep (the largest herd in California), Mule Deer, Desert Tortoise, Panamint Alligator Lizard and Cottonball Marsh Pupfish inhabit this roadless area. Other species found throughout the Death Valley region include Ringtail, Bobcat, Kit Fox, Badger, Chuckwalla, Panamint Rattlesnake, Mojave Desert Sidewinder and California Lyre Snake. The Death Valley area has a remarkable abundance of reptiles and birds (100 avian species are permanent or seasonal residents). The Owlshead Mountains to the south of DVNM, with two large dry lake beds, deep canyons, and rough mountains, are one of the more remote and pristine areas in the country. The Manson

Gang hung out at the Meyers Ranch in the BLM area — Charlie was captured there.

Status: A number of jeep trails intrude into this area and one in Butte Valley crosses it. Old mines also scar the area — particularly in the Warm Springs Canyon area. A toxic waste dump, being considered for the southern Panamint Valley, would, of course, impact the nearby Wilderness.

The Park Service should close all jeep trails in the area and protect this million-acre wilderness as one unit. The Cranston bill would transfer the 129,060 acre Owlsheads Wilderness to Death Valley NP, 58,480 acres of other adjacent BLM land to the Park as Wilderness, establish 117,980 acres as BLM Wilderness, and designate most of the present Monument as Wilderness. But, alas, the bill would divide this huge roadless area into several units and leave most jeep trails open. Mineralized areas have been excluded from Cranston's bill as a sop to rabidly anti-wilderness prospectors. This is an unnecessary but far too typical compromise. Conservation groups should also encourage the military to protect the wilderness values of their lands in this area.

Argus Range 199,000 acres

BLM WSA CDCA 132B (Argus Range)	80,000
BLM WSA CDCA 132 (Great Falls Basin)	14,000
China Lake Naval Weapons Center roadless	105,000

Description: East-central California north of Trona. The California Desert Protection League says that this roadless area "contains a great diversity of terrain, land forms and geological features: alluvial fans, broad canyons and washes, and narrow twisting canyons with steep walled sides." The Argus Range rears up west of the Panamint Valley, climbing from 1,600' to 8,741' on Parkinson Peak. Even though it is in the rainshadow of the Sierra Nevada, the range receives enough rainfall, because of its height, to boast perennial springs, streams and waterfalls with dense riparian vegetation. Vegetation ranges from Mojave Desert scrub to pinyon/juniper in the high country. A relative of Creosote, Fagonia, reaches the northern limit of its range here. *Mimulus rupicola*, listed by the California Native Plant Society as rare and endangered, grows in two canyons, and the Inyo Brown Towhee, a candidate for Endangered species listing, inhabits the riparian areas. There are reports of salamanders in the area, which would be a species new to science. Desert Bighorn Sheep were reintroduced in 1986.

Status: Small scale mining and ORVs are the principal threats to this area. BLM and local politicians oppose Wilderness designation, but the Cranston bill would establish two Wilderness Areas, divided by Homewood Canyon, of 79,300 acres (1,920 acres would be in the new Death Valley NP) and 8,800 acres (Great Falls Basin). BLM and the Navy are cooperating to control feral burros in the area.

Amargosa Range 221,000 acres	
Death Valley National Monument roadless	*166,000*
BLM WSA CDCA 148	*54,600*

Description: East-central California, southern part of Death Valley. This area includes the Black Mountains, the southern end of the beautiful Greenwater Valley and part of the Amargosa Range. The Black Mountains are so rugged that there are only two routes across them that do not require technical climbing. The California Desert Protection League says that in spring the Greenwater Valley "is a riot of wildflowers with even an occasional desert tortoise grazing amongst them." Golden Eagle, Prairie Falcon and Desert Bighorn Sheep are among the sensitive species. Rare plants include Death Valley Sandpaper Plant, Sticky Ring, Golden Carpet and Death Valley Sage. Elevations drop from 6,384' to sea level. The area offers extreme solitude. *Timbasha*, a sacred site of the Panamint Shoshone, is in the far south of the Greenwater Valley.

Status: 52,680 acres of BLM land will be declared Wilderness and added to Death Valley NP in the Cranston bill. The NPS proposes a 138,900 acre Wilderness. Active mining occurs around Ryan adjacent to the northern end of this area.

Greenwater Range 165,000 acres	
BLM WSA CDCA 147	*164,000*
Death Valley National Monument roadless	*1,000*

Description: East-central California just east of Death Valley NM and separated from the Amargosa Range roadless area by a dirt road. The Greenwaters are volcanic and virtually waterless; nonetheless, with good winter rains they offer one of the best spring wildflower displays in the desert. The green Creosote growing on black basalt is striking. Wildlife includes Golden Eagle, Prairie Falcon and Chuckwalla. The Greenwaters are an important travel corridor for Desert Bighorn from the Funeral Mountains to the Black Mountains. This area receives very little human use. 5,148' is the highest elevation.

Status: The Cranston bill would add 156,220 acres to Death Valley NP as Wilderness. BLM opposes Wilderness for this untracked area. Grandiose claims have been made about mineral wealth in the range, but no commercial extraction has occurred.

Ibex Hills 143,000 acres

Death Valley National Monument roadless	72,000
BLM WSAs CDCA 149 &149A	53,500
BLM WSAs CDCA 219 & 220	17,800

Description: East-central California in the southeastern corner of Death Valley NM southwest of Shoshone. The dirt Saratoga Springs road separates this area from the huge Panamint roadless area; paved Hwy 178 over Jubilee Pass separates it from the Amargosa Range roadless area. 4,749' Ibex Peak is the high point. The southern end of the Black Mountains, the Ibex Hills and Saddle Peak Hills constitute the area. The Amargosa River flows through the southern end. (The Saratoga Springs Pupfish is in Saratoga Springs which is accessible by cherrystem road in this area.) Vegetation and wildlife are typical of the Death Valley area. The rare Field Primrose grows south of Jubilee Pass.

Status: The access road to Saratoga Springs and surrounding mine-damaged country is excluded from the roadless area. ORVers from the Dumont Dunes regularly invade the Saddle Peak Hills.

The Cranston bill would add 43,060 BLM acres to Death Valley NP as Wilderness. BLM opposes Wilderness.

Nopah Range 134,000 acres (also in Nevada)	
BLM WSA CDCA 150	*116,000*
BLM roadless (NV)	*18,000*

Description: East-central California east of Death Valley NM next to the Nevada border. This area encompasses most of the Nopah Range, part of the Resting Spring Range, and the Chicago Valley between them. Two peaks in the area are popular with hikers for their exceptional views. The west face of the Nopahs, with bands of rusty red, brown and cream, is termed "unforgettable" by conservationists. Vegetation is diverse with Desert Willow, mesquite, cactus, Creosote and three rare plants — two buckwheats and an agave. Chicago Valley has riparian vegetation. Wildlife includes a small Bighorn herd, Prairie Falcon, Golden Eagle, Desert Tortoise, a wide variety of snakes and some unusual lizards.

Status: The Cranston bill would designate 110,880 acres as Wilderness; BLM originally proposed 78,880 acres for Wilderness but, under pressure from grazing, mining and development interests, dropped the Resting Springs Range and the western Chicago Valley portion from their recommendation in 1982.

Mojave Desert

The central part of the California Desert is part of the Mojave Desert. It is higher and slightly cooler than the torrid Colorado Desert to the south and is characterized by the unlikeliest-looking tree in the United States — the Joshua Tree, a yucca that took steroids and LSD. It is hot enough for Creosote Bush and cholla cactus in the lowlands, cool enough for pinyon and juniper in the highlands.

Kingston Range 270,000 acres	
BLM WSA CDCA 222	*270,000*

Description: Southeastern California north of Baker. This is a varied area southeast of Death Valley National Monument. Kingston Peak at 7,323' is the high point; the elevation drops to 600'. The Amargosa River, one of three perennial streams in the California Desert, provides habitat for the Amargosa Pupfish, Speckled Dace and Amargosa Toad. Terrain includes high peaks with White Fir (rare in the desert), and pinyon/juniper lower down; the limestone Valjean Hills; desert bajadas and washes with cactus, Creosote, and Joshua Tree; and sand dunes. The riparian areas along the Amargosa, Horsethief Springs and Salt Creek are particularly important. This area has a high concentration of Endangered species and unusual plant communities. Wildlife includes Vermillion Flycatcher, Desert Tortoise, Yellow-billed Cuckoo, Prairie Falcon, Desert Bighorn Sheep, Amargosa Vole (endemic), Kit Fox, Ringtail and Panamint Chipmunk.

Status: 255,290 acres of Wilderness are in the Cranston bill, but the Dumont Dunes are excluded because of the bleating of ORVers. Overgrazing occurs in parts of the area.

RM36: 650,000

Avawatz 101,000 acres

BLM WSA CDCA 221	*69,000*
Camp Irwin Military Reservation roadless	*32,000*

Description: Southern California northwest of Baker, and immediately north of the Soda Mountain roadless area and southeast of Death Valley National Monument. This roadless area contains most of the Avawatz Mountains with their rugged ridges, precipitous narrow canyons and colorful slopes, as well as a steep bajada clothed in Creosote and ending in a dry lake. Elevations range from under 800' on the playa to 6,154' on Avawatz Peak. White talc deposits add to the colorfulness of the area. Numerous springs provide good Bighorn habitat.

Status: The Cranston bill would designate 61,320 acres as BLM Wilderness and add 5,120 acres to Death Valley National Park. BLM, broken to heel in California by small miners and ORVers, opposes any Wilderness.

Soda Mountain 102,500 acres

BLM WSA CDCA 242	*102,500*

Description: Southern California west of Baker and north of I-15. The Soda Mountains have both gentle slopes and highly eroded, rugged ridges. Washes cutting into the mountains have steep, rocky, variegated walls. Several large dry lake beds (playas) are in this roadless area, including Silver Dry Lake which is a perfect example of a playa, and East Cronese Lake which often contains water and provides habitat for wintering and migrating shorebirds and waterfowl, including the Endangered Yuma Clapper Rail. This smorgasbord of birds attracts many raptors. The mountains provide good Desert Bighorn habitat. Creosote Bush is the dominant plant with barrel cactus, cholla and yucca also present. An "old growth," very tall Crucifixion Thorn stand inhabits the west end. At least one sensitive plant species is present, as are many archaeological sites.

Status: The Cranston bill would designate 92,690 acres as Wilderness; BLM is opposed to Wilderness here. The notorious Barstow-Vegas dirt bike race went through this area in 1983 and ORVers are slobbering mad in their opposition to Wilderness. The Blue Bell Mine area is cherrystemmed.

Old Dad Mountain 101,000 acres
BLM WSA CDCA 243 and additional roadless   *101,000*

Description: Southern California south of Baker and I-15. This is one of the most topographically varied areas in the California desert, with the crescent dunes of the Devil's Playground, Soda Lake (a Pleistocene lake which fills every 20 years or so), the terminus of the Mojave River, and precipitous Old Dad Mountain (4,250'). The largest Bighorn herd in the East Mojave (300 animals) is here. Soda Lake is the largest wilderness playa in California. There is a rich mesquite growth in the sand hummocks of the Devil's Playground.

Status: The Cranston bill would designate a 95,760 acre Wilderness. The BLM and its ORV, mining and grazing overseers strongly oppose Wilderness. The Barstow-Vegas dirt bike race passes through the northern end of the area. The Cranston bill excises the B-V course from the Wilderness. Soda Lake has obligingly swallowed several vehicles whole. One hopes the owners went down with their ships.

RM36: 1,970,000*

Kelso Dunes 215,000 acres

BLM WSA CDCA 250	*165,820*
Intermixed and adjacent private and state roadless	*49,000*

Description: Southern California in the East Mojave Desert south of Baker. The Kelso Dunes are the second highest in California and third highest in North America. This extensive dune field has a high species diversity with several endemics, and many wildflowers including Desert Lily, Desert Sunflower and evening primrose. The dunes have been closed to ORVs since 1972, but ORVers don't obey closures unless they are enforced. The Bristol Mountains to the west are essentially untouched. Broadwell Mesa, also in the western end of this roadless area, has a distinctive flat top and sheer sides. Just west of the mesa is one of the few natural arches found in the California Desert. This roadless area is separated from the Granite Mountains by only a pipeline corridor.

Status: Sen. Cranston's bill would designate 36,000 acres Wilderness in Mojave National Park and 129,820 acres BLM Wilderness.

Some mining threats remain. ORVers are fighting Cranston's bill and hope to "open up" the dunes for their "fun" again. (Claiming that ORVing off established roads in the desert is a legitimate form of recreation is akin to claiming the same for rape or mugging.) Even now, ORVers trespass on the dunes, their long-lasting tracks representing swaths of destruction. Livestock invasion of the dunes is also evident. The ranch at the base of the dunes allows its cattle to graze the dunes' sparse grasses and leave their ubiquitous pies in all but the most inaccessible reaches of these sand hills. The large acreage of private and state land should be a priority for acquisition.

RM36: 1,970,000*

Cady Mountains 122,000 acres

BLM WSA CDCA 251	*85,970*
Intermixed private and state roadless	*36,000*

Description: Southern California east of Barstow. The California Desert Protection League describes this as an area of "vast, windblown, sandy valleys and highly eroded volcanic ridges." Two springs make Cady important for Desert Bighorn Sheep. Other wildlife includes Prairie Falcon, Golden Eagle and abundant Mojave Fringe-toed Lizards. It is separated from the Kelso Dunes roadless area by a powerline corridor.

Status: The wildlife and wildness of the Cady Mountains are threatened by the growing population of Barstow, ORVs, mining and overgrazing. A macabre specific threat to this pristine area comes from the private firm of Patrick and Henderson who want to locate a commercial toxic waste dump on private land they own in the center of the WSA.

The Cranston bill would designate 85,970 acres of BLM lands as Wilderness. The checkerboard private lands should also be included in the Wilderness and acquired by the federal government. BLM opposes Wilderness for the Cadys.

RM36: 1,970,000*

Granite Mountains 135,000 acres	
BLM WSA CDCA 256	*99,804*
Intermixed state and private roadless	*35,000*

Description: Southern California north of I-40 midway between Needles and Barstow. This roadless area encompasses the Granite Mountains and portions of the Old Dad Mountains and Bristol Mountains. Elevations reach 6,738', with pinyon pine/juniper forest in the upper elevations, Creosote and yucca lower down. Famed for its granite boulders, similar to those in Joshua Tree NM, its considerable wildlife includes Bighorn, Golden Eagle, Prairie Falcon, Ringtail and Mule Deer. Numerous archaeological sites from the Chemehuevi and Serrano have been found. A gas pipeline separates it from the Kelso Dunes roadless area.

Status: The Cranston bill would designate 29,650 acres as Wilderness within the new Mojave National Park and 70,240 acres as BLM Wilderness. BLM has proposed a paltry 29,646 acres for Wilderness because of opposition from the local rancher and ORVers. Much of the area is checkerboard land owned by the state or Southern Pacific. It is likely that a land exchange can be arranged.

RM36: 1,970,000*

Southern Mojave & Colorado Deserts

The Colorado Desert in the southeastern corner of California is a western extension of Arizona's Sonoran Desert. Although many plants are shared, such as Creosote, palo verde, Ironwood and various cacti, the Saguaro and other typically Sonoran species are absent. The pattern of precipitation is the reason. Arizona's Sonoran Desert receives gentle winter rains from the Gulf of California and summer thunderstorms from the Gulf of Mexico. The Colorado Desert shares only the winter rains.

Sheep Hole 390,000 acres	
BLM WSA CDCA 305	135,827
Additional BLM and intermixed private, state roadless	254,000

Description: North of Joshua Tree National Monument and east of Twenty-nine Palms Marine Corps Base in southern California. This remote, essentially untouched area consists of the huge Sheep Hole Valley, Cadiz Valley, Calumet Mountains, the steep, granitic Sheep Hole Mountains, Kilbeck Hills, part of the Iron Mountains and part of Cadiz Playa. The high point is 4,613'. A special feature of this large desert wildland is the Cadiz Dunes, a low, unstable dune system that holds pockets of water and vegetation in its troughs. Galleta grass, Creosote and desert shrub are common plant types in the area. Wildlife includes Bighorn Sheep, Desert Tortoise and Prairie Falcon. Much of this area was part of Joshua Tree National Monument from 1936 until 1950, when it was removed from protection because of potential minerals.

Status: An access road from the south and salt evaporators on Cadiz Playa are cherrystemmed into the center of this area.

The Cranston bill would designate 177,000 acres of Wilderness for the Sheep Hole, with a 42,640 acre Cadiz Dunes Wilderness separate due to a vehicle way. BLM, for unfathomed reasons, opposes Wilderness even though this magnificent area has few conflicts (they originally supported Wilderness in the Desert Plan but changed their mind in an amendment). The entire area should be designated as a single Wilderness unit.

RM36: 1,100,000

Old Woman Mountains 150,000 acres

BLM WSA CDCA 299	*100,826*
Additional BLM and intermixed private,	
state roadless	*49,000*

Description: Southeastern California southwest of Needles, south of I-40 and north of the Colorado River Aqueduct; separated from the Turtle Mountains by a powerline corridor and from the Sheep Hole area by a railroad and dirt road. The California Desert Protection League writes, "The massive, fault-lifted Old Woman Mountains . . . are a wonderland of rockwalls, deep canyons, sandy washes, enclosed valleys and steep spires." The high point is 5,326'. Vegetation includes pinyon/juniper forest, yucca, nolina and barrel cactus. Abundant water (sixteen springs) supports a large Mule Deer population and Desert Bighorn Sheep. Other wildlife includes one of the most important populations of Desert Tortoises in California. The numerous Indian sites include burial areas.

Status: The Cranston bill would designate 146,110 acres as BLM Wilderness, but would exclude minor vehicle routes and an area with inconsequential mining impacts. BLM opposes any Wilderness in the Old Womans. Parts of the area have checkerboarded railroad lands. Unexploded military ordnance from World War II lies strewn about in a couple of areas.

RM36: 950,000*

Turtle Mountains 276,000 acres

BLM WSA CDCA 307	*144,500*
Additional BLM, state and private roadless	*131,000*

Description: Southeastern California south of Needles, west of US 95, north of the Colorado River Aqueduct. The Turtles are a fabulous volcanic range with spires, cliffs and crags in the northeast and rounded hills in the southwest. A large interior valley with numerous washes is a special attraction.

The surrounding bajadas are particularly lush. Mopah Springs has the northernmost occurrence of native Fan Palms. Wildlife includes Desert Bighorn, Desert Tortoise, Mountain Lion, Golden Eagle (two eyries), Prairie Falcon (two eyries), Bendire's Thrasher and Western Pipistrelle Bat (several roosts). Eleven springs provide dependable water. The high point is 4,313'.

Status: The Cranston bill would designate 144,500 acres as Wilderness. BLM proposes only 105,201 acres for Wilderness, leaving out much of the Upper Vidal Valley and most of the bajadas. Mining is a minor threat, as is grazing. The Parker 400 dirt bike race course is on some of the boundary roads.

RM36: 950,000*

Palen-McCoy 380,000 acres

BLM WSA CDCA 325	*225,000*
Additional BLM, private and state roadless	*155,000*

Description: Northwest of Blythe in southeastern California. The floor of this extensive interior valley in the hot, dry lower elevation Colorado Desert is desert pavement and Creosote Bush. It is cut by desert washes with Ironwood, palo verde and Smoke Tree, and is surrounded by four mountain ranges: Palen, with striated meta-sedimentary and meta-volcanic rock; McCoy, a ridge of striated meta-sedimentary rock; Granite, a steep granitic range rising north of the Palen Range with scarcely any break between them; and Little Maria, a small but complex limestone range. Other desert valleys, washes and bajadas enhance this diverse, spacious area. Crucifixion Thorn, Bighorn Sheep, Mojave Fringe-toed Lizard and Prairie Falcon are among the interesting resident species. The Midland Ironwood Forest in this area is the thickest such thicket in the state. The high point is 4,353' in the Granite Mountains. Numerous Indian sites have been found. The valley between the Palen and McCoy ranges was used for Gen. Patton's maneuvers during World War II. The nearly fifty-year-old scars are healing as this valley has rarely been visited since then.

Status: The Cranston bill would designate 214,420 acres as Wilderness. Hobby mining and ORVs present minor threats.

RM36: 1,500,000*

Coxcomb 188,000 acres

Joshua Tree National Monument Wilderness	
Area and additional roadless	*120,500*
BLM WSA CDCA 328	*58,700*
BLM WSA CDCA 334A	*4,000*
Additional BLM roadless	*5,000*

Description: Southern California east of Twenty-nine Palms; the eastern end of Joshua Tree NM and surrounding BLM lands, including the Coxcomb Mountains and Pinto Basin. The granitic Coxcombs are a complex range with steep walls, fin-like ridges and canyons. The valley between the Coxcomb and Pinto ranges is strewn with piles of granite boulders. This is an area of transition from Mojave Desert with Joshua Trees to Colorado Desert with Creosote, cholla cactus and Ocotillo. Bighorn are declining in the area. A small Desert Tortoise population remains, as does at least one Prairie Falcon nest.

Status: Formerly part of Joshua Tree NM, the BLM land (55,500 acres) would be added to the new Joshua Tree National Park as Wilderness by the Cranston bill.

RM36: 1,500,000*

Eagle Mountains 110,000 acres

Joshua Tree National Monument Wilderness Area	*55,600*
BLM WSA CDCA 334	*54,700*

Description: Southern California northwest of Desert Center and north of I-10; the southeastern corner of Joshua Tree NM. The BLM area was excised from the Monument in the 1940s for iron mining. The BLM part has an interior plateau of broad flat valleys drained by Big Wash. The massive, rounded mountains are colored gold, brown and tan. In the south are large exfoliated boulders of quartz monzonite. This lower elevation country represents the Colorado Desert as contrasted with the Mojave Desert preserved in the higher reaches of JTNM. Washes support dense stands of Ironwood, Smoke Tree, palo verde; slopes have Ocotillo, Bigelow Cholla, Mojave Yucca, Pencil Cholla and Silver Cholla. Scenic attractions include a palm oasis

with flowing water. Bighorn are declining and need further
protection on the BLM lands. Five square miles of the BLM
portion has Desert Tortoise densities of 20 to 50 per square mile.
The area also features Prairie Falcon eyries and several
springs.
   Status: The portion currently in the Monument is designated
Wilderness;   52,780 acres of the BLM land would receive
Wilderness status and be added to an expanded Joshua Tree
National Park under Sen. Cranston's California Desert bill.
BLM has proposed 42,700 acres for Wilderness. ORVs and
mineral exploration are threats.
   RM36: 1,500,000*

Hexie-Little San Bernardino Mts 328,000 acres

Joshua Tree National Monument Wilderness Areas	
and additional roadless	*260,000*
BLM, private roadless to south	*68,000*

   Description: Southern California north of Indio. The Hexie
Mts climb almost a mile above the below-sea-level Salton Sea
basin to a high point of 4,834' (Monument Mountain) on the
southern rim of Joshua Tree National Monument. Farther west,
Quail Mountain in the Little San Bernardinos attains 5,814'.
Here is an excellent example of Mojave Desert vegetation
(Joshua Tree, California Juniper, Singleleaf Pinyon), with
Colorado Desert vegetation (cactus, Creosote) in the lower ele-
vations.
   Status: The land south of the Monument and north of the
Colorado River Aqueduct is checkerboard private and BLM.
The Cranston bill would add much of it to the proposed Joshua
Tree National Park as Wilderness. There are currently four
separate Wilderness units in Joshua Tree NM in this roadless
area. The corridors are unnecessary (there are no through
roads); a single Wilderness Area of over 300,000 acres should be
established with the addition of the southern checkerboard
lands.
   RM36: 1,500,000*

Pinto Mountains 105,000 acres
Joshua Tree NM Wilderness Area and

| *additional roadless* | *53,800* |
| *BLM WSA CDCA 335* | *51,300* |

Description: Southern California southeast of Twentynine Palms. Twentynine Palms Mountain is 4,562'. Mojave Desert vegetation with excellent stands of Joshua Tree.

Status: The Cranston bill would add 51,300 acres (all of BLM WSA CDCA 335) to Joshua Tree National Park as Wilderness. Contiguous BLM lands are being trashed by ORVs.

Chuckwalla Mountains 197,000 acres

BLM WSA CDCA 348 and additional roadless   197,000

Description: Southern California south of Desert Center on I-10. The high point is 4,604' on Black Butte. These craggy mountains encircle a remote Fan Palm oasis, Corn Springs. Bajadas around the mountain support a rich growth of Ironwood. The Chuckwalla Bench, to the south, is an exemplary transition zone between the Mojave and Colorado Deserts, with exceptional cactus gardens that have not been looted by cactus poachers. *Opuntia munzii*, the largest cholla cactus in California, grows only in this area. The numerous springs support a high diversity and number of animals including Bighorn, Chuckwalla, Mule Deer, quail, Prairie Falcon and a core population of Desert Tortoise. The last Pronghorn in the California desert were here until World War II, and the area is a prime site for reintroduction. Intaglios and petroglyphs in the northwestern portion are sacred for the Cahuilla Indians. The California Desert Protection League says this area is "unequalled as an example of a Sonoran desert community in California."

Status: The Cranston bill would designate 165,200 acres as Wilderness (in two units, including an area outside this roadless area to the southwest). BLM has proposed only 57,312 acres for protection. Several dirt roads, including one to Corn Springs, are cherrystemmed.

RM36: 610,000

Lower Colorado River 462,000 acres (also in AZ)

See Arizona for description and status.

Santa Rosa Mountains <u>363,000 acres</u>

Designated Santa Rosa Wilderness Area (San Bernardino NF)	20,160
Designated Santa Rosa Mountains State Wilderness Area (Anza-Borrego State Park)	87,000
Additional San Bernardino NF, state, BLM, private, Indian Reservation roadless	256,000

Description: Southern California south of Palm Springs. This desert/mountain region has a complicated land ownership pattern rendering its protection difficult. It is an area of steep cliffs, highly eroded canyons, strewn boulders, a desert sink and sculpted desert hills. Vegetation makes a transition from Ocotillo, agave, Barrel Cactus and Creosote to pinyon pine and mountain mahogany. The Travertine Fan Palm grove is in the area. High quality desert riparian areas provide habitat for Least Bell's Vireo, a candidate federal Endangered Species. Elevations range from below sea level near the Salton Sea to 8,700' on the slopes of Toro Peak. The largest herd of rare Peninsular Bighorn Sheep in the US finds a home here.

Status: Wilderness designation is crucial for the BLM portion to link the FS and state areas together. ORVs are the major threat here, as they are on most public lands in southern California — the State Park recently closed them out of the Lower Willows area, the richest riparian zone in Anza-Borrego. More recently, the California State Parks System banned ORVs from roadless areas in all its Parks, except for the few with prior ORV management plans.

Only 53,240 acres of BLM Wilderness would be designated by the Cranston bill but conservationists are calling for 136,100 acres. Although many of the private land owners are willing sellers and much of the area is owned by the California Department of Fish & Game for Bighorn management, the checkerboard land ownership complicates protection. Some subdivisions on the edge pose a threat. A cherrystemmed primitive road for access to private land nearly divides the state Wilderness Area in half.

Vallecito Mountains <u>207,000 acres</u>

Designated Vallecito Mountains State Wilderness Area (Anza-Borrego Desert State Park)	82,000
Designated Whale Peak State Wilderness Area (Anza-Borrego Desert State Park)	34,000
Designated Carrizo Badlands State Wilderness Area (Anza-Borrego State Park)	19,200
Additional Anza-Borrego SP roadless	17,000
Carrizo Impact Area (military) roadless	28,000
BLM WSA CDCA 372	27,100

Description: Southern California northeast of San Diego. This central part of Anza-Borrego State Park, just south of State Highway 78 in Lower Borrego Valley, is an area of rugged topography with remote ridges and canyons. Elevations rise from sea level to 5,300' on Whale Peak. The only water in the area consists of intermittent tinajas. Wildlife present includes Mule Deer, Peninsular Bighorn Sheep, Badger, Kit Fox, Pallid Bat, Ringtail, Sora Rail, Golden Eagle, Prairie Falcon, Long-eared Owl, Red-legged Frog, Switak's Gecko, Desert Blind Snake, Lyre Snake, Red Diamond Rattlesnake, Desert Night Lizard and Desert Shrimp. A recent Sonoran Pronghorn skull was found in 1957. Pupfish were last found in Split Mountain in 1916 (their pools were silted in by a flood that year). Over a dozen uncommon species of plants are present, including the Elephant Tree, Sand Plant and the federally Endangered Borrego Bedstraw. Vegetation varies from Creosote and cactus to Singleleaf Pinyon Pine and California Juniper. Desert Thorn is common in Lycium Wash. Paleo-Indian sites of national significance are fairly common at the mouth of Harper Canyon. Sedimentary deposits in the south contain Pliocene mammal fossils, with petrified forests near Loop Wash. The west wall of Split Mountain is a nationally-known geological study site.

Status: Much of this area is protected as State Wilderness Areas but the rest suffers from ORV abuse. A half-dozen ORV corridors are cherrystemmed into the Wilderness. The Cranston bill would designate 27,100 acres as BLM Wilderness. The small Bighorn herd is infested with Parainfluenza 3, transmitted from domestic livestock and responsible for a high lamb mortality.

Nevada

Nevada. To most, the name conjures glittering casinos, top-less showgirls in elaborate headdresses, and "stars" like Wayne Newton. There's another Nevada, however. This is the Nevada scorned by the high-speed traveler on Interstate 80: the desolate waste of sagebrush steppe and seemingly barren mountain ranges in the distance.

These images have affected federal land management agencies and even the conservation movement. While the United States Forest Service was establishing Wilderness Areas in other Western states in the 1930s, '40s and '50s, they saw fit to designate only one such area in Nevada (and that was not until 1958) — the 64,667 acre Jarbidge Wilderness in far northeastern Nevada. I also recall a meeting in 1975 with the BLM's top staff in Washington, DC, to discuss Wilderness (this was before passage of the BLM "Organic Act" which mandated the Wilderness review). The head of resources, Roman Koenings, finally exploded in exasperation, "How many millions of acres of sagebrush flats do you want in the Wilderness System!?"

No national conservation group has ever treated Nevada as more than an afterthought; none has ever committed a portion of the resources to save the Nevada wilderness that they have allocated to other, more "scenic" states. Charles S. Watson, Jr., founder and sparkplug of the Nevada Outdoor Recreation Association (NORA), tells how the top brass of the Sierra Club shut him up in the early 1960s when he began agitating for inclusion of the BLM in the Wilderness Act. They were afraid such talk could torpedo chances for passage of the bill.

Small wonder, then, that Nevada's homegrown wilderness preservationists are a timid lot, not given to ambitious proposals or to playing political hardball. Neglected by na-

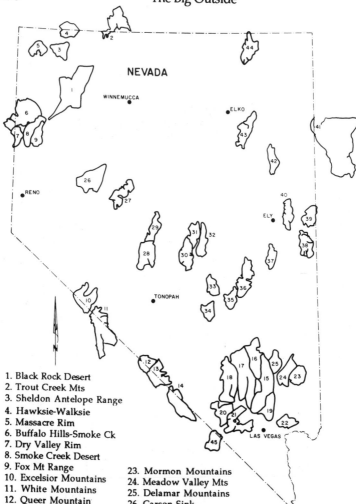

1. Black Rock Desert
2. Trout Creek Mts
3. Sheldon Antelope Range
4. Hawksie-Walksie
5. Massacre Rim
6. Buffalo Hills-Smoke Ck
7. Dry Valley Rim
8. Smoke Creek Desert
9. Fox Mt Range
10. Excelsior Mountains
11. White Mountains
12. Queer Mountain
13. Grapevine Mountains
14. Funeral Mountains
15. Sheep Range
16. Hole In The Rock
17. Desert-Pintwater Range
18. Spotted Range
19. Las Vegas Range
20. Mt. Stirling
21. Charleston Peak
22. Muddy Mountains

23. Mormon Mountains
24. Meadow Valley Mts
25. Delamar Mountains
26. Carson Sink
27. Clan Alpine Range
28. Arc Dome
29. Toiyabe Crest
30. Table Mountain
31. Horse Heaven
32. Antelope
33. Palisade Mesa
34. South Reveille
35. Quinn
36. Grant Range

37. South Egan Range
38. Wheeler Peak
39. Mt. Moriah
40. Schell Creek Range
41. S. Great Salt Lk Desert
42. Cherry Creek Range
43. Ruby Mountains
44. Jarbidge
45. Nopah Range

tional conservation groups, lambasted by ranchers and miners
who think they own the public lands of the state (Nevada was
the birthplace of the so-called "Sagebrush Rebellion"), played
for suckers by the "liberal" Democrats in their Congressional
delegation, the Toiyabe Chapter of the Sierra Club and Friends
of Nevada Wilderness (FNW) have operated cautiously. Even
during RARE II, when the Humboldt and Toiyabe NFs identified 2.1 million acres of roadless areas (there were actually 3.9
million acres of roadless areas on NFs in Nevada but FS land
use plans had already removed 1.8 million acres from consideration), conservationists asked only for a little more than 1 million acres as Wilderness. In response to this initial compromise,
the FS recommended a mere 11 areas with slightly more than
500,000 acres for Wilderness.

In addition to the diffidence of Nevada conservationists,
their other weakness has been a failure to organize the grassroots outside of the population centers of Reno and Las Vegas.
Assumed too often to be a wasteland of know-nothings, John
Birchers and wilderness despoilers, the small towns and rural
areas of Nevada do have Wilderness supporters. They have
shown up at Wilderness hearings, they have written letters.
Little effort, though, has been made to organize them or plug
them into the conservation activism of the two big cities. The
Nevada conservationists can't be blamed for this; they're volunteers, they work regular jobs and do their conservation work
at night, on weekends, and generally at their own expense.
They have fought the good fight and deserve praise.

The Wilderness Society and Sierra Club need to hire a
regional representative for Nevada, whose primary duty
would be grassroots organizing, both in the urban areas and the
hinterlands. Nevada conservationists would then be prepared
to go toe to toe with the cowboys and small miners. (It is encouraging to note that the present Sierra Club Regional Representative for Northern California and Nevada is devoting a
considerable share of her energy to Nevada.)

But, what good is Nevada? What really is there to preserve? Isn't it merely a desolate wasteland, miles on miles of
sagebrush steppe?

Beyond the bright lights of Las Vegas and Reno, off the
four lanes of the Interstate, away from the cat house and slot

machine emporium lies the real Nevada. The Great Basin. A land of basin and range after basin and range running generally on a north-south axis, caught between the Sierra Nevada-Cascades and the Rocky Mountains. Empty valleys carpeted in sage with herds of Pronghorn flashing the bright white of their rumps; valleys that stretch your eyes farther than you thought you could see. Valleys flowing like seas, breaking against the far mountains. Mountains rising up a mile or more to hidden glacier-gouged basins with tiny lakes glistening like turquoise in the dry air of this cold desert. Forests of Aspen, mountain mahogany or White Fir cloaking the high basins, the rolling summits. And above all, the patriarchs, gnarled, weathered and deeply wise from their millennial lives — Bristlecone Pines.

There are two Great Basins: one, a geographic region distinguished by internal drainage without an outlet to the sea through the surrounding river systems of the Colorado, Sacramento or Snake; and two, an ecological region of high desert, a cold, arid fastness characterized by Big Sagebrush. These Great Basins are both centered on Nevada but do not entirely coincide.

The geographic Great Basin is true basin and range country. Often the low point of a basin is a meandering stream, a marsh, a lake in various degrees of salinity, or a salt flat (playa). The entire state of Nevada, except for its southern tip draining into the Colorado River and its northeast where the Owyhee and Jarbidge Rivers herd the snowmelt into the Snake River, is part of this Great Basin. Much of the California Desert as well as that part of northern California east of the crest of the Sierra Nevada and Cascades is included. Western Utah is classic Great Basin topography, as is much of southeastern Oregon outside of the Owyhee drainage.

The ecological Great Basin roughly overlies the central and northern portions of the geographical Great Basin (the southern part of the geographical Great Basin is ecologically part of the much hotter Mojave Desert characterized by Creosote Bush and Joshua Tree). The Great Basin Desert is a cold, dry highland, dominated by sagebrush steppe and, higher, by

Wheeler Peak from Fortification Range, Nevada. Photo by Dave Foreman.

pinyon/juniper woodland and Aspen. It is a desert because the Sierra Nevada and Cascade mountain ranges capture the moist Pacific air and cast a rainshadow hundreds of miles east. This sagebrush desert laps over the divides into the Snake River drainage (the Owyhee country of Idaho and Oregon) and the Colorado Plateau of Utah, Arizona and New Mexico.

This vast, empty quarter lost between the great dividing ranges is one of the wildest and least populated areas in the temperate northern hemisphere. And with good reason. This is a lean, hungry land, with little fat to make men rich. Tiny Vermont produces more pounds of beef than does huge Nevada. Assignment to Nevada for a Forest Ranger is exile to Siberia — there is no industrial forestry to practice. So, even without priority status from conservation groups, Nevada boasts more roadless areas of 100,000 acres or more than does any other state except California (although it is important to note that Nevada has few truly large roadless areas).

Nevada's Big Outside is nonetheless threatened. Oil companies have begun tentative exploration for oil and gas. Urban ORVers probe deeper into the backcountry. Yellow-toothed trappers run their lines in the pinyon/juniper "pygmy forest" from the backs of motorized tricycles. But the gravest threats to the wild places of Nevada come from livestockmen and small miners, and from the federal agencies effectively in thrall to this rustic gentry. Destruction of wilderness is not as spectacular in Nevada as it is in the old growth forests of Oregon or the Grizzly habitat of Montana, but it is a slow, steady gnawing at the fabric of natural integrity like sheep grazing a mountain meadow in July.

Because of the weakness of state conservationists, Nevada is one of the last states without a comprehensive National Forest Wilderness Act. Friends of Nevada Wilderness and their allies are calling for 21 new NF Wilderness Areas with a total acreage of 1.5 million acres (an improvement in their proposal since RARE II). But many important NF wildlands are excluded from their proposal and generally their recommended boundaries are far from adequate. The anti-Wilderness Republicans in the Nevada delegation, Sen. Chic Hecht and Rep. Barbara Vucanovich, have grudgingly supported 4 Wilderness Areas totalling 137,000 acres. Nevada's supposedly pro-

Wilderness Congressman, Democrat James Bilbray, has proposed a bill of 14 areas with 731,000 acres, and Sen. Harry Reid, elected with Sierra Club support, endorses a total of only 600,000 acres. Things are obviously grim on the National Forest front. (In November, 1988, Hecht was defeated by Governor Richard Bryan, a Democrat. Bryan is even less a supporter of Wilderness than is Reid, but with three Democrats on the four-person Nevada delegation, a mediocre Wilderness bill is likely in the 1989-90 session.) *

The Bureau of Land Management has been somewhat better than the Forest Service on Wilderness in Nevada (although they, of course, have not been good). Out of 408 units totalling over 14 million acres considered for Wilderness Study Area status, 71 units of 3,388,516 acres were selected as WSAs. Studies and recommendations for or against Wilderness are ongoing for these areas (and are tallied with the individual area write-ups which follow). A Nevada BLM Wilderness bill lies in the distant future.

So . . . Is Nevada empty? Barren? Desolate? Is all the action in the casinos? All the beauty in the haughty showgirls? Are the sage-filled valleys and blue mountains yonder on the horizon good only for the sheepherder, the cowman, the trapper, the two-bit miner with a bulldozer?

Ask the Mountain Lion in the Grant Range. Ask the Bighorn in the Sheep Range. The Elk in the Schell Creek Range. The Lahontan Cutthroat in a stream cutting down from Toiyabe Crest. The Sage Sparrow lost in the immensity of the Black Rock Desert. The Golden Eagle riding the thermals over the Clan Alpine Range.

---

* Late in 1988, Congress passed a bill transferring almost a million acres of BLM land in Nevada to the Toiyabe National Forest. As we went to press in early 1989, Nevada BLM still did not have detailed maps showing what they had lost, but several BLM WSAs were included. What this means for possible Wilderness designation is anybody's guess. Three general areas were included in the transfer: the White Mountains/Excelsior Mountains region along the California border; the Spring Mountains west of Las Vegas; and the Hot Creek Range/Antelope Range area in central Nevada.

Listen to the answer whispered by the ancient limbs of the Bristlecone.

They know.

Northwestern Nevada

Northwestern Nevada is a land of shimmering salt flats, the remnants of Pleistocene lakes, and sloping tablelands carpeted with Big Sagebrush and its companions. The Pronghorn is king beneath this unfenced sky where roadless areas spill over into California and Oregon. BLM controls most of this acreage, although the Fish & Wildlife Service has one of their largest refuges — Sheldon Antelope Range — here. There are also two Indian Reservations with big wilderness in northwestern Nevada.

Black Rock Desert 640,000 acres	
BLM WSA 2-620	*319,594*
Additional BLM roadless	*320,000*

Description: Northwestern Nevada west of Winnemucca. The bed of prehistoric Lake Lahontan creates an immense basin surrounded by rough desert mountains where distance loses meaning. Sometimes the Black Rock is a perfectly flat and dry salt flat; at other times it is a shallow lake with abundant waterfowl. The Quinn River meanders from the north for 90 miles into the Black Rock before it disappears in a myriad of channels (an unusual float trip is possible in spring). Willow, Beaver and Muskrat live along the Quinn. Elevations range from 3,900' to 8,594' atop Pahute Peak. Scattered desert playas and expansive flats are lightly vegetated with saltbush, greasewood and sagebrush: isolated stands of mountain mahogany and Aspen inhabit the Black Rock Range (Big Mountain or Pahute Peak). Two rare plants live here: Winged Milk-vetch and Barneby Wild Cabbage. Pronghorn, Mule Deer, Mountain Lion, Kit Fox, Sage Grouse, Chukar (exotic) and "wild" horses are residents. Important paleontological (Woolly Mammoth, camel and prehistoric bison remains) and archaeological sites as well as remnants of emigrant trails tell stories of the past. Natural arches in the Pahute Peak Range, as well as badlands and hot springs distinguish this area.

Status: Conservation groups are proposing only 214,300 acres for Wilderness in two units: Black Rock Desert (174,300) and Pahute Peak (40,000). BLM supports the small conservationist proposal on the Black Rock but recommends only 25,200 acres for Pahute Peak. At the very least, this entire roadless area should be designated as Wilderness. With even a modicum of vision, a superlative 3 million acre Wilderness representative of the Great Basin could be designated here merely by closing minor and unnecessary dirt roads. This would include the Calico and Jackson Mountains, the High Rock Canyon region, and the southern part of Sheldon Antelope Range.

ORVs threaten the area. Prospecting and overgrazing occur on the edges. Some oil & gas and geothermal leases are within the roadless area.

Trout Creek Mountains 212,000 (also in Oregon)
See Oregon for description and status.

Charles Sheldon Antelope Range 124,000 acres
Charles Sheldon Antelope Range roadless (FWS)   120,000
BLM & Summit Lake Indian Reservation roadless   4,000

Description: Extreme northwestern Nevada, north of Summit Lake Indian Reservation in the southern part of Charles Sheldon Antelope Range. Features of this high, wild basaltic tableland, cloaked with sagebrush steppe and cut by dramatic canyons, include Rock Spring Table, Hell Creek, Blowout Mountain, Virgin Creek and Fish Creek Mountain. Pronghorn, reintroduced California Bighorn Sheep, Mountain Lion, Coyote, Bobcat, Mule Deer and Sage Grouse thrive here. The cirque-like south face of Blowout Mountain probably formed from an ancient volcanic explosion. Virgin Creek cuts a narrow-walled canyon. Elevations vary from under 5,000' to over 7,100'. Mountain mahogany adorns the highlands; Aspen, cottonwood and willow line the streams.

Status: Old ranching jeep trails and intermixed private lands present potential conflicts. The FWS recommends a 93,000 acre Wilderness. Conservation groups forthrightly propose a 234,000 acre Wilderness by closing unimportant dirt roads. Livestock should be removed and dirt roads closed throughout the Sheldon Refuge.

Hawksie-Walksie 144,000 acres (also in Oregon)
See Oregon for description and status.

Massacre Rim 112,000 acres

BLM WSA CA20-1013	110,000
Sheldon National Wildlife Refuge roadless	2,000

Description: Extreme northwestern Nevada northeast of Vya. This juniper-dotted sagebrush steppe plateau, broken by rim-bound drainages, slopes up from Massacre Lake. Elevations range from 5,500' to 6,800'. The western edge of the bench suddenly drops 1,000' in volcanic talus slopes. The southern boundary has smaller steep rims above Massacre Lakes Basin. Large flats have scattered dry lake beds. Features include over a dozen flowing springs with wet meadows; Pronghorn, Mule Deer, Sage Grouse, Prairie Falcon, Red-tailed Hawk and Brewer's Sparrow; "wild" horses; 4' diameter Utah Junipers; and many archaeological sites. Reintroduction of Bighorn Sheep is planned.

Status: Although the area is threatened by continued overgrazing, additional range "improvements," ORVs, archaeological site vandals and illegal firewood cutters, BLM proposes only a 23,260 acre Wilderness.

Buffalo Hills-Smoke Creek 387,000 acres (also in California)

BLM WSA 2-621/618 (Poodle Mt)	142,050
BLM WSA 2-619 (Buffalo Hills)	47,315
BLM WSA 2-619A (Twin Peaks)	91,405
BLM WSA 2-609 (Five Springs)	48,460
Additional BLM. state, private roadless	58,000

Description: Northwestern Nevada west of Gerlach and northeastern California east of Susanville. Buffalo Hills, Buffalo Creek, Twin Peaks, Smoke Creek and Five Springs Mountain form a large wilderness in the remote Smoke Creek

Desert north and west of its terminal playa. The Buffalo Hills are a circular basaltic plateau with large canyons radiating from the center. Some of the country outside the uplands is flat, some is rolling. Buffalo Creek Canyon has steep 1,000' talus slopes. The West Fork of Buffalo Creek, a year-around stream, drains Hole-in-the-Ground, a 200' deep, mile-wide volcanic caldera. Rush, Stony and Smoke Creeks are other perennial streams. Several seasonal lakes are up to 100 acres in size. Poodle Mountain is a recent volcanic vent. The Twin Peaks WSA is the most rugged part of this large roadless area. Elevations range from 3,850' to 6,911'. Wildlife includes Mule Deer, Pronghorn, Kit Fox, Mountain Lion, Sage Grouse, Valley Quail, Golden Eagle and Prairie Falcon, as well as Chukar (exotic) and "wild" horses. There is potential for Bighorn Sheep reintroduction. Vegetative zones are sagebrush steppe to juniper woodland. Willows form important riparian areas along the creeks.

Status: Conservationists should develop a million-acre Wilderness proposal for this part of the Smoke Creek Desert which would close jeep trails and minor dirt roads. But they are only calling for a 87,900 acre Wilderness for Poodle Mt. BLM opposes Wilderness for this outstanding area (except for a 54,970 acre piece in the Twin Peaks), and, during their inventory, sliced it into several roadless units determined by jeep trails and scattered range improvements. Although several cherrystemmed dirt roads (including one to the small Smoke Creek Reservoir) and jeep trails have tracked parts of the area, it remains very wild. The military conducts low level flights over the area. A few mining claims exist. Ranchers using public land in the area oppose protection. (What else is new?) The name, Buffalo Hills, reminds us that this area of Nevada, California and Oregon was home to the Oregon race of Bison. Reintroduction of Bison and Gray Wolf should be studied.

Dry Valley Rim 100,000 acres (also in California)

BLM WSA 2-615	95,025
Additional BLM, state, private roadless	5,000

Description: The northern Nevada-California border east of Susanville, CA. The Dry Valley Rim is a 17 mile-long, east-

facing fault block that rears 1,500' above the Smoke Creek
Desert to the east (with a sheer 400' to 600' rimrock wall).
Flat-topped summits characterize this area, and elevations
vary from 3,800' to 6,200'. The east slope is cut by short,
highly-dissected drainages; the west slope is more gentle, and
includes Skedaddle Creek (a perennial stream). Smoke Creek
is on the north side. Grass and sagebrush; Prairie Falcon,
Golden Eagle, Sage Grouse (important strutting grounds),
Pronghorn, "wild" horses and large wintering herds of Mule
Deer inhabit this area.

Status: BLM has recommended a 52,845 acre Wilderness.
Dry Valley Rim is separated from the Buffalo Hills-Smoke
Creek area to the north by a dirt road and from the Skedaddle
roadless area to the west by a very poor dirt road. It should be
part of a single million acre Wilderness.

Smoke Creek Desert 148,000 acres

BLM roadless	*122,000*
Pyramid Lake Indian Reservation roadless	*26,000*

Description: Northwestern Nevada southwest of Gerlach
and north of Pyramid Lake. The Smoke Creek Desert is a large
dry lake bed, bordered by desert piedmont and scrub, serving as
the basin for Smoke Creek, Buffalo Creek, Squaw Creek and
numerous intermittent drainages flowing from the Fox Range
and Buffalo Hills.

Status: BLM, in keeping with their assumption that
Wilderness can't be flat or open, refused to even study this
reservoir of tranquility for possible Wilderness recommendation. Conservation groups have obligingly neglected it as well.
(Those with a more-highly developed sense of natural aesthetics know that wilderness isn't limited to regions of
"spectacular grandeur" and that true wildness is often found in
the most godforsaken zones of the planet. Flat is beautiful.)

Fox Mountain Range 105,000 acres

BLM WSA 2-14	*75,404*
Pyramid Lake Indian Reservation roadless	*30,000*

Description: Northwestern Nevada north of Pyramid Lake. The Fox Range is between the Smoke Creek and San Emido Deserts. Elevations are from 3,900' to 7,608' on Pah Rum Peak. Vegetation includes Great Basin shrub steppe up to juniper with some riparian vegetation along Rodeo Creek. Steep canyons, rolling hills, bowl-shaped basins, granite outcrops, boulders and several small sand dune areas in the desert piedmont around the mountains constitute a varied landscape. Pronghorn, Mule Deer, Mountain Lion, "wild" horses and Sage Grouse occupy the landscape. The proposed National Desert Trail (hiking) would pass through the eastern edge.

Status: A few mining claims, and oil & gas and geothermal leases are the main threats. Low level military flights occasionally shatter the peace. Conservation groups are only asking for a 23,600 acre BLM Wilderness, and BLM opposes any Wilderness.

Western Nevada

South of Lake Tahoe, Nevada shares several large roadless areas with California. These areas represent a gradient from the cool Great Basin Desert to the hot Mojave Desert. The Toiyabe and Inyo NFs, BLM and Death Valley National Monument are the land managers.

Excelsior Mountains 232,000 acres (also in California)

Inyo National Forest roadless (NV)	116,370
BLM roadless (NV)	58,000*
Inyo National Forest roadless (CA)	47,300
BLM roadless (CA)	10,000

Description: The central California-Nevada border east of Mono Lake. This is an enticing low mountain range of volcanic cinder soils with a high point of 8,651'. It has no surface water (except in Teels Marsh), and is remote, harsh and seldom visited. The climate tends toward cool summers and cold winters with very little precipitation, most of that being snow. Vegetative types consist of Big Sagebrush and pinyon/juniper, with salt scrub around the alkali flat at Teels Marsh. The

BLM portion in Nevada is lower and made up of long, narrow basalt bluffs and flat valleys draining into Teels Marsh on the far east end. There are no trails. Archaeological sites are common. Wildlife populations are characteristically low, although there is a sizable herd of "wild" horses.

Status: There are no significant conflicts, although ORVs and fuelwood cutting represent possible threats. Friends of Nevada Wilderness proposes a 122,000 acre Wilderness Area.

*Some or all of the NV BLM portion of this roadless area was transferred to the Toiyabe NF late in 1988.

White Mountains 358,000 acres (also in California)
See California for description and status.

Queer Mountain 155,000 acres (also in California)
See California for description and status.

Grapevine Mountains 246,000 acres (also in California)
See California for description and status.

Funeral Mountains 287,000 acres (also in California)
See California for description and status.

Nopah Range 134,000 acres (also in California)
See California for description and status.

Southern Nevada

The southern tip of Nevada is a stronghold of the Mojave Desert, with sparse vegetation and extremely hot temperatures. Nonetheless, several ranges rise out of this geographic oven to create some of the finest forests and wildlife habitats in the state. Las Vegas may be the antithesis of natural beauty and serenity, but surrounding the glitzy strip is incomparable wilderness. The sprawling Desert National Wildlife Refuge, largest in the system (outside of Alaska) at over one and half *million acres, is the centerpiece of big wilderness here, but BLM and the Toiyabe NF have important areas, too.*

Sheep Range 468,000 acres

Desert National Wildlife Refuge roadless	*440,000*
BLM WSAs 5-201/165/16 etc.	*28,000*

Description: Southern Nevada north of Las Vegas. This superb desert mountain range rises out of the Mojave Desert at 2,500' to reach 9,750' on Sheep Peak. Joshua Tree, saltbush, Creosote and cactus populate the Mojave Desert lowlands, with pinyon/juniper, Ponderosa Pine and White Fir higher up, and a Bristlecone & Limber Pine forest on top. The world's largest population of Desert Bighorn Sheep (over 1,000 individuals) is found in the roadless areas on the Desert Wildlife Refuge, as is the greatest diversity of animal life in Nevada. Other species include Desert Tortoise, Gila Monster, Gambel's Quail, Golden Eagle, Mountain Lion, Bobcat, Mule Deer, Badger and the rare Kit Fox. Water is limited to a few springs. Only dirt roads separate the Sheep Range from the other large roadless areas on the DNWR. In 1936, Bob Marshall called what is now the Desert NWR and Nellis Air Force Range the finest desert wilderness in America. Temperatures range from 117° to below zero, and precipitation from 2" to 15" a year.

Status: The FWS proposes 440,000 acres for wilderness. BLM recommends none. The US Air Force continues to try to take over the Desert National Wildlife Refuge as a Military Operations Area (a military air zone). Conservationists have so far prevented exclusive control going to the military. Some of the BLM land was just exchanged to the Aerojet Corporation in a shady land exchange. Of course, the Desert NWR has been downwind of the Nevada Test Site for nearly 40 years. Radiation kills.

RM36: 2,670,000*

Hole In The Rock 277,000 acres

Desert National Wildlife Refuge roadless	*115,700*
BLM roadless	*140,058*
Nellis Air Force Range roadless	*21,000*

Description: Southern Nevada north of Las Vegas. This area largely consists of a broad desert valley between the Sheep and Desert mountain ranges. The southern end includes the large, dry Desert Lake. Elevations range from about 3,200' to over 6,200'. See Sheep Range for general description.

Status: The FWS proposes 115,700 acres for Wilderness. BLM proposes none.

RM36: 2,670,000*

Desert-Pintwater Range <u>467,000 acres</u>

Desert National Wildlife Refuge roadless	*372,000*
Nellis Air Force Range roadless	*65,000*
BLM roadless	*30,000*

Description: Southern Nevada north of Las Vegas. The Desert and Pintwater Ranges, with the Three Lakes Valley between them, lie west of the Sheep Range. High point is 6,400' on Quartz Peak in the Pintwaters. Lower elevations are about 3,200'. See Sheep Range for general description.

Status: The FWS proposes 339,500 acres for Wilderness. BLM proposes none. The Three Lakes Valley is used by the military for air to ground target practice. Although mostly roadless, the valley does show definite impacts from this use.

RM36: 2,670,000*

Spotted Range <u>354,000 acres</u>

Desert National Wildlife Refuge roadless	*318,000*
Nellis Air Force Range roadless	*27,000*
BLM roadless	*9,000*

Description: Southern Nevada northwest of Las Vegas and west of the Pintwater Range. This area includes parts of the Spotted Range and Emigrant Valley, Papoose Range, Ranger Mountains and Papoose Dry Lake. The high point is 6,300' on Aysees Peak in the Buried Hills. Low point is below 3,200'. See Sheep Range for general description.

Status: The FWS proposes 300,700 acres for Wilderness. BLM proposes none.

RM36: 2,670,000*

Las Vegas Range 207,000 acres

Desert National Wildlife Refuge roadless	164,600
BLM WSAs 5-216/217	39,224
Nellis AFB roadless	3,000

Description: Southern Nevada immediately north of Las Vegas. See Sheep Range for general description.
Status: FWS proposes 164,600 acres for Wilderness. BLM recommends none.
*RM36: 2,670,000**

Mt. Stirling 180,000 acres

BLM WSA 5-401 and additional roadless	147,000*
Additional BLM and private roadless	33,000*

Description: Southern Nevada west of Las Vegas in the Spring Mountains. A dirt road separates this area from the Mt. Charleston roadless area. Elevations in this rugged complex of canyons and ridges, that stretches from US 95 on the north to the Pahrump Valley on the south, vary from about 2,800' to 9,618'. This is a heavily vegetated range for Nevada with pinyon/juniper, Ponderosa Pine, White Fir and Bristlecone Pine. The fauna includes quail, Elk, Mule Deer, Mountain Lion, Bobcat, "wild" horses and burros. Potential for Bighorn Sheep reintroduction is high. See Charleston Peak for additional description.
Status: BLM proposes 40,275 acres for Wilderness.

*Some or all of the BLM land in this roadless area was transferred to the Toiyabe NF in late 1988.

Charleston Peak 200,000 acres

Toiyabe NF RARE I	40,430
Additional Toiyabe NF and intermixed private roadless	9,000
BLM WSAs 5-412/421	62,093*
Additional BLM and private roadless	88,000*

Description: The Spring Mountains in southern Nevada west of Las Vegas. Charleston Peak (11,919') is one of the most prominent peaks of the Mojave Desert, and the Spring Mountains are the only range in the southern Great Basin to rise above treeline. Lower elevations are about 3,200'. Moving upward, vegetation ranges from southern Mojave Desert scrub to Joshua Tree to scrub oak to pinyon/juniper to White Fir and Ponderosa Pine forests, and ultimately to one of the largest forests of Bristlecone Pine in the world. 27 species of endemic plants grow in the area. A dirt road separates the Charleston Peak roadless area from the Mt. Stirling roadless area. Some of the BLM portion is in the Red Rock Canyon National Recreation Lands, known for sheer cliffs (up to 1,000' high) and canyons of red Aztec sandstone. A large Desert Bighorn Sheep herd and a small herd of Elk use the area. Other wildlife includes Mule Deer, Mountain Lion, the Endangered Spotted Bat, and the endemic Palmer's Chipmunk. Feral burros compete with native wildlife. Brownstone Canyon is included on the National Register of Historical Places as an archaeological district due to its dramatic petroglyphs. This area receives very high precipitation for the Great Basin, up to 28" a year, with a snow depth of 6'.

Status: This roadless area is rather amoeba-shaped due to several cherrystemmed roads penetrating along canyons. The FS portion is likely to be included in a Nevada Wilderness bill (FNW proposes 47,000 acres). BLM proposes only 34,010 acres for Wilderness. Since BLM's La Madre Mountain WSA (5-412) abuts the sprawl of Las Vegas, impacts to it include, in addition to those from the standard ORV joy riders, the dumping of bodies by beefy guys in tight dark suits and sunglasses. This may be the only BLM area receiving ORV use by Cadillacs. Mining and oil & gas are specific threats.

* Some or all of the BLM portion of this roadless area was transferred to the Toiyabe NF late in 1988.

Muddy Mountains 116,000 acres

BLM WSA 5-229	*96,170*
Additional BLM roadless	*11,000*
Lake Mead National Recreation Area roadless	*9,000*

Description: Southern Nevada east of Las Vegas. Elevations range from 2,000' to 5,400'. The core of the Muddy Mountains is formed by limestone peaks and canyons with two valleys where orange, red and cream sandstone are exposed. Lower Mojave Desert plant communities (Creosote, Blackbrush, yucca, Joshua Tree) are complemented by large Desert Willows in the big washes. Gambel's Quail, Desert Bighorn Sheep, Mountain Lion, Bobcat and "wild" horses live here. Archaeological sites up to 4,000 years old, 600' high cliffs, sculpted sandstone formations, and Anniversary Narrows (a 600' deep canyon only 7 - 15' wide) are special attractions.

Status: BLM proposes only 36,850 acres for Wilderness. ORV use is a particular threat because of the proximity to Las Vegas (dirt bike racing occurs here). Additional threats include claims for nonmetallic minerals.

Mormon Mountains 163,000 acres
BLM WSA 5-161   *162,887*

Description: Southeastern Nevada southeast of Alamo. The Union Pacific tracks separate this area from the Meadow Valley Mountains roadless area. Mormon Peak is 7,411'. The low point is 2,200'. The BLM describes the area thusly: "Core is a tortuous collection of rugged limestone peaks, high cliffs, and deep remote canyons. Around core are lesser hills, canyons and dissected bajadas. On the south knife-like Moapa Peak stabs skyward, a beacon to climbers and scramblers. Caves provide spelunking." Vegetation ranges from Blackbrush, Bursage and Joshua Tree to pinyon/juniper with a small relict stand of large Ponderosa Pine near the summit of Mormon Peak. Fauna includes Desert Tortoise, Desert Bighorn Sheep, Mule Deer and Spotted Bat. The Meadow Valley Range Sandwort is a state protected plant. The many archaeological sites include agave roasting pits and petroglyphs.

Status: BLM recommends a piddling 23,690 acre Wilderness Area; conservation groups have asked for only 123,130 acres for Wilderness.

Meadow Valley Mountains 186,000 acres
BLM WSA 5-156   *185,744*

Description: Southeastern Nevada southeast of Alamo. Elevations range from 3,400' to 5,700'. BLM says, "Landforms include 30 miles of rugged Meadow Valley Mountains along western spine; the Bunker Hills, south; and central bajada stretching from Bunker Hills nearly to Hackberry Canyon. Mountains are jumbled, remote and extremely varied. A natural arch, cliffs, jagged peaks and hidden canyons. Conical Sunflower Mountain focal point. Hackberry Canyon has outstanding wilderness. Vigo Canyon has sculpted cliffs . . . vast desert vistas untrammeled by man." Vegetation includes Creosote Bush, Blackbrush, Joshua Tree, rabbitbrush and pinyon/juniper. Meadow Valley Range Sandwort and Nye Milkvetch are state protected plants. Large Barrel Cactus grow on the southern end of the roadless area. Desert Tortoise, Golden Eagle, Prairie Falcon, Desert Bighorn Sheep and Spotted Bat are some of the sensitive species in the area. "Wild" horses are also present.

Status: BLM recommends 97,180; conservation groups 166,500 acres for Wilderness. Aerojet Corporation has just acquired nearby BLM lands in the Coyote Springs Valley in a shady land exchange. This may have some impact on the Meadow Valley Mts.

Delamar Mountains 127,000 acres
BLM WSA 5-177   *126,700*

Description: Southern Nevada southeast of Alamo. This area is separated from the Meadow Valley Mountains by a minor dirt road and from the Sheep Range in the DNWR by a narrow paved highway. Elevations rise from 2,600' to 6,600'. The Delamars are a broad rolling plateau bounded by an abrupt cliff on the west, and with a multicolored caldera in the core. Desert bajadas, badlands and spectacular, twisting, cliff-lined canyons on the south constitute a varied landscape. Desert scrub dominated by Blackbrush is the most common vegetative community; Big Sagebrush, Joshua Tree, pinyon/juniper, grassland and salt desert scrub are also present, as is Nye Milkvetch, a state protected plant. Desert Tortoise find habitat here. This area is being considered for Desert Bighorn reintroduction.

Paleozoic fossils, and important archaeological sites, including an obsidian quarry, are of scientific interest.

Status: Peace and quiet is disturbed by low level military flights and ORVs. Conservationists recommend 102,490 acres for Wilderness. Aerojet has just acquired nearby BLM lands in the Coyote Springs Valley in a land exchange. This may adversely affect the Delamars.

Central Nevada

There is perhaps no better representation of basin and range than central Nevada where a series of long, narrow mountain ranges rise more than a mile above the similarly long, narrow valleys that divide them. This topography differs from the tablelands and sinks of northwestern Nevada but is ecologically part of the Great Basin Desert, too. The Toiyabe NF generally manages the higher ranges and BLM has the rest except for Carson Sink where land management is divided among four agencies.

Carson Sink <u>286,000 acres</u>

BLM, Navy, state, Fish & Wildlife Service
  roadless   *286,000*

Description: West-central Nevada north of Fallon. This little-known alkali flat is the terminus of the Carson River (and the remnant of Pleistocene Lake Lahontan). Here, in the midst of the surrounding Great Basin desert, sand dunes meet marshes. Elevations vary only from under 4,000' to about 3,870'. The roadless portion of the Sink is composed of parts of the Fallon National Wildlife Refuge, the state Stillwater Wildlife Management Area, a Navy bombing range, but mostly of BLM lands. It is one of the more important areas in Nevada for waterfowl and shorebirds, including White Pelican, Tundra Swan, White-faced Ibis, Bald Eagle, Peregrine Falcon, and several species of more common ducks, geese and "peeps." Other wildlife includes Coyote, kangaroo rat and horned lizard. Saltbush, greasewood, sand verbena and evening primrose are common desert plants in the area. The primary marsh area is roaded and diked on the Wildlife Refuge, and much of the roadless area stretching to the north does not receive water every year.

Status: The US Fish & Wildlife Service has discovered toxic contamination (selenium, arsenic, lead and boron) at Carson Sink similar to that at Kesterson NWR in California (a case that made national news). There was a large die-off of waterfowl and fish at Stillwater in 1987. The area has no water rights and depends entirely on run-off from Newlands Project irrigation; it has been drying up over the last 80 years — from over 170,000 acres of wetlands to less than 38,000 today. The Toiyabe Chapter of the Sierra Club has begun a major campaign to buy water rights from Newlands Project farmers to restore the marshes and dilute the toxics. Support is needed.

Carson Sink is a prime example of a large, biologically important wild area that has been neglected because it does not fit the classic conception of wilderness. BLM did not consider it for a WSA and conservationists have not pushed it.

A particularly gruesome assault on the area is from local good ol' boys who plunder ancient Paiute graves near the marshes. These ghouls rip apart the skeletons of the ancients in order to find artifacts.

Clan Alpine Range 196,000 acres
BLM WSA 3-102   *196,128*

Description: Central Nevada west of Austin. This major north-south trending volcanic range climbs from 3,600' in Dixie Valley to 9,966' on Mt. Augusta. Several small perennial and intermittent streams lined with riparian vegetation, numerous springs, colorful rock formations, high ridges with groves of mountain mahogany (rare in this part of Nevada), Aspen along the canyons, and pinyon/juniper forests are all included in this diverse area. Big Sagebrush and Shadscale predominant in the foothills. Sage Grouse, Golden Eagle, Prairie Falcon, Mule Deer, Mountain Lion, "wild" horses, and introduced Rainbow and Brown Trout dwell here. Desert Bighorn Sheep were reintroduced in 1986. Views extend to the Sierra crest 100 miles to the west. Good cross-country skiing attracts winter enthusiasts.

Status: BLM is recommending only 68,458 acres for Wilderness. ORVs, small-scale mining, continued overgrazing, fuelwood cutting and geothermal exploration are threats. Some lower elevation areas are severely cow-trashed (they may be outside this roadless area). Several cherrystem roads penetrate the area and crude, old jeep trails scar Mt. Augusta.

Arc Dome 250,000 acres	
Toiyabe National Forest roadless	*244,000*
BLM, private roadless	*6,000*

Description: Central Nevada north of Tonopah. Friends of Nevada Wilderness calls the imposing granite domes in the southern end of the Toiyabe Range "the backbone of Central Nevada." Topography varies from gently rolling, pinyon/juniper covered lowlands on the south through steep, rocky canyons up to glacial cirques around Arc Dome. The west slope is gentle with deep canyons; the east slope has cliffs and rocky, more rugged canyons. Elevations climb from 6,000' on the south to 11,773' on Arc Dome. Dense pinyon/juniper intermingles with Big Sagebrush and mountain mahogany. It is replaced by pockets of Aspen and Limber Pine higher up. The Reese, and North and South Twin Rivers spring from Arc Dome, with its 25" of annual precipitation (very high for the Great Basin). There are 18 other creeks in the area. Riparian vegetation is mostly cottonwood, willow, maple and birch. Many small, lush meadows adorn the higher elevations. Desert Bighorn Sheep, Mule Deer, Mountain Lion, Bobcat, Coyote, Sage Grouse, Blue Grouse and raptors prosper here. Fishing is popular. Some Aspens on the lower elevation west side have classic Basque sheepherder pornographic carvings.

Status: Cherrystem roads penetrate. The mining threat on the periphery is high, as is the potential for commercial cutting of pinyon/juniper. Probably a mere 100,000 acres or so of this area (considered one of the "jewels" of Nevada by conservation groups) will be designated Wilderness. Friends of Nevada Wilderness proposes only 146,000 acres and the FS recommends a thoroughly inadequate 94,400. Miners have convinced Sen. Harry Reid to drop a large part of Arc Dome in the North & South Twin River drainages from his Nevada Wilderness bill. These small, independent miners are the gravest threat to Arc Dome. Reid, who was elected to the

Senate with strong conservationist support, has proved with his Wilderness bill to be a major disappointment. He has shown a marked lack of enthusiasm for Wilderness since his election.

Toiyabe Crest <u>126,000 acres</u>

Toiyabe NF and BLM roadless	*126,000*

Description: Central Nevada south of Austin. The Toiyabe Range (north of the Arc Dome roadless area) is a high mountain ridge with elevations from 7,500' to over 11,000' located between two semi-arid valleys. The topography is steep and heavily dissected on the east; more gentle on the west. Vegetation rises from sagebrush, to pinyon/juniper, to stands of mountain mahogany, Aspen and occasional Limber Pine in the higher elevations. The Toiyabe Crest Trail runs the length of the area. A granite outcrop, "The Wild Granites," is on the crest, which is described by FNW as "a 400-foot wall of granite carved by wind and water into spectacular vertical spikes and columns." A small band of Desert Bighorn Sheep lives here, and several west slope streams contain the Endangered Lahontan Cutthroat Trout. Other wildlife includes Mule Deer, Mountain Lion, Bobcat, Golden Eagle, Blue Grouse and Sage Grouse.

Status: Cherrystem roads penetrate the area along several canyon bottoms. Mining is a threat throughout the area. The FS opposes Wilderness here and conservationists have asked for only 79,000 acres. A minor dirt road is all that separates Toiyabe Crest from Arc Dome. It should be closed and a single Wilderness of at least 400,000 acres established.

Table Mountain <u>190,000 acres</u>

Toiyabe NF RARE I	*170,000*
BLM roadless	*20,000*

Description: Central Nevada southeast of Austin in the core of the Monitor Range. Well-watered, rolling mountain uplands with steep, rocky canyons break into foothills and valley floor. Elevations rise from 7,000' to over 10,000'. One can walk for a dozen miles on a gentle plateau above 10,000' along a pre-

cipitous eastern escarpment. Higher elevation vegetation consists of expansive stands of grass and sagebrush broken by
extensive Aspen forests — not simply groves as exist elsewhere.
Lower elevation vegetation is pinyon/juniper, mountain mahogany and Big Sagebrush. Wildlife includes Mule Deer, Elk
(non-native and introduced in 1979), Mountain Lion, Bobcat,
Sage Grouse, Blue Grouse, and the Endangered Lahontan Cutthroat Trout in several large creeks. The highest Goshawk
nesting density in Nevada occurs here.

Status: Overgrazing is causing erosion. The Forest Service
has a burning desire to "manage" the area for wildlife
"improvement" — i.e., vegetative manipulation. Jeep trails
and old mines scar the area slightly. Conservationists support
a 125,000 acre Wilderness; the FS opposes Wilderness.

Horse Heaven 135,000 acres

Toiyabe NF RARE I	*115,000*
BLM, private roadless	*20,000*

Description: Central Nevada in the central Monitor Range
southeast of Austin. Rolling mountain uplands with steep,
rocky canyons break into foothills and valley floor. Elevations
range from 7,000' to 9,800'. Higher elevation vegetation consists of grass and sagebrush interspersed with Aspen groves;
lower elevation vegetation is pinyon/juniper, mountain
mahogany and Big Sagebrush. Wildlife includes Mule Deer,
Elk, Mountain Lion, Bobcat, Sage Grouse and Blue Grouse.

Status: Jeep trails and overgrazing impact the area.
National and state conservation groups are not proposing
Wilderness in this worthy but forgotten area. A poor dirt road
is all that separates Horse Heaven from Table Mountain. It
should be closed and a single 350,000 acre Wilderness established.

Antelope 144,000 acres

BLM WSA 6-231/241	*144,000**

Description: Central Nevada south of Eureka. A north-
south ridge one to two thousand feet above the valleys domi-

nates this remote range. The northern end has several perennial streams with mature riparian forests and extensive Aspen groves on the plateau-like top, while the central part is a barren interior valley. The southern part features flat-topped mountains covered with pinyon/juniper forest. Archaeological sites include a group of Shoshone wickiups.

Status: BLM has recommended 83,100 acres for Wilderness.

* Some or all of the BLM portion of this roadless area was transferred to the Toiyabe NF late in 1988.

Palisade Mesa 116,000 acres
BLM WSA 6-142/162   *115,350*

Description: Central Nevada east of Tonopah. This area in the Pancake Range consists of mesas, lava flows, volcanic craters and cinder cones, and includes Lunar Crater, a maar volcano (low relief, circular) which is on the National Natural Landmark Register. Large boulders form outcroppings on the mesa tops. Elevations rise from 5,000' to 7,394'. Vegetation is sagebrush steppe with scattered juniper on the mesas. Wildlife includes Golden Eagle, Prairie Falcon, other raptors, and small populations of Mountain Lion, Pronghorn, Bighorn Sheep, Mule Deer and exotic Chukar. Archaeological sites include a rock shelter with pictographs. *Astragalus callithrix* , a plant proposed for Threatened or Endangered status, is known in the area.

Status: BLM recommends 66,110 acres for Wilderness.

South Reveille 107,500 acres
BLM WSA 6-112   *107,500*

Description: Central Nevada east of Tonopah and north of Nellis Air Force Range. The southern and central parts of the Reveille Range are characterized by large expanses of high elevation valley bottoms surrounding mesas and mountain peaks, which are cut by narrow canyons. Elevations range from 5,000' to 8,910'. Sagebrush dominates below 7,000', pinyon/juniper above. Abundant wildlife includes Mule Deer, Pronghorn, Mountain Lion and various raptors.

Status: In accordance with the name it has earned, "Bureau of Livestock and Mining," BLM proposes only 33,000 acres for Wilderness protection.

Eastern Nevada

The alternating basins and ranges of eastern Nevada are not as symmetrical in their arrangement as are those of central Nevada, but this is still classic Great Basin landscape. The mountain ranges are far enough away from the rainshadow of the Sierra Nevada to support a thicker and more diverse forest than elsewhere in Nevada. The Humboldt NF generally has the higher ranges, while BLM manages everything else. Several of these limestone ranges hide caves of exceptional size and beauty.

Quinn 120,000 acres	
Humboldt NF RARE II	*101,000*
BLM roadless	*19,000*

Description: East-central Nevada east of Tonopah and southwest of Ely. A poor dirt road separates this area from the Grant Range roadless area. Vegetation is Sagebrush steppe through pinyon/juniper woodland to Aspen, White Fir, Limber Pine and Bristlecone Pine. The high crest holds snow into July in many years. Volcanic, as opposed to the limestone Grant Range, Quinn has more water in its canyons. The peaks and ridges, including the high point of 10,229', are unnamed. The low point is about 5,800'. Impressive rock cliffs buttress the canyons leading into the high country.

Status: Mining presents a possible threat. Exxon is exploring nearby for oil & gas — the area could be threatened if a strike is made. A 19,000 acre Wilderness was proposed in the 1988 Nevada Wilderness bill.

Grant Range 240,000 acres	
Humboldt National Forest roadless	*105,519*
BLM WSAs 4-166/158/199	*116,562*
Additional BLM roadless	*18,000*

Description: East-central Nevada east of Tonopah and southwest of Ely. This remote mountain range of limestone cliffs is cut by high-walled canyons. Benchlands and foothills are in the lower elevations. Troy Peak at 11,298' is the high point. The low point is under 5,000'. Vegetation includes sagebrush steppe, pinyon/juniper woodland, and, in the high country, large stands of Ponderosa Pine, Aspen, Limber Pine, White Fir and Bristlecone Pine (one of Nevada's best stands). Cottonwood grow along canyon bottoms. A healthy herd of Desert Bighorn Sheep lives here, and it is important Mule Deer winter range. Eyries are used by Golden Eagle, Kestrel, Turkey Vulture, Red-tailed Hawk, Ferruginous Hawk, Great Horned Owl, Long-eared Owl and Prairie Falcon. Other wildlife includes Ringtail, Gray Fox, Bobcat, Mountain Lion and Elk. Over 200 species of wildflowers, including a rare Nevada primrose and the state sensitive species Oneleaf Torrey Milk-vetch, and over a dozen tree species grow here. A poor dirt road separates it from the Quinn Canyon Range. John Muir wrote about climbing Troy Peak. Other visitors report a superb feeling of solitude.

Status: Threats include small mining operations and so-called livestock improvements. It is also threatened by current Exxon oil & gas exploration. The FS recommends a 43,100 acre Wilderness while BLM proposes an additional 37,542 acres for Wilderness. Conservationists are asking for 60,000 acres of Wilderness on FS lands. The dirt road between Quinn and Grant should be closed and a 400,000 acre Wilderness established.

South Egan Range 113,000 acres

BLM WSA 4-168	96,996
Additional BLM, private roadless	16,000

Description: Eastern Nevada south of Ely. This is an unusual mountain range for Nevada in that it is not a single ridge line, but a more complex series of ridges. Portions of the area are extremely wild and virtually inaccessible, characterized by steep slopes, massive limestone cliffs and White Fir forests. Long Canyon has an open bowl-like area. Vegetation is sagebrush steppe, pinyon/juniper, mixed conifer, scattered stands of Aspen and mountain mahogany, Bristlecone Pine along the ridgelines, and significant stands of Ponderosa Pine (unusual in the Great Basin). Riparian areas are abundant. Angel Cave is a 200' deep pit cave oddly located on the crest at 9,000'. Elevations range from 5,600' to over 9,600'. There are numerous archaeological sites. Red-tailed Hawk, Prairie Falcon, Golden Eagle, Kestrel, Turkey Vulture, Great Horned Owl and Long-eared Owl have eyries in the limestone cliffs. Gambel's Quail, rare in this part of Nevada, are found in the foothills. Additional species include Sage Grouse, Blue Grouse, Mule Deer, Mountain Lion, Bobcat and occasional Elk. This is a potential site for reintroduction of Bighorn Sheep.

Status: BLM opposes Wilderness designation for this area.

Wheeler Peak 160,000 acres

Great Basin National Park and Humboldt	
NF roadless	136,000
BLM roadless	24,000

Description: Eastern Nevada east of Ely. The new 77,100 acre Great Basin National Park encompasses a portion of the South Snake Range which culminates in 13,063' Wheeler Peak and several other peaks over 11,500'. Wheeler Peak offers a superb example of glaciation — a small permanent ice field, several small lakes, and U-shaped valleys with rushing streams. The area also has wild caves and the six-story high Lexington natural arch. Lehman Cave is on the edge of the roadless area. With 8,000' of relief, the crest drops down to sagebrush valleys on either side. A well-known ancient Bristlecone Pine forest (4,000 years old) thrives here. In 1964, a fiendish FS District Ranger, Don Cox, chainsawed down the oldest known Bristlecone Pine (4,900 years old) here. Fauna includes Rocky Mountain Bighorn Sheep, Mule Deer, Cougar, Beaver, Kit Fox, Pygmy Rabbit and Utah Cutthroat Trout. Vegetation includes a substantial forest (for Nevada) of Douglas-fir, White Fir, Limber Pine and Engelmann Spruce. Efforts to establish a Great Basin National Park on Wheeler Peak began in 1924. The Park was finally established in 1986 — late compromises cut nearly 100,000 acres from the originally proposed 174,000 acres.

Status: "Great Basin National Park" is a joke — allowing overgrazing and mining (on established claims), and including only a portion of one mountain range and no valleys — no basin! A true Great Basin National Park is needed that includes several mountain ranges and the intervening valleys — and excludes cows and prospectors. Despite the National Park, the Snake Range is not safe. Conservationists propose 42,000 acres of the South Snake Range outside of the Park for Wilderness.

Mt. Moriah 144,000 acres (also in Utah)	
Humboldt NF roadless (NV)	*97,000*
BLM roadless (partly in UT)	*47,000*

Description: Eastern Nevada east of Ely in the northern Snake Range. This complex mountain range, well-forested for Nevada, is crowned by 12,050' Mt. Moriah (Nevada's fifth highest peak), which sits on a high, geologically unique plateau over 11,000' in elevation with steep limestone canyons cutting away in all directions. John Hart, in **Hiking the Great Basin**, writes, "on the rounded peaks, more than on any other Great Basin peak, you have the sensation not just of height but of deep remoteness, of immersion in wilderness." The low point is 5,400'. Vegetation includes sagebrush steppe, pinyon/juniper, Aspen, mountain mahogany, Douglas-fir, White Fir, Limber Pine and Bristlecone Pine (including a young, vigorous Bristlecone forest). Rocky Mountain Bighorn Sheep and the rare Utah Cutthroat Trout live here, as do Pronghorn in the lower elevations.

Status: A portion is likely to be included in a Nevada Wilderness bill. The FS recommends 60,700 acres and conservationists 98,000 (including a bit of BLM land).

Schell Creek Range 145,000 acres	
Humboldt NF roadless	*134,000*
BLM, private roadless	*11,000*

Description: Eastern Nevada east of Ely. This long, high ridge above timberline is cut by several deep, rugged canyons with perennial streams. North Schell Peak reaches 11,890' and South Schell Peak 11,765'; elevations drop to 6,000' in the foothills. Impressive talus slopes flank the range. Wildlife includes many Mule Deer, a small herd of Elk, Pronghorn,

Beaver and Mountain Lion. Wild limestone caves include one where the remains of a Cave Bear were discovered in 1982. Sagebrush steppe and pinyon/juniper woodland grade up through Aspen stands and forests of Douglas-fir, Engelmann Spruce (very rare in Nevada) and White Fir to Limber Pine and Bristlecone Pine on top. Several streams have trout.

Status: Threats include continued overgrazing, mining, ORVs, and fuelwood and xmas tree cutting. Although the FS is opposed to Wilderness for this largely pristine mountain range, Friends of Nevada Wilderness supports a 120,000 acre Wilderness in one of their better proposals.

Cherry Creek Mountains 101,000 acres

BLM WSA 4-015 (Goshute Canyon)	*35,594*
Additional BLM roadless	*65,000*

Description: Northeastern Nevada north of Ely. Extensive limestone cliffs and bluffs, a large mountain basin, and a long, high ridge characterize this area which reaches 10,542' in elevation on Exchequer Peak, nearly a mile above the low point. Vegetation ranges from sagebrush steppe to pinyon/juniper; with mountain mahogany, cottonwood and willow along the canyons; and Aspen up to forests of White Fir and large stands of Bristlecone Pine on the summits. Wildlife includes Blue Grouse, Sage Grouse, Mule Deer, Mountain Lion, Bobcat, Yellow-bellied Marmot, Spotted Bat, Elk and Pronghorn. Nesting sites for raptors are present (both Peregrine Falcon and Bald Eagle are believed to use the area). "Wild" horses roam the area. Many creeks and springs support excellent riparian vegetation and the Bonneville Cutthroat Trout. Goshute Cave contains a wide variety of rare speleothelms, including blistered mammalaries and cave pearls.

Status: BLM is proposing a paltry 22,225 acre Wilderness in the Goshute Canyon area.

South Great Salt Lake Desert 1,144,000 acres (also in Utah)

See Utah for description and status.

Ruby Mountains 190,000 acres

Humboldt National Forest RARE II	*164,820*
Additional Humboldt NF, and BLM,	
private roadless	*25,000*

Description: Northeastern Nevada southeast of Elko. This glorious glacier-carved granite mountain range is the most classically scenic in Nevada. It includes sculpted peaks, U-shaped valleys with snow-fed streams, many lakes, and excellent views of Great Basin valleys and ranges in all directions. Ruby Dome at 11,400' is the high point. Vegetative types range from sagebrush to Bristlecone Pine. Mountain Goat (non-native) have been introduced. The other wildlife is characteristic of the Great Basin.

Status: Any Nevada Wilderness bill is almost certain to have at least a small Ruby Mountains Wilderness in it, with the FS proposing two separate units of 55,600 and 12,300 acres, and conservationists calling for 143,000 acres. Conservationists must insist that all life zones be included, not just the high slopes and glaciated crest. Commercial helicopter skiing promoters are trying to delete significant areas from the Wilderness.

Jarbidge 189,000 acres (also in Idaho)

Designated Jarbidge Wilderness Area	
(Humboldt NF)	*64,667*
Additional Humboldt NF roadless	*95,000*
BLM roadless (partly in Idaho)	*29,000*

Description: Northeastern Nevada north of Elko. These remote mountains are unusual for Nevada in that they have multiple ridges and are heavily forested. Eight peaks attain 10,000'. Other features include a glacial lake and the headwaters of the Jarbidge River, which flows into the Snake River. The west slope of the Jarbidge Mountains drops from 10,800' to 7,000' in two miles. Sagebrush steppe covers the lower country; mountain mahogany and Aspen the middle elevations; and Limber Pine and Subalpine Fir the higher. The precipitation of 30" a year is high for Nevada. Winter temperatures are extremely cold. California Bighorn Sheep were reintroduced into the area in 1981 but have been eliminated. The Forest Service blames predators, but they were probably of the pointy-toed, high-heeled, stetson-wearing kind. The local livestock gentry mounted a successful effort in the mid-1980s to prevent the Nevada Game & Fish Department from reintroducing Elk — the ranchers claimed the Elk would eat too much. Threatened Lahontan Cutthroat Trout inhabit the streams.

Status: This area includes Nevada's only designated Wilderness Area. All contiguous roadless lands should be added. Strong opposition to additional Wilderness comes from local ranchers and miners. Conservationists are asking for 54,000 acres of Wilderness additions; the FS proposes 26,400 acres.

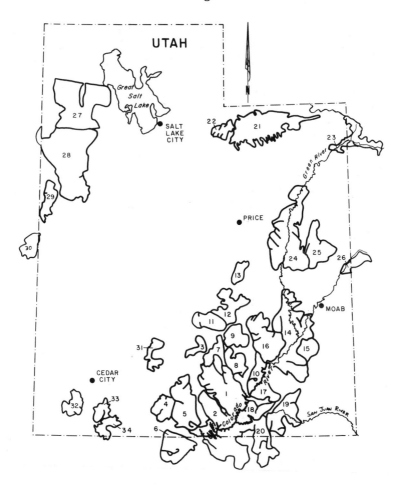

1. Escalante	13. Sids Mountain	24. Desolation Canyon
2. Kaiparowits	14. Canyonlands	25. Book Cliffs
3. Boulder Mountain	15. Salt Creek	26. Black Ridge Canyons
4. Paria-Hackberry	16. Dirty Devil	27. N. Great Salt Lk Desert
5. Wahweap-Canaan Pk	17. Mancos Mesa	28. S. Great Salt Lk Desert
6. Paria Canyon	18. Wilson Mesa	29. Deep Creek Mts
7. Steep Ck-Oak Ck	19. San Juan River	30. Mt. Moriah
8. Mt. Pennel	20. Navajo Mountain	31. Casto-Table
9. Mt. Ellen	21. High Uintas	32. Pine Valley Mt
10. Little Rockies	22. Lakes	33. Zion
11. Wayne Wonderland	23. Yampa-Green	34. Parunuweap
12. Muddy Creek		

Utah

But for two quirks of history, Utah would today be far wilder and less populated than it is. After Joseph Smith was gunned down in 1844 by a mob in Carthage, Illinois, Brigham Young led the Mormon faithful west to a safer haven — the valley of the Great Salt Lake on the west slope of the Wasatch Mountains in what was then Mexican territory. The Mormons in Utah represented an approach to the frontier different than the rugged individualism that "won" the other lands west of the Alleghenies. The disciplined, centralized communism of the Mormons allowed them to prosper in the arid wilderness of the Great Basin and Colorado Plateau. The atomized, nuclear family approach to the conquest of the frontier would never have worked in Escalante, Blanding, Delta or, perhaps, even the Wasatch Front. It took the dedicated ant-like obedience and single-mindedness of the Mormons to civilize Utah.

Of course, the social and philosophical attributes which enabled the Latter-day Saints to achieve success in a harsh land did not oblige their descendants to preserve the natural world. Verily, the Mormons have outdone the gentiles in waging a holy war against the "howling wilderness."

To make matters worse for wilderness in Utah, the second land rush there featured a group even more hostile toward the Big Outside — the uranium miners who swarmed to the canyon country after World War II armed with Geiger counters and bulldozers in the last great grassroots mining boom.

Whereas the Mormons had settled valleys where they could divert nearby mountain streams for irrigation and had used the back of beyond for cattle grazing (as was done throughout the West), the uranium frenzy resulted in thousands of miles of rough road being ripped across fragile ground by bulldozer jockeys, hundreds of mine shafts dug, and tons of radioactive tailings piled haphazardly about. Today, these prospecting trails provide jeep access to wild places that otherwise could never have been reached by vehicle.

Nonetheless, despite the best efforts of the Mormon settlers and the uranium miners, and despite the Bureau of Reclamation ("Wreck-the-Nation") which drowned Glen Canyon in the early 1960s, Utah has some of the wildest, most remote land in the lower 48 states.

The several generally parallel ranges of the Wasatch Mountains run south through the center of Utah from Idaho nearly to the Arizona line. East of the Great Salt Lake, the Uinta Mountains run on a west-east course almost to the Colorado border. The Uintas and the northern part of the Wasatch properly belong in the Central Rocky Mountains Ecoregion (centered on Yellowstone), while the southern ranges of the Wasatch are part of the Southern Rockies Ecoregion (centered on Colorado). Because of their elevation (the Uintas exceed 13,000' and several sub-ranges of the Wasatch top 12,000'), both are well-watered and heavily forested.

The Wasatch Range divides the Great Basin in Utah's western half from the Colorado Plateau in the eastern half of the state. The Great Basin consists of a series of mountain ranges and intervening valleys (basins) that have no outlet to the sea. The most well-known of these basins is the Great Salt Lake. Several of the isolated ranges reach over 9,000' and the Deep Creeks hit 12,000'.

The Colorado Plateau, or Canyon Country, is like no other place on Earth. There are other deserts with areas of exposed sandstone, yes, but none where great rivers, like the Colorado, Green and San Juan, cut through with the meltwater of far mountains on their way to the sea.

In RARE II, the Forest Service identified 3,234,759 acres of roadless areas in Utah (most Utah National Forests are in the Wasatch and Uinta ranges). Conservationists, hoping to appear reasonable in a rather unfriendly social climate, asked for only 1.9 million acres as Wilderness. During what became a controversial process, the Utah Wilderness Association (UWA) negotiated a bill with the Utah Congressional delegation (all Republican and generally anti-wilderness at the time). The 1984 Utah Wilderness Act, as passed, included 749,550 acres of Wilderness (including a 460,000 acre High Uintas Wilderness).

UWA's critics complained that UWA had compromised too readily and had not included other conservationists in late discussions with the delegation. UWA replied that the bill was the best they could achieve at the time and that it was a starting point for additional Wilderness designations.

In January, 1986, the Bureau of Land Management released a massive draft environmental impact statement proposing Wilderness for 1.9 million acres out of 3.2 million acres of Wilderness Study Areas in Utah. Nearly 6 million acres had been considered for WSA status by BLM until 1980 and most observers felt that BLM's selection was marred by insouciant capriciousness at best or downright criminal disregard for the law — FLPMA — at worst.

Previous to the release of the Wilderness EIS, Utah conservation groups had been meeting to develop a single proposal. The UWA argued for a conservative, pragmatic approach, while the Utah Sierra Club, The Wilderness Society and the newly-formed Southern Utah Wilderness Alliance (SUWA) took a bolder stance. Negotiations finally broke down and the groups agreed to disagree. UWA proposed 3.8 million acres of BLM Wilderness while the other groups, forming the Utah Wilderness Coalition (UWC), called for 5.2 million. In a few cases, however, the UWA proposal for an area was larger than the UWC proposal. Earth First! offered a visionary proposal for 16 million acres of Wilderness in several very large preserves (this proposal includes Park Service and some Forest Service land as well). Local politicians, developers, miners, ranchers, jeepers and the rest of the rural establishment opposed the very concept of Wilderness.

BLM was overwhelmed with the responses it received (most favored the UWC proposal), and has yet to publish its final recommendations. When it does, negotiations will begin with the Utah Congressional delegation. Fortunately, Democrat Wayne Owens, who is friendly to Wilderness, is now a member of Congress from Utah. National conservation groups should make the fight to protect Utah's BLM lands a national campaign. Utah's National Parks (Canyon-lands, Capitol Reef, Arches, Zion, Bryce Canyon), Dinosaur National Monument and Glen Canyon National Recreation Area have not had Wilderness Areas established (although Congress has pro-

Deer Creek, Escalante roadless area, Utah.
Photo by Dave Foreman.

posals for all of them from the NPS and conservation groups).
Various bills to accomplish this continue to be discussed.

The threats to Utah's Big Outside are manifold. The
National Forests face logging, road-building and oil & gas exploration. The National Park units confront demands by local
boomers for more paved roads and tourist developments. Oil &
gas and tar sands development plans are a threat to Glen
Canyon NRA. BLM (and FS) areas suffer from continued overgrazing and developments like juniper chaining (to "improve"
forage), mineral exploration (uranium, tar sands, etc.), and
ORVs. Most distressing, however, is that weak-kneed BLM
managers have looked the other way as powerful mining companies and local politicians have illegally invaded wild
areas. *

Unfortunately, for wild things and those humans who love
them, Utah is still the frontier. At the close of World War II,
the largest single roadless area in the United States was a 9
million acre expanse of the Canyon Country centered on the
Colorado River. It stretched from the Paria River on the west
through Escalante and Capitol Reef to the Needles on the east.
The uranium boom began to carve it into smaller pieces and then
Glen Canyon Damn flooded its heart in the early 1960s.

Today the tragedy continues.

Colorado Plateau

*The Colorado Plateau is a spectacular but forbidding land-
scape of exposed sandstone slickrock carved by wind and water
into buttes, mesas, arches, natural bridges, goblins, hoodoos,
slot canyons, fingers, cliffs and grottoes. Big rivers, like the
Colorado, Green and San Juan, and smaller watercourses, like
Paria, Escalante, Muddy and Dirty Devil, cut phenomenal*

---

* It should be noted that this collusion was no monopoly of the
Reaganauts. Garry Wicks, Utah State BLM Director under the Carter
Administration and one of the most questionable individuals in the
history of the agency, drew WSA boundaries to coincide with the edges
of mining claims -- excluding the claims, even though there was no other
difference in the land on either side of the line. Conservationists
protested at the highest level but Secretary of the Interior Cecil Andrus
refused to look into it.

canyons deep into the rock. High mountain ranges rise above the red rock. It is little wonder that south-central and southeastern Utah was the last unexplored region in the lower 48 states. This is not a land tolerant of human frailty. As one patriarch noted, "It's a hell of a place to lose a cow." The Bureau of Land Management, National Park Service, Forest Service and Navajo Nation share management responsibility for the Big Outside here.

Escalante 620,000 acres

Glen Canyon NRA roadless	*327,380*
Capitol Reef NP roadless	*38,560*
BLM and intermixed state roadless	*254,000*

Description: South-central Utah north of "Lake" Powell (called "Foul" by true desert rats) and southeast of the town of Escalante. With Glen Canyon drowned beneath dead reservoir water, the Escalante is the heart of the Canyon Country. Sandstone arches, intricate and twisting canyons, slickrock uplands, pygmy forests of pinyon/juniper, sagebrush/grassland expanse, and the Escalante River with dense riparian forests of cottonwood, willow and Box Elder make this a wilderness of international significance. This extraordinary landscape reaches from Lake Foul on the south to the Burr Trail on the north, southern Capitol Reef on the east to the Hole in the Rock road on the west. Elevations reach 6,800' on Durffey's Mesa and King Bench in the northern part of the Escalante. The shoreline of the reservoir is at 3,700'. Bare rock covers up to 70% of large areas. A few Mule Deer and Mountain Lion reside in the Escalante, and Elk winter in the Deer Creek area in the northern part. Desert Bighorn Sheep were reintroduced to Glen Canyon NRA in 1981 and '82. Peregrine Falcon and Bald Eagle pass through, and seven other raptors, including the Golden Eagle, nest here. Introduced Brown and Rainbow Trout are in Deer and Boulder Creeks. Numerous archaeological sites have been discovered. This is a popular backpacking area.

Status: Portions of the Escalante will be protected by Wilderness designation despite the sulfurous anti-wilderness stance of locals in such backwater burgs as Escalante and Hanksville. (The good Saints of Escalante town have hung local "environmeddlers" in effigy from light poles on their main street.) However, the area will be broken into small preserves surrounded by lands open to exploitation unless conservation groups see the Escalante roadless area as a single Wilderness to be protected intact. By closing dirt roads, a three million acre Wilderness, stretching from Bullfrog to Bryce Canyon, could be protected.

The Pooh-Bahs of the local area and their hand puppets in Washington are screaming to pave the Burr Trail, which forms the northern border of much of this area. SUWA has fought hard against this but may have lost. A road across the heart of the Escalante was once proposed but appears to have died a welcome death. Oil & gas exploration, ORVs, pot hunting, firewood cutting, and mining for coal, uranium, tar sands and hardrock minerals are eternal threats to the entire area. An additional threat is BLM's penchant for "improving" road access to trailheads.

Cattle grazing is destroying riparian communities and canyon bottom mixed scrub/grassland communities throughout the area. Grazing cannot occur in a non-degrading manner in this arid country; the cows gotta go.

BLM proposes 110,680 acres for Wilderness; UWA 160,000 acres for BLM lands; UWC 163,380. The Park Service proposes 34,000 acres Wilderness and 4,580 acres Potential Wilderness Addition for the part of Capitol Reef NP in this roadless area, and 253,105 acres for Wilderness and 48,250 acres as Potential Wilderness Additions for the part of Glen Canyon NRA in this roadless area.

RM36: 8,890,000*

Kaiparowits 360,000 acres

BLM roadless (Fiftymile Mt WSA 4-79, etc.)	207,000
Glen Canyon NRA roadless	153,000

Description: South-central Utah south of the town of Escalante and north of Lake Foul. Kaiparowits Plateau (or Fiftymile Mountain) is a high, remote plateau cloaked in a vast pinyon/juniper pygmy forest in the north, with much exposed slickrock in the south. The Straight Cliffs above Fiftymile Bench form a remarkable escarpment along the Hole in the Rock road on the east side (which separates this road-less area from the Escalante roadless area). A dirt road di-vides the area from other large roadless areas on the west. The Rogers Canyon system cuts the plateau to the south. Woolsey Arch and other rock formations dot the area. The high eleva-tion is 7,650' along the Straight Cliffs; the elevation at the reservoir is 3,700'. Communities of Aspen, maple and oak occur in some of the canyons. Big Sagebrush grows throughout. Mule Deer are common. Other wildlife includes Mountain Lion, Desert Bighorn Sheep and Lewis Woodpecker. Numerous Anasazi archaeological sites have been identified.

Status: A great conservation victory of the 1970s was the defeat of coal stripmining and a huge powerplant on Kaiparo-wits. This ill-conceived Frankenstein's monster could be resur-rected and conservationists must be vigilant. Overgrazing, ORVing, looting of archaeological sites and fuelwood collecting are ongoing problems.

Because the last four miles of the Hole in the Rock Road are nothing more than a jeep trail over slickrock, it could be ar-gued that the Escalante and Kaiparowits form a single roadless area of one million acres. At the very least, the lower 20 miles of the road should be closed and a million acre Wilderness es-tablished. Better yet would be to close intervening dirt roads from the Henrys to Paria for a 3 million acre Preserve.

BLM proposes 92,441 acres for Wilderness, dropping the Straight Cliffs; UWA & UWC 146,000; the NPS proposes 58,755 acres Wilderness and 1,040 acres Potential Wilderness Addition for the GCNRA portion of Kaiparowits.

RM36: 8,890,000*

Boulder Mountain 110,000 acres
Dixie NF roadless   *110,000*

Description: South-central Utah south of Torrey. This is the wildest part of the superlative Aquarius Plateau. Largely over 10,000' (with some points at 11,000'), this deeply forested area rises above the Escalante country to the south and Capitol Reef to the east with vistas even extraordinary in a state known for scenery. Numerous lakes, streams and meadows; forests of Ponderosa Pine, Aspen, Limber Pine, Blue and Engelmann Spruce, Subalpine and White Fir, Douglas-fir and some Bristlecone Pine make this the finest high country left in Utah outside of the High Uintas. Wildlife includes Blue Grouse, Golden Eagle, Turkey, Mountain Lion, Bobcat, Mule Deer and Elk. This roadless area is separated from the Oak Creek-Steep Creek roadless area by a newly-paved state highway.

Status: The US Forest Service has been pillaging the Aquarius Plateau with logging and road-building during the last twenty years. Boulder Mountain is the last significant part of the high country remaining in a natural condition. Unfortunately, the FS now has evil plans for Boulder Mountain (which was not even inventoried in RARE II because it had allegedly been covered in a completed land use plan). A major campaign is needed to save it. SUWA has proposed the entire area (110,000 acres) for Wilderness and has sued the FS to stop the Windmill timber sale on Boulder Mountain.

Paria-Hackberry 186,000 acres

BLM WSA 4-247	*135,822*
Additional BLM, state roadless	*50,000*

Description: South-central Utah south of Bryce Canyon National Park. This classic Utah canyon country in the upper reaches of Paria Creek and its tributaries, including Hackberry Canyon, has numerous arches, natural bridges and other sandstone erosional features. No Mans Mesa, rising isolated one thousand feet above surrounding lands, has relict (ungrazed) vegetation. Elevations run from 4,700' up to 7,200'. The primary vegetation in this slickrock area is pinyon/juniper with some Big Sagebrush, and Ponderosa Pine at higher elevations. The area includes 50 miles of riparian vegetation. Wildlife is sparse, featuring Mule Deer and a few Cougar; Speckled Dace inhabit the streams. Ravens croak overhead.

Status: Grazing is a continuing impact. Oil & gas exploration threatens. ORVs are allowed up the Paria River and Hackberry Creek, and jeep trails and rough dirt roads penetrate the roadless area. A potentially serious threat is the possible location of a uranium mill (to process uranium from the Grand Canyon) within the southern boundary of this roadless area.

Paria-Hackberry is the western end of a wild backcountry area of 3 million acres, including Capitol Reef and the Henrys on the east and Escalante, Wahweap & Kaiparowits in the center, that is broken only by jeep trails and a few dirt roads. This entire region should be designated as a single Wilderness Area and all vehicles prohibited.

BLM proposes only 59,270 acres for Wilderness (excluding the Paria River); UWA 136,000; UWC 158,750.

*RM36: 8,890,000**

Wahweap-Canaan Peak 367,000 acres

BLM WSA 4-248 (Wahweap)	144,166
BLM WSA 4-78 (Death Ridge)	66,710
BLM WSA 4-77 (Mud Spring Canyon)	41,116
Dixie NF, state, private and additional	
* BLM roadless*	110,000
Glen Canyon NRA roadless	5,500

Description: South-central Utah north of Glen Canyon City on the western end of the Kaiparowits Plateau and leading up to the high country near the Aquarius Plateau. The Cockscomb, a sharp, double-ribbed, north-south ridge, forms the western part of the area and has the southern high point of 6,742' near The Gut. Coyote, Wahweap, Last Chance and Warm Creeks cut the plateau to the south; the low point of 4,040' is at the confluence of Coyote and Wahweap. The northern part of the area consists of benches and narrow ridges cut by deep canyons. Cretaceous bedrock with fossils, including dinosaur bones, underlies this northern part. Canaan Peak, in the Dixie NF, is the high point of the area at 9,293'. This is a diverse area for the canyonlands, with vegetation primarily of pinyon/juniper, Shadscale, desert shrub and Big Sagebrush, except near Canaan Peak where there is Ponderosa Pine, Engelmann Spruce, White Fir and Douglas-fir. Some of the junipers are 1,400 years old. There are isolated ungrazed mesas and two sensitive plant species. Wildlife is limited but includes Mule Deer, Pronghorn, Mountain Lion, Black Bear and Blue Grouse (north). Up to 13 species of raptors nest in the area. An abandoned shack on Four Mile Bench is believed by locals to be haunted.

Status: Threats include coal mining, oil & gas leasing and ORVs. A few cherrystem dirt roads and jeep trails penetrate, but it is a unified roadless area. BLM divided it into three WSAs based on these intrusions. A good example is the Four Mile Bench dirt road which BLM indicates cutting the area in half from west to east. In actuality, the dirt road only penetrates half way and a full nine miles of wild mesa and canyon landscape connect Wahweap WSA to the Death Ridge and Mud Spring Canyon WSAs to the north. Conservation groups should not be misled by BLM and should propose a unified Wilderness Area here. (Although we would propose that this entire roadless area be part of a three million acre Escalante Wilderness. See Paria-Hackberry for general discussion).

BLM proposes only 70,380 acres for Wilderness (excluding the eastern portion for coal mining); UWA 134,000 (Wahweap), 62,870 (Death Ridge), 51,000 (Mud Spring Canyon); UWC 151,240 (Wahweap), 56,000 (Death Ridge), 62,000 (Mud Spring Canyon). The NPS does not propose any Wilderness for the GCNRA portion.
RM36: 8,890,000*

Paria Canyon 290,000 acres (also in Arizona)
See Arizona for description and status.

Steep Creek-Oak Creek 173,000 acres

Capitol Reef National Park roadless	66,320
BLM WSA 4-61; additional BLM and state roadless	36,500
Dixie NF roadless	70,000

Description: South-central Utah northeast of the town of Boulder. This area consists of the upper Muley Twist Canyon-Oyster Shell Reef portion of the Waterpocket Fold and Oak Creek in Capitol Reef National Park, the upper parts of Deer Creek and The Gulch on BLM and Dixie NF land, and the east slope of Boulder Mountain on the Dixie NF. The high point is 9,670' on the Dixie NF; The Gulch drops to 5,400' at the Burr Trail. The Gulch portion is a northern extension of the Escalante country. Below the slickrock, cottonwoods and willows line the creeks; higher, pinyon/juniper and Big Sagebrush grade into Ponderosa Pine, Aspen and a bit of mixed conifer.

Wildlife is limited and characteristic of the Colorado Plateau, although Elk are present and Mule Deer find critical winter habitat. Reintroduction of Bighorn Sheep is proposed for the Park. Seven raptor species nest within the area.

Status: This area is separated from the huge Escalante roadless area by the Burr Trail, a dirt road currently proposed for paving by the political powers of southern Utah. Not only should this paving be fought (as SUWA and other groups are doing), but the Burr Trail should be closed to vehicles in order to include Steep Creek-Oak Creek in a 3 million acre Escalante Wilderness. Oil & gas, uranium, overgrazing, ORVs, looting of Anasazi ruins, and poaching threaten this area. The FS wants to log ancient Ponderosa Pine in high portions of the roadless area; conservation groups are appealing.

BLM proposes an 18,350 acre Steep Creek Wilderness; UWA 20,000; UWC 21,900. The NPS proposes two units of Wilderness (28,110 + 4,470 acres Potential; and 35,010 +320 acres Potential) in Capitol Reef NP. SUWA is developing a Wilderness proposal for the NF lands.

RM36: 8,890,000*

Mt. Pennel 170,000 acres

BLM WSA 5-248 and state roadless	162,000
Capitol Reef National Park roadless	8,180

Description: South-central Utah north of Bullfrog Marina in the Henry Mountains. The last mountain range in the 48 states to be discovered by Anglos, the Henrys are sharp, ragged peaks broken by narrow canyons. They were formed by massive volcanic intrusions pushing up through many sedimentary layers. Mt. Pennel, the second highest peak in the range and the highest in this roadless area, rises out of badlands and slickrock to 11,371'. Ten miles of perennial streams cross the area. Lower elevation vegetation consists of grass and sagebrush. Above 7,000', oak, pine, spruce, Subalpine Fir, Douglas-fir and Aspen form a complete vegetation gradient for the region. *Sclerocactus writhiae* is an Endangered cactus in the area. A free-roaming Bison herd makes this mountain range unique in Utah. Other wildlife includes Mule Deer, Coyote and Mountain Lion.

Status: Mineral and oil & gas exploration, ORVs, overgrazing and inane opposition to Wilderness from locals threaten the Henrys. An immediate threat is the BLM's plan to chain several thousand acres of pinyon/juniper. (Chaining involves dragging a ship's anchor chain between two bulldozers to rip out the vegetation to "open" it up for improved cattle grazing. BLM and the FS commonly employ this "range improvement" technique on pygmy forests in the Southwest and Great Basin.) SUWA is appealing. BLM hopes to double grazing use in the Henrys through chaining, fencing and new water developments.

The Henrys should be added to a 3 million acre Escalante Wilderness by closing dirt roads.

BLM opposes Wilderness; UWA calls for a 99,000 acre Wilderness; UWC 143,125. The NPS proposes 6,050 acres for Wilderness and 700 acres as Potential Wilderness Additions for Capitol Reef NP.

RM36: 8,890,000*

Mt. Ellen 128,000 acres

BLM WSA 5-238 and state roadless   128,000

Description: The Henry Mountains just north of Mt. Pennel (see for general description) in south-central Utah. Elevations in this roadless area drop from 11,615' to 4,600'. The Henrys are in the center of the area with the highest average visibility in the United States; views in all directions are exceptional. Mt. Ellen is the southeastern limit for the Great Basin variety of Bristlecone Pine.

Status: Same as Mt. Pennel. Mainstream conservation groups should at least propose the closure of a few dirt roads to combine Mt. Ellen with Mt. Pennel for a single Wilderness Area. Bolder conservationists should insist that the Henrys be part of a 3 million acre Escalante Wilderness.

BLM proposes a 58,480 acre Wilderness; UWA 97,000; UWC 128,350.

RM36: 8,890,000*

Little Rockies 145,000 acres

Glen Canyon NRA roadless   60,000

BLM WSA 5-247 and intermixed state roadless	85,000

Description: South-central Utah between the Henry Mountains and Lake Foul north of Bullfrog. The Little Rockies are considered to be part of the Henrys. Mt. Holmes and Mt. Ellsworth (8,235') are the high points. (See Mt. Pennel for general description.) *Dalea epica*, a species of indigo brush in the area, is a candidate for Endangered species listing. Blackbrush is the predominant vegetation in the lower elevations of the Henrys, although over half the area is barren rock outcrop. Some stream stretches have perennial flows. Wildlife is not abundant but includes Desert Bighorn Sheep.

Status: See Mt. Pennel. BLM proposes a 38,700 acre Wilderness; UWA 52,000; UWC 60,070. The NPS proposes 34,795 acres for Wilderness and 640 acres as Potential Wilderness Addition for Glen Canyon NRA.

*RM36: 8,890,000**

Wayne Wonderland 188,000 acres	
Capitol Reef NP roadless	*94,000*
Fishlake NF roadless	*54,000*
BLM and state roadless	*40,000*

Description: South-central Utah north of Torrey. The high point is the 11,306' summit of Thousand Lake Mountain; the low point is under 5,000' in the South Desert. The topography of this roadless area varies from the forested slopes of Thousand Lake Mountain down to the slickrock of the Waterpocket Fold in the north end of Capitol Reef National Park and out into the badlands of the South Desert. Several intermittent streams flow across the unit, west to east, from the high country into the Fremont River. The Park Service describes it as "perhaps the most ruggedly beautiful and remote rockscape in America." The streams cut deep, twisting canyons through yellow, orange, buff, red, brown, tan, white, black, grey and green rocks. The South Desert has volcanic features. Cactus and Fremont Barberry predominate in the desert, with pinyon/juniper and then oak, Ponderosa Pine, Douglas-fir, then Aspen, Engelmann Spruce and Subalpine Fir growing higher up. A handful of lakes sparkle in the high country. Cottonwood and willows grow along the watercourses. Critters in the NF include Elk, Black Bear, Mountain Lion, Mule Deer and raptors. Wildlife populations are low in the lower elevations; species are representative of the Colorado Plateau.

Status: Several poor dirt roads are cherrystemmed into the NF portion; and there are some jeep trails in the Park and BLM parts. Capitol Reef National Park was saddled with commercial livestock grazing at its creation. Fortunately, a dedicated and creative staff at Capitol Reef has developed a plan to buy out more than 90% of the commercial AUMs (animal unit months). This program will remove cattle from all but a small part of the Park.

The FS has proposed a land exchange which would transfer part of their land in the roadless area to a private individual. The Park Service proposes only a 64,290 acre Wilderness (and 4,240 acres of Potential Wilderness Additions); BLM and the FS propose no Wilderness. Only minor dirt roads separate this area from the Muddy Creek area in the southern portion of the San Rafael Swell. A million acre San Rafael Swell Wilderness could be established by closing these unnecessary roads.

RM36: 1,930,000*

Muddy Creek 242,000 acres

BLM WSA 6-7 and additional BLM roadless	240,000
Capital Reef National Park roadless	1,610

Description: Central Utah in the San Rafael Swell south of I-70, west of Green River. Elevations drop from 7,000' to 5,000'. Sandstone, limestone and shale formations produce a highly colorful topography here with tight, twisting canyons, and slickrock. Vegetation is mainly composed of pinyon/juniper and desert shrub, but large areas are rock outcrop. Two Endangered plants inhabit the area and six others are being considered for Endangered status. Muddy Creek is a perennial stream which has cut a canyon several hundred feet deep. It offers an exciting float trip — "technical innertubing" — during spring runoff through the seven-mile long sheer gorge known as the "Chute of Muddy Creek." Water is otherwise scarce. Low populations of Mule Deer and Desert Bighorn are present. Other wildlife (Bobcat, Coyote, fox, Prairie Falcon, etc.) is characteristic of the Colorado Plateau woodland. Roundtail Chub and Speckled Dace live in the river.

Status: There are potential threats of uranium mining and oil & gas leasing. ORVers have discovered the San Rafael country and are ripping up the canyons. BLM proposes two small Wilderness Areas: 31,400 acres for Muddy Creek and 25,335 for Crack Canyon (separated by a jeep trail); UWA concurs with two units: 63,500 for Muddy Creek and 49,500 for Crack; UWC recognizes the unity of this area and calls for a single 215,000 acre Wilderness.

*RM36: 1,930,000**

Sids Mountain 101,000 acres

BLM WSA 6-23, state and private roadless   101,000

Description: Central Utah west of Green River and north of I-70 in the San Rafael Swell. The colorful badlands and mesas of this part of the San Rafael Swell are cut by an intricate complex of canyons with massive sandstone walls, long and twisting routes, and fingered tributary canyons. Between the canyons and mesa top are flat to rolling parklands; unusual rock formations are scattered throughout the area. Elevations range from 6,800' down to 5,100'. Pinyon/juniper and desert scrub are the primary vegetative communities. Small pockets of Douglas-fir grow high on Sids Mountain. The perennially flowing San Rafael River has cottonwoods and offers an excellent canoeing adventure through its "Little Grand Canyon." Desert Bighorn Sheep were reintroduced to this area in 1978, and it is considered crucial habitat (Utah's second largest population of Desert Bighorn Sheep live in the San Rafael Swell region). Peregrine Falcon and Bald Eagle are present as are Mountain Lion.

Status: Oil & gas exploration presents a threat. Conservation groups and Joe Bauman, a popular columnist for the *Deseret News*, have proposed a new National Park for the San Rafael which would include this roadless area. ORVs are a major problem — the BLM's Wilderness proposal of 78,408 acres cuts the area into four units with ORV corridors effectively destroying it as a Wilderness. The UWA proposes 85,000 acres and UWC 90,000. By closing jeep trails and minor dirt roads, a

half-million acre Wilderness National Park could be established north of the Interstate.
  RM36: 1,930,000*

Canyonlands 805,000 acres

Designated Dark Canyon Wilderness (Manti-La Sal NF)	45,000
Canyonlands NP and Glen Canyon NRA roadless	410,000
BLM and intermixed state roadless	320,000
Manti-La Sal NF roadless	30,000

Description: Southeastern Utah southwest of Moab. One of the great Wildernesses of North America is formed where the Colorado and Green Rivers cut through sandstone mesas to their confluence. Cataract Canyon, Dark Canyon, the Maze, Fins, Needles, Island in the Sky, Orange Cliffs, Horseshoe Canyon, Labyrinth Canyon and Stillwater Canyon are some of the renowned features of this wonderland of sandstone slickrock, arches, buttes, cliffs and canyons. Elevations are from 7,700' down to the Lake Foul reservoir line at 3,700'. Dark Canyon is 2,000' deep. In addition to the Colorado and Green Rivers, perennial water is found in several canyons, including Dark. Large areas of this vast wildland are very dry with springs far apart. Low precipitation produces a pygmy forest of pinyon/juniper with Big Sagebrush and Blackbrush, while barren rock covers much of the landscape. In moist areas in the canyons, riparian "jungles" are formed of dense reed grass, Trailing Virgins Bower, willow, tamarisk (an invading and destructive small tree from the Middle East, also known as salt cedar) and cottonwood. Scattered stands of Douglas-fir and Ponderosa Pine grow in the higher elevations. Wildlife includes Bighorn Sheep, Pronghorn, Mountain Lion, Black Bear, Ringtail, Pinyon Mouse, Red-spotted Toad, Midget Faded Rattlesnake and other species of the Colorado Plateau woodland. The Colorado and Green Rivers support the Endangered Colorado Squawfish and Threatened Razorback Sucker. Anasazi archaeological sites, including some of the finest rock art in North America, abound. The visual range exceeds 100 miles in the summer. It is a popular backpacking and river running area.

Status: Jeep trails penetrate the area (White Rim, Flint Trail, Elephant Hill); some are significant intrusions, on the borderline of being "roads." They should be closed. Motorboats are currently permitted on the rivers. They should be prohibited. Uranium mining, ORVs, pot hunting, poaching and overgrazing are continuing threats. Major threats arising in recent years include proposed tar sands mining on the west side and the siting of a nuclear waste repository on the east side (now slated for Nevada but the vagaries of American politics could still lead to its placement here). The major obstacle to protection of this area has been its fragmentation into separate pieces based on managing agency. Conservation groups should at least propose an intact million acre Canyonlands Wilderness. Far better would be a single two and a half million acre Wilderness established by closing several dirt roads.

In 1936, Bob Marshall identified a 9 million acre roadless area stretching from the Canyonlands to Escalante. In 1936, Secretary of the Interior Harold Ickes proposed a 4 million acre National Monument along the Colorado River including Glen Canyon, the Escalante, and the area up to what is now Canyonlands NP. Glen Canyon Damn ripped the heart out of that great wilderness but we can still save the pieces. An 800,000 acre Canyonlands National Park was proposed in the 1960s (after Glen Canyon Damn) but late compromises cut the Park to 337,570 acres. There is a possibility that the Park will be enlarged.

BLM proposes 155,590 acres of Wilderness in 5 units; UWA 169,030 for BLM areas; UWC 229,620 for BLM areas. The Park Service proposes 195,060 acres for Wilderness and 22,740 acres as Potential Wilderness Additions in 7 units divided by jeep trails and the Colorado & Green Rivers in Canyonlands NP; and 72,005 acres Wilderness and 26,925 as Potential Wilderness Additions in GCNRA. Conservationists propose closing many of the jeep trail corridors for a single 304,320 acre Canyonlands NP Wilderness (which includes the NPS Salt Creek roadless area described below).

RM36: 8,890,000*

Salt Creek <u>124,000 acres</u>

Canyonlands National Park roadless   *63,360*

BLM WSA 6-169	25,780
BLM WSA 6-167	32,640
Manti-La Sal NF roadless	2,000

Description: Southeastern corner of Canyonlands National Park in southeastern Utah south of Moab. This area is cut off from the main Canyonlands roadless area by a primitive dirt road. It features the Needles, Salt Creek, Six Shooter Peak, Bridger Jack Mesa, slickrock domes, pinyon/juniper woodland, open sagebrush parks and a small Mule Deer population. Salt Creek cuts 600' deep into the sandstone. The high point is 7,400'. See Canyonlands for full description.

Status: This area should be made part of a larger Canyonlands Wilderness by closing the dirt road. BLM proposes a 5,290 acre Bridger Jack Mesa Wilderness; UWA 42,690 for BLM areas; UWC 58,420. The NPS proposes a 55,640 acre Wilderness with 7,720 acres of Potential Wilderness Additions. Conservation groups would add this area to a single Canyonlands NP Wilderness.

RM36: 8,890,000*

Dirty Devil-Fiddler Butte 413,000 acres

BLM Dirty Devil WSA 5-236A	63,560
BLM French Spring-Happy Canyon WSA 5-236B	25,640
BLM Fiddler Butte WSA 5-241	73,100
Glen Canyon NRA roadless	51,000
Additional BLM, state roadless	200,000

Description: Southeastern Utah east of Hanksville and west of Canyonlands National Park. This is a region of slickrock cut by thousand foot deep canyons. Mesas, buttes, spires, domes, sand dunes and benchlands characterize the area. Most of the area is bare rock; Blackbrush, pinyon/juniper and small riparian areas are the vegetative communities elsewhere. Cliffs are graced by hanging gardens of Eastwood Monkey Flower, Colorado Columbine, Maidenhair Fern and Giant Helleborine. The Dirty Devil River is perennial, as are a number of springs and seeps. Wildlife includes Desert Bighorn Sheep, Pronghorn, Mule Deer, Beaver, Dwarf Shrew, Golden Eagle, Bell's Vireo and Chuckwalla (at its northern limit).

Raptors find excellent nesting sites on the cliffs. Superb panels of rock art remain. The generally unpolluted air of this region gives it outstanding visibility.

Status: In 1976, as BLM began their wilderness review, they set aside more than 400,000 acres in the Dirty Devil for consideration. Unfortunately, a sleazy alliance between BLM and the uranium industry allowed the Cotter Corporation into the area. Between 1976 and 1980, more than 50 miles of road were bladed into the WSA and hundreds of exploratory wells were punched. The Dirty Devil country is the showcase example of BLM malfeasance in their wilderness program. The Dirty Devil is also threatened by tar sands and oil & gas development.

The Dirty Devil area should be restored at the expense of Cotter Corporation and both BLM and Cotter employees should face felony charges and prison sentences. Years of hard labor on a chain gang repairing the damage they did would be a fitting punishment. The minor dirt road separating the Dirty Devil region from the Canyonlands complex should be closed and a 2.5 million acre Wilderness established.

BLM proposes a 61,000 acre Dirty Devil Wilderness and a 32,700 acre Fiddler Butte Wilderness; UWA proposes separate 61,000 acre Dirty Devil, 25,000 French Spring-Happy Canyon, and 87,000 Fiddler Butte Wildernesses; UWC proposes a single Dirty Devil-French Spring 169,800 acre Wilderness and a separate 85,000 BLM Fiddler Butte Wilderness (BLM opposes Wilderness in the French Spring area because it might have potential for tar sands development). The NPS proposes a 21,625 acre Wilderness in GCNRA. This is, however, a single roadless area, albeit broken by very poor (and illegal) "roads."
RM36: 8,890,000*

Mancos Mesa 193,000 acres

Glen Canyon NRA roadless	*84,000*
BLM WSA 6-181	*109,000*

Description: Southeastern Utah east of Bullfrog Marina across Lake Foul. High point is 6,500'; low is 3,700' on the reservoir. Several canyons (with depths up to 800') cut Mancos Mesa and drop into the former Colorado River canyon (now Lake Foul). Most of the surface is Navajo sandstone. Vegetation is largely Blackbrush with scattered pinyon/juniper, and cottonwoods in the canyons. Wildlife includes Desert Bighorn Sheep, deer mice, cottontail, Common Raven, Canyon Wren and Side-blotched Lizard.

Status: BLM allowed thirty miles of uranium exploration road to be bladed into the Mancos Mesa area while they were studying it for Primitive Area designation in the 1970s. BLM proposes 46,120 acres for Wilderness; UWA concurs; UWC proposes a 108,700 acre BLM Wilderness. The NPS proposes a 41,700 acre Wilderness for GCNRA.

RM36: 8,890,000*

Wilson Mesa 188,000 acres

Glen Canyon National Recreation Area roadless	*108,000*
BLM roadless	*80,000*

Description: Southeastern Utah in the crotch between the Colorado and San Juan arms of Lake Foul. This is an area of classic slickrock mesas and canyons, which includes the Hole in the Rock trail.

Status: BLM did not designate this roadless area a WSA, and opposes Wilderness for it. ORVs, pot hunting, overgrazing, poaching — the standard threats for Utah — continue to encroach on the area. UWA proposes a 73,000 acre Nokai Dome-Mikes Canyon Wilderness on BLM land; UWC 80,000 BLM. The NPS proposes a 81,910 acre Wilderness with 640 acres of Potential Wilderness Additions.

RM36: 8,890,000*

San Juan River 371,000 acres

BLM Grand Gulch Instant Study Area	*107,920*
Glen Canyon NRA roadless	*32,000*
Navajo Indian Reservation roadless	*170,000*
Additional BLM, state roadless	*61,000*

Description: Southeastern Utah west of Mexican Hat. The canyon of the San Juan River includes the famed Goosenecks and wonderful side canyons like Grand Gulch, Slickhorn and Oljeto. Cedar Mesa rises north of the river. Imposing walls of sheer sandstone, arches, pools, hanging gardens, waterfalls and

views of Monument Valley to the south from high points are
some of the features of this area. The San Juan is a fast, red
river noted for its "sand waves" and is popular for rafting.
Backpacking is popular in Grand Gulch. Elevations drop from
6,400' to the reservoir at 3,700' (the largest rapids on the San
Juan were drowned by Lake Foul). Pinyon/juniper, sagebrush
and Blackbrush communities adorn the mesas; elsewhere there
is considerable bare rock. Cottonwood and willow populate
bottomlands in the canyons. Low populations of Desert Bighorn
Sheep, Mule Deer and Mountain Lion live here. Other wildlife
includes Spotted Skunk, Ringtail, Midget Faded Rattlesnake,
Bald Eagle and the Threatened Razorback Sucker. Temperatures range from 110° to below zero. Anasazi sites — some as yet
unmolested by Bishop Love and his pot-hunting cronies —
abound.

Status: Oil & gas leases, firewood cutting, ORVs, pothunt-
ing and excessive recreational use (rafting and backpacking) are
problems. BLM proposes a 105,520 acre Grand Gulch Wilderness; UWA 131,120 on BLM; UWC 136,120 BLM. Grand Gulch
was one of the few BLM Primitive Areas established prior to
the passage of FLPMA. As such it was made an Instant Study
Area (ISA) by FLPMA. The NPS proposes a 13,010 acre
Wilderness with 360 acres of Potential Wilderness Additions.
The Navajo Tribe should be encouraged to protect the wilderness qualities of their portion of this area.
RM36: 8,890,000*

Navajo Mountain 850,000 acres (also in Arizona)
See Arizona for description and status.

Northeastern Utah
*Northeastern Utah includes superlative high mountains
and equally superlative deep canyons north of the Colorado
Plateau in the Central & Southern Rocky Mountains Ecoregions.
The Wasatch & Ashley NFs, Dinosaur NM, the Unitah-Ouray
Indian Reservation and the BLM are involved here.*

High Uintas 843,000 acres
*Designated High Uintas Wilderness (Ashley &
    Wasatch NFs)*   460,000

Additional Ashley & Wasatch NFs roadless   383,000

Description: East of Salt Lake City in northeastern Utah. The Uintas are the largest east-west mountain range in the 48 states and the finest mountain area in Utah. Kings Peak at 13,528' is the highest point in Utah, and many other peaks exceed 13,000' and 12,000' (the crest averages 11,000' high). The peaks are distinctively red. Elevations drop to 8,000' in the river canyons. This landscape, shaped by glaciation, has over 250 lakes and 2,000 tarns, many meadows, rushing streams, a large area above timberline, scenic cirques and basins, and extensive Lodgepole Pine forests on its lower slopes. Other vegetation includes Engelmann Spruce, Douglas-fir, Subalpine Fir, Aspen and large expanses of alpine tundra. Black Bear, Elk, Moose (southernmost natural population in North America), Wolverine, River Otter, Canadian Lynx, Pine Marten, Pika, Mink, Mountain Lion, Osprey, Goshawk and Pileated Woodpecker are some of the distinctive mammals and birds; biological (not political) potential for Grizzly and Gray Wolf reintroduction is excellent. Arctic Grayling, Rainbow and Golden Trout (introduced), and native Cutthroat populate the streams. The first rendezvous of the mountain men was held on the north slope of the Uintas in 1825.

Status: The lower elevation Lodgepole Pine forests (largely left out of the Wilderness) are falling victim to Forest Service timbering and roading. The Forest Service is also promoting oil & gas leasing on the north slope, and oil companies like AMOCO are moving in. Some areas adjacent to the Wilderness boundary have already been leased. These north slope forests are crucial to the overall ecological integrity of the Uintas because they provide necessary wildlife habitat. UWA has made protection of the threatened parts of the Uintas a priority, although a national effort is needed. Acid rain has become a problem recently.

One bit of good news is that the Wasatch NF has closed three domestic sheep allotments and plans to reintroduce Rocky Mountain Bighorn Sheep.

RM27: 1,109,120

Lakes 112,000 acres

Wasatch NF roodless   *112,000*

Description: East of Salt Lake City in northeastern Utah. This lake dotted high country in the western end of the Uinta Mountains is separated from the High Uintas roadless area by a narrow paved road over a 10,600' high pass. See High Uintas for general description.

Status: The Forest Service has established a 60,000 acre backcountry area with no logging. Oil & gas leasing is a threat here as it is in the High Uintas. The Utah Wilderness Association is campaigning for the restoration of several alpine lakes that were enlarged with dams for irrigation storage early in the century.

Yampa-Green 250,000 acres (also in Colorado)
See Colorado for description and status.

Desolation Canyon 763,000 acres

BLM WSAs (68A/68B/67) with intermixed state & private	*502,100*
BLM roadless north of Sand Wash	*59,000*
State & private roadless to west	*12,000*
Uintah & Ouray Indian Reservation & Navy Oil Reserve roadless	*190,000*

Description: Eastern Utah north of the town of Green River and south of Ouray. This multifaceted and wildlife-rich area centered on Desolation & Gray Canyons of the Green River is beloved by boaters as the "Green River Wilderness." It is far more than simply a marvelous wilderness float trip, however. The UWA points out that only the Grand Canyon forms a more extensive canyon system. Moreover, the high country of the Tavaputs Plateau is sublime in its own right. Desolation Canyon is over a mile deep in places. Elevations vary from 4,000' along the river to 9,600' on the Roan Cliffs. The thousand foot high Book Cliffs are to the south and west. Balanced rocks, arches, waterfalls, caves and alcoves dot the river canyon. The high country has Douglas-fir, Ponderosa Pine, mountain mahogany and a few Aspen stands; healthy riparian forests of Fremont Cottonwood, willow and Box Elder grow

along the river; and large areas of pinyon/juniper, Big Sage-
brush/Shadscale and Black Greasewood flourish in the mid
elevations.   (There are 13 vegetative types in the area.)
Several side canyons to the Green form impressive drainages of
their own: Rock Creek, Jacks Creek, Flat Canyon, Range Creek,
Price River and Rattlesnake Canyon.   Elk, Black Bear, Mountain Lion, Rocky Mountain Bighorn Sheep, Goshawk, Peregrine
Falcon, Prairie Falcon, Golden Eagle, Bald Eagle, Long-billed
Curlew, Yellow-billed Cuckoo, White-faced Ibis and Midget
Faded Rattlesnake are among the sensitive species in this area.
Bony-tailed Chub, Humpback Chub and Colorado Squawfish
are Endangered fish species which find some of their best remaining habitat in this part of the Green.   Channel Catfish are
abundant and Rock Creek provides a high quality fishery for
Rainbow and Brown Trout (non-native).   Other wildlife includes a large herd of Mule Deer (the bottoms provide important winter range), Beaver, Turkey, Ruffed and Blue Grouse,
Lazuli Bunting, Lewis Woodpecker, many ducks and geese, Collared Lizard and Leopard Lizard.   Archaeological sites of the
Fremont culture include major petroglyph panels and ancient
granaries.

Status: Conservation groups have justly made this area a
priority in the BLM Wilderness review. Efforts should also be
made to gain tribal Wilderness designation for the east bank of
the canyon. Motors are allowed on rafts; these should be prohibited.   Additionally, some float trip operators use charter
flights to haul their passengers into Sand Wash. These flights
go over the roadless area. Oil & gas, coal and other mining are
possible threats to the roadless area and have already impacted considerable acreage around the roadless area.   Dirt
roads cherrystemmed into the roadless area should be closed —
particularly the one from Swaseys Rapid upriver to Nefertiti.

Float trips generally put in at Sand Wash, more than 30
river miles south of the last bridge over the river at Ouray. For
this reason, some conservation groups and the BLM have ignored the superb wilderness character of the river and adjacent
benchlands and flats north of Sand Wash. This area, while not
as spectacular as the deep canyon, is in some respects even
wilder and provides finer wildlife habitat, including rookeries
for Great Blue Heron and Black-crowned Night Heron, Prairie

Falcon eyries, and numerous waterfowl (the Ouray National Wildlife Refuge is just to the north). Indeed, the wildest riverine bottomlands in the West may be along this stretch of the Green. These 30 miles of the Green above Sand Wash are a contiguous part of the Desolation roadless area and should be included in Wilderness recommendations and considered for an expansion of the Ouray NWR. If not protected, roads, oil & gas, livestock grazing, and the other slow but steady destroyers of wilderness will whittle away, and this part of the Green will not long remain wild. It will be another sad chapter in "The Place No One Knew" story.

Additional wildlands are separated from the Desolation Canyon wilderness by dirt roads (such as the Book Cliffs area discussed below). These primitive roads should be closed and a 2.2 million acre Wilderness established.

BLM proposes a 242,000 acre Desolation Canyon Wilderness and a 33,690 acre Turtle Canyon Wilderness; UWA calls for a 600,000 acre Wilderness in two units for Desolation and the Book Cliffs; UWC 362,000 for Deso (but including some of the river north of Sand Wash) and 33,800 for Turtle Canyon. Additionally, the Green has been proposed for National Wild & Scenic River designation. It richly deserves this protection as well as Wilderness, but again, the less-scenic though ecologically-richer bottomlands north of Sand Wash and including all of the Ouray NWR should be included.

RM36: 2,420,000*

Book Cliffs 300,000 acres	
BLM WSAs (060-100B/C)	136,040
State, Uintah-Ouray IR and additional	
BLM roadless	164,000

Description: Eastern Utah north of 1-70 and immediately east of the Desolation roadless area (a minor dirt road separates them) in the Book and Roan Cliffs. Deep canyons slice the area to the north, south and east. Flat-topped benches and ridges form the uplands. The high point is 8,050' and elevations drop to 5,500'. Vegetation varies from desert shrub and pinyon/juniper to forests of Douglas-fir and Ponderosa Pine. Willow Creek forms a striking canyon system on the north in the state and Indian land. See Desolation for a more complete description.

Status: In its inventory, BLM hacked this area into several units based on jeep trails in Cottonwood and other canyons (it claimed they were roads), and now, kowtowing to the oil industry, stoutly opposes any Wilderness designation. Oil & gas exploration and development surround the area and threaten it with roads, drilling and other impacts. The Book Cliffs State Forest and the Indian lands are an integral part of this wilderness and should be included in any proposal.

The UWA includes most of the BLM land here in their two-unit Desolation Wilderness proposal; indeed, the dirt road between the two should be closed. Other dirt roads should also be closed for a single 2.2 million acre Wilderness. UWC proposes three separate Wilderness Areas of 61,000 (Coal Canyon), 50,000 (Flume Canyon) and 20,350 acres (Spruce Canyon).

RM36: 2,420,000*

Black Ridge Canyons   115,000 acres (also in Colorado)

See Colorado for description and status.

Western Utah

The western third of Utah lies in the Great Basin and is more akin to Nevada than to the rest of Utah. Desert ranges crowned with Bristlecone Pine rise high above salt flats in the basins below. Little happens here. A few paved highways and dirt roads built for mining or grazing cut through the valleys and penetrate canyons in the mountains. Additional areas in the Utah Great Basin beyond those described here could become large roadless areas with minor road closures. In the southwest, the Southern Wasatch Highlands and Colorado Plateau intermingle with the Great Basin around Zion National Park. The military, BLM, Dixie NF and Zion NP are the primary players here.

North Great Salt Lake Desert 850,000 acres

BLM (with scattered state & private) roadless	540,000
Hill AFB roadless	160,000

Wendover AFB roadless	*150,000*

Description: West of Salt Lake City and north of I-80 in northwestern Utah. This surreal landscape of glistening salt flats became a huge, shallow lake during the wet years of the early '80s, with waves lapping against the sandbags on the Interstate, reminding us that this is the bed of Pleistocene Lake Bonneville. Elevations are between 4,000' and 5,000'. Bonneville Speedway is outside the roadless area on the western edge. The BLM, with uncharacteristic eloquence, describes the area thusly: "Ecologically and geologically the North Salt Desert is unique. To some it is desolate though beautiful; to some a place to be avoided and feared; to others 'A kind of goodness in itself that is worth preserving.' It is in fact a historical narrative, a map and skeletal remains of the landlocked sea that once was Lake Bonneville."

Status: The North Salt Desert is a victim of the "Sierra Club Calendar" syndrome. Although BLM identified a very large WSA here, conservation groups were content to drop it from any proposal for Wilderness because it was "just salt flats." Status of the Air Force Bases is uncertain (they are used for air operations).

RM36: 1,700,000

South Great Salt Lake Desert 1,144,000 acres (also in Nevada)

Wendover Air Force Range and	
Dugway Proving Grounds (UT) roadless	*842,000*
Wendover USAF Auxiliary Field (NV) roadless	*12,000*
BLM roadless (UT)	*275,000*
BLM roadless (NV)	*12,000*
Fish Springs NWR roadless (UT)	*3,200*

Description: Western Utah south of I-80 and the Western Pacific tracks. The South Great Salt Lake Desert is not a place for a sufferer of agoraphobia. The vastness of empty space and the unrelieved monotony of miles and miles of salt flat in every direction is unparalleled in North America. Most would find this terrain oppressive; nonetheless it is a remarkable reservoir of silence — of wildness. Like its counterpart to the north, this area is largely a flat expanse of clay and sand impregnated with salt. Together, these areas encompass two million acres broken only by an Interstate Highway and railroad corridor.

Status: Although BLM identified all of their lands in this roadless area as "roadless," they did not further consider any of them for Wilderness study; no conservation group protested. The Air Force base is an aerial bombing and gunnery range; no doubt there is unexploded ordnance on the ground and other signs of use. The Dugway Proving Grounds are used for germ warfare experiments. It is unknown if any activity has occurred in the part of Dugway that is part of this roadless area; if so, human predators may be small here. The Great Salt Lake Desert is an awesome landmark on the planet. Until we as human beings appreciate the beauty and worth of such terrible places, we will be aliens in the natural world despite our appreciation for the Yosemites and Tetons, and will find no more appropriate use for them than testing bombs and anthrax.

RM36: 1,600,000

Deep Creek Mountains 179,000 acres

BLM WSA with intermixed state and private	72,366
Additional BLM, state, private roadless	90,000
Goshute Indian Reservation roadless	17,000

Description: West-central Utah between the towns of Callao and Ibapah. The Deep Creeks are one of the more stunning Great Basin ranges, rising up 8,000' above the Great Salt Lake Desert to an elevation of 12,101' on Haystack Peak. BLM says they are characterized by "sheer granite cliffs and glacial cirques at the higher elevations." Their great elevation gradient gives the Deep Creeks five vegetation zones: Montane Conifer (White & Subalpine Fir, Engelmann Spruce, Douglas-fir, Ponderosa & Limber Pine); Pinyon/juniper (Utah Juniper, Bluebunch Wheatgrass, Singleleaf Pinyon, Big Sagebrush); Sagebrush-grass and Desert Scrub (Big Sagebrush, Shadscale, Mormon Tea, Snakeweed, Winter-fat, Saltbush); and riparian along seven perennial streams. Bristlecone Pine, which include both very large, ancient individuals as well as significant stands of young, vigorous trees, grow on high ridges. Four potential Endangered or Threatened plants are in the area.

Wildlife includes Mule Deer, Mountain Lion, Peregrine Falcon, Golden Eagle, Utah Cutthroat Trout and Giant Stonefly. Rocky Mountain Bighorn Sheep were reintroduced in 1984.

Status: Wilderness designation for the Deep Creeks is a high priority for Utah conservation groups, with the UWC proposing 76,000 acres. BLM proposes a 50,984 acre Wilderness and would like to acquire about 6,000 acres of state land for addition to the Wilderness. BLM currently has an ORV closure on 52,738 acres except for 15 miles of existing ways. Mining, continued grazing and ORVs are threats to the high country proposed for protection but even more so for the lower elevation foothills and valleys ignored in the Wilderness proposals. An additional 55,000 acres of Goshute, BLM and private land (mostly in Nevada) perhaps should be included in this roadless area — the separating vehicle route may only be a jeep trail.

Mt. Moriah 144,000 acres (also in Nevada)
See Nevada for description and status.

Casto-Table 100,000 acres

Dixie National Forest RARE II	*93,440*
Additional Dixie NF, and BLM, state,	
private roadless	*6,500*

Description: South-central Utah east of Panguitch on the Sevier Plateau. Mt. Dutton is 11,041'. Vegetation ranges from pinyon/juniper to Ponderosa Pine and spruce/fir in the higher elevations. Several streams drain the high country. Mule Deer, Elk, Pronghorn, Mountain Lion, Turkey, Blue Grouse and Golden Eagle populate this high tableland.

Status: A number of dirt roads are cherrystemmed into this amoeba-shaped roadless area. ORVs, logging and roading will soon reduce its size.

Pine Valley Mountain 125,000 acres

Designated Pine Valley Mountain Wilderness	
(Dixie NF)	*50,000*
Additional Dixie NF, and BLM, private roadless	*75,000*

Description: Southwestern Utah north of St. George. This laccolithic mountain rises 6,000' above the valley. The high point, Signal Peak, is 10,360'. Engelmann Spruce, Aspen, Douglas-fir, Limber Pine and fairly young Bristlecone Pine are in the high country, while oak and mountain mahogany are down slope. Along with a major Mule Deer herd, wildlife includes Mountain Lion, Black Bear, Uinta Chipmunk, Yellow-bellied Marmot, Beaver, Turkey, Golden Eagle and Peregrine Falcon. Native trout inhabit the streams.

Status: Private developments threaten adjacent lands. Recreational horse use is damaging meadows in the Wilderness.

Zion 100,000 acres

Zion National Park roadless	*88,300*
BLM, state, private roadless	*12,000*

Description: Southwestern Utah south of Cedar City. Here is extraordinary scenery of huge sandstone monoliths and canyons, including The Narrows of the Virgin River — 2,000' deep and 20' wide. Textbook examples of tectonic activity — crossbedding, folding, sheer walls, and block faulting — and of the erosional power of wind and water are visible. Elevations drop from over 7,000' to under 4,000'. High country forests of Douglas-fir, Aspen, White Fir and Ponderosa Pine drop to pinyon/juniper/oak woodland and sagebrush. Riparian zones harbor cottonwoods and Box Elder. The Northern Black Hawk reaches its northern limit here. Other rare species include Spotted Bat, Ferruginous Hawk, Peregrine Falcon, Prairie Falcon and the endemic Zion Snail. Mule Deer, Bobcat, Beaver and Cougar live here, too. There are numerous archaeological sites and fossil footprints in the sandstone.

Status: The Park Service proposes 72,600 acres for Wilderness with 7,900 acres of potential additions. BLM recommends 6,199 acres for Wilderness; UWC 9,860.

Parunuweap 128,000 acres (also in Arizona)

Zion National Park roadless (UT)	*22,100*
BLM Canaan Mt WSA 4-143 (UT)	*46,428*
BLM Parunuweap Canyon WSA 4-230 (UT)	*32,080*

Additional BLM roadless (UT)	21,000
Designated Cottonwood Point Wilderness Area	
(BLM, AZ)	6,500

Description: Southwestern Utah and northwestern Arizona east of St. George. Spectacular Parunuweap Canyon is carved by the East Fork of the Virgin River. Canaan Mountain is a plateau with cliffs of Navajo sandstone that tower 2,000' above the surrounding desert. From the top, amidst slickrock, balanced rocks and pinnacles, a panorama of Zion, the Pine Valley Mts and the Arizona Strip stretches out. There are four vegetative zones (although slickrock predominates): Ponderosa Pine, Douglas-fir, Aspen, Gambel Oak, manzanita on the plateau; pinyon pine, Utah Juniper, Utah Serviceberry, live oak; sagebrush, rabbitbrush; and riparian groves in the canyons of willow, cottonwood, Box Elder, along with hanging gardens of Maidenhair Fern, Cliff Columbine and Scarlet Monkey Flower. Wildlife includes Desert Bighorn Sheep, Mule Deer, Cougar, Desert Shrew, Lewis Woodpecker, Bald Eagle and nesting Peregrine Falcon and Prairie Falcon. Speckled Dace is the only fish.

Status: The NPS proposes a 19,800 acre Zion NP Wilderness with 1,040 acres of potential additions. Continued grazing is the major intrusion; with ORVs and firewood cutting secondary problems. BLM recommends 47,500 acres for Wilderness in Utah; UWC 93,200.

Colorado

To most Americans, Colorado is The Rocky Mountain State. The Rockies reach their greatest height in Colorado, with 53 peaks exceeding 14,000', and, perhaps more than mountains in any other state, Colorado's are developed for recreation. Technically, the mountains in Colorado are the Southern Rockies, which extend into Utah, northern New Mexico and southern Wyoming. (The Central Rockies are around Yellowstone, and the Northern Rockies are in Montana, Idaho and Canada.) Although high and precipitous, the Colorado Rockies provide excellent habitat for Elk, Mule Deer, Mountain Lion, Rocky Mountain Bighorn Sheep and Black Bear. Wolverine and Lynx reach the southern limits of their ranges in Colorado, and at least one Grizzly Bear survived in southern Colorado until recently. Moose and Mountain Goat, neither native to Colorado, have been transplanted to several parts of the state. The Continental Divide runs through Colorado and hundreds of streams spill off either side, forming the headwaters of the Colorado, Rio Grande, Arkansas, South Platte and other major rivers.

Considering the rugged character of the Colorado Rockies and how much land they cover (two-fifths of the state), it is disappointing that Colorado has few very large roadless areas. Only one — the Weminuche — approaches one million acres in size. The most likely explanation is that Colorado was one of the principal mining frontiers in the mid- and late-1800s. Not only do old mining towns and diggings speckle the mountains, but the miners pioneered roads over passes that split the Colorado Big Outside into many smaller pieces.

Mining no longer dominates Colorado, but its ruins are ubiquitous. Additionally, current mining plans threaten several important roadless areas and even a few designated Wilderness Areas.

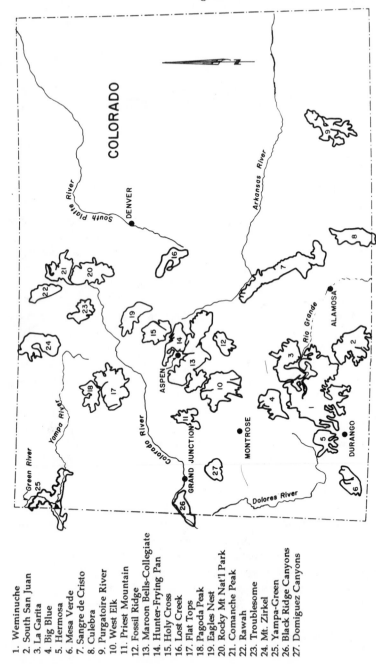

COLORADO

Below the high peaks and ridges rising above timberline, Colorado has lovely forests of Douglas-fir, Colorado Blue and Engelmann Spruce, Ponderosa and Lodgepole Pine, White and Subalpine Fir, but they are not economical to harvest. Nevertheless, the US Forest Service has encouraged a timber industry in Colorado dependent upon the National Forests. As a result, timber "management" with its attendant clearcuts and roads is slicing into the wildlands of the Southern Rockies with deadly results for sensitive species and.watersheds. Timber sales in Colorado's National Forests, as in most National Forests, are usually below cost sales — the federal government (and the taxpayer) spends more money offering and preparing the sale than it receives in fees from the logging contractor. Moreover, logging is damaging Colorado's huge Elk herds which bring in $60 million a year from hunting (more than the annual timber harvest is worth).

An even greater threat to wilderness is Colorado's insatiable thirst. Pork barrel water development has already severely damaged the high country, as Denver and other Front Range cities divert water from the West Slope through tunnels under the Continental Divide to fuel their growth. Although Denver is on the Great Plains and receives the same annual precipitation as does Tucson, Arizona, Denverites refuse to believe they live in a semi-arid bioregion and demand bluegrass lawns and trees. One-half of all the water Denver consumes is for watering lawns.

Another major threat to Colorado's roadless areas is recreation. Ski areas, condominiums, second-home subdivisions, golf courses, tennis resorts, convention centers, recreation reservoirs, campgrounds, highways and other facilities to help residents and visitors enjoy a "Rocky Mountain High" are spreading throughout the state. Most of the tourist towns like Aspen, Vail, Telluride and Breckenridge are in valleys which are — or were — prime winter range for wildlife. Ski areas, condos, trendy shops and gourmet restaurants displace Elk, Bighorn, Mountain Lion and other species. Such developments also interrupt migration routes for wildlife, fragment habitats, and overtax watersheds with sewage and airsheds with wood smoke and automobile exhaust. Many mountain areas in Colorado are laced with trails for jeeps, dirt bikes, all-terrain-vehicles (ATVs) and snowmobiles. Not only do these trails erode, damaging watersheds, but the noise created by the infernal combustion engines disturbs sensitive wildlife. Moreover, these vehicles allow poachers, litterbugs and other miscreants to reach the backcountry.

Despite these problems, Colorado has a somewhat more sophisticated electorate than have other Rocky Mountain states, and a large and active conservation community. After RARE II, Colorado took the lead in developing a National Forest Wilderness bill, and the Colorado bill, passed in 1980, became the prototype for the state NF Wilderness bills which followed. Among the precedents established were the compromise "standard release" language which dropped RARE II areas not designated as Wilderness from consideration for Wilderness (for approximately 10 years) as well as nullifying their protection from logging, roading and the like; and grazing management language (in the Committee Report) which allowed ranchers motorized access in Wilderness Areas for livestock management along with permission for the construction of new fences, stock ponds and other "improvements." Colorado conservationists endorsed this grazing language in order to get ranchers to support Wilderness designation. Ranchers still oppose Wilderness but now they have a stronger statutory right to continue to graze in Wilderness Areas.[1]

Out of Colorado's 6,539,201 acres of RARE II areas (second only to Idaho), conservationists, led by the Wilderness Workshop of the Colorado Open Space Council (COSC)[2], proposed over 5 million acres for Wilderness. The 1980 Colorado Wilderness Act designated 1,392,455 acres as Wilderness and left more than 650,000 acres for further study. Colorado conservationists have since pushed a second National Forest Wilderness bill, but that bill is tied up with questions about "Wilderness water rights." (Conservationists propose 1.2 mil-

---

[1] One of the authors of this book -- Dave Foreman -- pleads guilty to having supported this compromise; he has been punished with the giardiasis he carries.

[2] Now renamed the Colorado Environmental Coalition.

lion acres, but 700,000 acres seems to be the maximum that Colorado members of Congress will support.)

A Sierra Club lawsuit in 1985 established the concept of reserved water rights for Wilderness Areas. This resulted in a howl from traditional water users — ranchers and urban developers. Republican members of Congress, including Senators William Armstrong of Colorado and James McClure of Idaho, are trying to pin language onto all Wilderness legislation which would nullify the impact of the court's decision. Attorney General Edwin Meese, just before he was hooted out of office in 1988, issued an opinion against Wilderness water rights, with which Secretary of the Interior Donald Hodel concurred. Of course, conservationists are dissenting. Until this issue is resolved, there may not be a second RARE II bill for Colorado. (Much of Rocky Mountain National Park, and Dinosaur and Colorado National Monuments could also be designated as Wilderness in this bill.)

Not all of Colorado's wilderness is in the Rocky Mountains. Far western Colorado is part of the Colorado Plateau, and Dinosaur National Monument and the Bureau of Land Management have several big roadless areas there. Wilderness legislation is a possibility for Dinosaur (see above) but the BLM areas will probably wait for several years. The eastern two-fifths of Colorado is part of the Great Plains, where the thundering hooves of 60 million Bison have been replaced by the bucolic lowing of Herefords and the swishing drone of center-pivot irrigation systems. In all of the Great Plains, from Canada to West Texas, from the Mississippi to the Rockies, there are only four roadless areas over 100,000 acres. Two are in the badlands of South Dakota; one straddles the Little Missouri River in North Dakota; the other is the Purgatoire River Canyon in southeastern Colorado.

Colorado has the potential for significant wilderness preservation and restoration, including the reintroduction of Grizzly and Gray Wolf, but not only must conservationists overcome the traditional wilderness destroyers like ranchers, miners, loggers and ORVers, they must also deal with the explosive growth of the Front Range cities and the impossible demands for water and recreation these urban areas make on the Rocky Mountains.

Continental Divide, Weminuche Wilderness, Colorado.
Photo by Dave Foreman.

Southwestern Mountains

The San Juan Mountains of southwestern Colorado hold the largest complex of wild country in the state. The last Grizzly in Colorado was killed here in 1979 and the best habitat for reintroduction of the Grizzly in Colorado remains here — that is, if Forest Service logging and ski area development don't further degrade the San Juans first.

Weminuche 956,000 acres

Designated Weminuche Wilderness Area (San Juan and Rio Grande NFs)	459,172
Carson Peak roadless area (Rio Grande, San Juan and Gunnison NFs)	116,000
BLM WSA #030-241 contiguous to Carson Peak	18,860
Piedra roadless area (San Juan NF)	114,000
Additional Rio Grande & San Juan NFs roadless	227,000
Adjacent and intermixed private, state and FS roadless	21,000

Description: Along the Continental Divide in the San Juan Mountains northeast of Durango in southwestern Colorado. Several peaks in this vast high mountain area exceed 14,000', including those in the Needles and Grenadiers (Windom Peak at 14,091' is the high point), and Handies Peak (14,048'). The Weminuche has over 50 lakes (Emerald Lake is the second largest natural lake in Colorado) and nearly 200 miles of rushing streams — headwaters of the Rio Grande, San Juan, Animas, Los Pinos and Piedra Rivers. There are large areas above timberline as well as old growth forests (including a very large area of spruce/fir). Predominant tree species are Ponderosa Pine, Douglas-fir, Aspen, Engelmann & Colorado Blue Spruce, Subalpine & White Fir, and Gambel Oak. Lower elevations are below 8,000'. Significant wildlife populations include Elk, Cougar, Bighorn Sheep, Mountain Goat (introduced), Black Bear, River Otter (in the Piedra River), native Rio Grande Cutthroat Trout and raptors. There may be a remnant Grizzly Bear population. The West Needle Mountains include the steep-walled canyon of the Animas River and 13,000' high peaks of sheer granite. The Carson-Handies area on the north has massive volcanic peaks, large glaciated valleys and vol-

canic "beehive" cones of ash and lava (some sit astride Pole
Creek and form natural bridges).

Status: The unprotected National Forest lands are under
attack from road-building and logging. The Forest Service is
now destroying much of the Piedra roadless area to the south.
These unprotected areas are largely lower elevation forests
with more important habitat values than the high country,
which constitutes most of the protected portion. Along with
the South San Juan roadless area (separated only by US 160
over Wolf Creek Pass), the Weminuche is the priority in Colorado for Grizzly Bear reintroduction.

Conservationists propose a separate 49,000 acre Piedra
Wilderness and the FS proposes 41,000. Neither of these proposals connects to the existing Weminuche Wilderness, even
though the land between (Slide Mountain) is roadless and undeveloped. This is an outstanding example of fragmented
Wilderness proposals designed from a perspective of political
compromise instead of from an ecological standpoint
incorporating ideas of Island Biogeography. As part of negotiations on the remand of the San Juan Forest Plan, the FS has
agreed to drop plans for timber sales in the corridor between
Piedra and the Weminuche. And, in late 1988, Colorado conservationists were developing new boundaries for their Piedra
Wilderness proposal which would connect it to the Weminuche.

The 135,000 acre Carson Peak roadless area (FS & BLM) is
considered to be part of the Weminuche roadless area in this
inventory since it is separated from it only by the Stony Pass
jeep trail (which is, unfortunately, a popular one). Conservationists propose a 97,000 acre Carson Peak Wilderness while
the agencies propose a token 7,120 acre Wilderness. Extensive
logging threatens the east end of Carson Peak and ORVs are
ravaging it.

South San Juan 292,000 acres

Designated South San Juan Wilderness Area	
(Rio Grande & San Juan NFs)	*127,594*
Additional Rio Grande & San Juan NF roadless	*124,000*
Private roadless to south	*40,000*

Description: The southern San Juan Mountains east of Pagosa Springs in southwestern Colorado. The South San Juan has the largest extent of alpine tundra this far south in North America. It is a rolling area of waterfalls, easy peaks (13,300' Summit Peak is the highest), numerous lakes and the headwaters of the San Juan, Conejos and Chama rivers. The lowest elevation is about 7,500' on the northwest. Wind and water carving Cenozoic volcanics has left spires and cliffs on the west; valleys on the east are glacier-carved. Douglas-fir, Engelmann & Blue Spruce, Limber & Ponderosa Pine, White & Subalpine Fir are the most common trees. Bristlecone Pine (rare in Colorado) occur in the East Fork drainage. The last known Grizzly Bear in Colorado was killed here in 1979 (at the head of the Navajo River). The South San Juan has the southernmost Wolverine and Fisher populations in North America; also River Otter, Pine Marten, Bighorn Sheep, Mountain Lion, Bobcat and a large Elk herd. It is separated from the 956,000 acre Weminuche by a narrow paved highway over Wolf Creek Pass and from the Cruces Basin Wilderness Area in New Mexico by a minor paved highway and narrow gauge railroad over Cumbres Pass.

Status: Mixed conifer forests outside the designated Wilderness Area are being cut and roaded — particularly in the spectacular Chama Basin on the south. ORVs invade unprotected areas and sometimes the Wilderness. Private roadless land to the south is important wildlife habitat, but eventual subdivision and oil & gas exploration threatens it. Oil & gas is also a threat in the Chama Basin, Montezuma Peak and V-Rock areas. AMAX has plans to mine molybdenum.

The South San Juan is a prime area for Grizzly reintroduction. Major ski areas — East Fork and Wolf Creek Valley — are proposed adjacent to the north end of this area (around Wolf Creek Pass). They would destroy important habitat for Grizzly, Wolverine and other sensitive species, as well as further sundering the South San Juan from the Weminuche.

The FS opposes any additional Wilderness here, while conservationists campaign for 55,200 acres of additions.

La Garita 253,000 acres
Designated La Garita Wilderness Area

(Gunnison & Rio Grande NFs)	*103,986*
Additional Gunnison & Rio Grande NFs roadless	*149,000*

Description: South of Gunnison and north of Creede in southwestern Colorado. San Luis Peak is 14,014' and Stewart Peak is 13,983'. Although largely a rugged alpine area, La Garita includes Elk calving grounds and abundant wildlife — Bighorn Sheep, Black Bear, Mountain Lion, Mink, Pine Marten, Bald and Golden Eagle, and native Cutthroat Trout in lakes and streams. Extensive high tablelands have alpine tundra; lower elevations have old growth spruce/fir forest. The Wheeler Geological Area contains rock pinnacles and other formations carved from volcanic tuff. A paved state highway over Slumgullion Pass separates this area from the Carson Peak portion of the Weminuche roadless area.

Status: The standard logging threats affect La Garita. ORV travel to the Wheeler Geological Area is a continuing problem, as is overgrazing by livestock. The FS opposes any additional Wilderness here, while conservationists propose 25,000 acres of additions.

Big Blue 145,000 acres

Designated Big Blue Wilderness (Uncompahgre NF)	*97,235*
Additional Uncompahgre NF roadless	*36,000*
BLM WSA 3-217	*6,000*
Additional intermixed BLM and FS roadless	*6,000*

Description: East of Ouray in southwestern Colorado. The "Switzerland" of America is the chamber of commerce claim for this spectacular glacially carved area of 14,000' peaks, lakes and waterfalls which form the northern end of the San Juan Mountains. The fourteeners, Wetterhorn (14,015') and Uncompahgre Peak (14,309'), are among the best non-technical climbs in Colorado. Vegetation is similar to that of the Weminuche. Wildlife includes Elk, Black Bear, Pine Marten, White-tailed Ptarmigan, Turkey, Peregrine Falcon and Bald Eagle. Big Blue Creek is a noted trout fishery. Cow Creek Canyon is one of the wildest and most inaccessible canyons in the Rockies. Old mining ruins attest to the exploitative attitude which has governed human activity in this area.

Status: ORVs abound in the unprotected area; a rascally miner wants to bulldoze a road to his mining claim in the designated Wilderness. His plans would present a major challenge to Wilderness protection, but the FS has invalidated his bogus claim. Grazing by domestic sheep is a huge problem here.

BLM has recommend 1,500 acres of their lands for addition to the Wilderness; conservationists call for a 3,000 acre add.

Hermosa 147,000 acres	
San Juan NF roadless	*147,000*

Description: Southwestern Colorado north of Durango. Here in the western San Juan Mountains (La Plata Range) several peaks exceed 13,000', while the drainages of Hermosa, Junction and Bear Creeks drop to 7,000'. "Hermosa" is Spanish for "beautiful," and this area lives up to its name. It is the southwestern terminus of the Colorado high country with alpine tundra, rocky peaks, dense spruce/fir forest, flower-filled mountain meadows, open Ponderosa Pine parks, rolling groves of Aspen, and wide flat creek bottoms. In addition to an excellent native trout fishery and one of the largest Elk herds in the state, wildlife includes Black Bear and Mule Deer. The area provides both summer and winter range for Elk.

Status: Although conservationists proposed 147,000 acres for Wilderness during RARE II, neither conservation groups nor the FS are currently promoting Wilderness designation for Hermosa. Threats include logging, oil & gas leasing, dirt bikes and mountain bicycles.

Mesa Verde 136,000 acres	
Mesa Verde National Park roadless	*40,000*
Ute Mountain Indian Reservation & private roadless	*90,000*
BLM WSA 3-252	*6,320*

Description: Extreme southwestern Colorado southeast of Cortez. This high mesa north of the Mancos River has outstanding Anasazi and Basketmaker ruins dating from 550 CE to 1300 CE when the area was abandoned. The mesa gently slopes to the south and is heavily dissected by canyons cutting down to the Mancos River. Elevations drop from 8,500' to 5,800'. Oak brush, Ponderosa Pine/Gambel Oak and pinyon/juniper are the major vegetative types with Douglas-fir growing at upper elevations. Mule Deer, Mountain Lion, Bobcat, Coyote, Black Bear, Golden Eagle, Common Raven and Spotted Owl live here.

Status: Three small Wilderness Areas have been designated in the northern portion of the Park. Visitor roads to Chapin and Wetherill Mesas penetrate deeply into the roadless area. In the summer the roads receive heavy traffic but the tourists are restricted to the developed areas along them. Most of the backcountry of the Park was not designated as Wilderness because of the Park Service's desire for administrative access. There are some vehicle routes in the Park which are closed to all public use but may be used by the Park Service for fire suppression and archaeological site stabilization. The entire backcountry of the Park is closed to public entry to protect archaeological sites. Because of this public use closure, we have inventoried Mesa Verde as "roadless." The Ute Reservation portion wraps around the Park. It has some jeep trails and is grazed by cattle. Conservationists should work with the Ute Mountain Tribe to protect the roadless area on the Reservation.

Southeastern Mountains and Plains

The high desert of the San Luis Valley separates the San Juan Mountains on the west from the Sangre de Cristos to the east. Farther east, the Great Plains break against the Front Range of the Rockies.

Sangre de Cristo 418,000 acres

Great Sand Dunes National Monument	
Wilderness Area	*33,450*
Rio Grande & San Isabel National Forests roadless	*260,000*
BLM WSAs	*6,500*
Sangre de Cristo Grant (private) roadless	*40,000*
Private roadless to West (Baca Grant #4)	*20,000*
Additional BLM, private roadless	*58,000*

Description: South-central Colorado northeast of Alamosa. Rising from the giant sand dunes (700' high) of the San Luis Valley (7,600-8,000'), the Sangre de Cristo Mountains, a narrow, glacier-carved knife edge of a range, climb to over 14,000'.

The several 14,000' peaks include Crestone Peak at 14,294' and Blanca Peak, the highest in the roadless area at 14,345'. Here, elevation typically rises 7,000' in only three vertical miles. This leads to great diversity in vegetation — sagebrush steppe to alpine tundra, with pinyon/juniper, Ponderosa Pine, Dougfir, Limber Pine, spruce, fir, Aspen and Bristlecone Pine in between. The Sangre de Cristos have many lakes, waterfalls and lush valleys. Wildlife includes over 20 wilderness-related species such as Black Bear, Mountain Lion, Elk, Bighorn Sheep and Peregrine Falcon. The lower slopes offer winter range. About 60 lakes nestled in timberline basins feed numerous streams, some of which contain introduced Golden and native Cutthroat Trout. This popular climbing area affords eyestretching views of the Great Plains and the other mountains of southern Colorado. A skeleton in Spanish armor was found in a cave in this area in the 1850s.

Status: A jeep trail cuts across the north end of the FS area and the Medano Creek jeep trail crosses the area east from Great Sand Dunes. The entire area is threatened by ORV use. Logging and mining, particularly CO_2 and oil & gas leasing and development by ARCO, are threats. Subdivision is occurring on adjacent private lands with attendant damage to the area. The private Sangre de Cristo Grant takes in the southern end of the area including the south side of the Blanca Peak massif. Protection of this private land should be a priority.

Colorado conservationists are pushing hard for Wilderness designation of 256,000 acres; the FS has recommended 190,500 acres.

Culebra 125,000 acres (also in New Mexico)

San Isabel NF roadless (CO)	*31,000*
Private roadless (CO)	*85,000*
Private roadless (NM)	*9,000*

Description: East of San Luis in the Sangre de Cristo Mountains on the central Colorado-New Mexico border. This high mountain area is largely an old Spanish land grant. 14,047' Culebra Peak is the high point and the southernmost fourteener in the Rockies; several peaks top 13,000'. Mixed conifer forest (Engelmann and Blue Spruce, White and Subalpine Fir, Douglas-fir, Ponderosa Pine), Aspen and Bristlecone Pine, small lakes, streams and tundra make this a classic Southern Rockies area. The fauna is also typical of the Southern Rockies, including Turkey, Pine Marten, Elk, Mountain Lion and Black Bear.

Status: Logging and associated roading are steadily encroaching on the area. It will not last long as a large roadless area unless conservationists work for the entire area. Culebra is a textbook example of a major roadless area being ignored because of multiple land ownership. A minor dirt road (perhaps only a jeep trail) separates it from 35,000 acres of splendid high country around State Line Peak and Big Costilla Peak (both over 13,000') on private land in New Mexico. Closure of several additional dirt roads in New Mexico would add considerable acreage including the designated Latir Peak Wilderness Area and some of the recent Vermejo Park (Valle Vidal) addition to the Carson NF (see Latir-Ponil roadless area in New Mexico). Private lands in this area should be a major priority for acquisition by the Nature Conservancy or the National Park Service.

Purgatoire River Canyon 225,000 acres

Intermixed military, private and Comanche	
National Grasslands roadless	*225,000*

Description: Southeastern Colorado south of La Junta. The Purgatoire River Canyon is an excellent example of Shortgrass Prairie, exhibiting the typical vegetation of this formerly extensive ecosystem — Buffalo Grass and Blue Grama. It also includes a spectacular canyon system carved by the Purgatoire and its tributary, Chacuaco Canyon. There are major paleontological (dinosaur tracks) and archaeological sites. This is the only large roadless area remaining in the southern Great Plains — as such it is of exceptional ecological importance. (Three Great Plains roadless areas over 100,000 acres remain in Badlands National Park in South Dakota and the Little Missouri National Grasslands in North Dakota). This is one of the major habitat areas remaining for the increasingly rare Swift Fox.

Status: Much of the area outside of the canyon, which has been in private hands for over 100 years, was acquired by the

Army in the early 1980s for a tank maneuvering ground. They also picked up tracts in the canyon. The Army isn't using the area now and wishes to dispose of it (17,000 acres were recently transferred to the nearby Comanche National Grassland). Colorado conservationists are encouraging their members of Congress, several of whom are interested, to retain the land in federal ownership and to acquire more of it as a National Park or Wild & Scenic River. The Park Service studied the Purgatoire for Wild & Scenic River designation in 1982 and concluded that it qualified. The entire area, including the river canyons and the surrounding benchlands, should be protected, with Elk and Bison being reintroduced, as the Shortgrass Prairie National Park.

Central Mountains

North of the Gunnison River and south of the Colorado River, a huge block of mountains forms the central section of the Colorado Rockies.

West Elk 368,000 acres	
Designated West Elk Wilderness Area	
(Gunnison NF)	*176,092*
Additional Gunnison NF roadless	*157,000*
BLM, private roadless	*35,000*

Description: West-central Colorado northeast of Montrose. The high point of this lightly-used area is 13,035' on West Elk Peak; elevations drop to 6,500' on the north. Streams flow out from the center to all points of the compass, cutting numerous rugged canyons. Extensive meadows (wet & dry) and mixed-conifer forests (Douglas-fir, Engelmann & Blue Spruce, Subalpine Fir, Lodgepole & Limber Pine) with large Aspen stands clothe middle elevations; Ponderosa Pine and pinyon/juniper cover the lower elevations. Large Elk and Mule Deer herds make this a popular hunting area. Other wildlife includes Bighorn Sheep, Mountain Lion, Black Bear, Peregrine Falcon, Bald and Golden Eagle, and many hawks. The West Elks are used for biological research.

Status: As elsewhere, timbering, roading and ORVs threaten the unprotected area. "Aspen treatment" (clearcutting to "renew" Aspen stands, and incidentally provide pulp for a Louisiana-Pacific waferboard plant) is a particular threat to this area.

Priest Mountain 109,000 acres

Grand Mesa & Gunnison NFs roadless	103,000
BLM, private roadless	6,000

Description: North of Paonia in west-central Colorado on the eastern edge of Grand Mesa. Crater Peak, 11,327', is the high point. Ecologically, it is similar to West Elk.

Status: No one is publicly proposing this area for protection. The Forest Service has given dirt bikes the run of trails in the area. It is also threatened by extensive logging and continued overgrazing.

Fossil Ridge 101,000 acres

Gunnison NF roadless	91,680
Private, state roadless to west	9,000

Description: Northeast of Gunnison in central Colorado. A fossiliferous limestone ridge runs across the southern portion of this area of high peaks, stream-fed alpine lakes and steep forested slopes. Henry Mt. at 13,254' is the high point. Besides an important Elk herd, wildlife includes Golden Eagle and Peregrine Falcon. Although the area is far out of their normal range, Mountain Goats have been introduced. It is currently a study area for the role of limestone in buffering acid rain. Fossils aged 275-600 million years old have been found in the limestone.

Status: This is a Forest Service Wilderness Study Area, but the agency has recommended non-wilderness. Conservationists are only asking for a 57,000 acre Wilderness. ORVs and timber cutting are the main threats. Dirt bikes are rutting the trails and causing severe erosion.

Maroon Bells-Collegiate Pks-Raggeds 632,000 acres

Designated Maroon Bells-Snowmass Wilderness Area (White River and Gunnison NFs)	179,042
Designated Collegiate Peaks Wilderness Area	

(White River, Gunnison & San Isabel NFs)	166,638
Designated Raggeds Wilderness Area	
(White River and Gunnison NFs)	59,105
Additional White River, Gunnison & San	
Isabel NFs roadless	227,000
BLM WSA #070-392	330

Description: Central Colorado south of Aspen. This stunning high mountain area consists of three Wilderness Areas and their surrounding roadless areas. The Wildernesses are separated from one another by two jeep trails over high passes. The Taylor Pass trail divides the Maroon Bells from the Collegiates; the Schofield Pass trail separates the Maroon Bells from the Raggeds. This roadless area has an irregular shape due to cherrystem roads and other intrusions but it is currently an intact single area. It has a number of peaks over 14,000' including Mt. Harvard (14,420'), Maroon Bells (14,156'), and Snowmass Mt (14,092'), and is heavily glaciated, as evidenced by the cirques, ridges, U-shaped valleys and rock glaciers. Alpine tundra, alpine and subalpine meadows (with splendrous flower displays), Subalpine Fir, Engelmann Spruce, Blue Spruce, Douglas-fir and Aspen constitute the area's ground cover. The Sawatch Range (which includes the Collegiate Peaks) is the highest range in the US, with eight peaks over 14,000' and 65 over 13,000'. Numerous lakes and many rare and endemic plants are found here. Excellent summer and winter range for Bighorn Sheep, and winter range, calving areas and good summer and spring range for Elk add to the ecological significance of this area. Wolverine and Lynx head the list of sensitive species; also sensitive are Black Bear, Mountain Lion, Mink, Pine Marten, Pika, White-tailed Ptarmigan, Goshawk, Golden Eagle and native Cutthroat Trout. Mountain Goat have been introduced. The headwaters for many streams are fed by the deep snowpack.

The imposing glacial terrain of the Raggeds includes Peeler Basin, a hanging cirque. Treasury Mountain, the high point for the Raggeds, is 13,462'; the low point is under 7,000'. The Raggeds Wilderness is ecologically important because it contains high altitude lakes and ponds without fish (most alpine lakes in the West have had trout artificially introduced). A

rare, relict aquatic dragonfly, *Leucorrhinia hundsonica*, survives here because of the lack of exotic fish. Several rare and
endemic plants are also present.

Status: The three Wilderness Areas should be joined to form
one protected area, and the jeep trails closed. The Schofield
Pass jeep trail is such a brutal and dangerous route that six
people have died on it in recent years and the FS is now considering shutting it down. This initiative by the FS presents
the perfect opportunity for conservationists to argue that this
entire area is in reality one roadless area and should be protected as one large Wilderness Area. With minor road closures
and wilderness rehabilitation, a million acre Wilderness could
be established here in the heart of the Colorado Rockies. As
such, it would be a prime area for the reintroduction of Grizzly
and perhaps Gray Wolf.

ORVs and timbering threaten the unprotected portions.
The designated Wilderness Areas receive heavy and damaging
recreational use. A local tough has gained permission from the
Forest Service to use a bulldozer and six-wheel-drive truck to
haul out blocks of marble from his mining claim in the Maroon
Bells-Snowmass Wilderness Area. This precedent of mining in
Wilderness Areas needs to be blocked.

"Aspen treatment," mining and mountain bikes are threats
to the Oh-Be-Joyful roadless area adjacent to the Raggeds
Wilderness. Conservationists propose 5,500 acres of Wilderness
additions (Oh-Be-Joyful) while the FS opposes any additional
here. Domestic sheep overgraze the area.

Hunter-Frying Pan 168,000 acres

Designated Hunter-Frying Pan Wilderness Area	
(White River NF)	*74,250*
Designated Mt. Massive Wilderness Area	
(San Isabel NF)	*27,980*
Additional White River & San Isabel NF roadless	*66,000*

Description: East of Aspen and west of Leadville, between
the Maroon Bells-Collegiate-Raggeds and Holy Cross roadless
areas, in central Colorado. Mt. Massive at 14,421' is the high
point (and the second highest peak in Colorado). Populations
of native trout are healthy. The lower elevations on the

Arkansas River side have winter range for Elk and Mule Deer.
Other wildlife includes Black Bear, Bobcat, Mountain Lion,
Yellow-bellied Marmot, Pine Marten, Pika and Golden Eagle.
Vegetation is typical of the Southern Rockies.

Status: The FS and conservationists both propose only 8,000
acres of Wilderness additions.

Holy Cross 152,000 acres
Designated Holy Cross Wilderness Area
(White River & San Isabel NFs)   *122,600*
Additional White River & San Isabel NF roadless   *29,000*

Description: South of Vail in central Colorado. 14,005'
Mount of the Holy Cross (so-named from a cross-shaped snow-
field) is the high point; 24 other peaks exceed 13,000'. Glacial-
carved high country, alpine tundra, Engelmann Spruce and Subalpine Fir forests, and lush meadows create a diverse area.
Wildlife is typical of the Southern Rockies, and includes Lynx,
which is at the southern limits of its range. Holy Cross was
once a National Monument.

Status: The designated Wilderness Area and surrounding
lands are under serious threat of damming and water diversion
to supply Colorado Springs and Aurora with water for Star
Wars research and lawn watering. A major wilderness battle is
brewing here. Previous water diversions (Frying Pan-Arkansas
and Homestake) have already damaged the area. A notorious
ORV route goes to the Holy Cross City ghost town and the
jeepers are trashing fragile meadows in this part of the roadless area.

Lost Creek 126,000 acres
Designated Lost Creek Wilderness Area (Pike NF) *105,090*
Additional Pike NF roadless   *21,000*

Description: Southwest of Denver in the Kenosha and Tar-
ryall Mountains of central Colorado. Bison Mt. (12,427') is the
high point. The Forest Service describes this area thusly:
"Some of the most spectacular granite formations to be found in
Colorado, including domes, half domes, sheer walls, pinnacles,
spires, minarets, and even a natural arch are to be found . . . Lost

Creek . . . ducks in and out of huge granite slides or 'sinks' no less than 9 times." The Craig Creek Meadows in the northern part of the area have exceptional botanical diversity. The largest herd of Bighorn Sheep in Colorado resides here, and has provided a source for reintroductions elsewhere. Other wildlife and vegetation is typical of the Southern Rockies.

Status: Conservationists propose 11,000 acres of additions; FS nil.

Northern Mountains

From Denver's dramatic backdrop west for 130 miles, the northern Colorado Rockies encompass some of the most rugged and scenic ranges in the state.

Flat Tops 346,000 acres	
Designated Flat Tops Wilderness Area	
(White River & Routt NFs)	235,035
Additional White River & Routt NFs roadless	98,000
BLM WSA #070-425	3,360
Private, state & additional BLM roadless	10,000

Description: South of Craig in northwestern Colorado. This is an historic area. One of the first administrative actions to preserve wilderness occurred here in 1920 when Forest Service Landscape Architect ("Beauty Engineer") Arthur Carhart recommended leaving the Trapper Lake area wild instead of opening it to summer home leasing by the Forest Service. Carhart also helped Aldo Leopold refine his ideas for wilderness preservation, which led to the designation of the Gila Wilderness in New Mexico in 1924. In 1975, President Ford considered vetoing the Wilderness bill passed by Congress for the area because it was the conservationists' proposal instead of that of the Forest Service. Public pressure convinced him to sign it.

This high elevation plateau (average is 10,000') includes large rolling areas, deep forests of Engelmann Spruce, Douglas-fir and Aspen, large open parks, and steep cliffs and jagged peaks. This is an important area for Elk and Mule Deer. Other wildlife includes Bighorn Sheep, Black Bear, Marten, Beaver and White-tailed Ptarmigan. Native Cutthroat Trout live in the many lakes and streams. Sheep Mountain reaches 12,246' in elevation; the low point is about 7,500'.

Status: Continued grazing of domestic cattle and sheep conflicts with the large Elk and deer herds. Logging, road-building and ORVs are invading the unprotected FS area.

Pagoda Peak 126,000 acres

White River and Routt NFs roadless	105,500
Private & BLM roadless to north	20,000

Description: North of the Flat Tops Wilderness Area and south of Craig in northwestern Colorado. 11,257' Pagoda Peak is the high point. Over 5,000 Elk inhabit the area and it provides important calving grounds. Another 17 wilderness-associated species are present. Vegetation is similar to the Flat Tops. The paucity of trails helps make this one of the more pristine areas in Colorado.

Status: Conservationists propose a 105,700 acre Wilderness; FS & BLM oppose Wilderness here. Proposed logging, continued sheep grazing, possible oil & gas drilling, and extensive snowmobile use threaten the area.

Eagles Nest 170,000 acres

Designated Eagles Nest Wilderness Area	
(Arapaho & White River NFs)	133,688
Additional Arapaho & White River NFs roadless	36,000

Description: Northeast of Vail in the Gore Range in north-central Colorado. This is one of the most rugged mountain ranges in Colorado. Mt. Powell at 13,534' is its high point; there are 16 other peaks over 13,000', as well as numerous lakes. Wildlife populations are not high because of the high elevation but include Bighorn Sheep, Mountain Goat (introduced), and other mammals common to the Rockies. Eagles Nest is a popular recreation area. The Sierra Club's precedent-setting Meadow Creek lawsuit (after RARE I) to protect potential Forest Service Wilderness dealt with this area.

Status: The contiguous roadless areas are lower elevation and crucial for wildlife. As elsewhere in Colorado, they are being damaged by logging, roading and ORVs. The Denver

Water Board is pushing two major projects — East Gore Canal and Eagle-Piney — which would consist of huge pipelines and canals, running parallel to the range on the east and west sides, feeding into Dillon reservoir.

Rocky Mountain National Park 266,000 acres	
Rocky Mountain National Park roadless	*149,400*
Designated Indian Peaks Wilderness Area	
(Roosevelt & Arapaho NFs)	*70,374*
Additional Roosevelt & Arapaho NFs roadless	*46,000*

Description: Northwest of Boulder in north-central Colorado. Jagged peaks (Longs Peak reaches 14,256'), extensive areas of rolling alpine tundra, deeply forested U-shaped valleys, lakes, rushing streams, cirques and a few small glaciers characterize this quintessential Rocky Mountain high country. Vegetation ranges from Ponderosa Pine upward to Lodgepole to spruce/fir to tundra. It is a popular recreation area for backpacking and climbing. Wildlife includes Elk, Bighorn Sheep, Yellow-bellied Marmot, Pika, Marten, River Otter, Snowshoe Hare, White-tailed Ptarmigan, Golden Eagle and the Endangered Greenback Cutthroat Trout. Elevations drop to below 8,000'.

Status: Excessive recreational use is damaging the Indian Peaks Wilderness and the backcountry of Rocky Mountain NP as the two million residents of the Denver metroplex swarm to it. ORVs are damaging the unprotected NF roadless areas and logging is planned. The Wilderness Society considers Rocky Mountain NP to be one of the most threatened Parks in the country. They cite the Bald Pate condominium complex which will put 500 units as close as 25 feet from the Park boundary — in crucial winter habitat for Elk.

A particular threat occurs in the designated Indian Peaks Wilderness where a prominent Colorado water lawyer has acquired an old reservoir and access easement to it. He has upgraded the road to the reservoir through the Wilderness Area and plans further developments. Legal means to stop him appear to be hopeless.

Wilderness designation is needed for the NP area (NPS and conservationists propose a 140,428 acre Enos Mills Wilderness

— named for the "Muir of the Rockies," who was the force behind the National Park's establishment and was an early defender of the Grizzly Bear). Potential for Grizzly Bear reintroduction is high here, if wilderness restoration efforts can succeed on lands outside the Park.

Comanche Peak 182,000 acres

Designated Comanche Peak Wilderness Area	
(Roosevelt NF)	*66,464*
Additional Roosevelt NF roadless	*29,000*
Rocky Mountain National Park roadless	*86,500*

Description: The high country of the Mummy Range west of Ft. Collins in north-central Colorado. Hagues Peak at 13,560' is the high point; the low point is 7,600' along the Cache la Poudre River. There are several small glaciers. Vegetation ranges from Ponderosa Pine to Lodgepole and mixed conifer to alpine tundra. The Cache La Poudre River has deep canyons, waterfalls and lush meadows. The high country has many small alpine lakes. Wildlife includes Cutthroat Trout, Mule Deer, Elk, Bighorn Sheep, Black Bear, Mountain Lion, Blue Grouse and ptarmigan.

Status: The NPS proposes a 83,700 acre Wilderness; conservation groups recommend 86,000 in the Park.

Rawah 119,000 acres

Designated Rawah Wilderness Area (Roosevelt NF)	*73,109*
Colorado State Forest roadless	*38,000*
Additional Roosevelt NF roadless	*8,000*

Description: Medicine Bow Mountains north of Rocky Mt. National Park and west of Ft. Collins in north-central Colorado. This area is extremely popular for its spectacular scenery of rugged peaks, many lakes and lower elevation forests of Lodgepole Pine, spruce and fir. Wildlife includes Pine Marten, Black Bear, Beaver, Elk, Band-tailed Pigeon and native Cutthroat Trout.

Status: The Rawah Wilderness suffers from excessive recreational use. Snowmobiles use the state forest and timbering is proposed there.

Troublesome 117,000 acres

Routt & Arapaho NFs roadless	*99,000*
BLM WSA # 010-155	*12,000*
Additional BLM, and private roadless	*6,000*

Description: North of Kremmling in north-central Colorado along the Continental Divide. Parkview Mountain, at 12,296', is the high point. Featuring one of the lowest stretches of the Continental Divide in Colorado, this area has lower elevation forests much needed as wildlife habitat for Elk, Mule Deer, Black Bear, Prairie Falcon, Bald and Golden Eagle. There have been unconfirmed Grizzly sightings. Troublesome provides calving areas and winter range for Middle and North Parks' deer and Elk.

Status: Troublesome is under imminent threat of logging and roading. Louisiana-Pacific and the Forest Service propose 21 miles of road to carve it up. Conservationists propose 111,000 acres for Wilderness; FS & BLM oppose a Troublesome Wilderness (one sometimes thinks that the agencies consider all wilderness — designated or not — to be troublesome).

Mt. Zirkel 265,000 acres

Designated Mt. Zirkel Wilderness Area (Routt NF)	*139,818*
Additional Routt NF roadless	*124,000*
Private land to east	*1,000*

Description: The Sawtooth Range along the Continental Divide in north-central Colorado north of Steamboat Springs. The roadless area includes forty alpine lakes and summer Elk range. The high point is 12,180' Mt. Zirkel; low point is about 7,000'. Vegetation is diverse, from scrub oak and sagebrush parks to Aspen, Lodgepole Pine, spruce/fir, alpine tundra and meadows. Wildlife includes Sandhill Crane, Bald Eagle, Peregrine Falcon, Black Bear and a large Elk herd. It is an important watershed. An unusual configuration of trees, called the Ribbon Forest, is due to high snow accumulations. Livingston Park is an interesting glaciologic feature.

Status: Logging threatens the unprotected area. ORVs are a major threat to all of the undesignated area. Conservationists propose 49,000 acres of additions to the Wilderness; the FS only 9,000.

Colorado Plateau

In the western fifth of Colorado, the rivers pouring off the Rocky Mountains begin to cut down into the sandstone of the Colorado Plateau — the eastern extension of Utah's famous red rock Canyon Country.

Yampa-Green 250,000 acres (also in Utah)	
Dinosaur National Monument roadless	
(includes Utah)	163,000
BLM WSAs and roadless (includes Utah)	87,000

Description: Extreme northwestern Colorado north of Rangely and northeastern Utah east of Vernal. The magnificent canyons of the Yampa (48 miles) and Green (44 miles) Rivers include the Gates of Lodore, Split Mountain Gorge, Whirlpool Canyon, Steamboat Rock; soaring sandstone walls, and raging rapids (fearsome Warmsprings Rapid was created overnight by a flash flood). These canyons are popular for float trips. Impressive cottonwood trees grow in the spacious "holes" or "parks" through which the rivers flow between canyons. The modern conservation movement was born here during a protracted and successful struggle against building the Echo Park Dam in the mid-1950s. The Yampa is the last major undammed river in the Colorado River drainage.

Zenobia Peak on the rim is 9,006'; the low point along the Green River is 4,800'. Ponderosa Pine and Douglas-fir drop down from the high points into the canyons. Pinyon, juniper and sagebrush are common. Wildlife includes Rocky Mt. Bighorn Sheep, Mountain Lion, catfish in the Yampa & Green, trout in Jones Hole Creek. Two Endangered species of fish are present: Colorado Squawfish and Humpbacked Chub. Bald and Golden Eagles use the area. One of the healthiest populations of Peregrine Falcons in the country is here — it is used as a source of eggs for captive hatching and replenishment of the species elsewhere.

Status: Conservation groups propose that a few minor dirt roads be closed in the Monument and a 170,500 acre Wilderness be designated. The NPS proposes a 160,635 acre Wilderness. Conservationists propose 67,766 acres of the BLM areas for Wilderness; BLM proposes 36,240. (Wilderness proposal totals: conservationists — 238,266; agencies — 196,875.)

A dam (Juniper Mountain, with one million acre/feet of storage) is proposed upstream on the Yampa River; this must be stoutly resisted. Grazing is still permitted in the Monument, it should be terminated. Minor dirt roads around this roadless area should be closed for a much larger Wilderness area. There are some improved yet primitive campgrounds along the rivers for boaters.

Black Ridge Canyons 115,000 acres (also in Utah)

BLM WSA #070-113 (CO)	75,000
BLM WSA#060-118 and state roadless (UT)	40,000

Description: West of Grand Junction on the central Colorado-Utah border. This Colorado Plateau country features 13 arches (the second greatest concentration in the Southwest), sandstone side canyons, 43 miles of the Colorado River, exciting rapids and riparian forests along perennial streams. Westwater and Ruby Canyons of the Colorado make this area a magnet for whitewater boaters. The predominant vegetation is pinyon/juniper, sagebrush and cottonwood. A 450' cavern is cut by the stream in Mee Canyon. The canyons are popular for hiking, and have significant archaeological and paleontological sites. Colorado Squawfish, Humpbacked Chub and Razorback Sucker are extant but Endangered or Threatened fishes. Active Golden Eagle nesting sites and a rare butterfly, *Papilio indra minori*, are present. Desert Bighorn Sheep have been reintroduced. Other wildlife includes wintering Bald Eagle, Great Blue Heron and Ringtail.

Status: Conservationists propose 105,000 acres for Wilderness; BLM 100,000. All 43 miles of the Colorado here have been proposed for Wild or Scenic River designation. ORVs remain a major problem. A county road formerly separated the Westwater and Black Ridge Canyons WSAs, but it has been abandoned by the county at the request of the Mountain Island Ranch, which wholeheartedly supports Wilderness designation for the entire area and wishes to exchange their land on the Colorado River between the WSAs to BLM. The "road" is now gated and locked.

Dominguez Canyons 102,000 acres	
BLM WSAs 7-150/3-363 and additional	
BLM roadless	91,000
Uncompahgre NF roadless	11,000

Description: South of Grand Junction in west-central Colorado on the north side of the Uncompahgre Plateau. Elevations from 4,800' on the Gunnison River to 9,000' create a wide biological diversity. Two perennial streams cut slickrock canyons with numerous plunge pools. Vegetation on the ridges consists of Big Sagebrush and pinyon/juniper; Douglas-fir stringers and cottonwoods are in the canyons. Desert Bighorn Sheep have been reintroduced to the canyons; Elk, Black Bear and Mule Deer inhabit the high country; wintering Bald Eagles loiter along the Gunnison; and many species of raptors nest on the cliffs. The Threatened Uinta Basin Hookless Cactus and Endangered Spineless Hedgehog Cactus occur in Dominguez Canyon. Numerous archaeological sites include large petroglyph panels. Jurassic fossils are common, including the largest dinosaur yet discovered — Ultrasaurus.

Status: Some jeep trails and grazing "improvements" scar the area; both ORVs and overgrazing present future threats. Mining claims for precious metals have been staked. Conservationists propose a 90,000 acre Wilderness Area; BLM recommends 73,500. The proposed Dominguez Dam on the Gunnison River would impact the area.

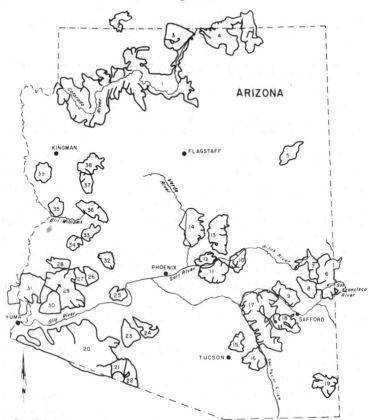

1. Grand Canyon
2. Parunuweap
3. Paria Canyon
4. Navajo Mountain
5. Painted Desert
6. Blue Range
7. Baldy Bill
8. Eagle Creek

9. Gila Mountains
10. Salt River
11. Superstition Mts
12. Four Peaks
13. Hellsgate
14. Mazatzal
15. Catalina Mts
16. Rincon Mts
17. Galiuro Mts
18. Mt. Graham
19. Chiricahua Mts
20. Cabeza Prieta

21. Bates Mountains
22. Ajo Mountains
23. Batamote-Sauceda Mts
24. Sand Tank Mts
25. Woolsey Pk-Signal Mt
26. Eagletail Mts
27. Little Horn Mts
28. New Water Mts
29. Kofa Mountains
30. Castle Dome Mts
31. Lower Colorado River
32. Bighorn Mountains
33. Harcuvar Mts East
34. Harcuvar Mts West
35. Mohave Wash
36. Arrastra Mountain
37. Aquarius Mts South
38. Aquarius Mts North
39. Black Mesa

Arizona

Political boundaries seldom follow ecological boundaries and Arizona is no exception. Within the human boundary of "Arizona" lie several natural provinces defined by R. G. Bailey in 1976: the Mexican Highlands Shrub Steppe (Sierra Madre and Chihuahuan Desert), Upper Gila Mountains Forest (Mogollon Rim), American Desert (Sonoran and Mojave Deserts) and Colorado Plateau. Each has its characteristic natives: oak, Chihuahua Pine, Coatimundi, Jaguar for the Sierra Madre; yucca and Javelina for the Chihuahuan Desert; Engelmann Spruce, Ponderosa Pine, Elk, trout for the Mogollon Rim; Saguaro, Gila Monster, Desert Bighorn for the Sonoran Desert; Joshua Tree and Desert Tortoise for the Mojave Desert; and Colorado Squawfish, Cliffrose, pinyon and juniper for the Colorado Plateau.

In nature, boundaries are fluid, open, interdigitating. Political boundaries try to be that way, too, but politicians defending the "nation" do their best to make such boundaries rigid, even to the extent of brick walls, concertina wire and machine guns. Nature enforces her boundaries more gracefully, with frost, precipitation and elevation. Plants and animals mix and meet new neighbors on the soft edges of natural provinces. Their easy integration makes one realize how fatuous, how ephemeral are the political affairs of our kind.

Yet, while our affairs may be fatuous and ephemeral in one sense, they are devastating in another. With cow, dirt bike, steel-jaw trap, thirty-ought-six, pickup truck, water pump, smelter, bulldozer, chainsaw and greenback, our kind has been ravaging Arizona since Padre Kino strode up the Rio Magdalena three centuries ago armed with Christianity and cattle. We have steadily accelerated the pace of destruction during the last hundred years until we are caroming out of control today.

Arizona has lost more of its old growth forest than has any other Western state; 95% of Arizona's riparian vegetation, crucial for wildlife, has disappeared; water tables have dropped and rivers (like the Santa Cruz through Tucson) have ceased to flow; the grass has gone into the livestockman's pocket and the soil to the Gulf of California. With this destruction of habitat and with campaigns of outright biocide, many of Arizona's leading citizens have disappeared into the mists of legend — Oso Gris, Lobo, El Tigre, Ocelot. . . .

Desert rats, canyon lovers and mountain freaks have been fighting to preserve Arizona since Teddy Roosevelt saw the Grand Canyon in 1903 and said, "Leave it as it is . . . The ages have been at work on it and man can only mar it." Unfortunately, we have not listened well to TR. Despite the best efforts of conservationists, little of Arizona has been left as it was.

Grand Canyon National Park still awaits Wilderness designation, as does the adjacent Lake Mead National Recreation Area. However, Organ Pipe Cactus and Saguaro National Monuments, and Petrified Forest NP have had reasonably good Wilderness Areas established. Wilderness proposals for Cabeza Prieta, Kofa, Imperial and Havasu National Wildlife Refuges were developed by the US Fish & Wildlife Service in the early 1970s, but Wilderness legislation has not been introduced. A joint Wildlife Refuge-BLM Wilderness bill for Arizona is now being discussed and may reach Congress in 1989.

The Forest Service evaluated 2,137,929 acres for Wilderness during RARE II in Arizona. Conservation groups recommended 2,154,674 acres for protection. The 1984 Arizona Wilderness Act was a political compromise granting protection to only 767,390 acres of National Forest land. A major failure of the bill was the omission of a Blue Range Wilderness. The Blue, in far eastern Arizona, was one of the earliest FS Primitive Areas and is the only one not yet designated as Wilderness (it may be included in the prospective BLM-NWR bill). Conservationists have continued their efforts to save wildlands on Arizona's six National Forests by appealing Forest Plans in order to halt destructive activities in released roadless areas.

Kofa National Wildlife Refuge, Arizona. Photo by Dave Foreman.

The 1984 Arizona Wilderness Act also included 265,000 acres of BLM Wilderness on the Arizona Strip — that part of the state north of the Grand Canyon. Pressure was intense to resolve the Wilderness question for this sprawling, unpopulated region because mining com-panies had discovered extremely high grade uranium ore in the area and a stalemate on Wilderness could have delayed their plans. Representatives of national conservation groups and Energy Fuels Nuclear, the principal mining company, worked out a compromise; Arizona's Congressional delegation took the ball and ran. The legislation opened several million acres around the Grand Canyon to uranium mining; the dozens of uranium mines now in operation and planned there are the legacy of this compromise (670,000 acres of former BLM WSAs have been blanketed with claims).

BLM identified a total of 2.1 million acres as Wilderness Study Areas in Arizona and has proposed 1,013,436 acres for Wilderness. The Arizona Wilderness Coalition recently issued a well-produced book outlining their comprehensive proposal of 2,222,091 acres for BLM Wilderness. Arizona Earth First! has countered with a 17 million acre Wilderness proposal for BLM lands, National Wildlife Refuges, the Grand Canyon and Blue Range.

The primary threats to Arizona Wilderness are continued overgrazing, ORVs, slob hunters and, in the White Mountains, Mogollon Rim and the Kaibab Plateau, logging. Additional threats to specific areas are mining, powerline corridors and urban sprawl.

Colorado Plateau

Northern Arizona is part of the Colorado Plateau, that extraordinary region of sandstone cut by the Colorado River and its tributaries. It is a land of rock, sometimes modestly clothed with Big Sagebrush, pinyon and juniper, but oft naked in a startling fashion. Grand Canyon and Petrified Forest National Parks; the Kaibab NF; the Navajo, Havasupai and Hualapai Indian Reservations; and BLM manage the land.

Grand Canyon 2,700,000 acres
Grand Canyon National Park roadless   1,131,508
Designated Saddle Mountain Wilderness Area

(Kaibab NF)	*40,600*
Designated Kanab Creek Wilderness Area	
(Kaibab NF & BLM)	*77,100*
Designated Mt. Logan Wilderness Area (BLM)	*14,600*
Lake Mead National Recreation Area roadless	*168,530*
Hualapai Indian Reservation roadless	*615,000*
Havasupai Indian Reservation roadless	*170,000*
Navajo Indian Reservation roadless	*180,000*
Additional Kaibab NF roadless	*15,000*
Additional BLM and intermixed state,	
private roadless	*288,000*

Description: Northwestern Arizona northwest of Flagstaff. The Grand Canyon of the Colorado with its side canyons and portions of its rims from Marble Canyon bridge to Lake Mead forms a single roadless area that is one of the most distinctive and awesome features of Earth. Two billion years of rocks lie exposed in this mile deep (8,200' to 2,400') chasm. Life zones range from Mojave Desert vegetation of Saltbush, mesquite and cacti in the depths of the Canyon to forests of Engelmann & Blue Spruce, White Fir, Douglas-fir and Aspen on the North Rim, with blackbrush, wolfberry, yucca, sagebrush, Cliffrose, pinyon, juniper, Ponderosa Pine and Gambel Oak in between. Precipitation varies from 25" on the North Rim (130" accumulation of snow is average) to 9" in the canyon bottom. Many miles of rough trail and one of the world's finest river float trips challenge the human visitor. Rampart and Vulture Caves have Ground Sloth dung. Bald Eagle, Peregrine Falcon, Speckled Rattlesnake, Bighorn Sheep, Mountain Lion, Spotted Bat, Pronghorn, Kit Fox, Beaver, Ringtail, Gray Fox, Bobcat, Bison, a world-famous herd of Rocky Mountain Mule Deer on the Kaibab Plateau, the endemic Kaibab Squirrel, and perhaps River Otter are some of the inhabitants. Desert species like Gila Monster, Desert Iguana, Sidewinder and Desert Tortoise reach the northeastern limits of their range in the Grand Canyon.

Status: Unprotected Forest Service and BLM roadless areas face severe and growing uranium mining pressure. Uranium mining also proceeds in adjacent areas surrounding the Canyon roadless area — the overall Grand Canyon region is being turned into an industrial zone threatened by radiation. In the 1984 Arizona Strip Wilderness Act, representatives of conservation groups, negotiating with a uranium company, Energy Fuels Nuclear, essentially agreed to allow uranium mining outside of designated Wilderness Areas in exchange for the designation of eight small BLM Wilderness Areas north of the Grand Canyon. Such is the nature of compromise environmentalism. Roads for uranium mining now provide access for pot hunters, poachers, trappers, off-road-vehicle (ORV) riders and other vermin.

Although the NPS has proposed 92% of the Park for Wilderness, the Park Service has largely sold out to commercial interests here. Excessive river use, especially by commercial outfitters using motorized rafts, is trashing the Colorado River corridor. Aircraft are as thick as flies on a dead cow in and above the Canyon. Aircraft restrictions have finally been developed, but they are inadequate. The Forest Service is logging the North Rim — right up to the edge (a bulldozer used in logging fell into the Canyon recently). Feral burros, officially eradicated, still compete with Bighorn Sheep.

The Bright Angel-Kaibab Trail corridor cuts across the canyon from the South Rim to the North. Although it is not a road, it is a heavily used and developed route that, some would argue, cuts the Grand Canyon wilderness in half.

Glen Canyon Damn upstream has restricted silt deposits and flushing floods with the result that beaches are disintegrating and becoming polluted, and the riverine ecosystem corrupted. The Damn has also lowered the water temperature, thereby devastating fish species like the Endangered Colorado Squawfish (which formerly grew up to 6' long and 100 lbs; survivors are much smaller and greatly depleted in number now), Endangered Humpback Chub, Loach Minnow, Little Colorado Spinedace and Threatened Razorback Sucker. The river now has a widely variable artificial flow controlled by sales of electricity.

Visibility is often limited in the Canyon due to air pollution from Los Angeles and coal-fired power plants in the Southwest. Air pollution, of course, has more nefarious impacts than veiling scenery.

Regrettably, neither conservation groups nor land managing agencies are looking at the Grand Canyon as a whole. Indeed, certain groups and individuals purporting to represent conservation interests have made shameful compromises. Teddy Roosevelt would be horrified if he could see what the Park Service, Forest Service and BLM have done to the Grand Canyon. An interagency, regional, programmatic, cumulative EIS on minerals and related land use in the entire Grand Canyon district is needed, along with an immediate moratorium on all further development.

RM36: 4,000,000

Parunuweap 137,000 acres (also in Utah)
See Utah for description and status.

Paria Canyon 290,000 acres (also in Utah)

Designated Paria Canyon-Vermilion Cliffs	
Wilderness Area BLM (AZ)	*90,046*
Designated Paria Canyon-Vermilion Cliffs	
Wilderness Area BLM (UT)	*19,954*
Additional BLM roadless (AZ & UT)	*180,000*

Description: Central Arizona-Utah border. This slickrock canyon complex west of Page includes portions of canyons carved in Navajo sandstone which are so deep and narrow that they seem like a sandstone analog to glacial crevasses. Buckskin Gulch is only a couple of feet wide in places and a hundred feet deep. Elevations drop from 7,356' to 3,200'. The canyon cuts through a plateau of slickrock and rolling sandy grassland dotted with sagebrush and pinyon/juniper. The brilliant Vermilion Cliffs rise 3,000' from House Rock Valley to the Paria Plateau. Paria Creek flows into the Colorado River at Lee's Ferry. Hikers, with no escape possible, face the danger of flash floods while in the canyons. Vegetation includes Sand Dropseed, Indian Ricegrass, Shadscale, Greasewood, Four-winged Saltbush and Golden Rabbitbrush in arid areas; willow, Fremont Cottonwood and Box Elder in the riparian zones; and Cliffrose, Apache-plume, pinyon/juniper and occasional Ponderosa Pine higher. Several state or federal Threatened or Endangered species live in the area, including Peregrine Falcon, Spotted Bat and Razorback Sucker.

Status: The designated Wilderness includes only Paria Canyon and the Vermilion Cliffs, leaving the central Paria Plateau unprotected. ORVs and overgrazing are damaging the area. The central plateau is a vitally needed addition to the Wilderness.

RM36: 8,890,000*

Navajo Mountain 850,000 acres (also in Utah)
Navajo Indian Reservation (AZ) roadless	*560,000*
Navajo Indian Reservation (UT) roadless	*290,000*

Description: Northern Arizona and southern Utah. This remote region to the south of "Lake" Powell and east of Page offers exceptional views of the Colorado Plateau from 10,000' high Navajo Mountain. Intricate, narrow, deep slot canyons flow from Navajo Mountain into the drowned San Juan River at 3,700'. Vegetation is sagebrush and pinyon/juniper with Ponderosa Pine in higher areas. Special features include Rainbow Bridge, Navajo Creek, Nokai Canyon, Skeleton Mesa and Navajo National Monument (with its exceptional Anasazi cliff dwellings).

Status: Protection is uncertain. Jeep trails and extensive livestock grazing are marring the land. The roadless area is nearly cut in half by dirt roads on Piute Mesa and to Navajo Mountain which come within five miles of "Lake" Powell. Another dirt road almost severs Nokai Canyon from Skeleton Mesa-Tsegi Canyon. Conservation groups need to work with the Navajo Tribe to gain recognition and protection for this huge wild area. 1,590,000 acres were designated as a BIA Roadless Area here in 1937 through the efforts of Bob Marshall, but that protective status was revoked in the early 1960s by the non-Indian staff of the Navajo Grazing Office. Since then developments and new pickup truck roads have halved the roadless area.

RM36: 8,890,000*

Painted Desert 140,000 acres
Petrified Forest National Park Wilderness

Area and additional roadless	50,000
Navajo Indian Reservation, private, BLM roadless	90,000

Description: Northeastern Arizona northeast of Holbrook. These barren, multicolored badlands north of I-40 have sparse Great Basin Desert vegetation, abundant petrified wood and many fossils. High point is 6,235' on Pilot Rock. Wildlife includes Pronghorn, Coyote and Bobcat.

Status: Overgrazing on adjacent private, BLM and Navajo land, and removal of petrified wood are problems.

RM36: 1,000,000

Central Mountains

The backbone of central Arizona is the Mogollon Rim. High plateaus stretch north of the Rim; broken mountains and canyons fall off to the south. Formerly this highland grew the world's largest Ponderosa Pine forest. Here is where most of Arizona's waters rise, and here Arizona appears less exotic than further to the south. Nevertheless, the influence of Mexico keeps the Mogollon Rim from being a typical part of the Rocky Mountains; biologically, the Mogollon Rim country mixes characteristics of the Rockies, Sierra Madre, Colorado Plateau, and Sonoran and Chihuahuan Deserts. This is largely National Forest — the Apache and Tonto NFs; although the Fort Apache & San Carlos Indian Reservations and BLM are also involved.

Blue Range-San Francisco 505,000 acres (also in New Mexico)

Designated Blue Range Wilderness Area (Gila NF, NM)	30,000
Blue Range Primitive Area (Apache NF, AZ)	180,139
Additional Apache & Gila NFs roadless (NM & AZ)	295,000

Description: The "Blue" is a rugged and little-visited area on the Arizona-New Mexico border west of the Gila Wilderness and north of Clifton, AZ. It consists of the deep canyons of the Blue and San Francisco Rivers and surrounding mountains along

the Mogollon Rim. Elevations range from 3,700' along the San
Francisco River to over 9,300' on Blue Peak. The Blue is similar
to the Gila (see New Mexico) in flora, fauna and geology, including rocky lower country covered with mesquite/grassland,
phasing upward to lush wet meadows in spruce/fir forest. The
southern (lower) part of the Blue has been severely overgrazed
but under recent protection is now coming back. The riparian
zones of cottonwood, willow, sycamore, walnut and mesquite (a
total of 32 broad-leaved trees and shrubs) along the San Francisco and Blue Rivers are of special biological importance. The
largest and healthiest herd of Rocky Mountain Bighorn Sheep
in the Southwest lives in the 1,600' deep canyon of the San
Francisco. Pronghorn roam the mesas above. There have been
reports of River Otter in the rivers. Javelina, Mountain Lion,
Elk, Bald Eagle, Peregrine Falcon, Common Black Hawk, Zone-
tailed Hawk, Osprey, Loach Minnow, Sonoran Mountain King
Snake, Arizona Coral Snake, Lyre Snake and Gila Monster are
other sensitive species. More than 200 species of birds breed
within a 50 mile radius of San Francisco Canyon — a number
which few other temperate non-marine areas can boast. The
Blue has the highest potential of any area in Arizona for Grizzly reintroduction. It would also be suitable as a reintroduction
site for Mexican Wolf.

   Status: Only a small part of this large area has received
Wilderness Act protection. Politically powerful ranchers in
eastern Arizona, along with timber interests and mining
corporations, have stridently fought Wilderness designation of
the Blue Range Primitive Area (the last remaining FS Primitive area) and conservation groups have not diligently cam-
paigned for the area because of its remoteness. The FS proposes
187,410 acres in Arizona to be added to the existing Blue
Wilderness (all of the Wilderness is currently in New Mexico)
but excludes San Francisco Canyon; the Arizona Wilderness
Coalition calls for 304,096 acres (including San Francisco
Canyon) and New Mexico conservationists have proposed
Wilderness for their part of San Francisco Canyon.

   Logging threatens the high country and severe overgrazing
continues throughout much of the area. ORVers stage supposedly macho (needing 8 cylinders to haul your fat ass through
wild country ain't macho) expeditions along San Francisco

Canyon — one of the most ecologically sensitive areas in the Southwest. A courageous effort by the Apache NF Supervisor to close San Francisco Canyon to ORVs was reversed in 1988 by the Regional Forester. The Gila NF is seriously considering the closure of the New Mexico portion of the canyon to vehicles as well. Conservationists must redouble their efforts to get the jeeps out! (ORVers have also looted important Mimbres archaeological sites in the canyon.) Mining potential presents a minor threat in the south. National as well as Arizona and New Mexico conservation groups should mount a major campaign to protect *all* of the Blue as Wilderness.

Although a double powerline crosses the San Francisco canyon near the Arizona-New Mexico border, we have not considered it to be a "road" since it is high above the river and does not have any road access within the canyon.

Baldy Bill 125,000 acres

Bear Wallow Wilderness Area (Apache NF)	*11,080*
Additional Apache National Forest roadless	*89,000*
Fort Apache Indian Reservation roadless	*25,000*

Description: Along the Mogollon Rim in east-central Arizona west of US 666 (across from the Blue Range) and south of Springerville. The Black River and several other trout streams cut canyons through this heavily forested area. Spruce/fir forest drops down to Ponderosa Pine to pinyon/juniper. Elevations range from 9,184' to under 5,000'. Mountain Lion, Black Bear, Elk, Mule Deer and Turkey are the big critters. The potential for Grizzly reintroduction is high. Terrain is similar to that of the nearby Blue Range.

Status: The Forest Service plans to clearcut most of the unprotected timbered area — which includes the finest old growth mixed conifer forest left in Arizona. A few jeep trails which formerly broke this area into several RARE II units are now washed out. Trail bikes are a threat, as is overgrazing. This is one of the choicest, but most overlooked, forested areas in Arizona. Conservation groups need to make it a major priority for preservation as an intact unit.

Eagle Creek 145,000 acres

Apache NF roadless	48,000
San Carlos Indian Reservation roadless	85,000
BLM, state, private roadless	12,000

Description: West of Clifton in southeastern Arizona. The Eagle Creek roadless area is the western end of the Greater Mogollon Highlands Ecosystem stretching from the Aldo Leopold and Gila in New Mexico through the Blue and Baldy Bill in Arizona. Eagle Creek and its tributaries form an exceptional riparian corridor through rough, lower elevation mountains. Elevations range from 7,113' on Elevator Mountain to under 4,000' on Eagle Creek. The higher reaches sport pinyon/juniper woodland and chaparral associations, while the lower country represents a transition between the Chihuahuan and Sonoran Deserts. The rich riparian zone is made up of Fremont Cottonwood, Arizona Sycamore, ash, willow, mesquite and Arizona Walnut. Considered with the adjacent Gila Box BLM WSA, Eagle Creek is the most important habitat in the United States for the Common Black Hawk. Bald Eagles have recently nested along Eagle Creek. There are 17 animal species in the area that are on state or federal Endangered or Threatened lists, or being considered for listing.

Status: Most of the FS land was inventoried in RARE II but recommended for non-Wilderness. Status of the San Carlos lands are uncertain. The lower part of Eagle Creek in this roadless area is private land owned by the Phelps-Dodge Copper Corporation. A dirt road separates this roadless area from the Baldy Bill area to the north; twisting, narrow US 666 is all that severs Eagle Creek and Baldy Bill from the Blue Range. An improved dirt road separates Eagle Creek from the Gila Box area to the south. The Arizona Wilderness Coalition has proposed that 151,680 acres of the Gila Box and the southern portion of this roadless area be studied for possible National Park designation. The study should be expanded to include all of the Apache NF land in this roadless area, and a cooperative agreement worked out with the San Carlos Apaches to protect their portion.

Continued grazing and ORVs are the primary threats.

Gila Mountains 194,000 acres

BLM WSAs 4-14/16 (Fishhooks-Day Mine)	32,524
Additional BLM roadless	71,000
San Carlos Apache Reservation roadless	69,000
State roadless	21,000

Description: Southeastern Arizona northwest of Safford. The Gila Mountains are a craggy range rising north of the Gila River from low rolling hills, and are punctuated by sheer cliffs, deep canyons and desert washes. Elevations range from around 3,200' to 6,629' on Gila Peak. This area has the farthest northeastern extension of the Saguaro; large areas of Creosote; a transition between oak/ juniper/ pinyon and mountain mahogany/oak scrub communities; and the largest existing stand of Lowell Ash, a candidate for Threatened species status. The uppermost watersheds are quite undisturbed by cattle grazing and have important climax vegetative communities needed by many mammals and birds. Wildlife includes Bald Eagle, Black Hawk, Javelina, Mule Deer and Mountain Lion. Numerous archaeological sites have been found.

Status: BLM chopped this area into several roadless areas due to the presence of minor, unmaintained vehicle ways. They are recommending only 10,883 acres for Wilderness. The Arizona Wilderness Coalition recognizes the unity of the area and has proposed an 80,000 acre Wilderness. Threats are additional grazing, ORVs and the pilfering and vandalism that comes with ORV use.

Salt River 110,000 acres

Designated Salt River Canyon Wilderness Area (Tonto NF)	32,800
Additional Tonto NF and Fort Apache Reservation roadless	77,000

Description: Central Arizona north of Globe. The precipitous canyon of the Salt River upstream of Theodore Roosevelt Reservoir has Sonoran Desert vegetation (Saguaro, etc.) phasing into pinyon/juniper. Elevations rise from 2,200' to 6,940'. The Salt offers a challenging whitewater float trip. Wildlife is similar to other Tonto NF areas.

Status: As in most Southwestern roadless areas, the unprotected area is being damaged by ORVs and overgrazing. More of the FS land should be added to the Wilderness and a hundred mile long stretch of the Salt River should be designated as a National Wild & Scenic River.

Superstition Mountains 269,000 acres

Designated Superstition Wilderness Area	
(Tonto NF)	*159,757*
Additional Tonto NF roadless	*96,000*
State roadless	*13,000*

Description: Central Arizona east of Phoenix. Weaver's Needle and the Lost Dutchman's Mine make this a well-known and popular area, replete with wild-eyed lunatics packing guns and treasure maps. Elevations rise from 1,700' to 6,266'. Very rugged topography and characteristically thorny Sonoran Desert vegetation (Saguaro, palo verde, mesquite) on the west leads into higher terrain with manzanita, ceanothus, oak, Arizona Cypress, mountain mahogany, pinyon/juniper and Ponderosa Pine in the east. The several perennial streams and springs have valuable riparian woodland. The typical Sonoran Desert/Southwestern Woodland fauna includes Phainopepla, Roadrunner, Verdin, Curve-billed Thrasher, Cactus Wren, Mountain Lion, Black Bear, Javelina, Bobcat, Whitetail and Mule Deer, Western Diamondback Rattlesnake and Gila Monster.

Status: The unprotected areas are threatened by overgrazing, ORVs and possible mining. Several rough dirt roads are cherrystemmed into the unprotected roadless area and there are several jeep trails cutting through it.

Four Peaks 100,000 acres

Designated Four Peaks Wilderness Area (Tonto NF)	*53,500*
Additional Tonto NF roadless	*46,500*

Description: Central Arizona northeast of Phoenix and north of the Salt River, in the southern Mazatzal Mountains between the Superstition, Mazatzal and Hellsgate roadless areas. The distinctive Four Peaks rise to 7,657'; the low point along the Salt River is 1,600'. Vegetation is Saguaro forest to Douglas-fir and Aspen. Black Bear, Mountain Lion, Mule Deer and Javelina roam the washes and slopes.

Status: The unprotected portion is open to ORV abuse and overgrazing.

Hellsgate 346,000 acres

Designated Hellsgate Wilderness Area (Tonto NF)	*36,780*
Designated Salome Wilderness Area (Tonto NF)	*18,950*
Additional Tonto NF roadless	*290,000*

Description: Central Arizona east of Payson and west of Young. This steep, convoluted country in the Sierra Ancha Mountains is sliced by formidable gorges. Tonto and Salome Creeks are perennial streams with important riparian zones. These creeks and their tributaries possess intricate, precipitous, narrow gorges that rival the best of the southern Utah Canyon Country. Elevations range from 2,200' to 7,000'. Vegetation is Saguaro through chaparral and pinyon/juniper to Ponderosa Pine. Wildlife includes Black Phoebe, Mule Deer, Black Bear, Mountain Lion and Javelina.

Status: The large roadless area between the two Wilderness Areas needs protection. ORVs, overgrazing and hobby mining threaten it. Several jeep trails penetrate it and one bone-jarring track crosses it. Range "improvements" also scar it. Conservation groups need to recognize the entire unit as one large roadless area deserving of protection.

Mazatzal 340,000 acres

Designated Mazatzal Wilderness Area (Tonto NF)	*251,912*
Additional Tonto NF roadless	*88,000*

Description: Central Arizona north of Phoenix. The roadless area consists of the northern end of the Mazatzal Mountains and the Verde Wild River west of the mountains. The high point is 7,904'; low is 2,000' on the Verde. The East Fork of the Verde cuts through the mountains. Topography ranges from craggy mountains and canyons to broad bajadas, flat-topped mesas and buttes, and open, flat country. Vegetation ranges from Aspen, Douglas-fir and Ponderosa Pine down to Saguaro,

Palo Verde, mesquite and other Sonoran Desert plants. Impressive stands of Arizona Cypress appear in the mid-elevation areas along with pinyon/juniper and chaparral. Occasionally deep snow accumulates in the mountains. The Verde is a fine float trip — one of the three possible in Saguaro country (the others being the Salt and Gila). Many Black Bear live here; this is one of the few places they can be seen among Saguaros. Gila Monster, Javelina, Mountain Lion, Mule Deer and Bald Eagle are other residents.

Status: Overgrazing continues in portions of the area, including the designated Wilderness. ORVs threaten unprotected areas. Air pollution from Phoenix increasingly degrades the entire area. Part of the Verde River in the Wilderness is a National Wild River; the rest of the Verde in the Wilderness as well as the East Verde River are proposed for that status.

RM27: 1,106,560

Sierra Madre

Southeastern Arizona is a zone of invasion from another nation — Mexico. It is basin and range like much of the western United States, but the basins are Chihuahuan Desert grassland with yucca and oak, and the ranges, despite their touch of the Rocky Mountains, are of the Sierra Madre in Mexico. These "Sky Islands" are among the most important habitats in the United States, supporting many species found nowhere else in our country. Strange kinds of pine and oak form forests alien to those expecting, say, Colorado. The Coronado NF, BLM, San Carlos Apaches, Saguaro National Monument and The Nature Conservancy manage the area.

Catalina Mountains 100,000 acres	
Designated Pusch Ridge Wilderness Area	
(Coronado NF)	56,933
Additional Coronado NF, state, private roadless	43,000

Description: Southeastern Arizona immediately northeast of Tucson. Rising from 2,800' along Canada del Oro, the Catalina roadless area climbs to 9,157' on Mt. Lemmon, forming the imposing skyline of Tucson. This well-watered desert mountain range has perennial streams, waterfalls and deep pools. Vegetation ranges upward from Saguaro/Ocotillo/palo verde to yucca grassland to oak savannah to pinyon/juniper to Ponderosa Pine/oak forest to Aspen, White Fir and Douglas-fir. Arizona Alder, Arizona Sycamore, Box Elder, cottonwood, willow, Arizona Walnut, Velvet Ash and other deciduous trees line the riparian zones. Wildlife includes Desert Bighorn Sheep, Mountain Lion, Black Bear, deer, Javelina and Coatimundi. A particularly rocky range, it is dissected by deep, precipitous canyons cutting in all directions. Summer temperatures hit 110° in the low country while the high country collects several feet of snow in the winter.

Status: Tucson's cancerous sprawl places great pressures on this roadless area; the Bighorn herd may not survive. Air pollution, suburban dog packs, excessive recreational use, and — most of all — encroaching subdivisions along the base of the mountains threaten the Wilderness. Ski area expansion and widening of the paved Mt. Lemmon Highway are damaging the adjoining Wilderness (the road to the top forms the eastern boundary of the roadless area). The additional FS roadless area should be added to the existing Wilderness (although a minor powerline, both underground and above ground, runs between) and adjacent state lands should be added to the NF Wilderness.

Rincon Mountains 217,000 acres

Saguaro National Monument Wilderness Area	60,000
Rincon Mountain Wilderness Area (Coronado NF)	38,590
Little Rincon RARE II (Coronado NF)	11,560
Additional Coronado NF roadless	24,000
Additional National Monument roadless	2,500
BLM, private and state roadless	80,000

Description: Southeastern Arizona immediately east of Tucson. A superlative Saguaro/palo verde/mesquite/Ocotillo forest leads up to oak and Amole (shin-dagger) to forests of Ponderosa Pine, Chihuahua Pine, Arizona White Oak, Arizona Cypress and Silverleaf Oak, then to Douglas-fir, White Fir and Aspen in the high country. This is a surprisingly well-watered range with streams hosting riparian woodlands of sycamore, willow and cottonwood dropping through nearly impassable canyons into the desert lowlands. Elevations range from under 2,700' to 8,666' on Mica Mountain. Wildlife includes Black Bear, Javelina, Mule Deer, Coues Whitetail Deer, Mountain Lion, Bobcat, tarantula, Desert Horned Lizard and Gila Monster.

Status: The unprotected Forest Service area is threatened by continued overgrazing and ORV abuse. Some adjacent private land is under threat of subdivision. A dirt road to Happy Valley is cherrystemmed in the FS portion, and several jeep trails penetrate the roadless area of mixed private, state and BLM land to the east. The Forest Service Wilderness and other FS land along with state, BLM and private land to the east down to the San Pedro River should be added to create a Saguaro Wilderness National Park of 350,000 acres; Ocelot, Jaguar, Jaguarundi and Mexican Wolf should be reintroduced into this preserve.

For a number of years, Park managers have been concerned with the lack of Saguaro reproduction. Recent research indicates that destruction of habitat for Sanborn's Longnose Bat in nearby caves may be the reason, since the bats pollinate Saguaros.

Galiuro Mountains 723,000 acres	
Designated Galiuro Wilderness Area (Coronado NF)	76,317
Designated Santa Teresa Wilderness Area (Coronado NF)	26,780
Designated Aravaipa Canyon Wilderness Area (BLM)	6,670
Needle's Eye BLM WSA 4-1A	9,485
Additional Forest Service, BLM, state, private and San Carlos Apache Reservation roadless	604,000

Description: Southeastern Arizona northeast of Tucson. This is a rugged area of extremely mixed ownership. The Galiuro Mountains reach 7,663' on Bassett Peak and the Santa Teresa Mountains reach 8,282' on Mt. Turnbull (on the San Carlos Reservation); the low point is about 2,300' along the Gila River on the northwest. Vegetation ranges from Ponderosa Pine and Aspen in the high country to Saguaro/palo verde and Creosote/bursage associations in the Sonoran Desert. There are

forests of Fremont Cottonwood, Arizona Sycamore, Netleaf
Hackberry, Velvet Ash, mesquite and Arizona Walnut in
riparian areas, some unusual alder/sycamore/oak riparian
forests, and extensive mesquite grasslands. The Table Top area
has the northernmost Blue Oak savannah, a very rare Alligator Juniper savannah, and desert grassland relatively undisturbed by grazing. Several canyon-bound perennial streams in a
desert setting (including scrumptious Aravaipa Creek) provide
crucial habitat for Endangered species of fish (the Gila Chub,
Spikedace and Loachminnow) and for Peregrine Falcon
(nesting). Aravaipa represents the best native fishery left in
Arizona. Other critters include Desert Bighorn Sheep, Ocelot,
Mountain Lion, Coues Whitetail Deer, Black Bear and infrequent, transient Mexican Wolf and Jaguar. Below Coolidge
Dam, the Gila River cuts a deeply incised canyon with numerous precipitous side canyons. This is an important part of this
roadless area and one of the more important riparian areas and
wild rivers in the state.

In a 1975 study, the FS identified the Galiuro Wilderness
as the least used unit in the Wilderness System.

Status: Conservationists are proposing a 27,520 acre addition to the Aravaipa Wilderness. BLM and conservationists
propose a 9,201 acre Needle's Eye Wilderness Area for the Gila
River canyon (an ancient 44 KV powerline runs through this
proposed Wilderness but is maintained by horseback and is
largely unnoticeable).

The Nature Conservancy manages the southern 50,000 acres
of this complex on their Muleshoe Ranch Preserve, and they
recently took over the George Whittell Wildlife Preserve on
both ends of BLM's Aravaipa Wilderness Area.

Only a small portion of this complex, however, is protected. The rest is vulnerable to overgrazing, poaching, ORVs,
road-building and mining. But the primary threat is the fact
that no agency or conservation group has recognized this area as
a single wilderness. Fragmentation will be its downfall. This
huge, untrammeled area has very high potential for Mexican
Wolf, Jaguarundi, Jaguar and Grizzly reintroduction. The
Ocelot population should be supplemented. This is a priceless
area and should be protected as a single 800,000 acre Wilderness Area.

Mt. Graham <u>208,000 acres</u>

Mt. Graham Wilderness Study Area (Coronado NF)	*62,000*
Additional Coronado NF roadless	*76,000*
State, BLM, private roadless	*70,000*

Description: An immense "Sky Island" mountain rising nearly 8,000' above Safford in southeastern Arizona. High Peak is 10,713' in elevation. The high country possesses a relict Ice Age forest of Engelmann Spruce, White Fir, Corkbark Fir, Douglas-fir, White Pine, Scouler Willow and Quaking Aspen which supports the Endangered Mt. Graham Red Squirrel and old growth-dependent Red-backed Vole. Other vegetative zones are the Ponderosa Pine/Arizona Pine/ Chihuahua Pine/Gambel Oak/Silverleaf Oak/Madrone forest and the Arizona Live Oak/Emory Oak/Alligator Juniper/ceanothus upper Sonoran association. Many perennial streams in precipitous canyons (with Arizona Sycamore, Box Elder, maple, ash, walnut) drop down to Chihuahuan Desert grassland and mesquite savannah. The densest population of Black Bear in the western United States occurs here. Thick-billed Parrots are present as are other Sierra Madrean species. Other wildlife includes Mountain Lion, Javelina, Coatimundi, deer, Mexican Spotted Owl and the Endangered Twin-spotted Rattlesnake. In short, this is a biological treasure trove.

Status: The roadless area is a horseshoe around an existing paved and graveled road up into the high country. Some selective logging was practiced previously in the high country adjacent to the road. Although this damaged the mixed conifer forest, it did not irreparably destroy it (a significant area of the high country was never logged). No timbering is now occurring. A number of cherrystem roads and jeep trails cut across the low desert to the base of the mountain and part way into some canyon bottoms. A large area of primarily state land (50,000 acres) to the west of the range and east of Aravaipa Creek should be added to the National Forest as part of the Wilderness to preserve its generally wild and roadless nature and to add a large expanse of Chihuahuan Desert to the diversity of the wilderness.

The primary threat to this area comes from an unexpected quarter: The University of Arizona proposes to place a dozen large telescopes on the summits of the range. This construction — if completed — will likely lead to the unraveling of the relict mixed conifer forest and the extinction of the squirrel and vole. Year-round human presence will disrupt the bears' feeding, mating and denning patterns. Conservation groups and the Arizona Game & Fish Department are engaged in a major struggle with the astronomers and their political supporters for the integrity of the mountain. Late in 1988, Arizona Senator Dennis DeConcini pushed through Congress a measure circumventing the National Environmental Policy Act and the Endangered Species Act, and allowing UA to build three telescopes. Construction is due to begin in 1989 but conservation groups have vowed to prevent it.

The scopes should be rejected, the existing road to the summit of the mountain closed, and state land contiguous to Mt. Graham added, for a 220,000 acre Wilderness. The FS proposes a 62,000 acre Wilderness.

Chiricahua Mountains 160,000 acres

Designated Chiricahua Wilderness Area	
(Coronado NF)	87,700
Additional Coronado NF, private, state roadless	72,000

Description: Southeastern Arizona north of Douglas. The most famous of the "Sky Islands" of southeastern Arizona, the Chiricahuas are a northern extension of the Sierra Madre of Mexico rising to 9,786' out of Chihuahuan Desert grassland at 4,600'. Vegetation zones include Engelmann Spruce and Aspen down to Ponderosa Pine, Chihuahua Pine, Arizona Pine, Gambel Oak, Silverleaf Oak, Arizona Cypress and Alligator Juniper to yucca and mesquite grassland, with rich riparian forests of Arizona Sycamore, walnut and cottonwood in the several well-watered canyons. This diversity of northern coniferous forest, Mexican pine/oak woodland, riparian zones and high desert creates an incredibly rich and diverse biota. Black Bear, Mountain Lion and Turkey are comparatively common. Mexican species include Javelina, Coatimundi, Coues Whitetail Deer (the densest population in the US), Elegant and Eared Trogon, Olive Warbler, Thick-billed Parrot (recently reintroduced), many species of hummingbirds, Mexican Chickadee (found only here in the US), Sulphur-bellied Flycatcher and Flammulated Owl. A Jaguar was killed nearby in 1987. In fascinating contrast, northern species like the Goshawk and Golden-crowned Kinglet nest here. Endemic subspecies include the Chiricahua Red Squirrel (a Mexican species not closely related to the Red Squirrel in the United States) and Chiricahua Green Rock Rattlesnake.

Status: Overgrazing, ORVs and heavy recreational use and development threaten the unprotected portion. There is excellent potential for reintroduction of Jaguar, Lobo (Mexican Wolf, a subspecies of Gray Wolf) and Ocelot. All of the contiguous roadless area should be added to the Wilderness as should wild country in Chiricahua National Monument, the Coronado NF Cochise Head area, and BLM's Dos Cabezas country to the north and northwest by closing dirt roads for a total Wilderness of 300,000 acres. (A 220,000 acre Chiricahua Wilderness was proposed by the first Presidential Conference on the Outdoors in 1928.)

Sonoran Desert

The symbol of the Sonoran Desert is the Saguaro, up to fifty feet tall and 200 years old. But the definer of the Sonoran Desert is rain. The surprising lushness of this arboreal (tree) desert is made possible by two rainy seasons — gentle winter rains from the Gulf of California and the Pacific, and summer thunderstorms (monsoons) from the Gulf of Mexico. Nevertheless, this is a desert with many days over 100° each year and only 12" to 2" of precipitation annually. The Sonoran Desert claims the southwestern quarter of Arizona and stretches south into Mexico. The Fish & Wildlife Service, with Cabeza Prieta, Kofa and Imperial National Wildlife Refuges; BLM; the Air Force and Marine Corps; the Tohono O'odham Indians; and the NPS, with Organ Pipe Cactus National Monument, divide the land.

Cabeza Prieta 1,627,000 acres

Cabeza Prieta NWR roadless	*817,000*
Goldwater Air Force Range roadless	*645,000*

Organ Pipe Cactus NM Wilderness & roadless	*46,000*
BLM WSA 5-40 (Gila Mts)	*8,765*
BLM roadless Yuma Desert	*10,000*
Contiguous roadless in Mexico	*100,000*

Description: Southwestern Arizona along the Mexican border between Yuma and Ajo, south of I-8. This peerless example of the Sonoran Desert is one of the most pristine large areas in North America. No native plant or animal has been extirpated; the two non-native birds and six introduced plants are rare. It is one of the driest and most remote areas in North America. The western end averages only 3" annual precipitation. Wildlife includes Desert Bighorn Sheep, Antelope Jackrabbit, Endangered Sonoran Pronghorn; Coatimundi and Javelina (western edge of range for both); Gila Monster, Desert Tortoise; Ferruginous Pygmy-owl, Crested Caracara, Tropical Kingbird; Tiger, Mojave, Western Diamondback and Sidewinder Rattlesnakes; Rosy Boa, Banded Sand Snake, Arizona Coral Snake; Flat-tailed Horned Lizard in the Yuma Dunes; Brown & White Pelican, Wood Stork and Magnificent Frigatebird as occasional overflyers; Sonoran Green Toad, Casque-headed Frog. Diverse Sonoran Desert vegetation includes Elephant Tree, Kearney Sumac, Saguaro, palo verde, Creosote, Ironwood, Organ Pipe Cactus, Senita and perhaps the largest Ocotillos in the USA. Six small, rugged, fault-block mountain ranges (of two kinds: a sierra-type of granitic and metamorphic rock, and a mesa-type of basaltic rock) are separated by wide alluvial valleys with sand dunes, lava flows and dry lake beds. This is one of the few desert areas encompassing a series of ranges with roadless valleys between them. The nearest thing to a road crossing Cabeza Prieta is a sandy jeep trail still known as the Camino del Diablo, or Way of the Devil, which bisects the area east-west. The Camino del Diablo was a feared route for Forty-niners and others in historic times and numerous graves mark this hot, waterless trail.

Status: The military uses the airspace for air-to-air gunnery training. This is disturbing to the visitor but has kept out ORVers, miners, ranchers and other riffraff. The Goldwater Range is, however, threatened by on-the-ground military operations and the possible siting of the Midgetman missile. A surprisingly large acreage is yet roadless on the military lands; most surface disturbing activities take place on the northern border of the military range, near the Interstate. The Marine Corps is more active with ground disturbing activities on the western end and have particularly impacted the portion of the Yuma Dunes in their range. (The Yuma Dunes are the prime habitat for the Flat-tailed Horned Lizard.) The Air Force has developed a resource management plan which will help protect the wilderness values of their land.

Although the Camino del Diablo and the Mohawk Valley public access "roads" divide Cabeza Prieta into three sections, we have considered this as one roadless area because these "roads," although regularly used, are quite primitive and require 4-wheel drive. The current Refuge administration does not fully appreciate the desert's pristine quality and has bladed jeep trails — supposed to be closed by their master plan and Wilderness proposal — for their administrative convenience. Some closed jeep trails are open to wealthy Bighorn Sheep hunters (who are the leading opponents of Wilderness designation). Such capricious actions by federal land managers were the impetus for the Wilderness Act.

The Camino del Diablo and all jeep trails in the area should be closed and blocked, and this entire area preserved as one Wilderness Area. The Sierra Club proposed this visionary idea in 1985 but has since backed down in an effort to appear "credible" with Arizona politicians, and is supporting a three unit Wilderness of 561,000, 161,000 (with military lands in the Tinajas Altas added) and 175,000 acres for a total of 894,000 acres; the USFWS proposes a three unit Wilderness of 833,500 acres.

Mexico Hwy 2 runs south of the international border separating the Cabeza from the Pinacate Desert and El Gran Desierto. (Approximately 100,000 acres of roadless land in Mexico are between Mexico Hwy 2 and the border. A Border Patrol route follows much of the border. Since this route requires 4 wheel drive and is not continuous — mountains interrupt it — we have considered the Mexican acreage an integral part of the Cabeza Prieta roadless area.) Although Pinacate is a Mexican National Park, management and patrolling is limited. A 6 million acre International Sonoran Desert Wilderness Park, en-

compassing Pinacate, the Gran Desierto, Cabeza Prieta and
Organ Pipe Cactus NM, should be established, and financial
support given to Mexico for protection of their part.

Bates Mountains 100,000 acres

Designated Organ Pipe Cactus National Monument
Wilderness Area   100,100

Description: Southwestern Arizona south of Ajo. This area
of the Sonoran Desert south of Ajo features Organ Pipe Cactus,
Saguaro, Ironwood; sloping bajadas and large desert washes.
See Cabeza Prieta for general ecological description. Kino
Peak, the high point, reaches 3,197'.
   Status: A poor dirt road separates this area from Cabeza
Prieta.

Ajo Mountains 160,000 acres

Organ Pipe Cactus National Monument Wilderness 102,300
Tohono O'odham Indian Reservation roadless   58,000

Description: Southwestern Arizona south of Ajo. This is a
relatively well-watered (10" a year), rugged Sonoran Desert
mountain range on the Mexican border with bajadas and plains
outwashing to around 1,600'. The high point is 4,808' atop Ajo
Peak. Organ Pipe Cactus, Saguaro and palo verde are replaced
at higher elevations by Ajo Oak, One-seed and Utah Juniper.
The few riparian zones around tinajas in the striking canyons
have hackberry trees and cattails. Much of this area consists of
the more arid bajadas below the mountains — here, the northern extension of the Central Gulf Coast phase of the Sonoran
Desert grades into the Arizona Succulent Desert phase. Desert
Bighorn, Javelina, Coues Whitetail Deer, Peregrine Falcon, Elf
Owl, Arizona Coral Snake, Mexican Black-headed Snake,
Desert Tortoise and Gila Monster are among the vertebrates
present.
   Status: The portion on the Reservation is overgrazed —
right to the crest of the Ajos. The Monument has not been
grazed by livestock since the mid-1970s and is recovering.

Batamote-Sauceda Mts 214,000 acres

BLM WSA 2-175 (Batamote Mts)	*56,385*
Goldwater Air Force Range roadless	*140,000*
Tohono O'odham Indian Reservation roadless	*18,000*

Description: Southwestern Arizona northeast of Ajo. This is a little-visited area of low but rugged desert mountain ranges, large bajadas and valleys, colorful cliffs and buttes, and desert washes accentuated by parallel bands of green. Elevations rise from 1,400' to 3,466'. The Lower Sonoran vegetation includes Organ Pipe Cactus (at the northeastern limit of its range), Saguaro, dense stands of cholla, Elephant Tree, Ironwood, palo verde and resplendent spring wildflowers. Gila Monster, Desert Tortoise, Desert Bighorn Sheep, Mountain Lion, Bobcat and Coues Whitetail Deer live here. Temperatures vary from 120° to (rarely) below freezing.

Status: BLM dropped their WSA because of opposition from Phelps-Dodge copper company. BLM claimed the area did not qualify because of the sights and sounds of nearby Ajo (a dying mining town) and its copper mines (the mines are now shut down). The military land is used for air to air gunnery practice (see Cabeza Prieta). Cattle graze throughout the area, and some jeep trails and water wells have been developed by ranchers. ORVs present an increasing problem.

Sand Tank Mountains 119,000 acres

Goldwater Air Force Range roadless	*76,000*
Tohono O'odham Indian Reservation roadless	*41,000*
BLM roadless	*2,000*

Description: Southwestern Arizona southeast of Gila Bend. See Batamote-Sauceda for general description. Squaw Tit at 4,021' is the high point; the low point is about 1,150'.

Status: Cattle graze both the military and Indian lands; there are some jeep trails and minor water developments used in the grazing operation on the edge of this roadless area but the core is quite pristine. It is an air to air gunnery range. A dirt road separates it from the Batamote-Sauceda area to the west.

Woolsey Peak-Signal Mountain 101,000 acres

BLM WSA 2-142/144	*73,930*

| BLM WSA 2-138 | 20,920 |
| Additional BLM & state roadless | 6,000 |

Description: Southwestern Arizona southwest of Phoenix. North of Gila Bend and the Painted Rock Reservoir on the Gila River in the stark, arid Gila Bend Mountains, Woolsey Peak, a large volcanic plug, rises 2,500' above the Gila River to 3,170' in elevation. Signal Mountain rises 1,200' above the surrounding bajada to 2,182'. A dozen basaltic mesas rise sharply in the central part of the area, as do rugged andesetic peaks and ridges in the west, and granitic formations in the east. Healthy Sonoran Desert vegetation of Saguaro/palo verde and Creosote/bursage with mesquite, Ironwood and acacia in the washes grows here. The easternmost population of Bigelow Nolina is here, as is essential Desert Bighorn Sheep and Desert Tortoise habitat. A vehicle route (not a road) in Woolsey Wash divides the two mountains.

Status: BLM proposes a 15,250 acre Signal Mt Wilderness and a 61,000 acre Woolsey Peak Wilderness. Conservation groups should call for closing the jeep route between the mountains and establishment of one Wilderness Area, but ask only for separate Wildernesses of 18,490 and 75,000 acres. Mining of dubious claims and ORVs are threats.

Eagletail Mountains 126,000 acres

| BLM WSA # 2-128 | 119,700 |
| Additional BLM and state, private roadless | 6,000 |

Description: Southwestern Arizona, west of Phoenix, east of Kofa NWR, and south of I-10. Distinctive peak profiles in this jagged basaltic desert mountain range rise to 3,300' above the desert plain at 1,200'. Free-standing Courthouse Rock is a prominent monolith on the north side of the range. Arches and windows are abundant, as are shallow caves which provide nesting for raptors. A perennial spring in a tight gorge creates a riparian habitat saturated with wildlife. A large flat wild area lies between the Eagletails and Cemetery Ridge to the south. Coyote, Desert Bighorn Sheep, Javelina and other wildlife typical of the Sonoran Desert live here. Palo verde/mixed cactus and Creosote/bursage are the main vegetative communities. A small relict population of juniper and oak on the north side of Eagletail Peak adds special importance to this part of the Sonoran Desert. Two plants are candidates for protection under the Endangered Species Act: *Peniocereus greggi* and *Opuntia wigginsi*.   A 10,000 year old rock art panel is present. This area affords a great feeling of spaciousness. Unfortunately, it also affords a startling view of a growing problem in southern Arizona: girdled Saguaros. Apparently, mice which ordinarily eat grasses are being forced by livestock overgrazing to eat cacti instead.

Status: BLM recommends 78,020 acres for Wilderness. The flat area is not proposed for protection and is threatened by overgrazing and ORVs. Conservation groups are proposing 97,000 acres for Wilderness. Minor dirt roads to west and south should be closed to combine the Eagletails with other BLM areas for addition to the Kofa NWR as a single one and a half million acre Wilderness.

   RM36: 740,000*

Little Horn Mountains 111,000 acres

BLM WSA 2-127	*91,930*
Additional BLM, state roadless	*19,000*

Description: Southwestern Arizona east of Kofa National Wildlife Refuge. The southern half of this roadless area consists of the highly dissected Little Horn Mountains, which reach 3,100'. The core of the range is a basaltic mesa cut by two 800' deep canyons and smaller side canyons exposing colorful red, yellow and buff Kofa volcanics, and featuring a large natural arch. The northern half of the roadless area is the Ranegras Plain, a rare pristine flat area — unmarred by tires or cows — which drops down to 1,300'. On the east are the rolling Nottbusch Valley and Palomas Plain with sandy washes. This provides key Bighorn Sheep habitat and migration routes, as well as good nesting areas on the cliffs for raptors. See Kofa for general description.

Status: BLM is recommending no wilderness for this outstanding area; conservation groups propose a 91,930 acre Wilderness. Mining and ORVs are threats. This should be combined with other BLM areas and the Kofa NWR for a 1.5 million acre Wilderness Area.

RM36: 740,000*

New Water Mountains 123,000 acres

BLM WSA 2-125	*58,600*
Kofa NWR and additional BLM roadless	*64,000*

Description: Southwestern Arizona, in the north end of Kofa National Wildlife Refuge south of I-10 and southeast of Quartzsite. This area consists of mesa-like basaltic mountains and typical Sonoran Desert vegetation. The Eagle Eye is a well-known large natural arch on the skyline that is visible from the Interstate. Black Mesa is a large flat-topped butte reaching 3,639'. A high density of Desert Bighorn Sheep and Desert Tortoise find habitat here. See Kofa for general description.

Status: ORVs and hobby mining threaten the BLM portion. A proposed powerline along I-10 would cut into the BLM WSA. BLM is proposing a 21,680 acre Wilderness and conservation groups a 24,200 acre BLM Wilderness which, with additional BLM lands, would be added to Kofa NWR. A powerline divides this area from the main Kofa roadless area to the south. Kofa NWR proposes about half of their acreage for Wilderness. An attempt by BLM to transfer the Kofa NWR north of the powerline corridor to BLM administration was defeated by conservation groups in Congress in 1988.

Kofa Mountains 597,000 acres

Kofa National Wildlife Refuge roadless	*377,000*
Yuma Proving Ground Marine Base roadless	*120,000*
BLM roadless	*100,000*

Description: Southwestern Arizona northeast of Yuma. The Kofa, Little Horn, Tank and Palomas mountains are volcanic desert ranges with jagged rock formations and natural arches. Large desert washes, alluvial plains and wide valleys divide the mountains. Signal Peak reaches 4,877' (with views of Mt. San Jacinto in California) and the lowest elevations are around 800'. Water is limited to rock tanks or potholes in the mountains, and a few seeps. Precipitation averages 3" to 8" a year. Kofa is a   crucial habitat for Desert Bighorn Sheep. Other wildlife includes Gila Monster, Desert Tortoise, Mule Deer, Kit Fox, Golden Eagle, Prairie Falcon, Gambel's Quail, Mourning and White-winged Dove. Mountain Lion and Javelina are rare. The only wild palms in Arizona (California Fan Palm) grow in the canyons of the Kofa Mountains. Vegetation is typical of the Sonoran Desert with Saguaro/palo verde, Creosote/bursage to yucca/grassland associations.   Also present is the Kofa Mountain Barberry, a rare indigenous plant. Turbinella Oak inhabits some of the canyons. Species at the western or southern limit of their range are Arizona Coral Snake, Black-tailed Rattlesnake, Curve-billed Thrasher and White Thorn Acacia.

Status: Several jeep trails, some well established in places, cross or penetrate this large area. ORV enthusiasts, posing as hunters, have mounted a major campaign to prevent Wilderness designation for the Refuge (which would close many of the jeep trails). Cattle were removed in the 1970s. Congress closed Kofa to new mining claims in 1988. The status of the Marine Base area is uncertain.

The Arizona Wilderness Coalition proposes a four-unit Wilderness of 653,260 acres in the Kofa NWR and adjacent BLM land, leaving open some of the jeep trails for "access." The FWS proposes a 543,980 acre Wilderness in several units. By closing minor dirt roads and jeep trails, a single Wilderness of 1.5 million acres, including the BLM areas to the east, could be established.

RM36: 740,000*

Castle Dome Mountains 200,000 acres

Kofa National Wildlife Refuge roadless	130,000
Yuma Test Station Marine Base roadless	70,000

Description: Southwestern Arizona, in the southern end of Kofa NWR, northeast of Yuma, including the eastern two-thirds of the rugged Castle Dome Mountains (east of the McPherson Pass road). Desert Bighorn Sheep thrive here. Distinctively-shaped Castle Dome Peak is 3,788' and a landmark for many miles. See Kofa Mts for detailed description.

Status: FWS has proposed most of this area for Wilderness. Several jeep trails enter the area. See Kofa Mts for more detail. The estimate of roadless acreage on the Marine base is rough. The McPherson Pass road should be closed and the western 50,000 acres of the Castle Dome Mountains combined with this area and incorporated into a 1.5 million acre Kofa Wilderness.

Lower Colorado River 462,000 acres (also in California)

Imperial National Wildlife Refuge roadless (AZ & CA)	24,000
BLM WSA 5-23B and additional roadless (AZ)	66,000
Yuma Proving Grounds Marine Base roadless (AZ)	235,000
Picacho State Recreation Area roadless (CA)	5,000
Ft. Yuma Indian Reservation roadless (CA)	2,000
BLM WSAs CDCA 356, 355A, 355 and additional BLM, private state roadless (CA)	130,000

Description: Southwestern Arizona and southeastern California between Yuma and Blythe, including 29 miles of the Colorado River and adjacent desert mountains in Arizona and California. Elevations rise from 200' to 2,772' on Mohave Peak (AZ) and 2,177' on Quartz Peak (CA). This area represents the best opportunity to preserve a portion of the lower Colorado River. This exceptionally diverse desert area ranges from backwater lakes (Island, Norton's and Adobe Lakes) and riparian vegetation along the Colorado (Cattail, Bulrush, Arrowweed, mesquite, willow, cottonwood) to arid, harsh Sonoran and Colorado Desert topography and vegetation (Saguaro, Ocotillo, palo verde, bursage, Desert Holly, Desert Lavender, Smoketree, Ironwood) in the rocky Trigo and Chocolate Mountains. This is the only roadless area that includes parts of the Colorado River below the Grand Canyon and features an ecological transect from the Sonoran Desert with Saguaro to the Colorado Desert without Saguaro. Yuma Wash and other large desert washes cut through the mountains. Cliffs rise 800' above stretches of the river. The mountains offer much-needed habitat for the beleaguered Desert Bighorn and for Mountain Lion. This is one of the few areas in the lower Sonoran Desert able to support a lion population — in this case the Yuma Puma, an Endangered subspecies. Gila Monster, Sidewinder, Beaver, Muskrat, Gray Fox, Peregrine Falcon, White Pelican, Sandhill Crane, Double-crested Cormorant, Osprey, Bald Eagle, Tundra Swan, Crissal Thrasher and other natives form a unique assemblage of creatures. Prime habitat for the Endangered Yuma Clapper Rail is here. The Endangered Colorado Squawfish and Threatened Razorback Sucker are present in the river. Abundant waterfowl, including herons, egrets, ducks and geese, feed on the river.

Status: The FWS has proposed Wilderness for most of the Imperial NWR roadless area (with the major exception of the river itself and backwater lakes and marshes — which they want to dredge to "enhance" waterfowl habitat); BLM has recommended 29,095 acres for Wilderness in Arizona. California BLM proposes a 5,418 acre Picacho Peak Wilderness, a 24,902 Indian Pass Wilderness, and no Wilderness for the Little Picacho area. The Cranston bill (see California introduction) would establish 7,300 acre Picacho, 34,420 acre Little Picacho and 35,320 acre Indian Pass Wildernesses. Arizona conservationists currently propose a 56,420 acre Imperial NWR-Trigo Wilderness including the crucial riparian zones, but not the river itself.

Unfortunately, the proposal from Arizona conservationists represents a scaling back of the original Wilderness proposal for Imperial NWR by the Sierra Club and Wilderness Society in 1972. At that time, 23,900 acres of the Refuge, including the Colorado River above Picacho State Recreation Area, were proposed for Wilderness. The river below Picacho was recommended for National Wild & Scenic River status. Conservation groups in Arizona and California need to return to this original stand and develop a comprehensive Wilderness proposal including the Colorado River and adjacent lands in both states.

Status of the Marine Corps Base land is uncertain (the estimate of what is actually wild & roadless here is rough). This area deserves far more attention from conservationists. FWS plans to ravage the Colorado River should be resisted through all effective means possible. ORVs and petty miners threaten the BLM lands (old mining districts are included). Motorboats should be prohibited from the Colorado River here.

A road to Picacho State Recreation Area is cherrystemmed through the California portion. Other dirt roads and jeep trails also penetrate this wide-open desert area, and motorboats are permitted on the river.

Selenium contamination has recently been reported in the river and fishing is not advised. Pelicans have little choice in the matter, however. Irrigated agriculture (in this case, the lettuce and melon fields around Blythe) carries the seeds of its own destruction with heavy metal and salt buildup. While it can be argued that there is justice in this, it is a terrible comment on our stewardship that we poison everything around us.

Nonetheless, read the chapter "Green Lagoons" (about the Colorado River delta in the 1920s) in Aldo Leopold's **A Sand County Almanac**. This roadless area is the closest we can come today.

Northern Sonoran & Mojave Deserts

The Sonoran Desert grades into the Mojave Desert in west-central Arizona. This is BLM country.

Bighorn Mountains 100,000 acres	
BLM WSA 2-100 *Hummingbird Springs*	*67,680*
BLM WSA 2-99 *Big Horn Peak*	*22,337*
Additional BLM, state, private roadless	*10,000*

Description: West-central Arizona west of Phoenix. This scenic Sonoran Desert range reaches 3,418' on Sugarloaf Mountain and 3,480' on Big Horn Peak. These peaks rise 1,800' above the desert plain, which includes a large roadless flat. Tight canyons twist through the mountains. Sheer cliff faces, fins, and a large natural arch are among the outstanding sights. Vegetation is diverse with Creosote/bursage on the flats, dense Ironwood, mesquite and acacia along the washes, and palo verde, Saguaro and other cacti on the higher ground. Four rare plants inhabit the area. Cliffs provide critical nesting habitat for Golden Eagle, Prairie Falcon, Barn Owl and Great Horned Owl. Other wildlife includes Desert Bighorn, Kit Fox, Desert Tortoise (crucial habitat), Gila Monster and Cooper's Hawk.

Status: A bulldozer scrape separates the two WSAs but it should not be considered a road. BLM proposes a 21,150 acre Big

Horn Wilderness but no Wilderness in the Hummingbird Springs area; conservation groups do little better with proposals of 22,337 and 31,500 acres respectively. Mining, ORVs and continued cattle grazing threaten the area. In a few years, urban development spilling over from the Phoenix abomination will lap up to these ranges — without Wilderness now, ORVers from these future subdivisions, with their trash, guns, and disregard for things natural will destroy much of the area.

Harcuvar Mountains East 101,000 acres

BLM WSA 2-75	*74,788*
Additional BLM, and state, private roadless	*26,000*

Description: West-central Arizona, between Phoenix and Parker Dam. Smith Peak at 5,242' is the highest part of the mountain mass. This large Sonoran Desert mountain rises sharply 2,800' from the desert floor; this roadless area is its eastern half. An unimportant paved road crossing over Cunningham Pass separates it from the Harcuvar Mountains West. Wildlife includes Desert Bighorn Sheep, Mountain Lion, Kit Fox and Golden Eagle. A special feature is an isolated and undisturbed area of interior chaparral with extensive stands of several native perennial grasses providing habitat to Fishhook Cactus, Gilbert's Skink, Rosy Boa and Desert Night Lizard. Vegetative communities also include Creosote/bursage, Saguaro/palo verde, mixed thorn scrub, and mixed riparian scrub.

Status: BLM proposes only 25,287 acres for Wilderness, and conservationists are asking for a mere 49,390 acres. Threats include, along with the standard ORVs and prospecting, additional electronic communication sites on the range's crest and the construction of a gas pipeline along the western boundary.

Harcuvar Mountains West 100,000 acres

BLM roadless areas 2-90,91,92	*91,979*
Additional BLM and state, private roadless	*8,000*

Description: The western end of the Harcuvar Mountains (see Harcuvar Mts East for general description). This area cul-

minates in Harcuvar Peak at 4,618'. It also includes the Granite
Wash Mountains.

Status: BLM dropped it from wilderness consideration because of mineral potential. Three rough jeep trails cross it.
Mining and ORVs threaten it.

Mohave Wash 125,000 acres

BLM WSA 5-7C/48/2-52 with state & private	113,245
Additional BLM and Havasu NWR, state, private roadless	12,000

Description: West-central Arizona east of Lake Havasu
City and Parker Dam in the Bill Williams Mountains. This
varied desert area includes Mohave Springs Mesa, Castaneda
Hills, Black Mountain and the Mohave Wash drainage. Elevations drop from 2,733' to under 500'. The Mojave Desert vegetation includes Creosote, Red Barrel Cactus, Boxthorn, Ocotillo,
with Ironwood, palo verde and Smoketree in the washes. Topographically, it consists of rough mountains, volcanic tablelands, large desert washes, and cliffs and spires along the Bill
Williams River on the southern edge of the area. An important
part of this roadless area is the marshland of the Bill
Williams River delta in Havasu NWR which provides crucial
habitat for the Endangered Yuma Clapper Rail and other sensitive and rare water birds. Wildlife includes Desert Bighorn,
Desert Tortoise and other typical Mojave Desert species.

Status: BLM proposes Wilderness for 55,018 acres in three
units broken by ORV corridors. The Arizona Wilderness Coalition unfortunately agrees, thereby giving dirt bikers and other
motorized weenies what they want at the expense of the land.
Moreover, neither the Arizona Wilderness Coalition nor the
FWS recognizes the importance of the Bill Williams marshes
and the need for Wilderness designation for that part of the
Havasu NWR. With a little vision, this area could be combined with the Arrastra Mountain WSA to the east and other
BLM roadless areas in the Bill Williams River country, simply
by closing a few jeep trails and unnecessary dirt roads, for a
million acre Wilderness. ORVs, trapping, overgrazing and
hobby mining are continuing and potentially major threats.
*RM36: 700,000**

Arrastra Mountain 225,000 acres

BLM Arrastra Mountain WSA 2-59	*123,930*
BLM Black Mt-Ives Peak WSA 2-204	*9,665*
BLM Tres Alamos WSA 2-205	*8,910*
Additional BLM, state & private roadless	*82,000*

Description: West-central Arizona east of Parker Dam. This is one of the most diverse and exceptional desert wildlands in North America. Arrastra Mountain in the Poachie Range rises to 4,807'; Ives Peak in the Black Mountains on the southeastern end of the area rises to 4,072'; and Sawyer Peak in the Tres Alamos hits 4,293'. The Big Sandy and Santa Maria Rivers (their elevations drop to 1,500' at the high water mark for Alamo Reservoir where they come together to form the Bill Williams River) are intermittent desert rivers with over 20 miles of rare riparian vegetation, including willow, Fremont Cottonwood, Arizona Sycamore, Arizona Walnut, Red Barberry, columbine, monkey flower and Cattail. The extensive mesquite bosque along the Santa Maria has been described by BLM as the "largest, healthiest undisturbed habitat of this type in the state." People's Canyon is a perennially flowing desert creek with lush vegetation — impenetrable and jungle-like in places — including Arizona Madrone far north of its normal range and an orchid and tropical fern found elsewhere in Arizona only in two sites in the southeastern part of the state. Narrow, winding canyons drop into the rivers from the mountains (Date Creek cuts a 200' deep gorge in the Tres Alamos WSA); there are also several perennial springs and tinajas with associated riparian vegetation. One spring creates several large pools and a 60' waterfall. The Artillery Mountains west of the Big Sandy are extremely rugged and dominated by the red spire of Artillery Peak.

This remote and little-used area has tremendous vegetative variety due to it being the juncture of the Sonoran and Mojave Deserts. Six distinct plant communities are present, and this may be the only place on Earth where Saguaro, palo verde, mesquite, Joshua Tree, oak and juniper grow side by side. It affords a large tract of prime Desert Tortoise habitat, and high potential for reintroduction of Desert Bighorn Sheep (they have already been reintroduced in the Ives Peak area). Among the 292 vertebrate species found in the area (high for a desert area) are Bald Eagle, Zone-tailed Hawk, Peregrine Falcon, Harris' Hawk, Snowy Egret, Osprey; Round-tailed Chub, Desert Pupfish, Gila Topminnow; Mountain Lion; Desert Tortoise and Gila Monster. The two dozen significant archaeological sites include exceptional petroglyph panels in Black Canyon, a winding volcanic gorge with springs in the northern part.

Status: BLM proposes 109,523 acres for Wilderness in the Arrastra Mt WSA but no Wilderness is recommended for the other two WSAs. Conservation groups have failed to see the unity here and feel bound by individual WSAs — they propose three separate Wilderness Areas of 133,100, 12,670, and 12,660 acres, thereby ignoring the wild state land joining the BLM areas. Arrastra Mountain should be made the core of a large Sonoran Desert Wilderness Preserve of 1 million acres by closing minor dirt roads in the area and adding roadless areas west to Mohave Wash.

A jeep trail cuts between Ives and Tres Alamos WSAs. Overgrazing, ORVs and hobby mining are threats. Morons on ATVs have discovered the Santa Maria. Protection for this unique Sonoran Desert riparian area is essential *now*.

RM36: 700,000*

Aquarius Mountains South 120,000 acres
Private, BLM, state roadless   *120,000*

Description: West-central Arizona east of Wickiup. This is an area of checkerboarded land ownership in the Aquarius Mountains. Mojave Desert vegetation phases into pinyon/juniper with elevations from 2,600' to 5,000'. See Aquarius Mts North for detailed description.

Status: See Aquarius Mts North. This area is divided from Aquarius Mts North by a minor dirt road, and from the Burro Creek BLM WSAs to the south by a dirt road, pipeline and powerline corridor.

RM36: 620,000*

Aquarius Mts North (Trout Creek) 190,000 acres

Mixed state, private roadless   *190,000*

Description: West-central Arizona east of Kingman. This is a virtually unknown area in the Trout Creek drainage of the Aquarius Mountains south of I-40 and east of US 93. Land ownership is checkerboarded state and private. Trout Creek is a spectacular canyon with perennial water. Vegetation ranges from Mojave Desert scrub to sparse Ponderosa Pine with extensive areas of pinyon/juniper in between, along with important riparian zones. Wildlife includes Black Bear, Mountain Lion, Bighorn, Mule Deer and Golden Eagle. Elevations range from 3,000' to 6,000'.

Status: Because of land ownership, little is known about this area, but it may be one of the more important wildlands in Arizona. There are a million acres of wild backcountry in the Aquarius Mountains between I-40 and the mining town of Bagdad to the south, crossed only by a handful of primitive dirt roads and jeep trails, and dotted with a few range "improvements" for cattle grazing. The southern end of the Aquarius Mts has BLM land, including two outstanding WSAs in the Burro Creek drainage. A roadless area of 120,000 acres lies between the Burro Creek country and this Trout Creek area (see Aquarius Mountains South). Conservationists should explore potential ways of preserving this entire region.

RM36: 620,000*

Black Mesa 145,000 acres

BLM Warm Springs WSA 2-28/29	*114,800*
Additional BLM, state, private roadless	*30,000*

Description: Northwestern Arizona, west of Kingman. Black Mesa is a huge basaltic mesa surrounded by sloping bajadas and colorful badlands. Canyons cut the mesa to the south; the largest of these, Warm Springs Wash, has three small warm springs. Farther south is a long flat plain littered with basaltic boulders which make travel difficult. The mesa rises 1,800' above the desert plain on the east. A fine array of Mojave Desert vegetation is represented, with impressive cholla cactus stands, Mojave Yucca and Bigelow Nolina on the mesa; Blackbrush, Mexican Bladdersage and other forbs in the northern part; and Creosote, mesquite, palo verde, Ocotillo, cactus, Smoke Tree and Cat Claw Acacia to the south. This is an important lambing area for Desert Bighorn. Other sensitive wildlife includes Kit Fox, Desert Rosy Boa, Gila Monster, Desert Tortoise, Gilbert's Skink, Desert Night Lizard, Le Conte's Thrasher, Peregrine & Prairie Falcon and Golden Eagle. Few humans visit this area.

Status: BLM recommends 90,600 acres for Wilderness; conservationists 94,180. Both conservationist and BLM proposals leave open a jeep trail from the south into the center of the area at the warm springs. This teeth-rattling vehicle route should be closed to protect the springs, which are valuable for wildlife. The large population of feral burros should be removed. BLM claims that the jeep trail to the warm springs is necessary for burro removal. If this is so, it should be open only for official use and permanently closed after the burros are eliminated. Mining is a major threat on the western side of the area. This area should be given high priority for protection.

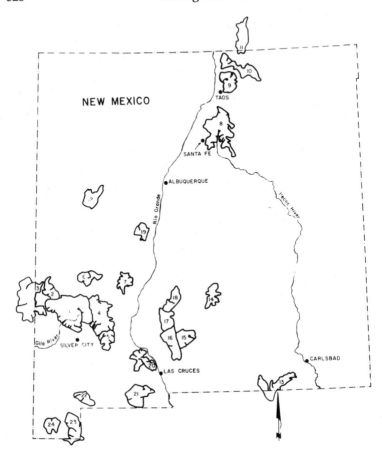

1. Gila
2. Devils Creek
3. Blue Range
4. Aldo Leopold
5. Sawyers Peak
6. Continental Divide
7. Apache Kid
8. Pecos
9. Wheeler Peak
10. Latir Pk-Ponil Ck
11. Culebra
12. El Malpais
13. Guadalupe Escarpment
14. Sierra Blanca
15. White Sands
16. San Andres Mts South
17. San Andres Mts Central
18. San Andres Mts North
19. Sierra Ladrones
20. Robledo-Las Uvas Mts
21. West Potrillo Mts
22. Cedar Mountains
23. Big Hatchet-Alamo Hueco
24. Animas Mountains

New Mexico

Our sense of wilderness aesthetics, of what is beautiful in wild nature, was formed largely in the European Alps. As a society we are still mired in that medieval approach to landscape appreciation. Even the Jim Watts and Ronald Reagans among us can marvel at the grandeur of the Tetons, the majesty of Mt. Rainier, the magnificence of the Colorado Rockies. As a nation, our first efforts at preservation were directed not towards wilderness or ecological integrity but rather towards the spectacles and curiosities of nature — Yosemite Valley, Yellowstone, the Grand Canyon.

It is far more difficult to preserve the commonplace, the wild area of unremarkable scenery, a plant or animal that does not inspire human emotions through its beauty or nobility. (It is one thing, for example, to protect the Bald Eagle, quite another to preserve Goodding's Onion.)

This being so, the first effort anywhere in the world to specifically preserve an area for its *wilderness* qualities is all the more noteworthy because it occurred in what is arguably the least spectacular of the Western states — New Mexico — and in an area — the headwaters of the Gila River — that, while not unattractive, is certainly not cut from the classic mold of the Alps. There are no peaks rising grandly above timberline, no jewel-like lakes shining in glacier-carved basins.

Land preservation in New Mexico represents a maturing of the European approach to nature appreciation. Sunsets here are stunning, there is a striking starkness about the land, the blending of three cultures — Indian, Spanish and Anglo — is quaint, but, overall, the spell this land casts is subtle, subliminal. While the hordes rush to Niagara Falls or the Alps, the finest of our kind — D.H. Lawrence, Aldo Leopold, Georgia O'Keeffe, Frank Waters, Mary Austin, Edward Abbey — have been drawn to New Mexico.

New Mexico has less potential Wilderness and fewer large roadless areas than do most western states, and it would behoove us to inquire into this lack. One might first suggest that although New Mexico is a very large state, fully one-third of it is in the Great Plains where mechanized agriculture and the private ownership of land virtually preclude large tracts of wilderness. But the same can be said for Colorado, Wyoming or Montana.

Two other factors offer better explanations. For one, New Mexico has been inhabited and used by Europeans longer than other areas of the West. The Spanish have been in northern New Mexico continuously since 1700 and thus, New Mexican villagers have used the high mountains for sheep pasturage and have diverted the streams for irrigation for almost three hundred years. More significantly, the first cattle frontier after Texas was New Mexico, and ranchers in New Mexico today tend to be more "Texan" than do ranchers in other western states. When the history of the cowboy is little more than 100 years long, a decade head start is significant.

The second factor, which is more important, is closely tied to this Texas ranching heritage. New Mexico's landscape and weather make her more accessible than is the rest of the West: her deserts are not as hot or barren as California's; her winters not as frigid or long as Montana's; her mountains lusher and better watered than Nevada's. In this gentler terrain, ranchers have been able to punch roads to more places than they have in other western states. Moreover, grazing in much of New Mexico is year-'round, unlike the Northern Rockies where ranchers herd their cows up into the mountains for only a few summer months and run the operation by horseback. To make much of arid New Mexico available for 12-month cattle grazing, stock ponds have been built to capture runoff; this requires road access.

So, the reason there is less of the Big Outside in New Mexico is because the land is dry, but not too dry; is rough, but not too rough; and because cattlemen here have had a longer time to fully exploit the public lands.

New Mexico, ecologically, is a complex state, a meeting-ground of ecosystems: the Great Plains from the east, the Chihuahuan Desert from the southeast, the Sierra Madre from the south, the Sonoran Desert from the southwest, the Great Basin and Colorado Plateau from the northwest, and the Rocky Mountains from the north.

Wilderness preservation has a long and active history in New Mexico. The Forest Service administratively established the first Wilderness Area — the Gila — here in 1924. New Mexico Sen. Clinton P. Anderson shepherded the Wilderness Act during its consideration in the Senate. The nation's first Wild & Scenic River — the Rio Grande — was established in 1968 in northern New Mexico. Except for White Sands National Monument and San Andres NWR, the National Parks and Wildlife Refuges in New Mexico which qualify have had Wilderness Areas established. The Bisti led the way for BLM Wilderness and New Mexico may also develop the first state-wide BLM Wilderness bill. Beating Colorado by a few days in 1980, New Mexico produced the first post-RARE II National Forest Wilderness bill.

This is not to say that by pioneering Wilderness preservation, New Mexico has fared well. Of 2,137,776 acres considered in RARE II, the New Mexico Wilderness Study Committee recommended 1,816,000 for Wilderness, but only 609,060 were designated in the 1980 New Mexico Wilderness bill (117,530 acres were left for further study). New Mexico BLM has recommended Wilderness for 761,159 acres (counting intermixed state and private lands). The New Mexico BLM Wilderness Coalition (including the Sierra Club and other groups), in an excellent 230-page book, has countered with a proposal for 1,879,289 acres. New Mexico Earth First! has upped the ante by calling for 5.3 million acres of BLM Wilderness. The New Mexico Congressional delegation may introduce a bill in 1989 and what it will be is anybody's guess. New Mexico conservationists are also discussing additional National Forest Wilderness legislation.

As elsewhere, the timbered roadless areas in New Mexico's National Forests are under attack by the Forest Service and the logging industry. Although timber sales in New Mexico are usually below cost, logging is a serious threat to roadless areas on the Gila, Santa Fe and Carson NFs.

Generally, however, it is ranching and off-road-vehicles (ORVs) which pose the most pervasive dangers to the Big Outside in New Mexico. Continued overgrazing; the construction of

Reeds Peak, Aldo Leopold Wilderness, New Mexico.
Photo by Dave Foreman.

additional fences, stock ponds and pipelines; and the destruction of pinyon/juniper forest by chaining and herbiciding threaten many areas. ORVs and the impacts they bring — soil erosion, poaching, trapping, etc. — are damaging sensitive habitats throughout the state. Mining and oil & gas development are problems for several specific areas.

Aldo Leopold challenged New Mexico and the nation in 1924 when he engineered the designation of the Gila Wilderness. That challenge — to radically alter our fundamental relationship with the land, to become again a plain member of the biotic community — has yet to be met.

Mogollon Highlands

The Mogollon Highlands, consisting of the Gila and Apache National Forests in west-central New Mexico and east-central Arizona, contain one of the key wilderness ecosystem complexes in the nation. This region is significant on the same level as are the greater Yellowstone, Northern Continental Divide, Central Idaho, Everglades and North Cascades ecosystems, and represents the best opportunity for an ecologically complete Wilderness in the Southwest. It is the area that taught Aldo Leopold to "think like a mountain."

Gila 736,000 acres	
Designated Gila Wilderness Area (Gila NF)	569,600
Additional Gila NF roadless	145,000
Gila Cliff Dwellings NM roadless	500
Private, state and BLM roadless to southwest	21,000

Description: Southwestern New Mexico north of Silver City. The Gila (*HEE-la*) was the first designated Wilderness Area anywhere in the world, receiving Forest Service administrative protection in 1924 at the urging of Aldo Leopold. It encompasses the rugged headwaters of the Gila River which form several spectacular riverine canyons; the Mogollon, Diablo and Jerky Mountain Ranges; and rolling mesa country with wide-open grasslands. Elevations range from 4,700' on the Gila River to 10,892' on Whitewater Baldy. This is the transition area between the Rocky Mountains, Mexico's Sierra Madre, the Chihuahuan Desert, the Sonoran Desert, the Great Plains, the

Great Basin and the Mexican Plateau. The fauna demonstrates this rich collection of ecotones — Mountain Lion, Black Bear, Elk, Rocky Mountain Bighorn Sheep, Mule and Whitetail Deer, Javelina, Coatimundi, Pronghorn, Arizona Coral Snake, Gila Monster, Turkey, Blue Grouse, Common Black Hawk, Zone-tailed Hawk, Red-faced Warbler, Goshawk, Mexican Spotted Owl and Bald Eagle. Vegetation includes riparian zones of Fremont and Narrowleaf Cottonwood, Arizona Sycamore, Arizona Walnut and Arizona Alder; up through chaparral (dominated by manzanita) and pinyon/juniper/oak woodland (including huge Alligator Junipers); Ponderosa Pine/Gambel Oak forest; to Engelmann & Colorado Blue Spruce, Douglas-fir, White & Corkbark Fir, and large Aspen stands. There are more species of deciduous trees here (over 20) than anywhere else in the West. Chihuahua Pine reaches its northeastern limit and the world's largest remaining virgin Ponderosa Pine forest is here. Because the high country was never glaciated, it has a different appearance than high country in other large western mountain areas. Over 300,000 acres of the designated Wilderness are no longer grazed by cattle or sheep, since the grazing leases have been retired. A number of archaeological sites, including several Mimbres phase cliff dwellings, are in the Wilderness.

Status: Logging, ORVs and overgrazing threaten the unprotected portions. Grazing is particularly atrocious along the Gila River in the Gila Wilderness, where it is damaging the riparian forest so essential for the biodiversity of the area; the cattle should be removed immediately. A couple of cowmen to the south of the Wilderness are agitating for "control" of Elk which are "robbing" them of "their" grass. ORVers are pushing for a road along the lower six miles of the East Fork of the Gila River, which was deleted from the Wilderness in 1980 at their insistence — several of them own cabins on a small private inholding up the East Fork. Small-scale mining poses a concern in the northeast, southeast and southwest corners of the roadless area.

The Gila is one of the best potential sites for reintroduction of the Grizzly Bear, Mexican Wolf, Jaguar and River Otter. The endemic and Endangered Gila Trout has been successfully restored to several streams in the Wilderness.

By closing a narrow gravel road (the North Star Road), the Gila and Aldo Leopold Wildernesses could be re-united into a single Wilderness Area of over 1.2 million acres. Several hundred thousand acres of additional wild country could be added by closing minor dirt roads to the north.

RM27: 1,327,360*

Devils Creek 100,000 acres

Gila National Forest roadless	100,000

Description: Southwestern New Mexico south of Reserve. This northern extension of the Mogollon Mountains is separated from the Gila Wilderness by a narrow but partly paved road and the old mining town of Mogollon. Mineral Creek, Devils Creek and the San Francisco River form deep canyons in the roadless area. Wildlife and vegetation are similar to that of the Gila Wilderness. Elevations range from 5,000' in canyon bottoms to 9,900' on the slopes of Bearwallow Mountain. The ghost town of Cooney, which was wiped out by the Apache Victorio in 1880, is included. Goodding's Onion is a State Threatened species present; the Spotted Owl also finds refuge here.

Status: The FS opposes protection, and proposes to build a high-grade logging road to Bearwallow which would cut through the Goodding's Onion habitat. Logging (of both mixed conifer and Ponderosa Pine), ORVs and grazing are steadily encroaching on this area. One jeep trail crosses it.

Blue Range-San Francisco 505,000 acres (also in Arizona)

See Arizona for description and status.

Aldo Leopold (Black Range) 409,000 acres

Designated Aldo Leopold Wilderness Area	
(Gila NF)	211,300
Additional Gila NF roadless	166,000
Private, state, BLM roadless to E & SW	32,000

Description: Southwestern New Mexico west of Truth or Consequences. The Black Range is a 9,000 to 10,000' high crest running north to south with steep canyons and rough ridges spilling down its sides. The high point is 10,165' McKnight Mountain, with low elevations of 6,000' along the east side. It is west of the Rio Grande Valley and directly east of the Gila Wilderness of which it was a part until split off by the North Star Road in the early 1930s. Deep mixed conifer forests along the crest give the range its name. Cottonwood/sycamore riparian forests (northeastern limit of Arizona Sycamore) and mesquite grassland cover the lower elevations. Ecologically it is similar to the Gila and Blue Range. An article in the *Denver Post Empire Magazine*, in 1976, billed the Black Range as "The Wildest Wilderness in the West."

Status: Logging threatens the northern part of this area. The southwestern portion was left out of the Wilderness Area in 1980 because of mining potential. Portions of the area are overgrazed, including some canyon bottoms important for their riparian vegetation. ORVs are penetrating some of the unprotected canyons. By closing the North Star Road, the Black Range could be combined with the Gila into a 1.2 million acre Wilderness Area.

RM27: 1,327,360*

Sawyers Peak 121,000 acres

Gila NF roadless	*73,000*
Private, state, BLM roadless	*48,000*

Description: Southwestern New Mexico south of Kingston and east of Silver City. South of the Aldo Leopold Wilderness (separated by a narrow paved road over Emory Pass), this area in the Mimbres Mountains is the southern extension of the Black Range. Like the Black Range, it is a crest cut by canyons to the west and east. High point is 9,668' Sawyers Peak; low point is about 5,500' near the Mimbres River. See Black Range for general description.

Status: Several old roads to abandoned mines and for grazing access are cherrystemmed into the roadless area. A few windmills and other range "improvements" are on the periphery of the area. The FS recommended against Wilderness for

the area in RARE II, and future timber sales in the mixed
conifer and Ponderosa Pine forests of the high country are a
definite threat. Exotic Iranian Ibex, introduced to the Florida
Mountains south of here 20 years ago, have been seen near this
roadless area. There is concern that they will spread into the
Black Range.

Continental Divide 170,000 acres

BLM WSA 2-44	*68,761*
Additional BLM, and private, state,	
Gila NF roadless	*101,000*

Description: Southwestern New Mexico south of Datil.
High grassland (up to 9,212' on Pelona Mountain) along the
Continental Divide drops into the southern San Agustin Plains
at 6,780'. Grassland roadless areas of this size are extremely
rare. Ponderosa Pine stringers line the canyons. Pronghorn, Elk,
Mule Deer, Turkey, Black Bear, Mountain Lion and wintering
Bald Eagle find homes here. The Bat Cave paleontological
site, in the northern part of the roadless area, has evidence of
some of the earliest domesticated maize in North America.
The proposed Continental Divide Trail will wind through this
area.

Status: BLM is proposing only 40,359 acres of the WSA for
protection. Even this has aroused strong rancher opposition.
Conservationists propose 94,501 acres of primarily BLM land.
Areas of state and private roadless land around the BLM WSA
should be acquired by the BLM for protection as Wilderness.

Jeep trails and grazing developments are minor intrusions.
One jeep trail crosses the area through Shaw Canyon.

Apache Kid 131,000 acres

Designated Apache Kid Wilderness Area	
(Cibola NF)	*45,000*
Additional Cibola NF roadless	*86,000*

Description: Central New Mexico north of Truth or Consequences. The southern portion of the San Mateo Mountains
forms a distinctive profile west of the Rio Grande with a series
of 10,000' peaks and interconnecting ridges which abruptly end

at the precipitous south face of Vicks Peak. Elevations range from 6,000' to 10,325' (Blue Mountain). Among the interesting geological features are several rock glaciers (talus slopes which behave like ice glaciers). Steep-walled canyons drop off to the west and east from the ridgelines. Ponderosa Pine and Gambel Oak, mixed conifer (Limber Pine, Douglas-fir, Engelmann & Blue Spruce, White Fir) and Aspen in the high country grade into mesquite, pinyon/juniper and mountain mahogany in the lower elevations. Narrowleaf Cottonwood, Arizona Alder, Live Oak and Netleaf Hackberry line the canyons. Very little surface water is present. Mountain Lion, Black Bear, Elk, Mule Deer and Turkey live here. The last Apache warrior, the Apache Kid, was gunned down on the upper slopes of Blue Mountain in 1909 by a posse of cowboys. He is buried in the high country near where he fell.

Status: The Forest Service, to their credit, proposed protection for the entire area in the 1980 New Mexico Wilderness Act but opposition from a politically powerful rancher, Reuben Pankey, who overgrazes the area, caused the Wilderness Area to be severely truncated. ORVs and grazing "improvements" may pose some threat along with possible minor logging in canyon bottoms in the future. Conservationists should press for additions to the designated Wilderness Area.

Rocky Mountains-Colorado Plateau

The Southern Rocky Mountains drop down from Colorado in two ranges — the Sangre de Cristos and the San Juans — on either side of the Rio Grande in northern New Mexico. The Colorado Plateau enters northwestern New Mexico from Utah and Arizona. The Carson and Santa Fe NFs largely control the Big Outside of the Rockies, while BLM and the Park Service have that of the Colorado Plateau.

Pecos 400,000 acres

Designated Pecos Wilderness Area (Santa Fe & Carson NFs)	223,333
Additional Santa Fe & Carson NFs roadless	151,000
Nambe Indian Reservation, BLM, private roadless	26,000

Description: North-central New Mexico in the Sangre de Cristo Mountains northeast of Santa Fe. The southern terminus of the true Rocky Mountains (and of once-extensively glaciated terrain), the Pecos is classic Rocky Mountain high country replete with lakes, trout streams, mountain meadows, glacial cirques, 13,000' high peaks above timberline (Truchas Peak is 13,102') and U-shaped valleys. As the name implies, the Pecos River begins here. Due to the steepness of terrain, vegetation quickly ranges upward from pinyon/juniper through Ponderosa Pine and Gambel Oak to thick mixed conifer forests (Engelmann and Blue Spruce, Limber Pine, White and Subalpine Fir, Douglas-fir) with an abundance of Aspen (the largest Aspen on record is here). Bristlecone Pine reaches its southeastern limit in the Pecos, and the grassland of the Great Plains touches the eastern side of this roadless area. Inhabitants include Black Bear, Mountain Lion, Elk, Rocky Mountain Bighorn Sheep, Mule Deer, Pika, Pine Marten (southern limit), Short-tailed Weasel, Grey Fox, Pileated Woodpecker, Blue Grouse, Spotted Owl and Wild Turkey. This is an extremely popular recreation area, but solitude can be found.

Status: The Santa Fe NF and Duke City Lumber are mounting a clearcutting and road-building assault on the rich spruce/fir forest of Elk Mountain on the southern end of the Pecos. Conservationists are fighting this travesty tooth and nail. Logging, firewood gathering and ORVs threaten the other unprotected portions of this roadless area. Mining interests kept the southwestern part out of the Wilderness Area. Sheep grazing continues in the high country each summer.

Wheeler Peak 120,000 acres

Designated Wheeler Peak Wilderness Area	
(Carson NF)	*20,000*
Columbine-Hondo Wilderness Study Area	
(Carson NF)	*43,276*
Taos Pueblo roadless	*45,000*
Additional Carson NF, and private roadless	*12,000*

Description: North-central New Mexico immediately northeast of Taos. Wheeler Peak is the highest point in New Mexico (13,160'); other 13,000' and 12,000' peaks form this area while lower elevations drop to 7,500'. Small lakes, cirques, avalanche chutes, trout streams and eye-popping views distinguish it. Mammals and birds present include Black Bear, Elk, Mule Deer, Rocky Mountain Bighorn Sheep, Mountain Lion, Yellow-bellied Marmot, Pika, Pine Marten, Blue Grouse and White-tailed Ptarmigan (rare in New Mexico).   The Columbine-Hondo area is connected to the Wheeler Peak Wilderness by a mile-wide unroaded ridgeline. The Taos Pueblo lands are closed to entry as a sacred area. Mixed conifer forest and alpine tundra are the primary vegetative types. Bristlecone Pine grow below timberline.

Status: The Carson NF has proposed only 27,032 acres of the Columbine-Hondo WSA for Wilderness.

Mining, ORVs and logging threaten the remainder of the NF area and the private land to the east. Construction of a road across the narrow neck connecting the Wheeler Peak area to the Columbine-Hondo has been a long-standing dream of the ski industry, which is big in this area. Taos Ski Valley wants to expand in unprotected roadless country adjacent to the Wheeler Peak Wilderness.

Latir Peak-Ponil Creek 214,000 acres

Latir Peak Wilderness Area (Carson NF)	20,000
Additional Carson NF roadless	5,000
Valle Vidal unit Carson NF roadless	48,000
Sangre de Cristo Grant (private) roadless	50,000
Philmont Boy Scout Ranch roadless	29,000
Additional private roadless	62,000

Description: North-central New Mexico north of the towns of Red River, Eagle Nest and Cimarron in the Sangre de Cristo Mountains. This area, with some of the highest and most scenic country in New Mexico (Latir Peak is 12,708') stretches across the Sangre de Cristos for 40 miles east-west from the Great Plains to the high tableland cut by the Rio Grande Gorge. There are several glacial lakes around Latir and many streams flow from the ridges above timberline.   Vegetation and wildlife are similar to the other Rocky Mountain areas in New Mexico.

Status: Complex ownership is the greatest obstacle to preservation of this roadless area. Logging is reducing the roadless acreage on the private lands; virtually the entire area is grazed by cattle and sheep; and ORVs fan out into the high country from the tourist resorts. Old mining activity dots the area and some new mining is possible.

.The Carson NF recently acquired by donation the Valle Vidal area east of the Latir Peak Wilderness Area and west of Philmont Scout Ranch. A network of low standard dirt roads cut this area in half over Costilla Pass, but the Forest Service has properly closed these roads and others to protect wildlife (the best trout fishing and Elk hunting in the state are here), so we have included this area in our inventory as "roadless" even though parts of it have been logged and there were through roads in it. Valle Vidal was formerly part of the huge Vermejo Ranch owned by Pennzoil, and operated as a company retreat (logging and grazing also occurred). Conservationists had hoped the Park Service could acquire the area as a new National Park, but the NPS botched the acquisition, and the FS got this magnificent area. Conservationists hope they will do a better job than they have with the rest of the Carson NF.

The small Rio Costilla Ski Area is cherrystemmed north of Latir Peak on the Sangre de Cristo Grant (a cooperatively managed area owned by local families tracing their ancestry in New Mexico back to the earliest Spanish settlers). A dirt road along Ponil Creek on Philmont Scout Ranch (used for supplying base camps) penetrates the eastern part of the area, and a rough dirt road to the Latir Lakes on the Sangre de Cristo Grant is also cherrystemmed. Obviously, this entire roadless area and other high country around it (including the Culebra roadless area to the north) needs to be looked at as a unit, with a joint management plan developed among the various owners to protect its wilderness and wildlife values.

Culebra 125,000 acres (also in Colorado)
See Colorado for description and status.

El Malpais 160,000 acres
Designated West Malpais Wilderness Area (BLM) 38,210
El Malpais National Monument roadless 105,000

Additional BLM, private, state roadless   *17,000*

Description: Western New Mexico south of Grants. The McCarty's Lava Flow is one of the youngest in the continental United States — only 500 to 1,000 years old (Pueblo Indian legends speak of a river of fire covering the fields their ancestors farmed). El Malpais (the "badlands" in Spanish) displays a wide variety of volcanic formations including cinder cones with craters, ice caves (with delicate ice crystal ceilings, ice stalagmites and smooth ice-rink-like floors), lava tubes (some 50' in diameter and several miles long), lava arches and collapsed vents. Ponderosa Pine groves grow in pockets in the flow, and on the volcanic craters with occasional intermixed Douglas-fir and Aspen. Several areas of healthy grassland of Blue Grama, Sand Dropseed and Ring Muhley survive. Other vegetation includes pinyon/juniper, Big Sagebrush, Four-wing Saltbush and oak brush. Numerous archaeological sites are present, including the old Zuni-Acoma trail. The largest natural bridge in New Mexico is immediately adjacent in the sandstone cliffs to the east. Elevations here in the southern part of the Colorado Plateau average about 7,000'. Wildlife includes Mule Deer, Pronghorn, Abert Squirrel, Mountain Lion, Bobcat, Turkey, Golden Eagle, Prairie Falcon, Peregrine Falcon and Black-tailed Rattlesnake. A few prairie dog towns are on the edge of the lava. This might be a potential reintroduction site for the Black-footed Ferret if captive breeding programs are successful. Desert Bighorn Sheep may be reintroduced. Supposedly, a now-deceased well driller operating in the Hole-In-The-Wall, an area of grassland and Ponderosa Pine in the center of the lava flow, pumped up several small, white, blind cave fish.

Status: On the last day of 1987, legislation was signed establishing the El Malpais National Monument and National Conservation Area under the management of the National Park Service and BLM, respectively. A 60,000 acre Cebolla Wilderness Area (just east of this roadless area) and a West Malpais Wilderness Area (in the western part of this roadless area), both under BLM management, were included, and the Park Service was directed to study the new Monument for possible Wilderness designation. Continued grazing is permitted in the

Monument until 1998, and is allowed in the BLM Wilderness indefinitely, as are hunting and trapping. Otherwise, this roadless area is comparatively well protected.

Chihuahuan Desert

The Chihuahuan Desert is the largest, yet least known, of America's deserts. With yucca, Lechuguilla, Ocotillo, Creosote Bush and barrel cactus, it flows into southern New Mexico from Texas and Chihuahua, dominating the lowlands from the Pecos River in the east to the Arizona border on the west. The mountains, like islands in a desert sea, are influenced by the Rocky Mountains from the north and by the Sierra Madre from the south. The BLM, Lincoln NF, Mescalero Apaches, Air Force and Park Service all manage important pieces of the Big Outside here.

Guadalupe Escarpment 258,000 acres (also in Texas)	
Carlsbad Caverns National Park Wilderness Area (NM)	*33,125*
Guadalupe Mountains National Park Wilderness Area (TX)	*46,850*
Lincoln NF roadless (NM)	*44,000*
Brokeoff Mountains BLM roadless 3-112 (NM)	*61,000*
Additional National Park roadless (NM & TX)	*27,000*
Additional private, BLM, state roadless (NM)	*26,000*
Additional private roadless (TX)	*20,000*

Description: Southeastern New Mexico west of Carlsbad, and west Texas east of El Paso. The "Guads" are best known for the extensive network of wild caves that lace this uplifted limestone reef. Carlsbad Caverns includes lengthy "backcountry" passages in addition to the developed tour routes. The surface of the escarpment is just as exciting, however, including fine Chihuahuan Desert vegetation (Ocotillo, Lechuguilla, Creosote, and cholla, prickly pear and barrel cactus) and riparian woodland (cottonwood, walnut, hackberry) in the lower elevations, pinyon/juniper/oak/madrone woodland at middle elevations, and culminating in a relict forest of Ponderosa Pine and Douglas-fir in GMNP. Guadalupe Peak at 8,749' is the highest point in Texas. Deep canyons, including

McKittrick Canyon, the only trout stream in Texas, cut the escarpment. Wildlife includes Elk, Mountain Lion, Javelina, and the largest Mule Deer herd in New Mexico. The exotic Barbary Sheep are reported in the area (they were released at various sites in New Mexico by the state Game & Fish Department in the early 1970s and have increased their range). Lower elevations (3,600') to the northwest in New Mexico (BLM's Brokeoff Mountains roadless area) include a series of alkali flats which sometimes form ephemeral lakes and include rare plants.

Status: There is strong opposition to Wilderness protection for the Lincoln National Forest roadless area between the National Parks by a coalition of ORV zealots, road hunters, small town boosters and local ranchers. The 1980 New Mexico Wilderness Act established a 21,000 acre Wilderness Study Area, but it was recently recommended for "no Wilderness" by the gutless Forest Service. (They had considered it for Primitive Area status as far back as the early 1930s and had supported it for Wilderness in the 1970s.) New Mexico conservation groups propose a 44,000 acre Wilderness here. Wilderness designation, or addition to Carlsbad Caverns NP, is vital for this "missing link" in the unified Guadalupe Escarpment Wilderness. Without protection, multiple "abusers" on the NF will divide this important wilderness.

The BLM is recommending only 14,516 acres of the untracked Brokeoff Mountains for Wilderness protection; conservation groups propose 66,350 acres, including the rugged mountain and canyon country as well as desert flats with ephemeral lakes. Inclusion of all of this area would greatly expand the diversity of Chihuahuan Desert ecosystems included in the greater Guadalupe Escarpment Wilderness. Roadless BLM and state land to the north of Carlsbad Caverns NP (Mudgetts WSA) in the Serpentine Bends of Dark Canyon is a key element in the eastern end of the Escarpment. BLM proposes no Wilderness; the NM BLM Wilderness Coalition proposes 2,230 acres. Congress should add 20,000 acres of the undeveloped state and BLM land in the area to the CCNP Wilderness.

A recently discovered cave in Carlsbad Caverns NP, Lechuguilla Caverns, has already been found to be the second-deepest cave in the US and may exceed Carlsbad Caverns in length. Underground Wilderness designation for this cave is currently being proposed. The Wilderness Areas established in both Carlsbad and Guadalupe Mountains NPs in 1978 were far too small. The CCNP Wilderness should be expanded to the north to shut down a jeep trail along the escarpment crest that continues into the NF roadless area. The GMNP Wilderness should be expanded to include lower desert country to the west in the Park, and ecologically important desert land on private land to the west should be added to the Park and the Wilderness (10,000 acres of this was added to the Park in 1988). The formerly proposed tramway up Guadalupe Peak appears to be dead.

Ranchers in New Mexico have pressured the NPS to allow "search and destroy" missions against Mountain Lions taking refuge in the National Parks. (The NPS has refused.) This provides a textbook example of an ecological island that is too small to contain and sustain its large mammals. (The NM Department of Game & Fish already employs a lion hunter full-time in the area as a subsidy to the sheepmen and cattlemen.) Potential oil & gas development presents some danger around the edges on NF, BLM, state and private land. ORVers and cave vandals (often the same individuals) are significant threats to the integrity of the complex.

Sierra Blanca 140,000 acres

Designated White Mountain Wilderness Area	
(Lincoln NF)	48,366
Additional Lincoln NF, state, private roadless	28,000
Mescalero Indian reservation roadless	64,000

Description: South-central New Mexico west of Ruidoso. Sierra Blanca at 12,003' is the southernmost area in the United States shaped by past glaciation. This extinct volcano rises 7,000' above the desert basin to the west and reaches into the arctic/alpine life zone, providing an exceptional wilderness transition from Chihuahuan Desert to tundra. Black Bear, Elk, Mountain Lion, Mule Deer and Southern Spotted Owl live here as does old-growth mixed conifer forest with the southeastern limit of Blue and Engelmann Spruce. An immense viewshed includes the Great Plains to the east, and White Sands, the San Andres Mountains and across the Rio Grande to the west.

Status: The status of this roadless area on the Mescalero reservation is uncertain. Roading and logging operations may be occurring and reducing it. Ski area expansion and small-scale mining may threaten the NF lands outside of the designated Wilderness.

White Sands 146,000 acres

White Sands National Monument roadless	*130,900*
White Sands Missile Range roadless	*15,000*

Description: South-central New Mexico west of Alamogordo. White Sands is a world famous complex of gypsum dunes formed by the wind blowing across calcium carbonate crystals (some several feet in length) on the dry bed of Lake Lucero. Moist areas between the dunes allow cottonwood trees to grow. Elevation is around 4,000'. Vegetated areas consist of seven Chihuahuan Desert associations, the main components of which are yucca, Iodinebush, Creosote, mesquite and various grasses. Precipitation averages 7" a year. Wildlife populations are low, as befits such an arid area. Both Peregrine and Prairie Falcon are present. An interesting phenomenon is the presence among several small mammal and lizard species of pale variations in the White Sands and dark variations in the Carrizozo lava flow to the north.

Status: The National Park Service has not proposed White Sands for Wilderness because it is an overflight and infrequent impact area for military missiles. There are no significant threats.

RM36: 1,200,000*

San Andres Mountains South 240,000 acres

San Andres National Wildlife Refuge roadless	*50,100*
White Sands Missile Range roadless	*190,000*

Description: South-central New Mexico southeast of Truth or Consequences. The San Andres Mountains, broken into three large roadless areas by maintained military roads, are perhaps the wildest part of New Mexico, and are the most extensive Chihuahuan Desert mountain range in the US. This precipitous north-south fault block range has many sheer canyons but little water.   Largely contained within the 3 million acre White Sands Missile Range, the San Andres have not been grazed by cattle for over 40 years and have very healthy populations of Mule Deer, Pronghorn and exotic Oryx.   (Oryx, as Big Don Schwarzennegger once commented, may be filling the ecological niche of the extinct Giant Ground Sloth — but are probably better eating.)   This was the prime area being considered for reintroduction of the Mexican Wolf, but the base commander rejected the plan in 1987 because of "security" problems. Desert Bighorn Sheep were present but were recently wiped out by an epidemic — this underscores the need to maintain many populations of rare species. They may be reintroduced. This desert mountain range is far wilder today than it was before the military took it over. Old roads in the canyon bottoms have been abandoned and the riffraff have been kept out. (Nonetheless, read Ed Abbey's novel **Fire on the Mountain** for a fictional treatment of the arrogant military take-over.) The first atomic bomb was exploded nearby — a range expert says that range conditions near Ground Zero are better than those of over ninety percent of New Mexico, making one wonder if cows are more dangerous than nukes. Vegetation is that of the Chihuahuan Desert (Creosote Bush, yucca, barrel cactus, cholla, mesquite) and grassland, up to oak and pinyon/juniper woodland, with hackberry and cottonwood in riparian areas. The high point is San Andres Peak at 8,239'; elevations drop to 4,000'.

Status: The only large-scale threat is the possible development of electronic or communication sites by the military. There is a high potential for reintroducing the Mexican Wolf, and conservationists need to lobby the military to allow this. The exotic Aoudad (a north African wild sheep brought to New Mexico by a poorly-considered and now repudiated exotic game introduction scheme of the NM Game & Fish Department) may be extending its range into the San Andres — all the better reason for returning the wolf.

RM36: 1,200,000*

San Andres Mountains Central <u>155,000 acres</u>
White Sands Missile Range and BLM roadless   155,000

Description: South-central New Mexico east of Truth or Consequences and separated from the San Andres Mountains South by a road; same general description and status. This area includes BLM land adjacent to the western boundary of White Sands Missile Range.

RM36: 1,200,000*

San Andres Mountains North 155,000 acres

White Sands Missile Range roadless	*155,000*

Description: Central New Mexico southeast of Socorro and separated from San Andres Mountains Central by a road; same general description and status as San Andres South. The elevation nearly reaches 9,000' on the slopes of Salinas Peak (which has a road to the top with a radio tower).

RM36: 1,800,000

Sierra Ladrones 109,000 acres

BLM WSA 2-16	45,308
Sevilleta National Wildlife Refuge and BLM	
* & private roadless adjacent to Sevilleta NWR*	60,000
Cibola NF roadless	4,000

Description: Central New Mexico north of Socorro. This rough desert peak, 50 miles south of Albuquerque, rises from 5,000' to over 9,000' elevation. Scattered Ponderosa Pine grow on top. Creosote Bush, Four-wing Saltbush and fairly healthy grassland up through pinyon/juniper constitute the other vegetation. The Sevilleta NWR portion is closed to grazing and public entry as a natural area. Pronghorn and Mule Deer are relatively common. Ladron is a potential Desert Bighorn Sheep reintroduction area. The Rio Salado Box Canyon is an attraction on the south side.

Status: BLM supports Wilderness protection of 34,124 acres. Conservation groups propose only 36,244 acres; this should be expanded.

Minor ORV use, fuelwood cutting and range "improvements" taint the edges. Former ranch roads and developments are fading on the Sevilleta NWR.

Robledo-Las Uvas Mountains 143,000 acres

BLM WSA 3-63	12,946
Additional BLM, state, private roadless	130,000

Description: South-central New Mexico immediately northwest of Las Cruces. This rugged mountain complex west of the Rio Grande (and touching it at one point) includes the limestone Robledo Mountains, with high cliffs, on the southeast and the bedded volcanic Las Uvas Mountains, with rim-rocked mesas, buttes and deep canyons, on the northwest. The Rough & Ready Hills, Cedar Hills and wide open spaces lie between the ranges. Vegetative types are Chihuahuan Desert, oak and juniper woodland, and riparian woodlands dominated by Netleaf Hackberry in the canyon bottoms (also cottonwood and associated riparian growth along the Rio Grande). Typical plants are Sotol, Creosote Bush, Apache-plume, barrel cactus, penstemon and Lyreleaf Greengages. Night Blooming Cereus and the Transpecos Rat Snake, a state Endangered species, inhabit the area. Other wildlife includes Golden Eagle (cliffs provide nesting spots), Peregrine Falcon, Bald Eagle, Scaled and Gambel's Quail, Mule Deer and Banded Rock Rattlesnake. Several caves are here, as are numerous archaeological sites, including a ten room pueblo. Elevations range from 5,876' on Robledo Mountain to less than 4,000'.

Status: Livestock graze throughout, and additional developments have been proposed. ORVs are a major threat and there are a variety of jeep trails in part of the area. Several roads penetrate the area giving it an irregular configuration. Additional threats from potential geothermal development and mining for building stone have arisen.

Conservation groups are proposing a 123,003 acre Wilderness. BLM opposes Wilderness protection for this area.

West Potrillo Mountains 260,000 acres

BLM WSA 3-52	143,145
Additional BLM roadless (includes scattered state and private tracts)	117,000

Description: South-central New Mexico west of Las Cruces. Just north of the Mexican border and west of the Rio Grande valley, the West Potrillos are a series of volcanic cinder cones (some with intact craters) and wide flats in between. This is a desolate, little-visited area with remarkably healthy Chihuahuan Desert grassland (yucca, Four-wing Saltbush, cholla, Ocotillo, Creosote) including large barrel cactus. There is no natural perennial water in the area, but plenty of solitude. Sand dunes and ephemeral ponds are present in Indian Basin. The very recent Aden Lava Flow occupies the northeast corner of the roadless area. Several archaeological sites have been found, and a rare mollusk and rare cactus species are present. Wildlife includes Mule Deer, Golden Eagle, Great Horned Owl (which nest in cinder cones), numerous quail and dove, and migrating ducks (in Indian Basin).

Status: Surprisingly, despite its lack of classic "wilderness" features, the core of the West Potrillos (162,820 acres) is proposed for Wilderness by the BLM, along with 27,277 acres of the Aden Lava Flow. Conservation groups propose a single Wilderness Area of 259,837 acres.

A few jeep trails penetrate the area and a couple cross it. ORVers and a local hobby rancher are strongly opposing Wilderness designation. There is interest in mining cinders from some of the cones.

Cedar Mountains 106,000 acres

BLM WSA 3-42	*14,911*
Additional BLM, state, private roadless	*91,000*

Description: Southwestern New Mexico southwest of Deming. This roadless area consists of a remote, little-known, low mountain range, rolling hills and adjacent plains on the Mexican border. Flying "W" Mountain, at 6,217', is the high point. 4,600' is the low point. The area's juniper woodland and Chihuahuan Desert includes the rare Night-blooming Cereus, as well as Tobosa and Burro Grass, Netleaf Hackberry, Four-wing Saltbush, Apache-plume, Tarbush, juniper (locally misnamed "cedar") and mesquite. Mule Deer, Pronghorn, Javelina, quail (abundant) and many species of raptors are the most noticeable critters. Superb 360 degree views and two large Animas phase pueblo ruins remain almost unknown to hikers.

Status: BLM opposes protection. Conservationists propose the entire 106,000 acres for Wilderness.

Continued overgrazing, possible construction of additional grazing "improvements," and ORV use are potential problems. A few jeep trails intrude — one of which was bladed in the spring of 1987, possibly with BLM connivance, to try to disqualify the area from Wilderness consideration.

Big Hatchet-Alamo Hueco Mountains	207,000 acres
BLM Big Hatchet WSA 3-35	65,872
BLM Alamo Hueco WSA 3-38	16,264
Additional BLM, state, private roadless	100,000
Contiguous roadless in Mexico	25,000

Description: Southwestern New Mexico on the Mexican border southeast of Lordsburg. Big Hatchet Peak is a rough, dry limestone peak that reaches 8,366' in elevation; the Alamo Hueco Mountains to the south are lower (high point 6,448') with low points under 4,300'. Springs in the Alamo Huecos attract many species of birds, including Elegant Trogon, Varied Bunting and Thick-billed Kingbird. This area is a northern extension of the Mexican Highlands Shrub Steppe Province — oak brush and juniper predominate on the mountains, Chihuahuan Desert vegetation (Ocotillo, Creosote, mesquite) prevails lower down and in the large flat expanses between the ranges, and Arizona Walnut grows in the canyons. Desert Bighorn Sheep, Coues Whitetail Deer, Javelina, Mountain Lion, Coatimundi, Montezuma Quail, Sonora Mountain Kingsnake and Giant Spotted Whiptail Lizard are some of the interesting vertebrates. Night Blooming Cereus and Scheer Pincushion are unusual cacti present. Caves in the Alamo Huecos have archaeological sites.

Status: BLM recommends 51,980 acres of the Big Hatchets for Wilderness; but does not recommend the Alamo Huecos because of mixed land ownership — a land exchange is needed to consolidate public land in this key biological area (rumors have it that such an exchange with Phelps-Dodge copper company is in the works). Conservation groups propose 91,219 acres of Wilderness for the Big Hatchets and 31,984 acres for the

Alamo Huecos. A unified 200,000 acre Wilderness should be established.

The major threat to the area is oil & gas exploration, with a secondary threat from grazing "improvements." There is minor ORV use and a few jeep trails. A poor dirt road almost divides the two ranges but they are connected by a several mile wide roadless corridor. Mexico should be encouraged to protect its lands in this roadless area.

Animas Mountains 101,000 acres

Private, state roadless	*94,000*
BLM Cowboy Spring WSA 3-007	*6,699*

Description: Extreme southwestern New Mexico south of Lordsburg. Largely private land (with some BLM and state patches), this is the finest extension of the Sierra Madre Mountains into the United States. It is not one of the "Sky Island" mountain ranges; it is directly contiguous with the Sierra Madre cordillera and has habitat for rare birds including Elegant Trogon, Thick-billed Parrot, Harris' Hawk, Common Black Hawk and Zone-tailed Hawk. More species of mammals are present here than in any National Park or Wildlife Refuge in the United States — including White-sided Jackrabbit, Coatimundi, Javelina, Black Bear, Coues Whitetail Deer, Pronghorn and . . . Mexican Wolf (a female denned and produced pups just north of the border in the early 1970s). Potential is high for reintroduction of Jaguar (which may be present on a transient basis along with Ocelot and Jaguarundi). Desert Bighorn Sheep may be reintroduced. The Animas is also one of the priority areas for Mexican Wolf reintroduction (or supplementation). Several species of rare rattlesnakes, including the very rare Ridge-nosed (federally listed as Threatened), live here. The area above 5,500' elevation has supposedly not been grazed for 10 years. The high country reaches 8,519' and sports fine Madrean oak/pine forest with good stands of Chihuahua, Arizona and Apache Pine. Dry Creosote desert flats abut the range on the east, while the west is bounded by a lush grassy valley. Riparian woodland of cottonwood, sycamore and walnut line the several perennial streams and springs. Rare Gray Oak savannahs enhance the vegetative diversity. An extremely wild and pristine area, the Animas are separated only by a dirt road (which is closed to the public) in the US and a paved road in Mexico from an even larger wild area in Mexico. This is one of the biologically most important areas in the US.

Status: The US Fish & Wildlife Service wants to purchase 322,000 acres in the Animas, including this roadless area, and make it a National Wildlife Refuge. Although the owner is interested in selling, nearby ranchers, with support from the powerful cow establishment of New Mexico, oppose this — evidently because of a dogmatic position against taking any rangeland "out of production." Conservationists need to strongly support the FWS in letters to their members of Congress. It is disturbing to note that this was part of the Coronado National Forest until it was traded to the Phelps-Dodge Corporation in the late 1950s for some nondescript pottage. Mexico should be encouraged to protect the ranges which provide a direct high elevation connection between the Animas and the bulk of the Sierra Madre.

BLM recommends the entire 6,699 acre Cowboy Spring WSA for Wilderness designation. In an excellent and visionary proposal, the New Mexico BLM Wilderness Coalition calls for acquisition of surrounding state land and the designation of a 40,989 acre Wilderness.

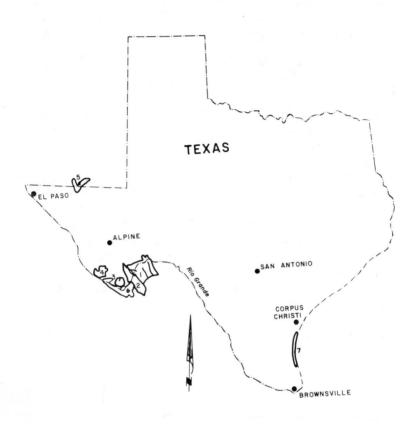

1. Lower Canyons of R G
2. Dead Horse Mountains
3. Chisos Mountains
4. Solitario
5. Guadalupe Escarpment
6. Mariscal-Santa Elena
7. Padre Island

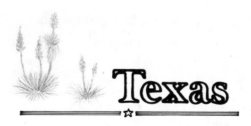

Texas

Texas. To many it is the epitome of the Wild West, the Frontier. But where is the wilderness? Where is the "wild" in this West? Texas has a greater variety of native ecoregions than does any other state, and is the only state that truly encompasses both Western and Eastern ecoregions. It is by far the largest of the lower 48 states. But compare it with California, a state smaller in area yet larger in population. California has nearly 6 million of its acres protected in the National Wilderness Preservation System; Texas has a mere 83,000.

The Lone Star State serves as a grim warning of what happens to wild country when there is little public land. Texas, more than any other of the United States, glorifies the private ownership of land. Given the history of Texas, we are fortunate that Big Bend and Guadalupe Mountains National Parks were acquired by donation or purchased out of private ranches; and that Padre Island National Seashore, Big Thicket National Preserve, several important National Wildlife Refuges and the National Forests of East Texas were purchased by the federal government.

The reason Texas had no public land to begin with was due to the agreement in 1845 whereby the independent Republic of Texas joined the United States as the State of Texas. Unlike all other states (except for the original thirteen), public lands in Texas were owned by the state, not by the federal government. As a result, these lands quickly passed into private ownership and were developed.

There are five Wilderness Areas in the East Texas National Forests, but the largest is only 12,700 acres, far too small to be included in this inventory. These areas were designated in 1984 after a long, hard-fought battle with the timber industry which rules East Texas and their champion, Congress-

Chisos Mountains and Sierra del Carmen, Texas & Mexico.
Photo by Dave Foreman.

man "Timber Charlie" Wilson. Dedicated conservationists in the Texas Committee On Natural Resources, the Lone Star Sierra Club and Texas Earth First! have continued to agitate for additional Wilderness Areas in the National Forests, but are currently occupied with trying to prevent the US Forest Service from conducting *cut and leave timber sales in the designated Wilderness Areas* under the pretext of Southern Pine Beetle control.

The only regions of Texas where large roadless areas remain are the Chihuahuan Desert in the far west and Padre Island on the southern Gulf Coast.

1978 saw the designation of 191.2 miles of the Rio Grande in West Texas as a National Wild & Scenic River, again after a long uphill struggle by conservationists. Since then, the local Congressman, at the behest of goat ranchers in the area, has regularly introduced legisla-tion to rescind the protection.

The anti-wilderness boys grow as big as their belt buckles in West Texas, and steady pressure from chamber of commerce honchos in the town of Alpine have prevented 559,000 acres of Big Bend National Park from being designated as Wilderness, although the proposal from the National Park Service and conservationists has been before Congress since 1974. (Big Bend was established as a National Park in 1945 after a decade-long fund-raising campaign which included Texas school children saving their lunch money for the acquisition fund.) A 46,850 acre Wilderness (scaled down from a larger recommendation at the insistence of local development interests) passed Congress in 1978 for Guadalupe Mountains National Park after a ten-year struggle by El Paso conservationists.

Threats to the Big Outside of Texas include ranching, oil & gas extraction, excessive National Park development, and private subdivision and tourist development.

Lower Canyons of the Rio Grande 890,000 acres (also in Mexico)

Black Gap State Wildlife Area, Rio Grande	
Wild & Scenic River, private roadless (TX)	190,000
Mexico roadless	700,000

Description: West Texas south of Sanderson. One of the half dozen wildest stretches of river in the United States, the Rio Grande east of Big Bend National Park forms a deep, rugged limestone canyon complex along the international border with Mexico. We consider it roadless from the La Linda bridge to Bone Watering. Major side drainages include Big Canyon, Reagan Canyon, Cañon de San Rosendo (Mexico), Cañon Caballo Blanco (Mexico), Palmas Canyon, Arroyo del Tule (Mexico), Panther Canyon and San Francisco Canyon. Elevations range from 3,988' on Cupola Mountain in Black Gap to 1,330' on the river at Bone Watering. Burro Bluff rises 1,000' out of the river; there are many other high cliffs, windows, spires, caves and assorted rock formations in the canyon. For 43 miles, walls up to 2,000' high rise on both sides of the river. Terrific (and intimidating) flash floods occur on the Rio Grande and the tributary canyons. This is difficult water for canoes, as aluminum carcasses wrapped around boulders attest.

Bighorn Sheep, Mountain Lion, Javelina, Peregrine Falcon, Summer Tanager, Green-winged Teal, Blotched Water Snake, Trans-Pecos Copperhead, Mottled Rock Rattlesnake, Big Bend Turtle, Red-spotted Toad, giant catfish, possibly Ocelot and Mexican Wolf live here. Lucifer, Broad-billed and Black-chinned Hummingbirds nest along the river (10 other hummingbird species are visitors). Chihuahuan Desert vegetation — Lechuguilla, Ocotillo, Creosote Bush, Blind Prickly Pear, cholla & barrel cacti, Sotol, yucca, Guayacan, Candelilla, Leather Stem — graces the area above the river; mesquite, willow and Giant Reed predominate along the river. The native Lanceleaf Cottonwood (a hybrid of Narrowleaf and Plains Cottonwoods) was wiped out by early-day woodcutters. Berlander Ash reaches its upriver limit here.

Status: While the entire river through this roadless area (72 miles) is protected as a National Wild & Scenic River, the surrounding lands in both the United States and Mexico are open for development. (The Wild & Scenic River designation continues for an additional 54 miles downstream from this roadless area.) Adjoining lands in the United States outside of Black Gap are private sheep and goat ranches. Several of the ranchers are interested in punching roads down to the river for private tourist development. This extraordinary area deserves to be part of an international Big Bend Park, with high priority given for Mexican Wolf, Jaguar, Ocelot and Jaguarundi reintroduction or supplementation.

The calculation of what is roadless in Mexico is rough.

Dead Horse Mountains 720,000 acres (also in Mexico)

Big Bend National Park roadless	*142,000*
Private land to east (Adams Ranch) roadless	*28,000*
Mexico (Sierra del Carmen) roadless	*550,000*

Description: West Texas southeast of Alpine. This roadless area is separated from the Lower Canyons by a narrow paved road and bridge providing access to a fluorspar mine at La Linda on the Rio Grande. It includes the Dead Horse Mountains, Boquillas Canyon on the Rio Grande (2,000' deep), and (in Mexico) the Sierra del Carmen. The finest stand of Giant Dagger Yucca in the US is here. Wildlife includes a relatively dense Mountain Lion population, Javelina, Pronghorn and Beaver. Ocelot have been seen in Boquillas Canyon within the last decade. Black Bear and introduced Elk are present in the National Park Mexico has established in the Sierra del Carmen, which rises to over 9,000' in elevation, and supports Ponderosa Pine, Limber Pine, Alligator Juniper, Douglas-fir and Aspen. The high point in the US part is Sue Peaks at 5,799'. River elevations are under 2,000'. Outstanding Chihuahuan Desert vegetation is present in the Big Bend portion. Groove-billed Ani, Green Kingfisher, Mississippi Kite and Zone-tailed Hawk are unusual birds found here. Fish include the Mexican Stoneroller and Chihuahua Shiner. Flora and fauna are generally similar to the Lower Canyons. Boquillas Canyon offers a fine canoe trip.

Status: Although most of this area is protected in Parks, Park management in Mexico is a much more casual affair than in the United States. Most of the Big Bend NP area has been recommended for Wilderness by the NPS. The 25 miles of the Rio Grande in this roadless area are part of the National Wild & Scenic Rivers System, as are the river stretches upstream and downstream. High priority for Mexican Wolf, Jaguar, Ocelot and Jaguarundi reintroduction or supplementation is needed.

The Adams Ranch has high wilderness and ecological values and should be acquired by the National Park Service for addition to Big Bend NP (it has recently been used as headquarters for a major smuggling ring which dealt in spotted cat skins from Latin America).

The calculation of what is roadless in Mexico is rough. Over half of the Mexican acreage in this roadless area is in the Parque Internacional Del Rio Bravo.

Chisos Mountains 186,000 acres

Big Bend National Park roadless   *186,000*

Description: Entirely within Big Bend National Park in West Texas south of Alpine. Vegetation zones begin with Chihuahuan Desert and rise to a relict forest of Ponderosa Pine, Gambel and Emory Oak, Arizona Cypress, Texas Madrone, Velvet Ash, Netleaf Hackberry, Douglas-fir and Aspen in the high country and canyons. Emory Peak, the high point, reaches 7,835', a mile above the lower elevations of the area. Perennial streams and important bird habitat give the Chisos ecological significance. Mountain Lion, Javelina, Yellow-nosed Cotton Rat, all four US species of skunk (Striped, Spotted, Hog-nosed and Hooded), Lucifer Hummingbird and 10 other hummingbird species, Flammulated Owl, Varied Bunting, Lyre Snake, Mexican Black-headed Snake and Trans-Pecos Copperhead live here. The Carmen Whitetail Deer, Colima Warbler and Drooping Juniper are found nowhere else in the United States. More birds are known from Big Bend National Park than from any other National Park area (380 species).

Status: The National Park Service has proposed most of this area as Wilderness and is managing it as such. Support should be given them to remove more of the tourist developments from the Basin area in the mountains. (Local boosters favor expanding the visitor facilities in the oak/juniper woodland of the Basin.) Mexican Wolf and border cats should be reintroduced.

Mariscal-Santa Elena Canyons 483,000 acres (also in Mexico)

Big Bend National Park roadless (TX)   *69,000*

Private roadless (TX)	*14,000*
Mexico roadless	*400,000*

Description: Southeastern Big Bend National Park and adjacent Mexico. Three roadless areas in Big Bend National Park are joined by contiguous roadless acreage in Mexico to form this large expanse of exceptional desert river wilderness. Santa Elena and Mariscal Canyons, cut through flat-topped mesas by the Rio Grande, have sheer walls rising out of the river. Santa Elena is 1,500 feet deep and less than 1,500 feet wide in places. Mariscal is just as sheer, but even deeper. The abrupt ending of Santa Elena Canyon is unmatched. See other Big Bend areas for general description.

Status: The three roadless areas in Big Bend NP are split in Texas by roads coming down to the river. They are joined together by a sprawling backcountry to the south in Mexico that includes half of the Parque Internacional Del Rio Bravo. Most of the Big Bend NP acreage is proposed for Wilderness by the NPS. The calculation of what is roadless in Mexico is rough.

Solitario 225,000 acres
Texas State Park and private roadless   *225,000*

Description: West Texas between Terlingua and Presidio. Because this area was until late 1988 entirely private land, details are rough. By all accounts, however, this area west of Big Bend National Park is as wild and scenic as the Park. Features include the Bofecillos Mountains, Solitario Peak, Panther Mountain, Bandera Mesa, Fresno Creek and Tapado Canyon. It is blessed with perennial streams, numerous springs and two 100' high waterfalls. The high point is 5,193' with lower elevations near 3,000'. Chihuahuan Desert vegetation and grassland, riparian woodland in the canyons, oak and juniper in the higher elevations are the vegetative types. Wildlife is similar to that of Big Bend NP and includes at least 11 Endangered species. Although not part of this roadless area (a paved state highway separates), 25 miles of the Rio Grande, including Colorado Canyon, are included in the new State Park.

Status: In 1988, the Texas Parks & Wildlife Commission voted to acquire the 215,000 acre Big Bend Ranch roughly overlapping most of this roadless area. The owner, oil magnate and philanthropist R.O. Anderson, has wanted to sell this ranch to the State of Texas or National Park Service as a public park for over 15 years but the offer has not been taken until now. It will be managed as a natural area, according to preliminary reports. Conservationists should encourage Texas Parks & Wildlife to close old dirt ranching roads in order to expand the size of the roadless area in the park. Portions of the roadless area outside of Big Bend Ranch (Bandera Mesa, Cesario Creek, Contrabando Creek) to the east and northeast should be priorities for public acquisition.

Guadalupe Escarpment 258,000 acres (also in New Mexico)
See New Mexico for description and status.

Padre Island 108,000 acres
National Seashore roadless   *108,000*

Description: South Texas Gulf Coast between Corpus Christi and Brownsville. Padre Island National Seashore protects the longest barrier island (75 miles are roadless) on the United States coast. Wide, clean (aside from the occasional tar ball) beaches, sand dunes, grassy flats and mud flats characterize the area. More than 350 species of birds, Loggerhead Turtle, Alligator, Portuguese Man-of-War jellyfish and many fishes frequent the island and its surrounding waters, which include Laguna Madre — the long, shallow bay between Padre Island and the mainland. There are only two coastal areas included in this inventory — the Everglades and Padre Island.

Status: The Park Service studied but did not recommend this island for Wilderness due to continuing offshore oil & gas extraction allowed in the National Seashore (production has been fairly limited). The Park Service allows dune buggies and other off-road-vehicles to drive along the beach. Once a cattle ranch, grazing has been terminated. Conservation groups have not pushed Wilderness designation. The island and surrounding waters should be designated as a Wilderness Area and motorized vehicles prohibited.

Southeast

Pity the poor South. Once it had the richest temperate forest on Earth with Tuliptrees more than 200 feet tall, Carolina Parakeets and Ivory-billed Woodpeckers, Black Bears and Eastern Panthers galore, Elk in the mountains and giant 'gators in the lowlands. . . .

But a century or two of Europeans changed all that. Lumbermen, swamp drainers, market hunters, cotton farmers, coal companies and mountaineers transformed the land into a pale imitation of Europe. More recently, tree farmers, oilmen, chemical companies, commercial fishermen and slick land developers have ground out the wildness in all but a few places.

Today, the Big Outside in the South is restricted to two swamps (the Everglades and Okefenokee) and to a handful of high, remote sections of the Southern Appalachians.

Preservation of things wild and natural comes harder in Dixie. There are fewer members of conservation groups per capita in the South than there are in any other region of the country, and Southern members of Congress, with rare exceptions, don't much care for things that you can't eat or put a price tag on.

Our generation can thank a few far-sighted Southern iconoclasts for what is left — folks like Marjory Stoneman Douglas, still going strong as she nears 100 years of age, who gave us Everglades National Park; and a band of New Deal idealists in Knoxville who gave us Great Smoky Mountains National Park.

Although Eastern conservationists began to suggest possible Wilderness protection for National Forest areas east of the Rockies before the Wilderness Act was passed in 1964, the Forest Service argued that no areas qualified, that there was a fundamental difference between National Forest lands East and

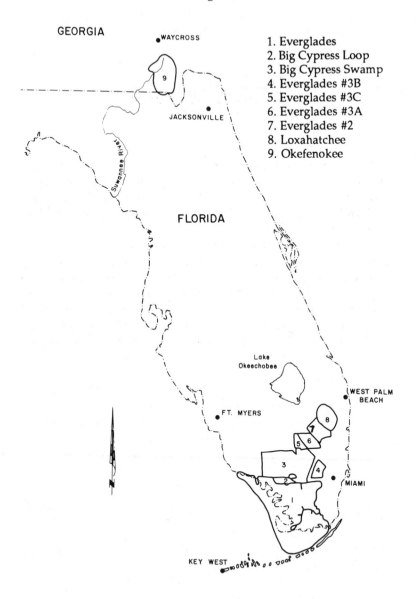

GEORGIA

• WAYCROSS

1. Everglades
2. Big Cypress Loop
3. Big Cypress Swamp
4. Everglades #3B
5. Everglades #3C
6. Everglades #3A
7. Everglades #2
8. Loxahatchee
9. Okefenokee

9

JACKSONVILLE •

Suwannee River

FLORIDA

Lake
Okeechobee

WEST PALM
BEACH •

• FT. MYERS

8

7

5   6

3

4

• MIAMI

2

1

N

KEY WEST •

West (except for Minnesota's Boundary Waters). In the West, they argued, National Forests had been withdrawn from the public domain and, although some minor uses may have previously been made of Wilderness Areas there, such as grazing, tie-hacking, old cabins and such, these areas were essentially pristine. The Eastern National Forests, on the other hand, had been purchased from private ownership and added to the system. They had been homesteaded, cleared and developed at various times during their history. Even if, under Forest Service management, the forests were growing up, old roads were fading, signs of habitation were disappearing, and the appearance of wilderness was being reestablished, these areas were not wilderness in the same sense as the Western wilderness. There was a qualitative difference. To include Eastern areas in the Wilderness System would tarnish the whole system and demean the pristine Western areas.

There was an element of sincerity in the Forest Service argument. Some foresters honestly believed it. Others used it in a Machiavellian way to keep their managerial hands from being tied. Yes, under Forest Service protection these Eastern areas were recovering from past abuse, but that didn't mean the Forest Service had no plans to abuse them again now that their trees were large enough to harvest.

Nevertheless, belying their own argument, the Forest Service had established three Wilderness Areas (called "Wild Areas" because they were under 100,000 acres) in the East before the Wilderness Act. They were Linville Gorge and Shining Rock in North Carolina, and Great Gulf in New Hampshire.

Utterly convinced that there was no potential Wilderness in the East (or on the National Grasslands), the Forest Service's first Roadless Area Review and Evaluation (RARE) in 1972 covered only National Forests in the 12 Western states (with three exceptions — one each in Florida, North Carolina and Puerto Rico). Eastern conservationists mobilized with the support of The Wilderness Society and submitted Wilderness proposals to Congress. An Eastern Wilderness bill was drafted; the Forest Service countered with a proposal for a separate, and lesser, system of Eastern National Forest "Wild Areas." After a substantial campaign, a bill was passed by Congress and signed by President Ford on January 3, 1975, establishing 16 full-fledged units of the National Wilderness Preservation System in Eastern National Forests and directing the Forest Service to study for possible Wilderness recommendation an additional 17 areas. (25 of these 33 areas were in states from West Virginia south.)

The dam had been broken. The Forest Service in RARE II considered National Forests in the East (and National Grasslands) equally with National Forests in the West. State-wide bills in the decade after RARE II have designated additional National Forest Wilderness Areas in most of the Eastern states with National Forests.

Two factors, unfortunately, work in tandem to reduce Wilderness designation in Eastern National Forests. First, the land use history of these recovered Wildernesses limits their size. As this book indicates, only a handful of National Forest roadless areas in the East exceed our floor of 50,000 acres. The lands that have recovered are small and isolated. It will require conscious planning to restore areas of several hundred thousand acres in the East to a general condition of roadlessness. This is, of course, the prerequisite for reestablishing the basis for ecological Wilderness with the full range of native species.

Second, Forest Service managers are under the same bulldozer and chainsaw mind-set in the East as they are in the West. Their job is to build roads and cut trees, not to restore and protect ecosystems. Areas in the Eastern National Forests that have recovered a degree of wildness and roadlessness are under the same threat of clearcutting and roading as are larger areas in the West. Even though Eastern National Forests are the logical cores for wilderness restoration, this will not be achieved with the support of the Forest Service, but by overpowering them in the same way conservationists overpowered them in 1974 on the Eastern Wilderness Act. It will be a far more difficult campaign.

The Eastern Wilderness Act in 1974 and subsequent Wilderness legislation was too late to give us big wilderness in the National Forests of the South (with a couple of exceptions which are described in the inventory). A number of National Wildlife Refuges in the South have received Wilderness designation (but not Loxahatchee or Great Dismal Swamp, which

Okefenokee Wilderness Area, Georgia.
Photo by Dave Foreman.

are two of the three Southern NWRs included in this inventory). The Smokies still await passage of a Wilderness bill that has been pending for nearly 20 years; Wilderness legislation passed for Okefenokee NWR in 1974 and Everglades National Park in 1978. Big Cypress National Preserve adjacent to the Everglades was expanded in 1988 by Congress, but Wilderness designation remains on hold.

The Everglades and Great Smoky Mountains confirm the key principles of Island Biogeography — that a preserve, unless it is truly large, will lose species; that it cannot stand alone. Diversion of water to Miami and its environs threatens to destroy the Everglades, and air pollution is killing the virgin forests in the Smokies saved from timber companies 50 years ago. Moreover, wide-ranging, wilderness-dependent species such as Eastern Panther, Ivory-billed Woodpecker, Red Wolf and Manatee can't survive in isolated natural "islands" even as large as the Everglades or Smokies. To maintain the fabric of the natural world, we have to set aside preserves large enough for these species and then connect them by corridors to other preserves so the gene pool doesn't grow isolated and inbred. The Everglades-Big Cypress and the Great Smoky Mts NP and surrounding National Forests are the prime areas in the South for large preserves.

Exciting things are happening in the South today, such as the work of ecologist Reed Noss at the University of Florida who has developed a comprehensive proposal for a system of core preserves, connecting corridors and buffer zones that would allow Florida Panther, Manatee, Black Bear and other imperiled wildlife to maintain healthy populations in a wild habitat; and of Dr. R.F. Mueller of Virginia Earth First!, who is calling for the restoration of large Wilderness Areas in the Appalachian Mountains by closing roads, healing clearcuts, and reintroducing Panther, Elk and other extirpated species.

Maybe the South can rise again.

Swamps

Swamps.   Wet, yucky, sweltering, snake-infested, mosquito-ridden, leech-filled hell holes.   Humphrey Bogart and the African Queen.   These common images associated with swamps tend to hide from the public the great plentitude and diversity of life which swamps hold thanks to their abundance of water. Thankfully, swamps are also a bit more difficult for the financial adventurer to exploit. As a result, the largest tracts of wildland left in the South are swamps. Tough in appearance though they may be, even the Southern swamps are delicate ecosystems vulnerable to human misuse.

Everglades 1,658,000 acres (Florida)

Everglades National Park east mainland roadless	174,300
Everglades National Park west mainland roadless	672,400
Florida Bay Everglades National Park	529,300
Big Cypress National Preserve Stairsteps Unit	
roadless	143,281
Private roadless to east	75,000
Cape Romano Aquatic Preserve	64,000
(Designated Everglades National Park	
Wilderness	1,296,500)*

Included in first three items above.

Description: Southern Florida southwest of Miami. "Unique" is an over-used word in describing natural landscapes, but if any natural region can be called "unique," it is the Everglades. There is, simply, no other place like it on Earth. Sawgrass prairie, alternately tinder dry and flowing wet, Baldcypress swamp festooned with epiphytes, Caribbean tropical hardwood hammocks, Slash Pine/Saw Palmetto forests, Paurotis Palms, Buttonwood thickets and mangrove keys distinguish it. This is the land of the American Alligator, American Crocodile, River Otter, Everglades Mink, Florida Panther, Cotton Mouse, West Indies Manatee, Bottle-nosed Dolphin, Black Bear, Snapping Turtle, Loggerhead Turtle, Indigo Snake, Liguus Tree Snail, Coon Oyster, Apple Murex, Strangler Fig, Gumbo Limbo, Royal Palm, Live Oak, Pond Apple, an incredible profusion of birdlife (300 species including Roseate Spoonbill, Great White Heron, Reddish Egret, White Ibis, Wood Stork, Anhinga, Magnificent Frigatebird) and fish (including Florida Spotted Gar, bonefish, mullet and tarpon), and . . . mosquitoes.

Status: The Everglades Ecosystem is one of the most threatened areas in America. By altering the water flow patterns of south Florida, humans have upset the ecological applecart. Efforts are being made to restore natural water flows and they should be strongly encouraged. Additionally, pollution from agricultural runoff is disrupting native plants and encouraging exotics which can tolerate it. As an indication of the damage being done to the Everglades, populations of water birds have crashed in recent years (The Wilderness Society reports that wading bird populations have declined by 90% since the 1930s).

A new threat is the Air Force, which hopes to begin low-altitude training dogfights for F-4s and F-16s over the Park.

Although motorboats ply the mangrove channels, Ten Thousand Islands and Florida Bay (even in the designated Wilderness), we have considered these areas roadless because they are *wild*; the many keys are off-limits to landing, the water is no deeper than nine feet over a vast area, and much of this marine landscape is designated as Wilderness. It is this Florida Bay Wilderness which links the two mainland roadless areas which are split on shore by the Flamingo road.

The area in Big Cypress Preserve is open to swamp buggies and airboats. These ORVs should be banned, and the Stairsteps Unit of Big Cypress immediately added to the Everglades Wilderness Area. Swamp buggies and airboats are prohibited in Everglades National Park.

Big Cypress Swamp Loop 55,000 acres (Florida)

Big Cypress National Preserve roadless   *55,000*

Description: Southern Florida between Miami and Everglades City. This roadless area is that part of Big Cypress Swamp National Preserve bounded by the Loop Road and Tamiami Trail.

Status: This is the only part of Big Cypress Swamp National Preserve currently closed to motorized vehicles, including swamp buggies and airboats.

Big Cypress Swamp 583,000 acres (Florida)

Monument Unit Big Cypress National

Preserve roadless	282,714
Everglades Wildlife Management Area	
(Conservation Area #3) and Florida State	
Miccosukee Indian Reservation roadless	300,000

Description: Southern Florida west of Miami. The Big Cypress Swamp is the northern extension of the Everglades and is separated from the main Everglades roadless area merely by the Tamiami Trail highway. Baldcypress swamp and Sawgrass prairie mix here in an interdigitating mosaic (see Everglades for general description). Big Cypress is even more crucial for survival of the Endangered Florida Panther (down to 30 individuals) than Everglades National Park.

Status: Big Cypress National Preserve may have the dubious distinction of being the most poorly managed unit in the National Park System. Swamp buggies and airboats have the run of this area. Primitive campgrounds along the highways are RV slums with trash covering the ground. Oil exploration was permitted by the Interior Department until a conservationist lawsuit halted it in 1988. Speeding vehicles on Tamiami Trail and Alligator Alley (highways cutting through the Everglades-Big Cypress complex) are the main sources of mortality for the Florida Panther.

Both highways should be closed (along with several other roads) and a 3 million acre Everglades Wilderness National Park established. Airboats and swamp buggies should be entirely banned in Big Cypress as well as the adjacent Wildlife Management Areas.

The eastern border of this roadless area is the Miami Canal and Levee 67A.

Congress added 115,000 acres of private land to Big Cypress National Preserve in 1988. Portions of the Conservation Areas in this roadless area and in some of those following are now federal land and part of Big Cypress National Preserve.

Everglades #3B 50,000 acres (Florida)

Everglades Conservation Area #3 roadless	50,000

Description: Southern Florida west of Miami. This roadless area is that part of Everglades Conservation Area #3 bounded by US 27, the Miami Canal and Levee #67C.

Status: See other Everglades units.

Everglades #3C 54,000 acres (Florida)

Everglades Conservation Area #3 roadless	*54,000*

Description: Southern Florida west of Ft. Lauderdale. This area is separated from the main unit of Big Cypress Swamp by Alligator Alley and from the next area by Mud Canal.

Status: See other Everglades units.

Everglades #3A 109,000 acres (Florida)

Everglades Conservation Area #3 roadless	*109,000*

Description: Southern Florida west of Ft. Lauderdale, that part of the Everglades Conservation Area #3 bounded by Alligator Alley, Mud Canal, US 27 and the Palm Beach-Broward County Line. Canals and road corridors separate this roadless area from the other roadless areas in the Everglades Conservation Areas.

Status: This area has some airboat trails, and has been subjected to the southern Florida flood and water management system which has diverted regular water flow to the cancerous sprawl along Florida's "Gold Coast."

Everglades #2 95,000 acres (Florida)

Everglades Conservation Area #2 roadless	*95,000*

Description: Southern Florida west of Pompano Beach, bounded by US 27, Levee 6, Levee 39 and Levee 36, between Loxahatchee NWR and Roadless Area #3A (see above).

Status: Similar to #3A.

Loxahatchee 143,000 acres (Florida)

Loxahatchee National Wildlife Refuge roadless	*143,000*

Description: Sawgrass prairie in the northern part of the 'Glades southwest of West Palm Beach in southern Florida (Water Conservation Area #1). The key habitat for the Endangered Everglades (Snail) Kite is here as are tree islands of Red Bay, Wax-myrtle and Holly. Alligator, Florida Sand-hill Crane, Osprey, Great White Heron, Bald Eagle, Peregrine Falcon, Masked Duck, Fulvous Whistling-Duck, Roseate Spoonbill, Limpkin, Everglades Mink, Florida Panther and Florida Water Rat reside in Loxahatchee. About half of the area is closed to all public entry.

Status: Loxahatchee is entirely enclosed by canals and levees (#39, 7 & 40). Although water levels are artificially managed (as is true throughout the Everglades-Big Cypress complex), this is a wild area. A portion of the area is open to airboats and hunting — it should be closed to airboats.

Okefenokee 400,000 acres (Georgia, partly in Florida)

Designated Okefenokee National Wildlife Refuge Wilderness (GA)	353,981
State, private & additional Refuge roadless (GA & FL)	46,000

Description: Southeastern Georgia south of Waycross. Okefenokee is THE SWAMP, and is the home of Pogo, Alligator, River Otter, Black Bear, Bobcat, 'coon, armadillo, Snapping Turtle and maybe a Florida Panther or two. Here also can be found 225 species of birds — including Barred Owl, Red-cockaded Woodpecker, Prothonotary Warbler, Sandhill Crane, Osprey, Anhinga, Wood Duck, Wood Stork and various herons, egrets and ibis. Other denizens include 54 species of reptiles, 32 of amphibians and 37 of fish. Slash & Longleaf Pines, gum and bay are common trees. Baldcypress forests, watery prairies, piney islands, open "lakes" and superlative canoe trips characterize this nationally significant Wilderness. Okefenokee is the source of the Suwannee and St. Marys Rivers and varies from 128' to 103' in elevation. Peak-bagging opportunities are accordingly limited.

Status: Motorboats are allowed in portions of the designated Wilderness. They should be banned. All portions of the swamp and adjacent pine woods, out to the encircling paved highways, should be made wilderness recovery areas. The Refuge is surrounded by huge industry tree farms — all in pine.

Great Dismal Swamp 102,000 acres (Virginia and North Carolina)

Great Dismal Swamp National Wildlife Refuge
  "roadless" *   102,000

see status below

Description: Eastern border of Virginia-North Carolina southwest of Norfolk. This large swamp is centered on the unusually pure waters of Lake Drummond. A remnant of the Atlantic White Cedar forest survives here. Many species reach their northern limit in the Great Dismal Swamp. Rare forms include Dismal Swamp Short-tailed Shrew and Dismal Swamp Log Fern. Black Bear, Bobcat, River Otter, Whitetail Deer and 92 nesting species of birds are among the fauna. A million Robins use it for a winter roost. Baldcypress, gum, magnolia, pawpaw, poplar, oak, holly and juniper are among the flora. Formerly owned by George Washington and Patrick Henry, it is no longer in their hands.

Status: This swamp is cut by numerous ditches with "roads" on the spoil banks that are closed to motorized vehicles but are open to bicycles and walking. Motorboats are permitted on the Feeder Ditch as access to Lake Drummond. Perhaps the Great Dismal Swamp should not be considered "roadless," but it presents a remarkable opportunity for wilderness restoration.

Atchafalaya Swamp (Louisiana)

Description: South-central Louisiana. This 800,000 acre area of swamp and bayou is crossed by only one road — I-10 — but is so cut up by canals (used by powerboats) and oil & gas pipelines, wells, and other development that we, with regret, have not included it in our inventory as roadless. It is, to be sure, an important natural area retaining considerable wildness and important wildlife habitat. Additional information for future editions of this book would be appreciated.

Appalachian Mountains

Backbone of the Eastern states, the Appalachians run from Alabama to Maine and provide a pathway for northern species to reach the high country of the South. In the Southern Appalachians, the most diverse temperate forest on Earth developed. The Southern Appalachians also represent the largest block of federal land in the East with Great Smoky Mountains National Park and contiguous National Forests in North Carolina, Tennessee, Georgia and South Carolina totalling 4 million acres — the Southern Appalachian Highlands Ecosystem. This, obviously, presents an opportunity for wilderness restoration on a grand scale.

Although included with the lowlands of the South in this book, the Appalachians form their own bioregion and are ecologically and culturally distinct. The Central Appalachians were, of course, ravaged by coal companies (and continue to be so ravaged today). Except for West Virginia's Cranberry Wilderness, there is no Big Outside in the Appalachians between the Great Smoky Mountains and New York State.

Great Smoky Mountains West 227,000 acres (North Carolina & Tennessee)

Great Smoky Mts. National Park roadless (NC)	138,600
Great Smoky Mts. National Park roadless (TN)	86,200
Private and Cherokee IR roadless (NC)	2,500

Description: South of Knoxville, TN, west of Asheville, NC. The Southern Appalachians have the most diverse temperate deciduous forest on Earth. The Smokies have more species of deciduous trees (130) than does all of northern Europe (80). This is a botanist's haven with over 1,400 species of flowering plants. The Smokies harbor the most extensive virgin forest in the East; it is composed of Red Spruce/Fraser Fir and cove hardwoods. A total of 200,000 acres in this and the Great Smoky Mountains East roadless area have never been logged. This area has the southernmost extension of spruce/fir forest in Eastern North America. Rhododendron thickets in the high country are famous for their color. Other trees include Fraser Magnolia, Black Locust, Black Cherry, Black Walnut, Eastern Sycamore, Eastern White Pine and Eastern Hemlock.

10. Great Dismal Swamp
11. Great Smoky Mts West
12. Great Smoky Mts East
13. Cohutta
14. Southern Nantahala
15. Cranberry

Wildlife includes Wild Turkey, Ruffed Grouse, Blackburnian
Warbler, Raven, Mink, Bobcat, Red Fox, Southern Flying
Squirrel, abundant Black Bear, and Endangered Red-cockaded
Woodpecker and Indiana Bat. There are more species of sala-
manders in the Smokies than anywhere else in the world. The
streams have 70 species of fish, including native Eastern Brook
Trout. The Smokies kept the Black Bear from extinction in the
Southern Appalachians and even today provide a nucleus
breeding area supplying areas outside the Park with bears.
The Smokies arguably afford the best backpacking east of the
Rockies (although Adirondack aficionados would differ). The
high point in this roadless area is 6,600' on the slopes of Cling-
mans Dome (there are 16 peaks over 6,000' in the two roadless
areas). Elevations drop to under 1,300'. Although the Smokies
are in the South, winter temperatures in the high country can
drop to -20°. The nearly 80" of annual precipitation gives birth
to many streams and waterfalls.

Status: Wilderness legislation is pending. Locals pushing
for a road north of Fontana Reservoir in the roadless portion of
the Park have held up the Wilderness bill through North
Carolina Senator Jesse Helms. Had it not been for Helms,
Wilderness designation for the Park would have passed in
1988. Conservationists must continue to fight for Wilderness.
Furthermore, Fontana Dam should be removed, Fontana Reservoir drained and the land added to the Park. Additionally,
The Newfound Gap-Clingmans Dome paved roads should be
closed, along with the Spruce Mountain and Parson Branch one
way dirt roads. This would restore a single Wilderness of
500,000 acres, making it a prime area for reintroduction of Eastern Timber Wolf, Panther, Elk and other extirpated species.

Acid rain is beginning to damage the old growth spruce and
fir on the crest of the Smokies. The Fraser Fir stands in the
Park have become infested with an aphid, the Balsam Woolly
Adelgid (an exotic), which is destroying them. Non-native
wild boar are upsetting the natural environment in the area,
ripping up vegetation and competing with bears for mast. They
should be eliminated.

The Forest Service presents another major danger to the
Smokies. Logging has doubled on the surrounding National
Forests in the last 10 years and 1,400 miles of new logging roads

have been built. This sawlog mania is further isolating and impoverishing one of the premier biological areas on Earth. It is just as important to stop the Forest Service's destructive behavior in the East as in the West.

Great Smoky Mountains East 163,000 acres (North Carolina & Tennessee)

Great Smoky Mts. National Park roadless (NC)	87,400
Great Smoky Mts. National Park roadless (TN)	71,500
Private and Cherokee IR roadless (NC)	4,000

Description: Separated from Great Smokies West (see for general description) by the Newfound Gap highway. High point is 6,621' Mt. Guyot.

Status: Wilderness legislation is pending. Even with Wilderness designation for much of the Park, the Park will remain as a habitat island and subject to floral and faunal depauperation. Major wilderness restoration efforts are needed throughout the Southern Appalachians in order to protect the ecological health and integrity of core wildland units such as Great Smoky Mountains National Park. See Great Smokies West for general status.

Cohutta 56,000 acres (Georgia & Tennessee)

Designated Cohutta Wilderness Area (Chattahoochee NF, GA)	35,247
Designated Cohutta Wilderness Area (Cherokee NF, TN)	1,795
Designated Big Frog Wilderness Area (Cherokee NF, TN)	7,972
Designated Big Frog Wilderness Area (Chattahoochee NF, GA)	83
Additional Chattahoochee and Cherokee NF and private roadless (GA & TN)	11,000

(13,000 acres total in TN; 43,000 in GA)

Description: Georgia-Tennessee border west of Copper Hill. The Cohutta consists of rugged Southern Appalachian mountains, and the canyons of the Jacks and Conasauga Rivers (two of the most prolific trout streams in Georgia). In contrast to the Southern Nantahala, habitats are medium to low elevation. Waterfalls and rocky gorges are special features, as are several stands of virgin forest, including some very large Yellow-poplar (Tuliptree) and Eastern Hemlock. Slopes and ridges are second growth oak/hickory forest recovering rapidly and remarkably from heavy logging 60 years ago. In another 60 years there will be a semblance of "old growth" throughout the area, according to Clemson forestry professor Robert Zahner. Wildlife includes Black Bear, Whitetail Deer, Bobcat, Turkey, Ruffed Grouse, Coosa Bass, three species of trout, and boar (not native); 40 species of rare plants. Big Frog Mountain (4,200') is the high elevation; Jacks River at 950' is the low point.

Status: The contiguous roadless acreage should be added to the designated Wilderness to prevent Forest Service logging and roading. Surrounding unpaved roads should be closed to add an additional 50,000 to 70,000 acres of land to the Wilderness as Wilderness Recovery Areas (total acreage would be 110,000 to 130,000).

Southern Nantahala 60,000 acres (Georgia & North Carolina)

Designated Southern Nantahala Wilderness Area (Chattahoochee NF, GA)	12,439
Designated Southern Nantahala Wilderness Area (Nantahala NF, NC)	10,900
Additional Chattahoochee & Nantahala NFs, and private roadless (NC & GA)	37,000

(39,000 acres total in NC; 21,000 in GA)

Description: North Carolina-Georgia border northwest of Clayton, GA. The Appalachian Trail winds through this botanically diverse, scenic high mountain area. Standing Indian Mountain (5,500') is the high point. The North Carolina portion is characterized by high ridges, averaging 4,000' to 5,000' in elevation. They were formerly covered with large expanses of wildfire-maintained native plant communities termed "heath balds." These ericaceous shrubs are losing out to invading forest trees due to over 60 years of fire protection that has not permitted lightning fires to burn. Slickrock ridges and steep slopes (gneiss bedrock outcroppings) are common, and are dominated by dwarf forests of White Oak, Chinkapin, Mountain Ash and pine. Small patches of virgin oak forests occur above cliffs, where they were inaccessible to loggers. In coves between cliffs are patches of virgin hemlock and disjunct northern hardwood forest types, which are rare this far south. The diversity of environmental niches results in an incredibly rich diversity of flora and fauna, relics of Arcto-tertiary species second only to interior China. The high elevations record the highest precipitation in Eastern North America, circa 120" annually. The Georgia portion is lower in elevation and, like the Cohutta, is characterized by second growth oak/hickory forests recovering from extensive logging between 1900 and 1920. There are several unique bog habitats here that support not only Endangered species like Bog Turtle and Manna Grass, but rare combinations of species that occur nowhere else on Earth.

Status: The 37,000 roadless acres adjacent to the Southern Nantahala Wilderness need immediate protection; the Forest Service has four timber sales scheduled in the North Carolina portion of the area during 1988-90. This may be the most threatened roadless area of any size in the Southern National Forests; local and national conservation groups should rally to its defense by recognizing that the Southern Nantahala could form the core for a large (100,000+ acres) wilderness recovery area in the southern Appalachians.

Cranberry 82,000 acres (West Virginia)

Designated Cranberry Wilderness Area	
(Monongahela NF)	*35,864*
*Additional Monongahela NF "roadless"**	*45,000*
Cranberry Glades Botanical Area roadless	
(Monongahela NF)	*750*

*see status below

Description: Eastern West Virginia north of Richwood. This high, dissected plateau, ranging from 2,300' to 4,600' in elevation, is an area of lush forest with precipitation in excess

of 45" per year. The forest types range from complex mixed
mesophyte at lower elevations to boreal/montane with Red
Spruce at the highest elevations. There are also high elevation bogs with reindeer moss and other muskeg vegetation. Numerous northern and disjunct plants such as Dwarf Dogwood,
Goldthread, Buckbean and Bog Rosemary grow here. Five
species of birds, the Hermit Thrush, Olive-backed Thrush,
Mourning Warbler, Northern Water Thrush and Purple Finch
reach their southernmost breeding limits. Bobcat, Black Bear,
Turkey and Beaver are common and the land can support up to
50 deer per square mile. Other wildlife includes Mink, Snowshoe Hare, Red Fox and Brown Recluse Spider. The streams
(headwaters of the Williams and Cranberry Rivers) support
trout, except in much of the designated Wilderness where naturally acidic waters prevent their reproduction. Cranberry is
surrounded by a wide buffer zone of roaded but extremely rugged
wildland. This is an eastern area in which we will be able to
see how the return of wilderness old growth fosters the recovery
of indigenous species. It is a popular backpacking area.

Status: The 45,000 acres outside of the designated Wilderness Area constitute the Cranberry Backcountry and contiguous
NF lands. There are dirt roads in this area but they have been
closed to public use for over 50 years, thereby largely eliminating their practical purpose as "roads." They should be permanently closed to all use, including Forest Service administration
and logging (which continues to occur in the Backcountry). By
also closing the dirt road along the Williams River and dirt
roads on Gauley Mountain, an additional 50,000 acres could be
added for a total Wilderness and Wilderness Recovery Area of
130,000 acres. Gray Wolf, Fisher, Panther and Elk should be
reintroduced.

Specific threats include timber sales and coal mine development in the areas surrounding the designated Wilderness,
including the Backcountry.

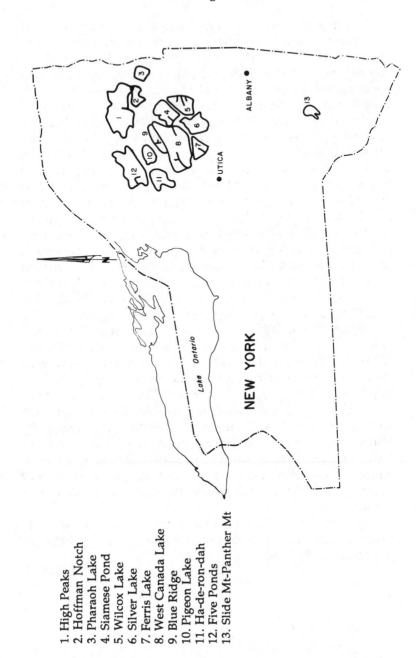

1. High Peaks
2. Hoffman Notch
3. Pharaoh Lake
4. Siamese Pond
5. Wilcox Lake
6. Silver Lake
7. Ferris Lake
8. West Canada Lake
9. Blue Ridge
10. Pigeon Lake
11. Ha-de-ron-dah
12. Five Ponds
13. Slide Mt-Panther Mt

Northeast

More than three hundred and fifty years ago the Pilgrims stepped off the Mayflower into "a hideous and desolate wilderness." Seeing New England as a stronghold of Satan and the indigenes as his worshippers, they launched into the conquest of the wild with all the fervor their religion could muster. Roderick Nash in **Wilderness and the American Mind** quotes Edward Johnson in 1654, saying that "the admirable Acts of Christ" had transformed Boston from "hideous Thickets" where "Wolfes and Beares nurst up their young" into "streets full of Girles and Boys sporting up and downe."

In those "hideous Thickets" cloaking New England, Eastern White Pine grew 250 feet tall. So excellent were these great conifers that the Royal Navy reserved them for use as masts for His Majesty's Ships. The Timber Wolf, Eastern Panther, Wolverine and other wilderness-dependent species that "nurst up their young" in primal New England were eradicated as ruthlessly as were the native humans. Farley Mowat, in **Sea of Slaughter**, describes the ruination of the New England/Newfoundland/Gulf of St. Lawrence bioregion with gruesome but accurate detail.

Surprisingly, much of New England is wilder today than it was 100 years ago or even 150 years ago. Fields marked by stone walls have grown up into forest again; there are rumors of Panther and Caribou. Abandoned dirt roads in the mountains are fading.

Nowhere else in the United States are the opportunities for sweeping wilderness restoration greater than in northern New York, Vermont, New Hampshire and Maine. The land is more resilient here than in the arid West, and the pressures for de-

Mt. Ktaadn from West Branch Penobscot River, Maine.
Photo by George Wuerthner.

velopment have not been so strong until recently. With the wisdom and foresight which established Adirondack Park 100 years ago, wilderness recovery areas of a million acres or more could be put together in the Northeast today from privately-owned timber lands. (In Pennsylvania, where there is currently no roadless area of 50,000 acres, the opportunity exists on state forest lands in the north-central part of the state for wilderness restoration of an area of a quarter of a million acres.) Unless conservationists act swiftly, though, this opportunity will slip through our fingers. Second home development, and the demand for wood for paper pulp and biomass energy production (wood chip boilers) are at an all-time high. The opening of I-93 through Franconia Notch has placed northern Vermont and New Hampshire within four hours of Boston — making second home development an even greater threat to wildlands. Who will get the regenerating Northeastern forest — "Wolfes and Beares" or Boston yuppies and pulpers?

It is the choice of this generation whether we see New England and New York as vibrant, diverse and beautiful in their natural state or as the "hideous and desolate wilderness" which so terrified the Puritans; whether we choose wilderness or unbridled development.

New York

There is little to be proud of in American history for the four decades following the Civil War. During this period business became the business of America, and New York City became its capital. Nonetheless, during this era and from the city of Mammon itself came one of the great chapters in American wilderness preservation. With the enthusiastic support of the New York City Chamber of Commerce, the Governor of New York signed a bill in 1885 establishing the Adirondack Forest Preserve in the northern part of the state. In 1894, the New York State Constitutional Convention enshrined protection of the Adirondacks in that state's highest law. (Louis Marshall, father of Bob Marshall, was one of the leaders of that effort.)

However, a pristine wilderness was not being preserved. Moose, Timber Wolf, Panther, Lynx and Beaver were already gone or virtually so. Little virgin forest remained. Streams had been heavily damaged by logging.

But the protection afforded the land has succeeded. Moose, Raven and Beaver have returned. Bald Eagle and Peregrine Falcon have been reintroduced. Rivers and streams are healing themselves, and forests are growing tall.

Adirondack Park is a complex preserve. Some 3,700,000 acres of its 6 million acres are privately owned. Although there are large blocks of state land, private inholdings complicate preservation for key areas. The Adirondack Park Agency, created in 1970, was instructed to develop a master plan for management of the Park. Not only did the agency have management authority over state lands, but (to a limited degree) they were able to control development on private lands through strict zoning. Obviously, the Adirondack Park Agency has been unpopular with some of the local residents, who would find kindred spirits in any Idaho mill town bar.

The master plan involved the classification of state lands into nine categories. These include Wilderness (with regulations as strict as for federal Wilderness Areas), Primitive, Wild River, and Canoe (almost as well protected as Wilderness). Wild Forest classification permits the retention of some truck trails and allows snowmobiles, among other non-wilderness uses. Nevertheless, some Wild Forest is quite primitive and qualifies as "roadless" in this inventory. By 1979, slightly over one million acres (45% of the state land) had been designated as Wilderness. Additions to the Wilderness classification are being continually made as private lands are acquired or non-conforming uses are removed from state lands. Catskill State Park, less than 100 miles north of New York City, also has designated Wilderness Areas, including one large enough for this inventory.

Sadly, though, all is not well even in the Adirondack Wilderness Areas. Acid precipitation is destroying the lakes, streams and forests. As it does so, restoration of Moose, Timber Wolf, Panther, Lynx, Wolverine . . . becomes moot. There is no better example than in the Adirondacks of the painful fact that wilderness cannot be preserved in isolation, that the damage we wreak in industrial areas is also felt in protected wildlands. There is no preserve large enough to escape our poisoning of the air, water and land with the by-products of industrialization.

High Peaks 336,000 acres

Designated High Peaks State Wilderness Area (Adirondack Park) & private inholdings	197,215
Dix Mountain State Wilderness Area (Adirondack Park)	45,208
Private and Wild Forest roadless adjacent to Dix Mountain	54,570
Private roadless east of Raquette River	38,652

Description: Northern New York south of Lake Placid (north-central Adirondack Park). This is the high country of the Adirondacks, including the highest peak in New York State, Mt. Marcy (5,344'); dropping down to lower elevation swampland along the Saranac and Raquette Rivers. Mount Marcy and Algonquin are above timberline. Lake-Tear-of-the-Clouds, the source of the Hudson River, is at 4,300'. Some parts of this area are very wild, while others are heavily impacted by recreationists. Dramatic high cliffs in the area attract climbers. Major forest types for all of the Adirondack areas are Red Spruce/Balsam Fir at high elevations and in lower frost pockets; below that a mixed forest primarily of Beech, Yellow Birch and Sugar Maple, with a wider variety of hardwoods and hemlock at the lowest elevations. In addition, Black Spruce, Eastern Larch and other bog species occur in scattered poorly drained lowlands. Beaver, Raven, Moose, Fisher and Marten maintain a stronghold here. Sensitive species of wildlife found in the Adirondacks as a whole include Indiana Bat, Bald Eagle, Spruce Grouse, Common Loon, Short-eared Owl, Sedge Wren, Grasshopper Sparrow, Worm Snake, Bog Turtle, Round Whitefish and Eastern Sand Darter.

Status: Elk, Wolf, Lynx and Eastern Panther should be reintroduced to this and other Adirondack Wilderness Areas (5 Lynx were reintroduced in January, 1989, and 19 more will be released during the next two years). Acid rain is a severe problem in all the Adirondack areas, killing the lakes and perhaps the high altitude spruce/fir forests. Most Adirondack areas were roaded and logged in the past (although pockets of virgin forest exist); these "roadless" areas listed are recovering, and existing vehicle routes in them are no more than jeep routes. In the portions designated as "Wilderness" or "Primitive," vehicles are prohibited.

RM36: 380,000

Hoffman Notch 61,000 acres

Designated Hoffman Notch State Wilderness	
Area (Adirondack Park)	*36,231*
Wild Forest roadless	*24,324*

Description: Northern New York west of Schroon Lake (east-central Adirondack Park). This is an area of large diameter hardwoods and is dominated by three north-south ridges (Blue Ridge, Washburn Ridge and Texas Ridge) reaching over 3,000'. Hoffman Mountain, the high point in the area, was saved from a ski area in a referendum in 1967. There are eight lakes and ponds in the area.

Status: The area designated as Wilderness is protected; the remainder is not.

Pharaoh Lake 52,000 acres

Designated Pharaoh Lake State Wilderness	
Area (Adirondack Park)	*45,884*
Additional roadless	*6,465*

Description: Northern New York west of Ticonderoga (eastern Adirondack Park). The vegetation is generally White Pine/birch due to past forest fires. Many ponds and imposing rock outcrops adorn this area. Old hardwood stands survive in unburned coves. There are also areas of Red Pine and mixed northern hardwoods. Pharaoh Lake is one of the largest wilderness lakes in the Adirondacks. This is a low, rolling area with a high point of 2,557' on Pharaoh Peak.

Status: The area designated as Wilderness is protected; the rest is not.

Siamese Pond 141,000 acres

Designated Siamese Pond State Wilderness

| *Area   (Adirondack Park)* | *112,604* |
| *Wild Forest & private roadless* | *28,391* |

Description: Northern New York west of North Creek (south-central Adirondack Park). Rolling hills, Beaver ponds and mature second growth forest distinguish this area. Ice caves on Chimney Mountain are a rare feature. There are some 60 to 70 glacier-carved lakes and ponds in this area, including Thirteenth Lake which has landlocked salmon.

Status: Snowmobiles and ORVs trespass into the Wilderness.

Wilcox Lake 120,000 acres

Wilcox Lake Wild Forest & private roadless
  (Adirondack Park)   *120,000*

Description: Northern New York between the Siamese Ponds and Silver Lake Wilderness Areas (southern Adirondack Park) north of Northville. Rolling hills, Brook Trout streams and some very large trees characterize this area.

Status: This area is heavily laced with snowmobile trails and old logging roads.

Silver Lake 141,000 acres

Designated Silver Lake State Wilderness Area
  (Adirondack Park) and private inholdings   *106,900*
Wild Forest and private roadless to south,
  north & west   *34,130*

Description: Northern New York north of Gloversville (southern Adirondack Park). This is rolling, low country (only four mountains reach 3,000') with large second growth hemlock and hardwoods. Because this was one of the first areas acquired by the state in the Adirondacks, the logged areas have grown back to give a powerful impression of pristine forest. Swamps, beaver ponds and lakes are common.

Status: The designated Wilderness is protected; the remainder is not.

Ferris Lake <u>75,000 acres</u>

Ferris Lake Wild Forest (Adirondack Park) and private roadless	75,000

Description: Northern New York northeast of Utica (southwestern Adirondack Park). Many ponds, lakes and streams make this a prime area for water-loving species.
Status: Open to vehicles.

West Canada Lake <u>316,000 acres</u>

Designated West Canada Lake State Wilderness Area (Adirondack Park)	156,735
Designated Buell Brook State Primitive Area	10,900
Jessup River Wild Forest roadless	18,120
Black River Wild Forest roadless	75,000
Private and additional state roadless	55,300

Description: Northern New York southeast of Old Forge (southwestern Adirondack Park). Numerous lakes and streams in three watersheds (Hudson, Mohawk and Black), Red Spruce/Balsam Fir swamp and Beaver meadows make this an important area of wetlands. The state-designated Indian Wild River flows through it. Rolling hills, steep mountains, and large coniferous and deciduous trees characterize this diverse and productive landscape.
Status: Snowmobiles occasionally trespass in the Wilderness Area; jeep trails run to private inholdings in Black River Wild Forest.
RM36: 430,000

Blue Ridge <u>75,000 acres</u>

Designated Blue Ridge State Wilderness Area (Adirondack Park)	45,736
Moose River Wild Forest roadless	29,343

Description: Northern New York south of Blue Mountain Lake (central Adirondack Park). Some of the best old growth spruce and hemlock in the Northeast was blown down here in the 1950 hurricane, illustrating the fragility of tiny remnant ecosystems. The high point is 3,497' Blue Ridge.

Status: The designated Wilderness is protected; rest is not.

Pigeon Lake 62,000 acres

Designated Pigeon Lake State Wilderness Area	
(Adirondack Park)	*50,100*
Private roadless to north	*11,860*

Description: Northern New York north of Eagle Bay (west-central Adirondack Park). Low, rolling hills, many swamps, dense Red Spruce/Balsam Fir forest on West Mountain, and small tracts of old growth White Pine and virgin Yellow Birch mark this area.

Status: The designated Wilderness is protected; the private land is not.

Ha-de-ron-dah 89,000 acres

Designated Ha-de-ron-dah State Wilderness	
Area (Adirondack Park)	*26,528*
Private and Independence River	
Wild Forest roadless	*62,540*

Description: Northern New York northwest of Old Forge (western Adirondack Park). This rolling, swampy terrain features 100' high pines. Pin Cherry, Aspen and Bracken Fern dominate formerly burned areas.

Status: The designated Wilderness suffers from serious snowmobile invasion. The non-Wilderness portion has old logging roads that have been converted to hiking trails and snowmobile routes.

Five Ponds 203,000 acres

Designated Five Ponds State Wilderness Area	
(Adirondack Park)	*101,171*
Designated Pepperbox State Wilderness Area	
(Adirondack Park)	*14,625*
Wild Forest, private, other roadless	*87,000*

Description: Northern New York south of Cranberry Lake (west-central Adirondack Park). The high point is 2,489' Summit Mountain. There are excellent examples of glaciation here, including the well-developed Five Ponds esker. 50,000 acres of virgin White Pine and Red Spruce (the largest tract of virgin timber in the northeast) are located within this largely low, rolling area, as are nearly 200 lakes and ponds, alder swamps and Beaver ponds, and 48 miles of three designated Wild & Scenic Rivers — the main branch, West Branch and Middle Branch of the Oswegatchie River. This area once had the best Brook Trout fishing in New York, but the introduction of perch eliminated them, illustrating the dangers of non-native species. The Pepperbox Wilderness is trailless and one of the wilder places in the Adirondacks — it is largely a wet lowland with scattered spruce, fir and Red Maple. The Cranberry Wild Forest has boreal forest and bird species common to Canada. Bob Marshall's first wilderness experiences were in this roadless area.

Status: Snowmobiling is permitted in the Cranberry Wild Forest. Marshall proposed a 380,000 acre Wilderness here in the 1930s. The Adirondack Council is currently proposing acquisition of private property to designate a 160,000 acre "Bob Marshall Wilderness Area," which they say could be the outstanding Wilderness in the Adirondacks. Other conservationists have called for a 350,000 acre unified Wilderness.

RM36: 380,000

Slide Mountain-Panther Mountain 52,000 acres

Designated Slide Mountain-Panther Mountain	
State Wilderness Area (Catskill Park)	*38,745*
Proposed Wilderness addition & other roadless	*13,000*

Description: Southeastern New York west of Kingston in Catskill State Park. Slide Mountain is 4,180'; the low point is 1,100'. Oak/hickory forest grades to northern hardwoods with Red Spruce/Balsam Fir on the higher elevations. This wilderness produces the water supply for New York City. Just across a road from this roadless area is the 37,000 acre roadless area of the Big Indian-Beaverkill Range Wilderness Area & Balsam Lake Mountain Wild Forest.

Status: The designated Wilderness is protected; rest is not.

New England

Paper companies own a vast, once-logged but otherwise undeveloped area along the Canadian border in Maine, New Hampshire and Vermont which consists of northeastern spruce/fir and northern hardwoods forest, streams, lakes and mountains. Indeed, some 10 *million* acres in Maine may be uninhabited, according to wilderness expert and author George Wuerthner. This is the largest uninhabited area in the Lower 48. The "Northeast Kingdom" of Vermont, mostly paper company land, is the wildest and least populated part of that state. Much of northern New Hampshire (in private ownership) is probably wilder than the large roadless areas in the White Mountain National Forest. These areas have, of course, been logged, and some dirt roads remain in them, but the opportunity to restore significant wilderness in northern New England is greater than anywhere else in the United States. If these areas were transferred to public ownership, and closed to logging and motorized vehicles, wilderness would quickly begin to reestablish itself and wilderness-dependent species such as Wolverine, Panther, Lynx, Pine Marten and Caribou would likely return. The Fisher has already repatriated to northern New Hampshire. With careful wilderness restoration management and reintroduction of extirpated species, wilderness would return even sooner.

The opportunity for such restoration will never be better than it is today. The going price for timber company land is $200/acre; all of northern Maine (10 million acres) could be purchased for $2 billion — the price of the proposed Two Forks Dam in Colorado. More than enough money is currently in the federal government's Land & Water Conservation Fund to buy several million acres in northern New England for wilderness restoration and a new National Park(s). All that is lacking are popular demand and political will.

Now is the time for conservationists in New England and the nation to envision real wilderness, with its full complement of native species, existing once again east of the Rockies. The opportunity currently exists for wilderness on an Alaskan scale in New England.

1. Baxter State Park
2. Baxter North
3. Reed Mountain
4. Wildlands Lakes
5. St. John Ponds

6. St. John River South
7. St. John River North
8. Moose River
9. Redington Pond
10. Dead Diamond
11. Blue Mountain
12. Meachum Swamp
13. Kilkenny
14. Mahoosuc Range
15. Wild River-Kearsarge
16. Pemigewasset
17. Sandwich Range

If conservationists do not act swiftly, however, the opportunity will be lost. Forestry is becoming harsher on the corporate lands. Herbicides, larger clearcuts, shorter rotation times, more roads and heavier machinery are having a more devastating impact today than the "lighter" logging practices of the past. Relatively natural forests are being transformed into industrial tree farms. Moreover, developers like the Patten Corporation are already gobbling up paper company lands that are put on the market. If this continues, condominiums, ski areas, lodges, vacation resorts and second homes will ring the lakes and scar the mountains; loon and wolf will lose out once again.

In addition to the *potential* Big Outside in New England, there are several areas over 50,000 acres in size which are essentially roadless and undeveloped today. Baxter State Park in Maine and the White Mountain National Forest in New Hampshire are the principal areas of public ownership in New England. Baxter is largely protected but the White Mountain NF is under the same pressures of roading and logging as National Forests in other parts of the country.

The designated Wilderness Areas on the White Mountain NF were not easy to win. (See the discussion on Eastern National Forest Wilderness in the introductory remarks for the "Southern States.") The 1984 New Hampshire Wilderness Act was the worst one in the East. Of 262,257 acres in RARE II (conservationists proposed 495,596 acres for Wilderness and that figure is a far more accurate indicator of what was roadless), only 77,000 acres were protected in the bill. A special problem for Wilderness preservation in New Hampshire is that some so-called conservation groups — like the hut-operating Appalachian Mountain Club — essentially oppose Wilderness designation. Real conservation groups, including The Wilderness Society and Sierra Club, recently settled their appeal of the White Mountain NF Plan (which was one of the worst in the nation) with what they call a victory but what New England Earth First! calls a sell-out. Nonetheless, there are several large roadless areas on the White Mountain NF; their long-term prospects are varied.

There are apparently large roadless areas on timber company lands in Maine, New Hampshire and Vermont, and they are listed here as well.

Baxter State Park <u>200,000 acres (Maine)</u>	
Baxter State Park roadless	*120,000*
Private roadless to east	*80,000*

Description: Central Maine north of Millinocket. Baxter is the beau ideal of the North Woods: lakes, streams, Mt. Ktaadn, Black Bear, Moose and blackflies. Mt. Ktaadn, the highest point in Maine, is 5,268'. Seventeen other peaks are over 3,000'. The lowest elevations are below 500'. Henry David Thoreau climbed Ktaadn in 1846 and wrote about that experience in his wilderness classic **The Maine Woods**. Ktaadn's peak is the first place in the United States to be hit by the sun, and, along with other peaks in the Park, has extensive areas of alpine tundra. In this area of transition from northern hardwoods (Beech, Yellow Birch, Sugar Maple) to Red Spruce/Balsam Fir forest, some virgin forest remains. Sadly, this roadless area is a habitat island generally surrounded by a sea of clearcuts and other "managed forest." Glacial features include kames, eskers, drumlins, kettleholes and moraines. Moose are abundant here. Additional wildlife includes Whitetail Deer, Bobcat, Mink, Short-tail and Long-tail Weasel, Canada Jay and Spruce Grouse.

Status: A large area of seemingly roadless private land, east of the Park, including the Seboeis River and the East Branch of the Penobscot, is included in this roadless area. Lands in the Park are protected and managed much like federal Wilderness; those outside the Park are not. This additional acreage should be added to Baxter State Park as the core for a ten million acre Wilderness Preserve stretching to the north to include the St. John and Allagash Rivers. In one of the most visionary and praiseworthy initiatives from the mainstream conservation movement in recent years, The Wilderness Society has proposed a 3 million acre National Park or Preserve in this area.

Baxter North 90,000 acres (Maine)

Baxter State Park roadless	*55,000*
Private & Maine Public Reserve roadless to north	*35,000*

Description: Central Maine northwest of Patten. Baxter State Park and adjacent private and Maine Public Reserve Land north of the Baxter Park road form this roadless area. The countless streams, ponds and lakes include the East Branch Penobscot River, Webster Brook and Grand Lake. Elevations vary from 1,200' to 650'. The Baxter Park road separates this roadless area from the main Baxter roadless area. See Baxter Park for general description.

Status: Logging is allowed on 28,000 acres of Baxter Park lands in this area. The land north of the Park appears to be essentially roadless but is likely under some kind of timber "management." Baxter Park should be considerably enlarged with wilderness restoration the management goal. Logging should, of course, be entirely halted in Baxter State Park.

Reed Mountain 60,000 acres (Maine)

Big Reed Pond Preserve (The Nature Conservancy)	*3,800*
Private roadless	*56,000*

Description: North-central Maine north of Baxter State Park. There are only 6,000 acres of original (unlogged) forest in the entire state of Maine. Two-thirds of this is in the Reed Mountain roadless area. The Nature Conservancy recently acquired this 3,800 acre old growth forest around Big Reed Pond. Besides providing habitat for other North Woods species, Big Reed Pond is one of only ten ponds in the world to contain the Blueback Char. Other features in this area include Haymock Lake, Munsungan Lake, Mooseleuk Mountain and the Currier Ponds. This roadless area is just north of the Baxter North roadless area and separated from it only by a timber company dirt road.

Status: This important Nature Conservancy preserve provides additional argument for acquiring timber company land north of Baxter and creating a huge National Park. Without protection, surrounding lands which are returning to a roadless condition may be roaded and logged once again.

Wildlands Lakes 135,000 acres
Private roadless   *135,000*

Description: Central Maine south of Baxter State Park and west of Millinocket. The Appalachian Trail winds through this large area of forest, streams and lakes. Features include Rainbow Lake, Nahmakanta Lake and the Debsconeag Lakes.

Status: This area should be high priority for preservation in public ownership as part of a 10 million acre Maine Woods Wilderness National Park stretching north through Baxter Park to the Canadian border.

St. John Ponds 180,000 acres (Maine)
Private roadless   *180,000*

Description: Northwestern Maine north of Moosehead Lake. The headwaters of the St. John River and North Branch Penobscot, including the St. John Ponds, Big Bog, and the Baker Branch of the St. John River below Baker Lake, form a large roadless area of northeastern spruce/fir and northern hardwoods. Moose, Black Bear, Lynx, Marten, Fisher, Northeastern Coyote, Mink, River Otter, Fisher, Osprey, Common Loon and Furbish Lousewort live here.

A huge area of northern Maine is uninhabited, although the paper companies which own enormous tracts have certainly damaged it with continual cutting over the last century. Nonetheless, some areas of quite wild land remain and the opportunity exists for wilderness restoration on an unprecedented scale.

Status: Despite the presence of several cherrystemmed dirt roads, this large area appears to be essentially roadless. Conservation groups should establish a national priority to acquire ten million acres of paper company land, from Baxter State Park to the St. John River, to form a wilderness-oriented National Park. Dirt roads should be closed, logged areas restored and extirpated species like Gray Wolf, Woodland Caribou, Wolverine and Catamount (Eastern Panther) reintroduced. Such an area, in twenty years or less, could be one of the finest temperate zone Wildernesses in the world.

RM36: 2,800,000*

St. John River South <u>100,000 acres (Maine and Quebec)</u>

Private roadless	· *90,000*
Quebec roadless	*10,000*

Description: Northwestern Maine. Hardwood Mountain, Desolation and Corner ponds are landmarks. Elevations drop from 1,800' to 1,100'. The St. John River, a National Wild & Scenic River, is a classic wilderness canoe trip. The Baker Branch St. John River from Baker Lake (International Paper Road) north (downstream) to the Boise Cascade Road (confluence with the Southwest Branch St. John River) is essentially roadless. See St. John Ponds for general description.

Status: See St. John Ponds. The estimate for contiguous roadless land in Quebec is rough.

RM36: 2,800,000*

St. John River North <u>70,000 acres (Maine)</u>

Private roadless	*70,000*

Description: Northwestern Maine. A section of the St. John River north from the American Realty Road to low standard dirt roads coming in to either side of the river at Ninemile, the river's east side between Red Pine and Ninemile East campgrounds, and a larger area on the west bank north, including Linscott and Houlton ponds, appear to be essentially roadless. Elevations drop from 1,400' to 1,000'. See St. John Ponds for general description.

Status: See St. John Ponds.

RM36: 2,800,000*

Moose River <u>110,000 acres (Maine)</u>

Maine Public Reserve Land roadless	*14,000*
Private roadless	*96,000*

Description: Western Maine southwest of Jackman. Attean Mountain and Pond, Moose River, No. 5 Mountain, Holeb Falls, Tumbledown Mountain, Spencer Bale Mountain, Kirby Range and numerous small ponds are features of this roadless area south of the Canadian Pacific Railroad tracks. Several of the summits exceed 3,000'; the low point is 1,159' on Attean Pond.

Status: Minor dirt roads form the southwestern half of the boundary of this area.

Redington Pond 120,000 acres (Maine)
Private roadless 120,000

Description: Western Maine east of Rangeley. The Appalachian Trail passes through this mountainous region which includes several peaks over 4,000' including Crocker Mountain (4,168') and The Horn (4,023').

Status: Although several dirt roads penetrate this large area of private land, it appears to be essentially roadless.

West Branch Dead Diamond River-Crystal Mountain 60,000 acres (New Hampshire)
Private roadless 60,000

Description: Northern New Hampshire northeast of Dixville Notch. The land from Magalloway Mountain (3,359') south to Crystal Mountain (3,250') and the Swift Diamond River appears to be essentially roadless. Flora and fauna are similar to the Pemigewasset. Wildlife also includes Eastern Panther, Fisher and Moose.

Status: Several minor dirt roads penetrate, but do not cross this area of paper company land. Efforts should be made to acquire this area and other paper company or otherwise privately-owned roadless areas in northern New Hampshire and Vermont as the core for a large Wilderness National Park. Most of this particular roadless area is owned by Champion International; while their land is not formally on the market, Champion would probably listen to an offer.

Blue Mountain <u>100,000 acres (New Hampshire)</u>
Public and private roadless   100,000

Description: Northern New Hampshire north of Groveton. The area from Goback Mountain (3,523') east to Blue Mountain (3,720'), Dixville Peak and Owlhead Mountain is essentially roadless. The 45,000 acre Nash Stream watershed in this area is prime habitat for Moose and Panther — Moose have returned and there are increasing Panther sightings in the area. Fisher have also returned to the area. Flora and fauna are otherwise similar to the Pemigewasset.

Status: This former paper company land is penetrated, but not crossed by several dirt roads. Much of the area was recently purchased by public and private funds for "conservation," but the details may prove to be disappointing — logging, sand & gravel mining, and ORVs may be permitted.

Meachum Swamp <u>50,000 acres (Vermont)</u>
Private roadless   50,000

Description: Northeast Kingdom of Vermont north of Bloomfield. This is the country between Averill Lake-East Branch Nulhegan River and the Connecticut River. Landmarks are Bloomfield Ridge, Monadnock Mountain (3,139') and Sable Mountain (2,726'). Yellow Bog — the largest bog in Vermont — is an important feature. This area is the center of Vermont's recovering Moose population and has fine habitat for Gray Wolf and Panther, which were once present. Across the Connecticut River is the Blue Mountain roadless area.

Status: Although penetrated by minor dirt roads, this is a key part of the Northeast Kingdom National Park proposal.

Kilkenny <u>New Hampshire</u>
White Mountain NF and private roadless   70,000

Description: Northern New Hampshire between Lancaster and Berlin. This mountainous area includes Deer Ridge, Pilot Range, Pliny Range and Crescent Range. Mt. Cabot at 4,080' is the high point; Mt. Waumbeck also exceeds 4,000' and several

other peaks, including The Horn, approach that elevation.
Unknown Pond is one of several ponds in the area. See Pemigewasset for general description.

Status: About three quarters of the White Mountain NF
area was designated for backcountry management by the settlement on the Forest Plan. This means that commercial timber
sales will not be scheduled and semi-primitive recreation and
wildlife habitat will be stressed, although ORVs will be allowed on designated trails. The remaining part of this roadless
area in the White Mt NF is zoned for full-scale timber harvest.
The status of the private lands is unknown.

Mahoosuc Range 78,000 acres (Maine & New Hampshire)

Maine Public Reserve Land, Grafton Notch	
State Park, private roadless (ME)	*60,000*
Private roadless (NH)	*18,000*

Description: Central New Hampshire-Maine border east of
Berlin, NH, and northwest of Bethel, ME. The Appalachian
Trail runs along the crest of the Mahoosuc Range in this road-
less area. Several peaks exceed 3,700'; lower elevations near
the Androscoggin River drop to 1,100'. The Sunday River
watershed forms the the southeastern portion of the area.
Fauna and flora are similar to areas in the White Mountain
NF.

Status: The State of Maine is managing its lands in the
Mahoosuc as "wilderness." The private lands in Maine and
New Hampshire are unprotected and should be high priority
for public acquisition and preservation. The Sunday River Ski
Area is cherrystemmed in the southern part of this area, as is a
dirt road along the lower part of the Sunday River. US Highway 2 separates this area from the Wild River-Kearsarge
roadless area to the south.

Wild River-Kearsarge 110,000 acres (New Hampshire & Maine)

White Mountain NF & private roadless	*110,000*

Description: Central New Hampshire-Maine border south of Berlin. Carter Mountain at 4,832' is the high point. Seven other peaks exceed 4,000'. Elevations drop to under 1,000'. This area, with 20 miles of the Appalachian Trail, has spectacular views of the Presidential Range (Mt. Washington, etc.) which is to the west of Pinkham Notch. The valley of the Wild River, which is surrounded by high peaks, has the best habitat in the White Mt NF for Pine Marten and Lynx. Flora and fauna are similar to the Pemigewasset (see below).

Status: 35,000 acres in the Wild River country (northern part of this roadless area) are supposedly closed to motorized vehicles, but a "temporary" snowmobile trail goes through the heart of this roadless area. Over 40,000 acres south of the Wild River portion are being fragmented by FS roading and logging, which will cut the Kearsarge Mt area off from the rest of the roadless area (it may already have been separated by the time this is printed). Conservation groups have acquiesced in this destruction by cutting a quick deal on their appeal of the White Mt NF Plan. Additional areas around the Wild River "core" are also being roaded and logged by the FS. Snowmobiles and ORVs are a big problem. This may be the most threatened large roadless area east of the Rocky Mountains (except possibly for the Southern Nantahala in North Carolina/Georgia).

Hwy 113 in Maine should be closed to connect this area with the Caribou-Speckled Mountain roadless area of 16,000 acres (the FS is studying only 12,000 acres there for possible Wilderness designation). A 125,000-150,000 acre Wilderness could be established here if the Forest Service chainsaw mentality could be held in check.

Pemigewasset 125,000 acres (New Hampshire)

Designated Pemigewasset Wilderness Area	
(White Mountain NF)	*45,000*
Additional White Mountain NF roadless	*75,000*
Crawford Notch State Park roadless	*5,000*

Description: Central New Hampshire between Lincoln and Bartlett. A popular backpacking area, this is the largest National Forest roadless area east of the Mississippi. The high point is Mt. Lafayette at 5,249'; Mt. Lincoln is 5,108';

thirteen other peaks exceed 4,000'. Elevations drop to under 1,000' on the edges of the roadless area near large rivers. Many brooks and ponds, and 27 miles of the Appalachian Trail are in the "Pemi." This area was heavily logged at the turn of the century but is recovering, with large second growth forest now occurring. Franconia Notch forms the western boundary and Crawford Notch the east. Both are classic "notches" carved by continental ice sheets.

Rich, diverse lowland forests surround Sawyer Pond in the southeastern corner. Four basic forest types exist here: Northern Hardwoods (maple, ash, beech); Northern Hardwoods/Red Spruce (with some White and Black Spruce); Spruce/Fir (spruces and Balsam Fir); and Paper Birch/Aspen. Hardwoods and spruce/fir mixed with birch grow below 2,500'. In the high country, spruce/fir grows from 2,500-3,500'; spruce/fir krummholz (up to 300 years old) from 3,500-4,000'; sub-alpine vegetation above 4,000'; and alpine tundra above 5,000'. Wildlife includes Peregrine Falcon, Cooper's Hawk, Northern Harrier, Black Bear and Pine Marten. Prime habitat exists for Golden Eagle, Lynx, Wolverine, Eastern Panther and Gray Wolf — all of which should be reintroduced.

Status: Snowmobiles and other ORVs are allowed on 50,000 acres of the unprotected area. Logging is allowed on about 30,000 acres along the edges of the current roadless area. Three "huts" (lodges) accessible only by foot are in the area. The primary threats to the Pemi are acid rain, excessive numbers of hikers, and an unhealthy ecology because of extirpated species. Conservationists continue to push for protection of about 100,000 acres. The Kancamagus Highway to the south — a popular scenic drive and a zoo when the colors turn in the fall — should be closed and a single 220,000 acre Pemigewasset-Sandwich Wilderness created.

Sandwich Range 81,000 acres (New Hampshire)

Designated Sandwich Range Wilderness Area	
(White Mountain NF)	*25,000*
Additional White Mountain NF &	
private roadless	*56,000*

Description: Central New Hampshire northeast of Plymouth. Mt. Osceola at 4,315' is the high point; three other peaks are above 4,000'. Elevations drop to under 1,000'. Flora and fauna are similar to the Pemi, except that oaks reach their northern limit in the Sandwich Range. This roadless area is separated from the Pemi by the Kancamagus Highway.

Status: Logging, roading, snowmobiles and ORVs threaten the unprotected portion. A long-used snowmobile trail marks the eastern boundary of the Wilderness and divides it from the Mt. Chocorua Scenic Area (which is included in this roadless area). This area should be combined with the Pemigewasset (see above).

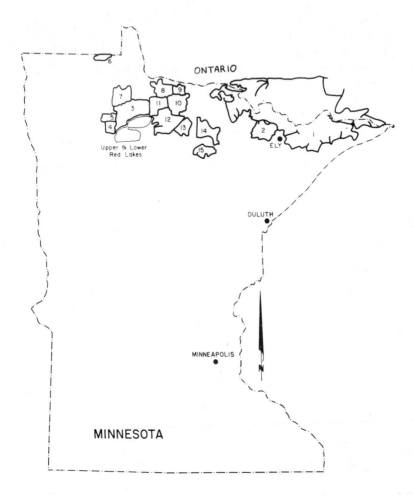

1. Boundary Waters-Quetico
2. Little Sioux
3. Red Lake Peatland
4. Red Lake Indian Res.
5. Carmelee-Hamre
6. Marvin Lake Peatland
7. Lost Lake Peatland
8. East Fk Rapid River
9. West Fork Peatland
10. Black River Peatland
11. Ludlow Peatland
12. Sturgeon River
13. SE Pine Island
14. Little Fork River
15. George Washington

Northcentral

The North Woods of Wisconsin, Michigan and Minnesota gave the timber industry its age of heroic legend. From the 1870s on, the exploitation of the virgin White Pine forests established a new scale for rapaciousness, and a gigantic folk hero — Paul Bunyan — had to be created to equal the deed. Never before had so much forest fallen so quickly. Even some within the timber industry became alarmed. Frederick Merk, in **History of the Westward Movement**, quotes the owners of the Black River Falls sawmill as telling the Minnesota legislature, "In a few years, the wealthiest portion of the pineries will present nothing but a vast and gloomy wilderness of pine stumps."

They were correct. Paul and the Blue Ox did their work well for the timber barons. The Northern Hardwoods and Great Lakes Pine Forests of northern Wisconsin were chopped to smithereens. There is no Big Outside left in that state. As someone from Madison has written, "I keep driving north in Wisconsin to get to the North Woods, but I never find them." There was a Big Outside once in Wisconsin, there may be again someday, but the largest Wilderness Area in 1989 is less than 20,000 acres on the Nicolet National Forest. By closing roads, by stilling the chainsaws, by encouraging Timber Wolf and Moose, ecological wilderness could come back. To do so, though, will require vision and self-restraint; something that a few far-seeing citizens of Wisconsin possess, but something alien to most of their forest rangers and politicians. Botanists at the University of Wisconsin have proposed establishing two biodiversity preserves (100,000 acres and 40,000 acres) on the Chequamegon National Forest where native old growth ecosystems could be reestablished. To his lasting credit, the Forest Supervisor supported the idea, but the Regional Forester overruled him. The botanists have appealed the rejection of their visionary proposal. More power to them.

In the Upper Peninsula of Michigan, where Nick Adams and his kid sister fished the Big Two Hearted River . . . well, Paul got that, too. But he missed a couple of places on the UP, places that offer a glimpse of what Michigan once was.

To really find the North Woods, one has to go all the way north in the Midwest, up to northern Minnesota, where glaciers scoured the southern end of the Canadian Shield to form the Boundary Waters. Make no mistake about it, Paul did his best to turn this area into a "wilderness of stumps," too. Despite Forest Service administrative protection for the Boundary Waters beginning in 1926, Paul's successors were permitted to swing their axes in much of it. In the 1964 Wilderness Act, Congress continued the exception. It was not until 1978, after a dreadful fight, that Congress finally protected the last great remnant of the North Woods, by outlawing logging in the Boundary Waters Wilderness. Nonetheless, this great Wilderness must be guarded constantly.

In western Minnesota, the North Woods give way to the Great Plains — first Tallgrass Prairie, then Shortgrass Prairie. In its own way, change came as rapidly to this treeless landscape as to the big woods. The Lakota had to step aside for civilization, and the Lakota depended on the buffalo for their freedom, reasoned Gen. Phil Sheridan. The answer was simple: Destroy the buffalo and destroy the Indian. George Armstrong Custer discovered that the warriors of the Plains wouldn't take it lying down. But after the great herds were gone, even the Ghost Dance couldn't bring back the freedom of rolling grass and distant thunder.

There are still spectacular thunderstorms and riveting sunsets on the Great Plains, blizzards sweeping down from the North Pole, and summer days hot enough to drive a man to his knees. But cattle have replaced Bison, Elk and Pronghorn. Farmers' dogs yap where Buffalo Wolves once howled. And the rotary irrigation pump squeaks where the medicine wheel marked sacred ground.

Only in Badlands National Park in western South Dakota and along the Little Missouri River in western North Dakota was the land hard enough to deflect civilization. Four areas

Seagull Lake in Boundary Waters Wilderness, Minnesota.
Photo by Kevin Proescholdt.

there whisper a reminder of what was, a short hundred years
ago.

As Aldo Leopold learned from his sojourn in Wisconsin, we
live in a world of wounds.

Minnesota

*We Westerners look down our noses on the states east of the
Rockies, considering them tame woodlots compared to our wide
open spaces and unpopulated mountains and deserts. But northern Minnesota is as wild and sparsely settled as most of the
West. Indeed, the third largest roadless area in the 48 states is
on the Superior National Forest; state and Indian lands to the
west of it compose an additional two million acre backcountry
of bog and northern forest crossed only by a handful of minor
roads. Moreover, this is the only place in the United States
outside of Alaska where the wolf has held its own.*

Boundary Waters-Quetico 2,752,000 acres (also in Ontario)

Designated Boundary Waters Canoe Area Wilderness (Superior NF & intermixed state, county and private)	972,537
Quetico Provincial Park roadless (Ontario)	1,175,169
Superior NF RARE II contiguous to BWCA	36,000
Additional Superior NF roadless	152,000
Voyageurs National Park roadless	219,128
Superior NF, state, private roadless contiguous to Voyageurs NP	85,000
LaVerendrye Provincial Park roadless (Ontario)	22,000
Sand Point roadless (Ontario)	90,000

Description: Northeastern Minnesota north of Ely and
southwestern Ontario. The Boundary Waters are an incompa-
rable lakeland wilderness — the North Woods personified.
Denizens include Gray Wolf, Black Bear, Moose, Lynx, Fisher,
Pine Marten, Common Loon, Osprey, Double-crested Cormorant,
Belted Kingfisher, merganser (Common, Red-breasted and
Hooded), Bald Eagle, dozens of species of songbirds, pike and
trout.

Here is the largest extent of virgin forest east of the Rockies, including a stand of Red Pine dating from a fire in 1595 CE. Two major forest types meet in the BWCA: the Northern Boreal Forest typified by Black & White Spruce, Balsam Fir, Paper Birch and Jack Pine; and the Great Lakes or Laurentian Forest of Red & White Pine, Red & Sugar Maple, and other northern hardwoods.

The high point is Eagle Mountain, at 2,301' the highest elevation in Minnesota. Several thousand lakes over 10 acres in size, several thousand miles of canoe trails, Beaver ponds, bogs, marshes, exposed rock and cliffs shape the beauty of this great Wilderness. This is the southern edge of the Canadian Shield, with some of the oldest exposed rocks in the world. At least four times in the last million years continental glaciers up to two miles thick passed over it, gouging and shaping its present character.

The Boundary Waters Canoe Area was the second area protected by the Forest Service for its wilderness values (in 1926), and the first Wilderness so protected by Congress, beginning in 1930. Several of the conservation movement's greats have fought for the BWCA, including Arthur Carhart, Aldo Leopold, Bob Marshall, Ernest Oberholtzer and Sigurd Olson. President Truman in 1949 closed the BWCA airspace under 4,000' to airplanes. Timber harvest was permitted in the BWCA under a special provision in the Wilderness Act until conservationists managed to pass the Boundary Waters Canoe Area Wilderness Act in 1978, which also eliminated snowmobiles from the area and banned motorboats from many of the lakes.

Voyageurs National Park, established in 1975, has 40% of its area in water, most of it in four large lakes: Rainy, Kabetogama, Namakan and Sand Point.

Status: The designated Boundary Waters Canoe Area Wilderness consists of three units. The 57,000 acre Caribou unit east of the main unit is separated by a paved road in Minnesota. However, it connects to the main unit through roadless country north of Gunflint Lake in Ontario and is included as part of this distinct roadless area. The third unit, the 114,000 acre Little Sioux, is southwest of the main unit and cut off by a gravel road. It is considered, therefore, in this inventory as a separate roadless area. The Boundary Waters Canoe Area Wilderness (all three units) totals 1,086,954 acres.

Several lakes in the BWCA and all the large lakes in Voyageurs NP are still open to motorboats. The NPS permits snowmobiles in Voyageurs on the large lakes when they are frozen (it should be when they are not frozen). The NPS is also supporting a proposed snowmobile trail down the length of the Kabetogama Peninsula — the major land area in the Park. An additional threat to Voyageurs comes from an arrogant yahoo who vows to build an 18-unit condominium on his private land in the Park. The NPS has condemned the land for acquisition, but the developer has sued.

Airplanes fly into the small lakes on the Kabetogama, and military jets scream through the skies above Truman's BWCA airspace reservation — Friends of the Boundary Waters Wilderness filed suit to halt the military flights in 1988. Unprotected contiguous roadless lands are being chewed up by logging and roading in Ontario all around Quetico and in Minnesota around the BWCA. Acid rain threatens the lakes and streams of the area. Excessive visitor use in the BWCA (the most heavily used Wilderness Area in the United States, with over 1 million visitor days a year) is damaging campsites and water quality, although strict visitor regulations by the FS are improving the situation. A radio station is proposing a 611' high FM tower on the east side of the BWCA, which would be visible 15 miles away. Friends of the Boundary Waters Wilderness (FBWW) reports that "interest in gold and other precious metals has now reached a fever pitch in the wilderness-edge area." The state is currently leasing mineral rights.

Over a quarter of a million acres of lands within the Superior NF (including private and state) contiguous to the Boundary Waters Wilderness or Voyageurs National Park appear to be essentially roadless. Although once logged, these lands are recovering and should be added to the designated Wilderness. Protection of these Superior NF lands should be a high priority for conservationists — the FS plans anything but protection.

The Friends of the Boundary Waters have appealed the Superior NF Plan over 1) its failure to remove truck portages from the BWCA as required by law; 2) excessive road-building (outside the BWCA) mandated by the plan; and 3) the impact on the Eastern Timber Wolf from logging outside the BWCA.

Commercial outfitters in Ontario have mounted an attack on the Quetico Park Wilderness with demands for aircraft landings, motorboat use on lakes, the extension of commercial trapping (trapping was due to be phased out), removal of areas from the Park, and construction of a road to Batchewoung Lake.

By closing a few roads and undertaking wilderness recovery management, a single 5 million acre International Wilderness could easily be established here. (Ernest Oberholtzer proposed a ten million acre International Peace Memorial Forest here in 1928.)

Little Sioux 179,000 acres

Designated Boundary Waters Wilderness Area
Little Sioux unit (Superior NF)	114,417
Additional Superior NF and private roadless	65,000

Description: Northeastern Minnesota west of Ely. This is a detached section of the BWCA. See BWCA for general description.

Status: 25 horsepower motorboats are allowed on large Trout Lake. Contiguous lands are under threat of logging and roading, and are open to snowmobiles and power boats.

Red Lake Peatland 350,000 acres

Red Lake State Wildlife Management
Area-Beltrami Island State Forest-Red Lake Indian Reservation roadless	350,000

Description: North-central Minnesota. North and east of the Upper and Lower Red Lakes lies a vast wild area of peatlands, lakes, bogs, streams and conifer forest that is broken by only a few roads. Most of this primitive landscape is in Minnesota State Forests or Wildlife Management Areas with scattered Red Lake Indian Reservation tracts and some Bureau of Land Management and private lands. (This is one of the few areas east of the Rockies with any blocks of BLM land left.) These peatlands, of the Forested Raised Bog type, were formed by peat accumulation in the bed of glacial Lake Agassiz at the end of the Pleistocene. They feature forested teardrop islands and ribbed fen patterns, and are particularly important for scientific study because they are not underlain with permafrost which complicates studies in other peat areas, and because of the delicate interaction between vegetation and hydrology which produces the patterned landforms. Twenty-five vascular plant and animal species in the peatlands are listed as Endangered, Threatened or of special concern. Insectivorous plants such as pitcher plants, sundews and bladderworts, and various species of orchids and ericaceous plants are common. Wildlife includes Gray Wolf, Moose (perhaps the highest concentration in the lower 48), Northern Bog Lemming, Black Bear, Snowshoe Hare, Lynx, Elk, Whitetail Deer, Great Gray Owl, Northern Sandhill Crane, Yellow Rail and Palm Warbler. One of the highest concentrations of breeding songbirds in the US is here. Woodland Caribou made their last stand in Minnesota in the peatlands; they should be reintroduced. Forest types include Great Lakes spruce/fir and pine. Elevations in this flat terrain average a little more than 1,000' above sea level.

The largest of these apparently roadless units is immediately north of Upper and Lower Red Lakes between state highways 72 and 89.

Status: This area and the other peatland roadless areas listed have snowmobile trails crossing them, although there are sizable areas without even this impact. The Minnesota Department of Natural Resources has proposed protecting 233,508 acres of this particular area for scientific study and smaller portions of some of the others. Presumably most of the forests in this region have been logged at one time or another for pulpwood. Conservationists should make preservation of all of the generally roadless areas in this region a major priority. The northern Minnesota peatlands represent one of the wildest blocks of country east of the Rocky Mountains and an opportunity to preserve a true wilderness ecosystem in the Midwest of several million acres. Combined with the nearby Boundary Waters area, this is the finest habitat remaining for the Gray Wolf in the lower 48 states.

One threat to the peatlands is a recurring proposal to mine them for peat which would be burned as an energy source in power plants.

Red Lake Indian Reservation Peatlands 63,000 acres
Red Lake Indian Reservation roadless   *63,000*

Description: West of Lower Red Lake in north-central Minnesota. See Red Lake for general description and status.

Carmelee-Hamre Peatlands 58,000 acres
Red Lake IR-Carmelee and Hamre State Wildlife
   Management Areas roadless   *58,000*

Description: West of Upper Red Lake in north-central Minnesota. See Red Lake for general description and status.

Marvin Lake Peatlands 57,000 acres (also in Manitoba)
Undesignated state-owned Consolidated
   Conservation lands and private roadless   *57,000*

Description: West of Lake of the Woods along the Manitoba border in north-central Minnesota. See Red Lake for general description and status.

Lost Lake Peatlands 159,000 acres
Red Lake State Wildlife Management Area-
   Beltrami Island State Forest-Red Lake IR roadless 159,000

Description: South of Warroad in north-central Minnesota. Separated from the 350,000 acre Red Lake roadless area by a dirt road, this includes several ecologically significant peatlands such as Mulligan Lake Peatland. See Red Lake for general description and status.

East Fork Rapid River Peatlands 135,000
Pine Island State Forest-Red Lakes IR roadless   *135,000*

Description: Southeast of Baudette in north-central Minnesota. The East Fork Rapid River flows through this roadless area. See Red Lake for general description and status.

West Fork Peatlands 76,000 acres
BLM-Red Lake IR-Pine Island SF roadless   *76,000*

Description: West of International Falls in north-central Minnesota. The West Fork of Black River flows through here. This area includes the ecologically significant North Black River Peatland, a former BLM Wilderness Study Area. Conservationists should demand BLM protection for this area. See Red Lake for general description and status.

Black River Peatlands 170,000 acres
Pine Island State Forest roadless   *170,000*

Description: Northwest of Big Falls in north-central Minnesota. This area includes the botanically rich South Black River Peatland. See Red Lake for general description and status.

Ludlow Peatlands 155,000 acres
Pine Island State Forest-Red Lake SWMA-BLM-
*   Red Lake IR roadless*   *155,000*

Description: Northeast of Upper Red Lake and east of State Hwy 72 in north-central Minnesota. It includes the biologically important Lost River Peatland. See Red Lake for general description and status.

Sturgeon River Peatlands 265,000 acres
Pine Island State Forest roadless   *265,000*

Description: Between US 71 and State Hwy 72 east of Upper Red Lake in north-central Minnesota. See Red Lake for general description and status.

Southeast Pine Island Peatlands 87,000 acres

Pine Island State Forest roadless	87,000

Description: South of Big Falls between US 71 and State Hwy 6 in north-central Minnesota. See Red Lake for general description and status.

Little Fork River Peatlands 150,000 acres
Koochiching State Forest roadless	150,000

Description: Southeast of Big Falls in north-central Minnesota. The Little Fork River is in this area. Myrtle Lake Peatland is a designated National Natural Landmark. See Red Lake for general description and status.

George Washington 86,000 acres
George Washington State Forest roadless	86,000

Description: East of Bigfork in north-central Minnesota. This area is different from the other peatlands due to its greater relief. It has numerous lakes, mixed peatlands and forest. Some elevations approach 1,500'. See Red Lake for general description and status.

Status: This roadless area is crisscrossed with snowmobile trails, penetrated by several dirt roads, and has quite a bit of private land intermixed.

Michigan
The Upper Peninsula of Michigan (or the "UP") has long been considered the backcountry vacation land of the Midwest. Although abused by logging and mining, the UP still has several good-sized wildernesses, including a few stands of virgin forest and a handful of wolves. Wilderness restoration could create significant preserves here. Michigan conservationists achieved passage of the Michigan Wilderness Act in 1987 which established nine Wilderness Areas totaling 89,000 acres on the Hiawatha and Ottawa NFs in the UP, and one Wilderness Area of 3,395 acres in the Manistee NF in Michigan's Lower Peninsula. 105,000 acres were considered in RARE II. Previously, Wilderness Areas had been established

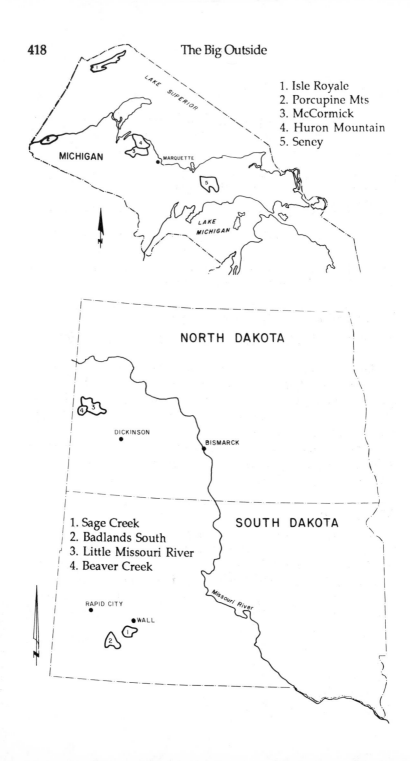

1. Isle Royale
2. Porcupine Mts
3. McCormick
4. Huron Mountain
5. Seney

LAKE SUPERIOR

MICHIGAN

MARQUETTE

LAKE MICHIGAN

N

NORTH DAKOTA

DICKINSON

BISMARCK

SOUTH DAKOTA

1. Sage Creek
2. Badlands South
3. Little Missouri River
4. Beaver Creek

Missouri River

RAPID CITY

WALL

N

in Isle Royale National Park and Seney National Wildlife Refuge in the UP.

Isle Royale 133,000 acres	
Designated Isle Royale National Park	
Wilderness Area	131,880
Contiguous Isle Royale National Park roadless	1,200

Description: The large island in the northwestern part of Lake Superior 20 miles south of the Canadian mainland. Biologists have found here a classic situation for studying Wolf-Moose-Beaver interactions. Wildlife also includes Red Fox, Lynx, Snowshoe Hare and Mink. This is a transition area between northern hardwood forest and coniferous forest, with Balsam Fir and White Spruce forming a climax forest near the lakeshore, Yellow Birch and Sugar Maple forming a climax forest in warmer areas, and subclimax Aspen, White Birch and scattered conifers growing in burned areas. The long forested ridges have sizable lakes and hundreds of swamps, ponds and bogs between them. Over 50 species of fish live in streams on the island, including Brook and Rainbow Trout in 25 miles of trout streams. The island contains 20 inland lakes and 170 miles of hiking trails. The high point is Mount Desor at 792' above lake level and 1,394' above sea level. Important archaeological sites of primitive copper mining date back 4,500 years.

Status: Isle Royale is fairly well protected as a National Park Wilderness Area. Park Service management has been mixed, but the short visitor season saves it from excessive development ideas.

Copper mining flourished from 1850 until 1899 (the forest was logged and burned to expose copper deposits). Summer homes then became popular after 1900 until Isle Royale became a National Park in 1940. Given these intensive impacts, the degree to which wilderness has recovered on the island gives hope for similar recovery efforts in the Upper Peninsula of Michigan and in northern Wisconsin.

The Timber Wolf population has seriously declined in recent years, due at least in part to canine parvovirus brought in from outside. This tragedy is another reminder of the fragility of island populations and of the danger of counting on a few wild areas to suffice as habitat for Threatened, Endangered or sensitive species.

Porcupine Mountains 50,000 acres

Designated Porcupine Mts State Wilderness Area	46,246
Additional State Park roadless and adjacent	
Lake Superior	4,000

Description: The northwestern part of Michigan's Upper Peninsula, northeast of Ironwood. This wild stretch of mountains rises in a series of rugged parallel ridges along the lakeshore of Lake Superior. The high point is 2,023' Government Peak. Lakes (including splendid Lake of the Clouds), rushing streams and rivers, ponds and swamps fill much of the area between mountain ridges. White Pine and northern hardwoods predominate. Here is the largest tract of virgin Northern Hemlock, Yellow Birch and Sugar Maple in the Lake States. Black Bear are common. A major campaign by the citizens of Michigan resulted in the legal protection of this area in 1944. An earlier effort to designate the Porkies as a National Park twinned with Isle Royale failed. It is now listed as a National Natural Landmark.

Status: The Porkies are largely protected as a state Wilderness Area, but management could be better and more effective. By closing a scenic road and restoring areas of the adjacent Ottawa NF, a significant wilderness could be recreated. Wolves and other extirpated wildlife should be reintroduced.

McCormick 89,000 acres

Designated McCormick Wilderness Area	
(Ottawa NF)	16,850
Escanaba River State Forest roadless	8,320
Private roadless	64,000

Description: Upper Peninsula of Michigan east of L'Anse. The Sierra Club says, "McCormick is probably the best and largest living example of the original Michigan forest . . . Climax white pine and maple forests dominate the area . . . Disturbance in the area is minimal." Rocky outcroppings tower

over lakes, streams and wetlands frequented by Moose, Black
Bear, Bobcat, River Otter, Common Loon, Bald Eagle, Pileated
Woodpecker and possibly Gray Wolf. The cascading Yellow
Dog River is among the most pristine streams in the Upper
Midwest and has a thriving trout population.

Status: The private lands and Escanaba State Forest are
open to logging, but there is not much activity at this time.
Protection of these roadless lands adjacent to the designated
Wilderness, including acquisition of the private land, should be
a high priority for conservationists. A dirt road is all that
separates this area from the Huron Mountain roadless area. By
closing it and several other old logging roads, a 200,000 acre
Wilderness could be established.

Huron Mountain 74,000 acres

Huron Mountain Club roadless (private)	*25,000*
Escanaba River State Forest roadless	*7,040*
Additional private and state roadless	*42,000*

Description: Upper Peninsula of Michigan northwest of
Marquette. The Huron Mountains, almost 11 miles of roadless
shoreline along Lake Superior including the mouth of the Huron
River, numerous streams, several large lakes, and a fine expanse of northern forest characterize this largely privately
owned area. Wildlife and vegetation are similar to other UP
roadless areas.

Status: 12,000 acres of the Huron Mountain Club are
managed as "wilderness." (Aldo Leopold was contracted to develop a management plan for it in the 1930s.) The state forest
and private lands (mostly owned by timber companies) outside
the Huron Mountain Club are protected only by their remoteness
and low timber value, and could soon be destroyed by roading,
logging and ORVs. There are some old dirt logging roads penetrating the area. It is separated from McCormick by a dirt
road.

Seney 131,000 acres

Designated Seney National Wildlife Refuge	
Wilderness Area	*25,150*
Additional Seney NWR roadless	*26,880*

Lake Superior State Forest and private roadless	79,000

Description: Upper Peninsula of Michigan between Seney and Manistique in the Great Manistique Swamp. Open marshes with sedges and rushes, and sandy knolls and ridges with mature Red Pine are characteristic of this area. Wildlife includes nesting Canada Geese, Wood Duck, Sandhill Crane, Bald Eagle, Sharp-tailed Grouse, Pileated Woodpecker, Black Bear, River Otter, Beaver, Mink, Bobcat and occasional Gray Wolf. Elevations rise from 650' to 780'.

Status: The Lake Superior State Forest lands are open to logging, roading and ORVs, but they are not being ravaged at this time. As for all the Michigan areas, Seney should be considered the core of a major wilderness restoration project of several hundred thousand acres.

North and South Dakota

Once considered wasteland, South Dakota's Badlands eventually were recognized as the finest remnant of the Great Plains. Established as a National Monument in 1939, Badlands was made a National Park in 1978. The Sage Creek Wilderness Area was designated by Congress in 1976. In the 1880s, Theodore Roosevelt took up ranching along the Little Missouri River in North Dakota. Between the two units of Theodore Roosevelt National Park, the Little Missouri National Grasslands and adjacent and intermixed private land have two large roadless areas.

Sage Creek 102,000 acres (South Dakota)	
Designated Sage Creek Wilderness Area	
(Badlands National Park)	*64,250*
Buffalo Gap National Grassland and	
private roadless	*38,000*

Description: Southwestern South Dakota south of Wall. The Sage Creek Basin, with its badlands, Shortgrass Prairie, Bighorn Sheep, Pronghorn, Bison, Prairie Dog, Badger, Mule Deer, Golden Eagle, Prairie Rattlesnake, juniper, yucca and cottonwood, is probably the best remaining example of the Great Plains. Elevations range from 2,600' to 3,100'.

Status: Buffalo Gap National Grassland should be added to Badlands National Park and designated part of the Sage Creek Wilderness Area. This area should be considered as a reintroduction site for the Black-footed Ferret if captive breeding results in a large enough population for eventual release into the wild. Elk and Gray Wolf also should be reintroduced here. Sage Creek should be the core for a restored Great Plains Wilderness National Park.

Badlands South 125,000 acres (South Dakota)

Badlands National Park roadless	*87,000*
Buffalo Gap National Grassland roadless	*20,000*
Pine Ridge Indian Reservation roadless	*18,000*

Description: Southwestern South Dakota southwest of Wall. In a 1979 agreement with the Oglala Sioux tribe, the South Unit of Badlands National Park, on the Pine Ridge Reservation, was transferred to management by the National Park Service. According to the Park Service, "This stunning landscape of high grassy tableland and spectacular buttes is the scene of much Sioux history. The Ghost Dances at Stronghold Table in 1890 were a prelude to the bloodshed at Wounded Knee, 25 miles south of here." Cottonwood Creek and several other creeks drain the high mesas. Elevations range from 2,600' to 3,200'. See Sage Creek for general description.

Status: Several old dirt roads penetrate this area. They should be permanently closed and the area designated as a Park Service Wilderness Area. Buffalo Gap Grassland should be added to Badlands National Park as the core of a major Great Plains Wilderness National Park.

Little Missouri River 150,000 acres (North Dakota)

Magpie RARE II area (Little Missouri National Grasslands)	*37,240*
Private and additional Little Missouri National Grasslands roadless	*113,000*

Description: Western North Dakota northwest of Dickinson, along the Little Missouri River immediately north of the Theodore Roosevelt National Park Elkhorn Ranch unit. This badlands and river bottom area is an excellent representation of the Great Plains Shortgrass Prairie Ecoregion. Vegetation includes Western Wheatgrass, several species of needlegrass, Little Bluestem, Blue Grama and sedges. The canyons and ravines grow Green Ash, Box Elder, American Elm, Rocky Mountain Juniper, skunkbrush, wild rose and wolfberry. Big Sagebrush, Ponderosa Pine, Limber Pine, Paper Birch and Black Cottonwood are less common. Wilderness-dependent wildlife includes Cougar, Lynx, Elk, Bighorn Sheep, Peregrine Falcon, Golden Eagle and Prairie Falcon. The cats are very rare. Mule Deer and Pronghorn are also present. Some 20 miles of the Little Missouri River are in the roadless area; side drainages include Magpie, Whitetail, Porcupine, Prairie Dog and Cinnamon Creeks. Elevations range from around 2,200' to 2,800'.

Status: This roadless area is penetrated by a few dirt roads and jeep trails, but appears to meet our criteria for roadlessness. Conservation groups proposed the Magpie area for Wilderness during RARE II but Congress has taken no action. The FS opposed Wilderness for Magpie during RARE II. Threats include continued overgrazing and ORVs.

The Little Missouri National Grasslands offer perhaps the best opportunity in the United States for significant wilderness restoration on the Great Plains. A 1,000,000 acre Wilderness National Park should be established along the Little Missouri River between the North and South Units of Theodore Roosevelt National Park; Bison, Gray Wolf and Grizzly should be reintroduced. If captive breeding programs are successful, this would be a good location for re-establishment of Black-footed Ferret (last seen here in 1969). This region of mixed Forest Service and private land consists of several RARE II areas and is broken only by dirt roads.

Beaver Creek 54,000 acres (North Dakota)

Bell Lake RARE II area (Little Missouri National Grasslands)	*11,980*
Private and additional Little Missouri National Grasslands roadless	*42,000*

Description: Western North Dakota northeast of Beach. This roadless area consists of Beaver Creek, Bell Lake Creek and Cooks Peak west of the Little Missouri River and south of the Magpie roadless area (separated by an unpaved road). See Magpie for general description.

Status: Proposed for Wilderness in RARE II by conservationists; Wilderness opposed by FS. See Magpie for general status.

APPENDIX A
Roadless Areas by Size

Rank	Area Name	State(s)		Acreage
1	River of No Return	ID	MT	3,156,000
2	High Sierra	CA		2,800,000
3	Boundary Waters	MN	CAN	2,752,000
4	Grand Canyon	AZ		2,700,000
5	Bob Marshall	MT		2,485,000
6	South Absaroka	WY		2,190,000
7	Selway-Bitterroot	ID	MT	1,813,000
8	Everglades	FL		1,658,000
9	Cabeza Prieta	AZ	MX	1,627,000
10	Glacier Peak	WA		1,607,000
11	Pasayten	WA	CAN	1,191,000
12	Wind River Range	WY		1,171,000
13	Panamint Mountains	CA		1,166,000
14	Absaroka-Beartooth	MT	WY	1,154,000
15	S Great Salt Lake Desert	UT	NV	1,144,000
16	Olympic Mountains	WA		1,060,000
17	Weminuche	CO		956,000
18	North Absaroka	WY		950,000
19	Lower Cyns of Rio Grande	TX	MX	890,000
20	Navajo Mountain	AZ	UT	850,000
21	N Great Salt Lake Desert	UT		850,000
22	High Uintas	UT		843,000
23	Canyonlands	UT		805,000
24	Desolation Canyon	UT		763,000
25	Yosemite North	CA		744,000
26	Mt. Baker	WA	CAN	742,000
27	Gila	NM		736,000
28	Galiuro Mountains	AZ		723,000
29	Dead Horse Mountains	TX	MX	720,000
30	Sawtooths	ID		700,000
31	North Glacier	MT	CAN	660,000
32	Black Rock Desert	NV		640,000
33	Maroon Bells-CollgtePks	CO		632,000
34	Saline-Last Chance	CA		631,000
35	Escalante	UT		620,000
36	Salmon-Trinity Alps	CA		620,000
37	Owyhee Canyons	ID	OR	619,000
38	Kofa Mountains	AZ		597,000
39	Hells Canyon	OR	ID	591,000
40	Big Cypress Swamp	FL		583,000
41	White Clouds-Boulders	ID		550,000
42	Gallatin Range	WY	MT	525,000

43	Cottonwood Mts	CA		524,000
44	Blue Range-San Francisco	AZ	NM	505,000
45	Mariscal-Santa Elena	TX	MX	483,000
46	Bechler-Pitchstone	WY	ID	468,000
47	Sheep Range	NV		468,000
48	Desert-Pintwater Ranges	NV		467,000
49	Alpine Lakes	WA		464,000
50	Great Rift-Craters of Moon	ID		463,000
51	Lower Colorado River	AZ	CA	462,000
52	Gros Ventre	WY		455,000
53	Eagle Cap	OR		452,000
54	Cloud Peak	WY		443,000
55	South Glacier	MT		430,000
56	Three Sisters	OR		424,000
57	Sangre de Cristo	CO		418,000
58	Dirty Devil-Fiddler Bt	UT		413,000
59	North Lemhis	ID		410,000
60	Aldo Leopold	NM		409,000
61	Kalmiopsis	OR	CA	408,000
62	Okefenokee	GA	FL	400,000
63	Pecos	NM		400,000
64	Anaconda-Pintlar/Saphr	MT		391,000
65	Sheep Hole	CA		390,000
66	Buffalo Hills-Smoke Ck	NV	CA	387,000
67	San Rafael	CA		381,000
68	Palen-McCoy	CA		380,000
69	South Madison Range	MT		375,000
70	San Juan River	UT		371,000
71	West Elk	CO		368,000
72	Wahweap-Canaan Peak	UT		367,000
73	Santa Rosa Mountains	CA		363,000
74	Alvord Desert	OR		361,000
75	Italian Peaks	ID	MT	360,000
76	Kaiparowits	UT		360,000
77	White Mountains	CA	NV	358,000
78	Spotted Range	NV		354,000
79	Bruneau-Jarbidge Rivers	ID		350,000
80	Red Lake Peatland	MN		350,000
81	Flat Tops	CO		346,000
82	Hells Gate	AZ		346,000
83	Mazatzal	AZ		340,000
84	High Peaks	NY		336,000
85	Sespe	CA		335,000
86	Teton Range	WY		334,000
87	Hexie-Li'l San Berdo Mts	CA		328,000
88	Inyo Mountains	CA		327,000
89	Marble Mountains	CA		320,000
90	West Canada Lake	NY		316,000
91	Book Cliffs	UT		300,000

92	Great Burn	ID	MT	295,000
93	South San Juan	CO		292,000
94	Paria Canyon	AZ	UT	290,000
95	Funeral Mountains	CA	NV	287,000
96	Carson Sink	NV		286,000
97	Mallard-Larkins	ID		285,000
98	Carson-Iceberg	CA		279,000
99	Hole In The Rock	NV		277,000
100	Turtle Mountains	CA		276,000
101	Secesh River	ID		273,000
102	Kingston Range	CA		270,000
103	Superstition Mts	AZ		269,000
104	Rocky Mountain NP	CO		266,000
105	Mt. Zirkel	CO		265,000
106	Sturgeon River Peatland	MN		265,000
107	Raven's Eye	ID		263,000
108	West Potrillo Mts	NM		260,000
109	Yolla Bolly-Middle Eel	CA		260,000
110	Guadalupe Escarpment	NM	TX	258,000
111	La Garita	CO		253,000
112	Pioneer Mountains	ID		250,000
113	Salt River Range	WY		250,000
114	Yampa-Green	CO	UT	250,000
115	Arc Dome	NV		250,000
116	Siskiyous	CA		249,000
117	Grapevine Mountains	CA	NV	246,000
118	West Pioneer Mts	MT		243,000
119	Muddy Creek	UT		242,000
120	Big Horn-Weitas	ID		240,000
121	Palisades	WY	ID	240,000
122	San Andres Mts South	NM		240,000
123	Grant Range	NV		240,000
124	Mt. Rainier	WA		233,000
125	Sheepshead Mts	OR		232,000
126	Excelsior Mountains	NV	CA	232,000
127	Diamond Peak	ID		230,000
128	Ventana	CA		230,000
129	Great Smoky Mts West	NC	TN	227,000
130	Solitario	TX		225,000
131	Grayback Ridge	WY		225,000
132	Arrastra Mountain	AZ		225,000
133	Purgatoirie River	CO		225,000
134	Ishi	CA		225,000
135	Amargosa Range	CA		221,000
136	Cougar Lakes	WA		219,000
137	Rincon Mountains	AZ		217,000
138	Kelso Dunes	CA		215,000
139	Batamote-Sauceda Mts.	AZ		214,000

140	Latir Peak-Ponil Creek	NM		214,000
141	Domeland	CA		212,000
142	Trout Creek Mts	OR	NV	212,000
143	West Big Hole	MT	ID	210,000
144	Mt. Graham	AZ		208,000
145	Las Vegas Range	NV		207,000
146	Vallecito Mountains	CA		207,000
147	Big Hatchet-Alamo Hueco	NM		207,000
148	Five Ponds	NY		203,000
149	Baxter State Park	ME		200,000
150	Castle Dome Mts	AZ		200,000
151	Wenaha-Tucannon	WA	OR	200,000
152	Charleston Peak	NV		200,000
153	Argus Range	CA		199,000
154	Chuckwalla Mountains	CA		197,000
155	Clan Alpine Range	NV		196,000
156	Peace Rock	ID		196,000
157	Goat Rocks	WA		196,000
158	Gila Mountains	AZ		194,000
159	Mancos Mesa	UT		193,000
160	Mount Jefferson	OR		191,000
161	Aquarius Mts North	AZ		190,000
162	Commissary Ridge	WY		190,000
163	Ruby Mountains	NV		190,000
164	Table Mountain	NV		190,000
165	Myotis	OR		190,000
166	Jarbidge	NV	ID	189,000
167	Wayne Wonderland	UT		188,000
168	Wilson Mesa	UT		188,000
169	Coxcomb	CA		188,000
170	Chisos Mountains	TX		186,000
171	Meadow Valley Mts	NV		186,000
172	Paria-Hackberry	UT		186,000
173	Central Plateau	WY		185,000
174	Comanche Peak	CO		182,000
175	St. John Ponds	ME		180,000
176	Mt. Stirling	NV		180,000
177	Borah Peak	ID		179,000
178	Little Sioux	MN		179,000
179	Deep Creek Mountains	UT		179,000
180	Mission Mountains	MT		176,000
181	French Creek-Patrick Butte	ID		175,000
182	Needles	ID		173,000
183	Steep Creek-Oak Creek	UT		173,000
184	Black River Peatland	MN		170,000
185	Eagles Nest	CO		170,000
186	Mt. Pennel	UT		170,000
187	Continental Divide	NM		170,000
188	Hunter-Fryingpan	CO		168,000

189	Sky Lakes	OR		166,000
190	Greenwater Range	CA		165,000
191	Great Rift-Wapi	ID		164,000
192	Mokelumne	CA		164,000
193	Mormon Mountains	NV		163,000
194	Great Smoky Mts East	NC	TN	163,000
195	Ajo Mountains	AZ		160,000
196	Chiricahua Mountains	AZ		160,000
197	El Malpais	NM		160,000
198	Wheeler Peak	NV		160,000
199	Lost Lake Peatland	MN		159,000
200	Basque Hills	OR		159,000
201	Allan Mountain	MT	ID	158,000
202	Little Bighorn	WY	MT	155,000
203	Ludlow Peatland	MN		155,000
204	Queer Mountain	CA	NV	155,000
205	San Andres Mts Central	NM		155,000
206	San Andres Mts North	NM		155,000
207	Selkirks	ID		155,000
208	Holy Cross	CO		152,000
209	Little Fork Peatland	MN		150,000
210	River of No Return South	ID		150,000
211	Old Woman Mountains	CA		150,000
212	Little Missouri River	ND		150,000
213	Smoke Creek Desert	NV		148,000
214	Hermosa	CO		147,000
215	White Sands	NM		146,000
216	Black Mesa	AZ		145,000
217	Little Rockies	UT		145,000
218	Schell Creek Range	NV		145,000
219	Big Blue	CO		145,000
220	Eagle Creek	AZ		145,000
221	Mt. Moriah	NV	UT	144,000
222	Antelope	NV		144,000
223	Hawksie-Walksie	OR	NV	144,000
224	Loxahatchee	FL		143,000
225	Robledo Mountains	NM		143,000
226	Ibex Hills	CA		143,000
227	Diablo Mountain	OR		142,000
228	Siamese Pond	NY		141,000
229	Silver Lake	NY		141,000
230	Crazy Mountains	MT		140,000
231	North Madison Range	MT		140,000
232	Painted Desert	AZ		140,000
233	Sierra Blanca	NM		140,000
234	Soldier Mts-Lime Creek	ID		139,000
235	Parunuweap	UT	AZ	137,000
236	Mesa Verde	CO		136,000

237	Deep Lake	WY	MT	135,000
238	East Fork Rapid River	MN		135,000
239	Granite Mountains	CA		135,000
240	Horse Heaven	NV		135,000
241	Wildlands Lakes	ME		135,000
242	Cabinet Mountains	MT		134,000
243	Nopah Range	CA	NV	134,000
244	Isle Royale	MI		133,000
245	Apache Kid	NM		131,000
246	Seney	MI		131,000
247	Pahsimeroi	ID		130,000
248	Snowcrest Range	MT		130,000
249	Mt. Ellen	UT		128,000
250	Cascade Mountain	MT		127,000
251	Delamar Mountains	NV		127,000
252	Eagletail Mountains	AZ		126,000
253	Lost Creek	CO		126,000
254	Pagoda Peak	CO		126,000
255	Toiyabe Crest	NV		126,000
256	Badlands South	SD		125,000
257	Baldy Bill	AZ		125,000
258	Culebra	CO	NM	125,000
259	Mohave Wash	AZ		125,000
260	Pemigewasset	NH		125,000
261	Pine Valley Mountains	UT		125,000
262	Washburn Range	WY		125,000
263	Chas Sheldon Ant Rng	NV		124,000
264	Salt Creek	UT		124,000
265	Piper Mountain	CA		124,000
266	New Water Mountains	AZ		123,000
267	Cady Mountains	CA		122,000
268	Sawyers Peak	NM		121,000
269	Quinn	NV		120,000
270	Aquarius Mts South	AZ		120,000
271	Wilcox Lake	NY		120,000
273	Redington Pond	ME		120,000
274	Rawah	CO		119,000
275	Sand Tank Mountains	AZ		119,000
276	Troublesome	CO		117,000
277	Palisade Mesa	NV		116,000
278	Muddy Mountain	NV		116,000
279	Black Ridge Canyons	CO	UT	115,000
280	Garnes Mountain	ID		115,000
281	South Egan Range	NV		113,000
282	Lakes	UT		112,000
283	Massacre Rim	NV		112,000
284	Mt. Leidy	WY		112,000
285	Little Horn Mountains	AZ		111,000
286	Boulder Mountain	UT		110,000

287	Eagle Mountains	CA		110,000
288	East Pioneers	MT		110,000
289	Salt River Canyon	AZ		110,000
290	Stony Mountain	MT		110,000
291	Wild River-Kearsarge	NH	ME	110,000
292	Moose River	ME		110,000
293	Everglades #3A	FL		109,000
294	King Mountain	ID		109,000
295	Priest Mountain	CO		109,000
296	Sierra Ladrones	NM		109,000
297	Padre Island	TX		108,000
298	South Reveille	NV		107,500
299	Bear Creek	ID		107,000
300	Cedar Mountains	NM		106,000
301	Big Snowy Mountains	MT		105,000
302	Fox Mountain Range	NV		105,000
303	Tenderfoot-Deep Creek	MT		105,000
304	Mount Thielsen	OR		105,000
305	Pinto Mountains	CA		105,000
306	Catlow Rim	OR		104,000
307	Tobacco Root Mts	MT		104,000
308	Red Buttes	CA	OR	104,000
309	Mt. Adams	WA		103,000
310	Stump Creek	ID		103,000
311	Soda Mountain	CA		102,500
312	Bates Mountains	AZ		102,500
313	Dominguez Canyons	CO		102,000
314	Great Dismal Swamp	VA	NC	102,000
315	Sage Creek	SD		102,000
316	Woolsey Peak-Signal Mt	AZ		101,000
317	Harcuvar Mts East	AZ		101,000
318	Avawatz	CA		101,000
319	Fossil Ridge	CO		101,000
320	Sid's Mountain	UT		101,000
321	Animas Mountains	NM		101,000
322	Cherry Creek Mts	NV		101,000
323	Old Dad Mountain	CA		101,000
324	Bighorn Mountains	AZ		100,000
325	Blue Mountain	NH		100,000
326	Casto-Table	UT		100,000
327	Catalina Mountains	AZ		100,000
328	Devils Creek	NM		100,000
329	Dry Valley Rim	NV	CA	100,000
330	Four Peaks	AZ		100,000
331	Harcuvar Mts West	AZ		100,000
332	Jacks Creek	ID		100,000
333	Lassen East	CA		100,000
334	Red Mountain	ID		100,000

335	Zion	UT		100,000
336	St. John River South	ME	CAN	100,000
337	South Warner	CA		100,000
338	Everglades #2	FL		95,000
339	Baxter North	ME		90,000
340	Ha-de-ron-dah	NY		89,000
341	McCormick	MI		89,000
342	Southeast Pine Island	MN		87,000
343	George Washington	MN		86,000
344	Cranberry	WV		82,000
345	Sandwich Range	NH		81,000
346	Mahoosuc Range	ME	NH	78,000
347	West Fork Peatland	MN		76,000
348	Blue Ridge	NY		75,000
349	Ferris Lake	NY		75,000
350	Huron Mountain	MI		74,000
351	St. John River North	ME		70,000
352	Red Lake Indian Res. Ptlnd	MN		63,000
353	Pigeon Lake	NY		62,000
354	Hoffman Notch	NY		61,000
355	W Br Dead Diamond River	NH		60,000
356	Southern Nantahala	GA	NC	60,000
357	Reed Mountain	ME		60,000
358	Carmellee-Hamre Ptlnd	MN		58,000
359	Marvin Lake Peatland	MN	CAN	57,000
360	Cohutta	GA	TN	56,000
361	Big Cypress Swamp Loop	FL		55,000
362	Everglades #3C	FL		54,000
363	Beaver Creek	ND		54,000
364	Pharoah Lake	NY		52,000
365	Slide Mountain	NY		52,000
366	Everglades #3B	FL		50,000
367	Meachum Swamp	VT		50,000
368	Porcupine Mountains	MI		50,000

APPENDIX B
Roadless Areas by State

Rank	Area Name	State(s)		Acreage
4	Grand Canyon	AZ		2,700,000
9	Cabeza Prieta	AZ	MX	1,627,000
20	Navajo Mountain	AZ	UT	850,000
28	Galiuro Mountains	AZ		723,000
38	Kofa Mountains	AZ		597,000
44	Blue Range-San Francisco	AZ	NM	505,000
51	Lower Colorado River	AZ	CA	462,000
81	Hells Gate	AZ		346,000

83	Mazatzal	AZ		340,000
94	Paria Canyon	AZ	UT	290,000
103	Superstition Mts	AZ		269,000
130	Arrastra Mountain	AZ		225,000
137	Rincon Mountains	AZ		217,000
138	Batamote Mts	AZ		214,000
143	Mt. Graham	AZ		208,000
148	Castle Dome Mts	AZ		200,000
157	Gila Mountains	AZ		194,000
160	Aquarius Mts North	AZ		190,000
194	Ajo Mountains	AZ		160,000
195	Chiricahua Mountains	AZ		160,000
215	Black Mesa	AZ		145,000
216	Eagle Creek	AZ		145,000
229	Painted Desert	AZ		140,000
251	Eagletail Mountains	AZ		126,000
255	Bady Bill	AZ		125,000
257	Mohave Wash	AZ		125,000
265	New Water Mts	AZ		123,000
268	Aquarius Mts South	AZ		120,000
273	Sand Tank Mountains	AZ		119,000
284	Little Horn Mountains	AZ		111,000
285	Salt River	AZ		110,000
310	Bates Mountains	AZ		102,500
315	Woolsey Peak	AZ		101,000
316	Harcuvar Mts East	AZ		101,000
323	Bighorn Mountains	AZ		100,000
324	Catalina Mountains	AZ		100,000
325	Four Peaks	AZ		100,000
326	Harcuvar Mts West	AZ		100,000
2	High Sierra	CA		2,800,000
13	Panamint Mountains	CA		1,166,000
25	Yosemite North	CA		744,000
34	Saline-Last Chance	CA		631,000
35	Salmon-Trinity Alps	CA		620,000
43	Cottonwood Mts	CA		524,000
65	Sheep Hole	CA		390,000
67	San Rafael	CA		381,000
68	Palen-McCoy	CA		380,000
73	Santa Rosa Mountains	CA		363,000
77	White Mountains	CA	NV	358,000
85	Sespe	CA		335,000
87	Hexie-Li'l SB Mts	CA		328,000
88	Inyo Mountains	CA		327,000
89	Marble Mountains	CA		320,000
95	Funeral Mountains	CA	NV	287,000
98	Carson-Iceberg	CA		279,000
100	Turtle Mountains	CA		276,000

102	Kingston Range	CA		270,000
108	Yolla Bolly-Middle Eel	CA		260,000
116	Siskiyou	CA		249,000
117	Grapevine Mountains	CA	NV	246,000
127	Ventana	CA		230,000
131	Ishi	CA		225,000
135	Amargosa Range	CA		221,000
140	Domeland	CA		212,000
144	Vallecito Mountains	CA		207,000
152	Argus Range	CA		199,000
153	Chuckwalla Mountains	CA		197,000
166	Coxcomb	CA		188,000
189	Greenwater Range	CA		165,000
190	Mokelumne	CA		164,000
201	Queer Mountain	CA	NV	155,000
208	Old Woman Mountains	CA		150,000
223	Ibex Hills	CA		143,000
236	Granite Mountains	CA		135,000
241	Nopah Range	CA	NV	134,000
262	Piper Mountain	CA		124,000
266	Cady Mountains	CA		122,000
286	Eagle Mountains	CA		110,000
300	Pinto Mountains	CA		105,000
305	Red Buttes	CA	OR	104,000
311	Soda Mountain	CA		102,500
317	Avawatz	CA		101,000
318	Old Dad Mountain	CA		101,000
327	Lassen East	CA		100,000
328	South Warner	CA		100,000
17	Weminuche	CO		956,000
33	Maroon Bells	CO		632,000
57	Sangre de Cristo	CO		418,000
71	West Elk	CO		368,000
82	Flat Tops	CO		346,000
93	South San Juan	CO		292,000
104	Rocky Mountain NP	CO		266,000
105	Mt. Zirkel	CO		265,000
111	La Garita	CO		253,000
112	Yampa-Green	CO	UT	250,000
132	Purgatoirie River	CO		225,000
173	Comanche Peak	CO		182,000
183	Nest	CO		170,000
187	Hunter-Fryingpan	CO		168,000
207	Holy Cross	CO		152,000
213	Hermosa	CO		147,000
217	Big Blue	CO		145,000
235	Mesa Verde	CO		136,000
252	Lost Creek	CO		126,000
253	Pagoda Peak	CO		126,000

257	Culebra	CO	NM	125,000
274	Rawah	CO		119,000
275	Troublesome	CO		117,000
278	Black Ridge Canyons	CO	UT	115,000
292	Priest Mountain	CO		109,000
312	Dominguez Canyons	CO		102,000
319	Fossil Ridge	CO		101,000
8	Everglades	FL		1,658,000
40	Big Cypress Swamp	FL		583,000
224	Loxahatchee	FL		143,000
293	Everglades #3A	FL		109,000
337	Everglades #2	FL		95,000
360	Big Cypress Loop	FL		55,000
361	Everglades #3C	FL		54,000
365	Everglades #3B	FL		50,000
62	Okefenokee	GA	FL	400,000
354	Southern Nantahala	GA	NC	60,000
359	Cohutta	GA	TN	56,000
1	River of No Return	ID	MT	3,156,000
7	Selway-Bitterroot	ID	MT	1,813,000
30	Sawtooths	ID		700,000
37	Owyhee Canyons	ID	OR	619,000
41	White Clouds	ID		550,000
50	Great Rift	ID		463,000
59	North Lemhis	ID		410,000
75	Italian Peaks	ID	MT	360,000
79	Bruneau-Jarbidge	ID		350,000
92	Great Burn	ID	MT	295,000
97	Mallard-Larkins	ID		285,000
101	Secesh River	ID		273,000
107	Raven's Eye	ID		263,000
113	Pioneer Mountains	ID		250,000
120	Big Horn-Weitas	ID		240,000
128	Diamond Peak	ID		230,000
154	Peace Rock	ID		196,000
176	Borah Peak	ID		179,000
180	French Creek-PB	ID		175,000
181	Needles	ID		173,000
191	Great Rift-Wapi	ID		164,000
202	Selkirks	ID		155,000
209	River of No Return S	ID		150,000
233	Soldier Mountains	ID		139,000
246	Pahsimeroi	ID		130,000
279	Garnes Mountain	ID		115,000
294	King Mountain	ID		109,000
298	Bear Creek	ID		107,000
308	Stump Creek	ID		103,000
329	Jacks Creek	ID		100,000

330	Red Mountain	ID		100,000
149	Baxter State Park	ME		200,000
174	St. John Ponds	ME		180,000
237	Wildlands Lakes	ME		135,000
269	Redington Pond	ME		120,000
287	Moose River	ME		110,000
331	St. John River South	ME	CAN	100,000
338	Baxter North	ME		90,000
345	Mahoosuc Range	ME	NH	78,000
350	St. John River North	ME		70,000
355	Reed Mountain	ME		60,000
243	Isle Royale	MI		133,000
244	Seney	MI		131,000
339	McCormick	MI		89,000
349	Huron Mountain	MI		74,000
366	Porcupine Mountains	MI		50,000
3	Boundary Waters	MN	CAN	2,752,000
80	Red Lake Peatland	MN		350,000
106	Sturgeon River	MN		265,000
177	Little Sioux	MN		179,000
184	Black River Peatlands	MN		170,000
198	Lost Lake Peatlands	MN		159,000
203	Ludlow Peatlands	MN		155,000
210	Little Fork River	MN		150,000
238	East Fork Rapid River	MN		135,000
341	Southeast Pine Island	MN		87,000
342	George Washington	MN		86,000
346	West Fork Peatlands	MN		76,000
351	Red Lake Indian Res.	MN		63,000
357	Carmellee-Hamre	MN		58,000
358	Marvin Lake Peatlands	MN	CAN	57,000
5	Bob Marshall	MT		2,485,000
14	Absaroka-Beartooth	MT	WY	1,154,000
31	North Glacier	MT	CAN	660,000
55	South Glacier	MT		430,000
64	Anaconda-Pintlar	MT		391,000
69	South Madison Range	MT		375,000
118	West Pioneer Mts	MT		243,000
142	West Big Hole	MT	ID	210,000
179	Mission Mountains	MT		176,000
200	Allan Mountain	MT	ID	158,000
230	Crazy Mountains	MT		140,000
231	North Madison Range	MT		140,000
242	Cabinet Mountains	MT		134,000
247	Snowcrest Range	MT		130,000
249	Cascade Mountain	MT		127,000
288	East Pioneers	MT		110,000
289	Stony Mountain	MT		110,000

301	Big Snowy Mountains	MT		105,000
302	Tenderfoot-Deep Ck	MT		105,000
306	Tobacco Root Mts	MT		104,000
129	Great Smoky Mts West	NC	TN	227,000
192	Great Smoky Mts East	NC	TN	163,000
211	Little Missouri River	ND		150,000
362	Beaver Creek	ND		54,000
258	Pemigewasset	NH		125,000
290	Wild River-Kearsarge	NH	ME	110,000
332	Blue Mountain	NH		100,000
344	Sandwich Range	NH		81,000
356	W Br Dead Diamond R	NH		60,000
27	Gila	NM		736,000
60	Aldo Leopold	NM		409,000
63	Pecos	NM		400,000
109	West Potrillo Mts	NM		260,000
110	Guadalupe Escarpment	NM	TX	258,000
121	San Andres Mts South	NM		240,000
139	Latir Peak-Ponil Ck	NM		214,000
145	Big Hatchet-AH Mts	NM		207,000
185	Continental Divide	NM		170,000
196	El Malpais	NM		160,000
204	San Andres Mts Cen.	NM		155,000
205	San Andres Mts North	NM		155,000
214	White Sands	NM		146,000
225	Robledo Mountains	NM		143,000
232	Sierra Blanca	NM		140,000
245	Apache Kid	NM		131,000
267	Sawyers Peak	NM		121,000
270	Wheeler Peak	NM		120,000
295	Sierra Ladrones	NM		109,000
299	Cedar Mountains	NM		106,000
320	Animas Mountains	NM		101,000
333	Devils Creek	NM		100,000
32	Black Rock Desert	NV		640,000
46	Sheep Range	NV		468,000
48	Desert-Pintwater	NV		467,000
66	Buffalo Hills	NV	CA	387,000
78	Spotted Range	NV		354,000
96	Carson Sink	NV		286,000
99	Hole In The Rock	NV		277,000
114	Arc Dome	NV		250,000
122	Grant Range	NV		240,000
125	Excelsior Mountains	NV	CA	232,000
146	Las Vegas Range	NV		207,000
150	Charleston Peak	NV		200,000
155	Clan Alpine Range	NV		196,000
161	Ruby Mountains	NV		190,000

162	Table Mountain	NV		190,000
165	Jarbidge	NV	ID	189,000
169	Meadow Valley Mts	NV		186,000
175	Mt. Stirling	NV		180,000
193	Mormon Mountains	NV		163,000
197	Wheeler Peak	NV		160,000
212	Smoke Creek Desert	NV		148,000
218	Schell Creek Range	NV		145,000
220	Mt. Moriah	NV	UT	144,000
221	Antelope	NV		144,000
239	Horse Heaven	NV		135,000
250	Delamar Mountains	NV		127,000
254	Toiyabe Crest	NV		126,000
263	Charles Sheldon AR	NV		124,000
271	Quinn	NV		120,000
276	Palisade Mesa	NV		116,000
277	Muddy Mountain	NV		116,000
280	South Egan Range	NV		113,000
281	Massacre Rim	NV		112,000
297	South Reveille	NV		107,500
303	Fox Mountain Range	NV		105,000
321	Cherry Creek Mts	NV		101,000
334	Dry Valley Rim	NV	CA	100,000
84	High Peaks	NY		336,000
90	West Canada Lake	NY		316,000
147	Five Ponds	NY		203,000
227	Siamese Pond	NY		141,000
228	Silver Lake	NY		141,000
272	Wilcox Lake	NY		120,000
340	Ha-de-ron-dah	NY		89,000
347	Blue Ridge	NY		75,000
348	Ferris Lake	NY		75,000
352	Pigeon Lake	NY		62,000
353	Hoffman Notch	NY		61,000
363	Pharoah Lake	NY		52,000
364	Slide Mountain	NY		52,000
39	Hells Canyon	OR	ID	591,000
53	Eagle Cap	OR		452,000
56	Three Sisters	OR		424,000
61	Kalmiopsis	OR	CA	408,000
74	Alvord Desert	OR		361,000
126	Sheepshead Mountains	OR		232,000
141	Trout Creek Mountains	OR	NV	212,000
159	Mount Jefferson	OR		191,000
163	Myotis	OR		190,000
188	Sky Lakes	OR		166,000
199	Basque Hills	OR		159,000
222	Hawksie-Walksie	OR	NV	144,000

226	Diablo Mountain	OR		142,000
304	Mount Thielsen	OR		105,000
307	Catlow Rim	OR		104,000
259	Badlands South	SD		125,000
313	Sage Creek	SD		102,000
19	Lower Canyons RG	TX	MX	890,000
29	Dead Horse Mountains	TX	MX	720,000
45	Mariscal-Santa Elena	TX	MX	483,000
133	Solitario	TX		225,000
170	Chisos Mountains	TX		186,000
296	Padre Island	TX		108,000
15	S Gr. Salt Lake Desert	UT	NV	1,144,000
21	N Gr. Salt Lake Desert	UT		850,000
22	High Uintas	UT		843,000
23	Canyonlands	UT		805,000
24	Desolation Canyon	UT		763,000
36	Escalante	UT		620,000
58	Dirty Devil	UT		413,000
70	San Juan River	UT		371,000
72	Wahweap	UT		367,000
76	Kaiparowits	UT		360,000
91	Book Cliffs	UT		300,000
119	Muddy Creek	UT		242,000
158	Mancos Mesa	UT		193,000
167	Wayne Wonderland	UT		188,000
168	Wilson Mesa	UT		188,000
171	Paria-Hackberry	UT		186,000
178	Deep Creek Mountains	UT		179,000
182	Steep Creek-Oak Ck	UT		173,000
186	Mt. Pennel	UT		170,000
219	Little Rockies	UT		145,000
234	Parunuweap	UT	AZ	137,000
248	Mt. Ellen	UT		128,000
260	Pine Valley Mts	UT		125,000
264	Salt Creek	UT		124,000
282	Lakes	UT		112,000
291	Boulder Mountain	UT		110,000
322	Sid's Mountain	UT		101,000
335	Casto-Table	UT		100,000
336	Zion	UT		100,000
314	Great Dismal Swamp	VA	NC	102,000
367	Meachum Swamp	VT		50,000
10	Glacier Peak	WA		1,607,000
11	Pasayten	WA	CAN	1,191,000
16	Olympic Mountains	WA		1,060,000
26	Mt. Baker	WA	CAN	742,000
49	Alpine Lakes	WA		464,000
124	Mt. Rainier	WA		233,000

136	Cougar Lakes	WA		219,000
151	Wenaha-Tucannon	WA	OR	200,000
156	Goat Rocks	WA		196,000
309	Mt. Adams	WA		103,000
343	Cranberry	WV		82,000
6	South Absaroka	WY		2,190,000
12	Wind River Range	WY		1,171,000
18	North Absaroka	WY		950,000
42	Gallatin Range	WY	MT	525,000
47	Bechler-Pitchstone	WY	ID	468,000
52	Gros Ventre	WY		455,000
54	Cloud Peak	WY		443,000
86	Teton Range	WY		334,000
115	Salt River Range	WY		250,000
123	Palisades	WY	ID	240,000
134	Grayback Ridge	WY		225,000
164	Commissary Ridge	WY		190,000
172	Central Plateau	WY		185,000
206	Little Bighorn	WY	MT	155,000
240	Deep Lake	WY	MT	135,000
261	Washburn Range	WY		125,000
283	Mt. Leidy	WY		112,000

APPENDIX C
Largest Roadless Areas in United States

By Robert Marshall and Althea Dobbins

The fight to save the wilderness has grown during the past ten years from the personal hobby of a few fanatics to an important, nation-wide movement. All over the country, people are beginning to protest in a concerted manner against the invasion of roadless tracts by routes of modern transportation. Encouragingly enough, a number of these protests have been heeded, and several splendid roadless areas have thus been saved. Others have been preserved by federal and state officials before any protest had to be launched. Yet others, unfortunately, have been invaded either because nobody happened to realize that invasion was imminent, or because no one was aware that there was a significant area to be saved.

The battle to protect the wilderness is a critical one. Definitely there have not been enough large roadless tracts safely reserved from invasions. There is important need to make a study at an early date concerning which officially designated roadless areas should be enlarged, and which areas on which official action has not been taken should be established.

As a step preliminary to such a study, it is necessary to know what are the potential roadless areas which still can be saved. With this objective in mind, we have made a rough analysis of all the forest areas in the United States, embracing 300,000 acres or more, which have not yet been invaded by routes of mechanized transportation. We have made a similar study of desert areas embracing 500,000 acres or more, under the assumption that a considerably larger area is needed in open country than in forest country to give one the feeling of the wilderness. The study of such areas was made from the accurate road maps for all National Forests, National Parks, and Indian Reservations, as kept by the federal bureaus administering these lands; from the excellent maps of the New

York State Conservation Department; from the most accurate available automobile maps; and from the knowledge of a number of people familiar with specific localities which are not well mapped. We wish to extend our appreciation to the following for their kind assistance: Lee Kneipp and Helen Smith of the U.S. Forest Service; H.S. Teller of the National Park Service; E.H. Coulson and J.P. Kinney of the Indian Service; Depue Falck of the Grazing Division of the Interior Department; and William G. Howard of the New York State Conservation Department. As this is only a preliminary study, we realize there will be a number of mistakes. This is especially true of the desert areas where existing road maps are unusually poor. We would greatly appreciate any corrections which the readers of this article can make.

In drawing the boundaries of our roadless areas, we placed the edge one-half mile back from all roads, under the assumption that this distance was necessary to isolate the more annoying influences of mechanization. Where a stub road penetrated into a wilderness area, we drew our boundaries half a mile back from the road on each side, thus in effect eliminating a finger reaching into such wilderness area for a width of approximately one mile.

In view of the fact that most people do not visualize areas in terms of acres, we would like to point out that 300,000 acres is not a roadless area in any pioneering sense. Actually, a 300,000 acre tract is only about 21 1/2 x 21 1/2 miles, something which a reasonably good walker could traverse readily in a day if there were a trail. A desert area of 500,000 acres is only 27 1/2 x 27 1/2 miles, across which even a poor horseman could ride in a day. Of course, most of these areas are not square, but are much attenuated, so that a 300,000 acre area might have the dimensions of approximately 47 miles by 10 miles, instead of 21 1/2 miles by 21 1/2 miles.

The following table and map indicate those forest areas in the United States of 300,000 acres of more and those desert areas of 500,000 acres or more which are not yet accessible to mechanized transportation.

FOREST AREAS

1. Arrostock-Alagash	Maine	2,800,000
2. Northern Cascade	Washington	2,800,000
3. Salmon River	Idaho	2,800,000
4. High Sierra	California	2,300,000
5. South Fork of Flathead	Montana	2,000,000
6. Selway	Idaho-Montana	2,000,000
7. Upper Yellowstone	Wyoming	2,000,000
8. Upper St. John	Maine	1,300,000
9. Olympic	Washington	1,200,000
10. Superior	Minnesota	1,200,000
11. Wind River Mountains	Wyoming	1,200,000
12. Beartooth	Montana-Wyoming	960,000
13. Absaroka Range	Wyoming	930,000
14. Siskiyou	Oregon	830,000
15. Sawtooth	Idaho	820,000
16. Sysladopsis	Maine	780,000
17. San Juan	Colorado	690,000
18. Umpqua	Oregon	640,000
19. North Yosemite	California	630,000
20. Dead River	Maine	600,000
21. High Uinta	Utah	580,000
22. East Grey River	Wyoming	560,000
23. Foss River	Washington	550,000
24. Gila	New Mexico	530,000
25. North Glacier	Montana	480,000
26. Marble Mountains	California	440,000
27. Moose River	New York	430,000
28. Bechlor River	Wyoming	420,000
29. Madison Range	Montana-Wyoming	430,000
30. South Fork of Salmon	Idaho	410,000
31. White River	Colorado	410,000
32. Salmon-Trinity Alps	California	410,000
33. Okefenokee	Georgia	400,000
34. South Yosemite	California	400,000
35. Mt. Marcy	New York	380,000
36. Cranberry-Beaver River	New York	380,000
37. Gros Ventre	Wyoming	370,000
38. Goat Rocks	Washington	370,000
39. South Glacier	Montana	340,000
40. Tonto Basin	Arizona	340,000
41. Wallowa	Oregon	330,000
42. Eagle Cap	Oregon	320,000
43. Electric Peak	Wyoming-Montana	320,000
44. Pintlar	Montana	320,000
45. Blue River	Arizona	310,000

46. Big Horn	Wyoming	310,000
47. Mission Range	Montana	310,000
48. Teton Range	Wyoming	300,000

DESERT AREAS

101. Colorado River	Utah-Arizona	8,890,000
102. Owyhee	Idaho-Ore.-Nevada	4,130,000
103. Grand Canyon	Arizona	4,000,000
104. Nevada Desert	Nevada	2,670,000
105. Book Cliffs	Utah-Colorado	2,420,000
106. North Mohave Desert	California	1,970,000
107. San Rafael Swells	Utah	1,930,000
108. Red Desert	Wyoming	1,900,000
109. Sevier Lake	Utah	1,900,000
110. Little Snake River	Wyoming-Colorado	1,800,000
111. Carrizozo Plains	New Mexico	1,800,000
112. North Salt Lake Desert	Utah	1,700,000
113. South Salt Lake Desert	Utah	1,600,000
114. South Mohave Desert	California	1,500,000
115. White Sands	New Mexico	1,200,000
116. Black Mesa	Arizona	1,200,000
117. West Mohave Desert	California	1,100,000
118. Painted Desert	Arizona	1,000,000
119. Guano Lake	Oregon-Nevada	980,000
120. East Mohave Desert	California	950,000
121. Harqua Hala Desert	Arizona	740,000
122. Bill Williams River	Arizona	700,000
123. Kingston Range	California-Nevada	650,000
124. Bruneau River	Idaho-Nevada	650,000
125. Cignus Peak	Arizona	620,000
126. South Pass	Wyoming	610,000
127. Salton Sea	California	610,000
128. Summer Lake	Oregon	540,000
129. Monument Butte	Wyoming	540,000

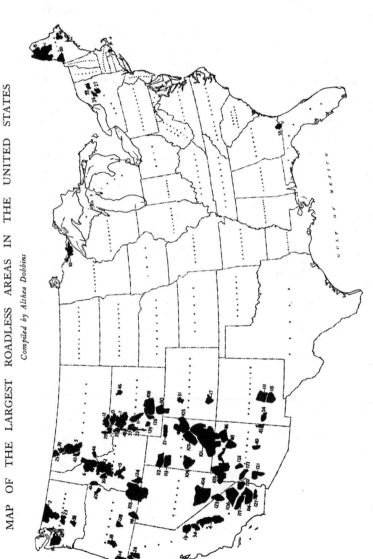

MAP OF THE LARGEST ROADLESS AREAS IN THE UNITED STATES

Compiled by Althea Dobbins

Showing 48 Forest Roadless Areas exceeding 300,000 acres and 29 Desert Roadless Areas exceeding 500,000 acres which are still inaccessible to mechanized transportation.

APPENDIX D
Bob Marshall's 1927 Roadless Area Inventory

1927

Area	Sections	Acres
Central Idaho	11,982	7,668,480
Northern Cascades	5,368	3,435,520
Central Sierra	4,541	2,906,240
Flathead	3,689	2,360,960
Northwestern Wyoming	2,285	1,462,400
Olympic	2,251	1,440,640
Columbia-Rainier	2,120	1,356,800
Gila	2,074	1,327,360
Seven Devils	1,881	1,203,840
Southern Cascade	1,861	1,191,040
South Yellowstone	1,782	1,140,480
Boise-Sawtooth	1,766	1,130,240
Northeastern Utah	1,733	1,109,120
Prescott-Tonto	1,729	1,106,560
Santa Barbara	1,715	1,097,600
Beartooth-Absaroka	1,522	974,080

Future

Area	Sections	Acres
Central Idaho	7,490	4,793,600
Central Sierra	3,673	2,350,720
Flathead	3,471	2,221,440
Northwestern Wyoming	2,285	1,462,400
St. Joe-Clearwater	2,189	1,400,960
South Yellowstone	1,755	1,123,200
Prescott-Tonto	1,729	1,106,560

Note: Areas listed under "1927" were the existing million acre roadless areas on the National Forests that Marshall roughly calculated at that time. Those listed under "Future" were presumably what would exist if Forest Service road-building plans at that time were carried out. Areas listed under "1927" but not under "Future" evidently would no longer exist as a million-plus acre roadless areas after such development. Marshall listed these areas by number of sections roadless. We've calculated the acreage. This information was found on a hand-lettered card in the Robert Marshall papers at the Bancroft Library, University of California, Berkeley.

APPENDIX E
Conservation Groups

There is a broad spectrum of organizations working for the preservation of wilderness and natural diversity in the United States. These groups use an array of tools and tactics in defense of ecological integrity which include: land purchase and management; Congressional lobbying; development of Wilderness proposals; filing of appeals and lawsuits; influencing federal and state land management; public education, economic analysis and scientific research supporting the need for nature preserves; public demonstrations; civil disobedience and ecotage (monkeywrenching). We feel that all of these approaches are legitimate and proper depending on the circumstances. Just as diversity is important in ecosystems, so it is important in social change movements. No one group, no one set of tactics is adequate for halting the headlong destruction of natural diversity now occurring. Concerned individuals should choose the group(s) with which they feel most comfortable. Today, during the white-hot crisis of eco-catastrophe, where one-third of all species may become extinct during the next two or three decades, there is no time for complacency or armchair conservation. All who value "wild things and sunsets" must act now — whether by writing letters or pulling up survey stakes. Involvement with one or several of the following organizations is a good way to resist the industrial destruction of the wild, although many individuals have fought the good fight for natural diversity on their own.

We list below only those groups devoting significant energy to wilderness and natural diversity issues in the lower 48 states. State chapters or regional offices for the national groups can be contacted through the national addresses given. Listing of these groups does not necessarily mean they agree with the views expressed by the authors in this book, nor does it mean that the authors entirely agree with the positions or approaches taken by the individual groups. In certain cases, we believe these groups need to take a more hard-line, less compromised stand on wilderness and natural diversity issues. Nonetheless, we include them in our listing in the hope that concerned activists who are willing to courageously promote the protection of *all* that remains wild (and then some) will become involved with and strengthen some of these groups.

National Groups

The Wilderness Society, 1400 Eye St., Washington, DC, 20005 (202-842-3400). The Wilderness Society is the only national group focusing entirely on wilderness and public lands issues in the United States. Regional offices cover all sections of the US.

The Sierra Club, 730 Polk St., San Francisco, CA 94109 (415)776-2211. Although the Sierra Club covers many environmental issues, it directs considerable attention to wilderness issues. Local Sierra Club chapters and groups are active in all parts of the United States and Canada.

The Nature Conservancy, 1800 North Kent St., Arlington, VA 22209 (703)841-5300. The major approach of The Nature Conservancy's headquarters office, field offices and state chapters is the purchase and management of ecologically sensitive areas.

Earth First!, PO Box 5871, Tucson, AZ 85703 (602)622-1371. Earth First! has many autonomous groups and task forces throughout the United States. *The Earth First! Journal* (address above) covers no-compromise environmentalism and biocentric wilderness preservation.

Society for Conservation Biology, c/o Blackwell Scientific Publi-cations, Three Cambridge Center, Suite 208, Cambridge, MA 02142. The Society for Conservation Biology is primarily made up of profes-sional ecologists concerned with the preservation of natural diversity.

National Audubon Society, 950 Third Ave., NY, NY 10022 (212-832-3200). Some local Audubon chapters work on wilderness and natural diversity issues; Endangered, Threatened and rare species are a general priority.

Defenders of Wildlife, 1244 Nineteenth St, NW, Washington, DC 20036. The national staff and field representatives work on Endangered species and habitat.

American Rivers, 801 Pennsylvania Ave, SE, Suite 303, Washing-ton, DC 20003 (202-547-6900). The only national group focusing on Wild & Scenic River preservation.

Arizona

Arizona Wilderness Coalition, PO Box 60576, Phoenix, AZ 85082. Coordinates wilderness and wild river preservation efforts in Arizona.

California

California Wilderness Coalition, 2655 Portage Bay East, Suite 5, Davis, CA 95616 (916)758-0380. Coordinates wilderness preservation efforts in California.

Friends of the River, Bldg. C, Fort Mason Center, San Francisco, CA 94123 (415)771-0400. Works for wild river and watershed protection in California.

California Desert Protection League, 3550 West Sixth St, Suite 323, Los Angeles, CA 90020. Coordinates wilderness preservation ef-forts in the California Desert.

Colorado

Colorado Environmental Coalition, 777 Grant St., Suite 606, Den-ver, CO 80203 (303-837-8701). Coordinates wilderness preservation efforts in Colorado.

Eastern States

Preserve Appalachian Wilderness (PAW), POB 36, Jefferson, NH 03583 (603-586-4432). A grassroots group working for wilderness restoration, wildlife reintroductions and large wilderness preserves in the East.

Idaho

Committee for Idaho's High Desert, PO Box 463, Boise, ID 83701. Coordinates wilderness preservation efforts for Idaho's BLM lands.

Idaho Conservation League, PO Box 844, Boise, ID 83701 (208-345-6933). Coordinates wilderness preservation efforts in Idaho.

Minnesota

Friends of the Boundary Waters Wilderness, 1313 Fifth St. SE, Suite 329, Minneapolis, MN 55414 (612-379-3835). The watchdog group for the Boundary Waters and other northern Minnesota wildernesses.

Montana

Alliance for the Wild Rockies, Box 8731, Missoula, MT 59807 (406-721-3621/549-0882). A new group fighting for the preservation of all roadless areas in the Northern Rockies of Montana, Idaho, Wyoming and Canada.

Montana Wilderness Association, Box 635, Helena, MT 59624. Coordinates wilderness preservation efforts in Montana.

Nevada

Friends of Nevada Wilderness, PO Box 8096, Reno, NV 89507 (702-322-2867). Coordinates National Forest wilderness preservation efforts in Nevada.

Nevada Outdoor Recreation Association, PO Box 1245, Carson City, NV 89702 (702-883-1169). Works on BLM wilderness issues in Nevada and throughout the United States.

New Mexico

New Mexico BLM Wilderness Coalition, PO Box 712, Placitas, NM 87043 (505)867-3062). Coordinates BLM wilderness preservation efforts in New Mexico.

New Mexico Wilderness Study Committee, 1409 Gold Ave SW, Albuquerque, NM 87104. Coordinates National Forest wilderness preservation efforts in New Mexico.

Oregon

Oregon Natural Resources Council, 1050 Yeon Bldg, 522 SW 5th Ave, Portland, OR 97204 (503)223-9001. Coordinates wilderness preservation efforts in Oregon.

Texas

Texas Committee on Natural Resources, 4144 Cochran Chapel Road, Dallas, TX 75209 (214-352-8370). Coordinates wilderness preservation efforts in Texas.

Utah

Southern Utah Wilderness Alliance (SUWA), Box 518, Cedar City, UT 84720 (801)586-8242. Focuses on the Canyon Country of southern Utah.

Utah Wilderness Coalition, PO Box 11446, Salt Lake City, UT 84147. Represents the Sierra Club, Wilderness Society, SUWA and many other groups on wilderness issues in Utah.

Utah Wilderness Association, 455 East 400 South #306, Salt Lake City, UT 84111 (801-359-1337). An independent wilderness group in Utah.

Washington
  Washington Wilderness Coalition, PO Box 45187, Seattle, WA 98145
(206-633-1992). Coordinates Washington wilderness preservation efforts.
Wyoming
    Wyoming Wildlife Federation, Box 106, Cheyenne, WY 82003. Not
just a hunter group, WWF has also been active recently in efforts to
protect public lands from various agency-sponsored development
schemes.
    Greater Yellowstone Coalition, Box 1874, Bozeman, MT 59715.
Monitors land use and coordinates various efforts to protect the Greater
Yellowstone Ecosystem of northwestern Wyoming, southwestern Montana and extreme eastern Idaho.

APPENDIX F
Further Reading

    The history and the current issues of wilderness preservation are
covered in many periodicals and books. The following are the most important in our opinion.

Periodicals
    To keep up-to-date on threats to large roadless areas and on ef-
forts to preserve them, the reader is encouraged to regularly consult the
newsletters, magazines and newspapers published by local and
national wilderness preservation groups.
    Regular newsletters and alerts are produced by virtually all state
and local wilderness groups; by Sierra Club, Nature Conservancy and
Audubon Society state chapters; and by local Earth First! groups. Their
addresses are listed in Appendix E. These are the best sources for the
activist interested in a particular region.
    The Earth First! Journal is unique in covering the news of direct ac-
tion environmentalism, articulating provocative biocentric arguments for
preserving natural diversity, and presenting visionary proposals for the
preservation of ecological wilderness.
    The periodicals of other national conservation groups are good
sources of information. Wilderness, published by The Wilderness
Society, is far and way the best full-color, glossy magazine dealing with
wilderness issues. TWS also publishes an informative newsletter for
National Forest activists, and a variety of reports on specific issues.
The Sierra Club publishes a general interest glossy magazine, Sierra,
and several useful newsletters, including the National News Report, a
biweekly summary of conservation news heavy on the Congressional

scene, and *Public Lands*, from the volunteers on the Public Lands Committee. The National Audubon Society's magazine, *Audubon*, is internationally known for its stunning wildlife photos, but it also includes some surprisingly good reports on natural diversity issues. Also valuable is the *Audubon Activist*, an excellent issues-oriented newsletter from the national office. *The Nature Conservancy Magazine* does a fine job of reporting on that organization's efforts to acquire crucial natural habitats. *Defenders*, from Defenders of Wildlife, is outstanding for its coverage of wildlife issues.

General outdoor magazines, such as *Backpacker, Canoe* and *Outside*, sometimes have information on threatened wildlands. One might even periodically browse through the innumerable cheap dirt bike, ORV and snowmobile magazines available in drug stores to see what they are up to.

For those concerned with wild places in the Rocky Mountain states, *High Country News* (Box 1090, Paonia, CO 81428) is a good news source.

Conservation Biology, published by the Society for Conservation Biology, is somewhat technical but is indispensable for keeping up with the latest scientific arguments for natural area preservation. *Natural History* (Central Park West at 79th St, NY, NY 10024) frequently has articles of import for conservationists working on natural diversity issues.

See Appendix E for addresses.

Books

A tantalizing buffet of books covers the history, issues and arguments of and for wilderness preservation. The best source for conservation books is the Earth First! Bookstore in the back pages of *The Earth First! Journal*. Nearly one hundred titles pertaining to various aspects of nature preservation, including many titles otherwise hard to find, are available there for mail order purchase. These books are selected and commented on by one of the authors of this book, Dave Foreman. Write PO Box 5871, Tucson, AZ 85703 for a sample issue of *Earth First!*. Most of the books mentioned below are available through the Earth First! Bookstore.

For the general history of wilderness preservation, two books are essential. Roderick Nash's **Wilderness and the American Mind** (Third Edition, Yale University Press 1982) is the classic study of the development of American attitudes toward wild nature. It also has a wealth of information on the history of efforts to preserve wilderness and the arguments advanced by preservationists. **The Battle for the Wilderness** (Westview Encore Reprint, 1984) is the definitive study of the wilderness preservation movement by the premier environmental journalist of our time, Michael Frome. It also articulates a variety of arguments for wilderness preservation. For the recent history of wilderness preservation, **The Wilderness Movement and the National Forests: 1964-1980** (Forest History series, FS 391, 1984) by Dennis M. Roth is the best source available. **Endangered**

Rivers and the Conservation Movement (University of California Press, 1986) by Tim Palmer is the basic work on the history of wild river preservation. Howie Wolke's **Wilderness on the Rocks** (Ned Ludd Books, available late 1989) is a critical analysis of the failure of the wilderness preservation movement, and a well-reasoned argument for the need for a broader effort to protect wilderness as a biological entity.

Several excellent general conservation histories and biographies of John Muir, Aldo Leopold and Bob Marshall are available through the Earth First! Bookstore.

For a quick yet thorough grounding in the ecological arguments for large nature preserves, see **On the Brink of Extinction: Conserving the Diversity of Life** (Worldwatch, 1987) by Edward C. Wolf. The Wilderness Society and Ecological Society of America have prepared a booklet essential for all forest activists, **Conserving Biological Diversity in our National Forests**. It is available from The Wilderness Society. For those interested in delving more deeply into the literature of conservation biology, **Conservation Biology: An Evolutionary-Ecological Perspective** (Sinauer Associates, 1980) edited by Michael Soule and Bruce Wilcox, and **Conservation Biology: The Science of Scarcity and Diversity** (Sinauer Associates, 1986) edited by Michael Soule are highly recommended.

For general studies of the destruction of the land since the dawn of agriculture, it is hard to beat **Deserts on the March** (University of Oklahoma Press, 1935, revised 1959) by Paul B. Sears, and **Topsoil and Civilization** (University of Oklahoma Press, 1955, revised 1974) by Vernon Gill Carter and Tom Dale. More recently, William R. Catton's **Overshoot** makes a convincing but disturbing case for humans overshooting the carrying capacity of Earth. It is mandatory reading for those concerned about the health of our planet.

The best source for information on Forest Service road-building is *Save Our National Forests: A Citizens' Primer to Stop US Forest Service Destruction,* a tabloid written by Howie Wolke for Earth First! (available free). Earth First! plans to soon publish a tabloid on the biological impacts of roads.

For the effects of logging and the value of old growth forests, see Wolke's tabloid. **Timber and the Forest Service** (University Press of Kansas, 1987) by David A. Clary is a penetrating study of how the timber industry captured the Forest Service. The Wilderness Society has published several excellent reports on old growth forests and Forest Service logging practices. **Secrets of the Old Growth Forest** (Peregrine Smith Books, 1988) by David Kelly with color photographs by Gary Braasch is a lovely and informative argument for preserving the Pacific Coast ancient forest. Legendary Texas conservationist, Edward C. Fritz, excoriates FS clearcutting in **Sterile Forest: The Case Against Clearcutting** (Eakin Press, 1983).

Sacred Cows at the Public Trough (Maverick Publications, 1983) by Denzel and Nancy Ferguson, and *Save Our Public Lands*, a tabloid by Lynn Jacobs are the basic texts on public lands livestock grazing. **Sacred Cows** may be out of print, but Jacobs' informative tabloid is available free from PO Box 5784, Tucson, AZ 85703. Jacobs is currently at work on a book about grazing for R.E. Miles Publishers.

William K. Wyant devotes several chapters in **Westward In Eden: The Public Lands and the Conservation Movement** (University of California Press, 1982) to mining and energy extraction on the public lands. His is a readable but authoritative account of the exploitation of the public lands by special economic interests. Jeff Radford, a former public relations man for the BLM, tells the truth about federal coal leasing in **The Chaco Coal Scandal** (Rhombus, 1986).

There are several excellent books dealing with the damming of America's wild rivers (in addition to the aforementioned **Endangered Rivers** by Palmer). Marc Reisner creates one of the best conservation histories with his **Cadillac Desert: The American West and its Disappearing Water** (Penguin, 1986), an anecdotal, accurate and thorough history of the Corps of Engineers, Bureau of Reclamation and others who have built dams, irrigation canals, levees and those who have profited from them. Donald Worster, one of the best environmental historians, gives us in **Rivers of Empire: Water, Aridity & the Growth of the American West** (Pantheon, 1985) the same story as **Cadillac Desert**, but weaves an intriguing and convincing theory of history (hydraulic civilization) through it.

Peter Matthiessen's **Wildlife In America** is an American classic. It discusses how we have laid waste to the original non-human inhabitants of this continent. It is fortunately back in print in a somewhat updated version. Farley Mowat, in his no-holds-bared style, tells the story of wildlife destruction in New England, the Gulf of St. Lawrence and Newfoundland in **Sea of Slaughter** (Atlantic Monthly Press, 1984). David Brown discusses the destruction of wolf, **The Wolf in the Southwest: The Making of an Endangered Species** (University of Arizona Press, 1983), and Grizzly, **The Grizzly in the Southwest: Documentary of an Extinction** (University of Oklahoma Press, 1985) in the Southwestern states. *The Independent Grizzly Bear Report*, a 16 page tabloid by bear expert Doug Peacock, is crammed with information on the Great Bear and its plight (free from Earth First!).

Alfred W. Crosby offers a brilliant and original view of history and ecology with **Ecological Imperialism: The Biological Expansion of Europe, 900 - 1900** (Cambridge University Press, 1986). It is difficult to properly understand either the so-called "Age of Exploration" and resulting European imperialism or the invasion of exotic plants and animals and the displacement of natives without taking Crosby's thesis into account.

Michael Frome consistently reminds us of the reality that designating an area as Wilderness does not necessarily save it. He edits

Issues in Wilderness Management (Westview Press, 1985), the result of the First National Wilderness Management Workshop. **Wilderness Management** (US Forest Service, 1978) by John C. Hendee, George H. Stankey and Robert C. Lucas is the basic source for students of wilderness management. In his classic, **Desert Solitaire** (various editions), Edward Abbey takes on industrial tourism and National Park mismanagement, a theme he returns to in his later non-fiction works.

Last Stand of the Red Spruce (Island Press, 1987) by Robert A. Mello dissects acid rain and its effects on pristine areas.

The arguments for preserving wild nature for its own sake are developed in **The Arrogance of Humanism** (Oxford University Press, 1978) by ecologist David Ehrenfeld, in **Deep Ecology** (Peregrine Smith Books, 1985) by Bill Devall and George Sessions, in any of Abbey's books, and in several books published in the last year (see Earth First! Bookstore for titles and information). Of course, Aldo Leopold's **A Sand County Almanac** (various editions) remains the most important book on conservation. Everyone interested in wilderness and natural diversity should read it.

American Geographic Publishing (Box 5630, Helena, MT 59604) publishes an excellent line of wilderness books featuring striking full-color photographs and well-researched text. Wilderness author George Wuerthner has several books with them. **Utah Wildlands** by Stewart Aitchison (Utah Geographic Publishing, Box 8325, Salt Lake City, UT 84108) is a superb book on the wilderness issues of that state.

APPENDIX G
A Note on the Research

Research sources for **The Big Outside** fall into several categories:

People

A number of knowledgeable individuals assisted us in our inventory, and reviewed various parts of our data as well as drafts of the text. Ron Kezar and Bart Koehler were enthusiastic about the project from the beginning and offered us their coast to coast expertise on American Wilderness. Michael Frome, the dean of American environmental journalists and one of the living experts on North American wilderness, not only graciously contributed his Foreword to the book, but also reviewed the text for accuracy and clarity. We are grateful to Mike not only for his support of this project, but for his continuing inspiration and encouragement. Jasper Carlton of the Earth First! Biodiversity Task Force also reviewed the entire text.

A handful of local wilderness experts significantly assisted us with their particular states. They are Saguaro Sam and Dale Turner (Arizona), Mark Pearson (Colorado), Kevin Proescholdt (Minnesota), Michael Kellett (Michigan), Jamie Sayen (New England), Janine Stuchin and Bill Pearson (New York), Shaaron Netherton (Nevada), Ric Bailey (Oregon and Washington) and Clive Kincaid (Utah). Each of these folks put in hours of work on the inventory. The book would have been far more difficult for us without their eager assistance. The accuracy of it would have suffered as well.

Many other wilderness experts provided additional information and comments for their regions: ARIZONA — Jim Notestine, Bob Lippman and Don Lyngholm; CALIFORNIA — Jim Eaton, Garth Harwood, Nancy Morton, Judy Anderson, Rod Mondt, Sally Miller, Roland Knapp, Pamela Bell and Bill Devall; COLORADO — Tony Povilitis and Reed Noss; IDAHO — Randy Morris, George Wuerthner, Tom Robinson and Scott Ploger; MONTANA — Randal Gloege, George Wuerthner and Bill Cunningham; MIDWEST — Jan Green, Jim dale Vickery; NEVADA — Rose Strickland, Sally Kabisch, Ron Kezar and Charles Watson, Jr.; NEW ENGLAND — Michael Kellett, Mark Shepard and George Wuerthner; NEW MEXICO — Big Don Schwarzennegger, Angie Berger, Jim Norton, Steve Marlatt, Bob Tafanelli, Kelly Cranston and Ron Mitchell; NEW YORK — George Wuerthner and Bart Koehler; OREGON — Don Tryon, Andy Kerr, Kate Crockett and George Wuerthner; SOUTH — Ernie Dickerman, R.F. Mueller, Reed Noss, Bob Zahner, David Wheeler, Dale Jackson, Ray Payne and Nancy Jo Craig; UTAH — Rodney Greeno, Fred Swanson, Elliott Bernshaw and Stewart Aitchison; WASHINGTON — Mitch Friedman, Ed Grumbine, Karen Coulter, Rick Johnson and Larry Svart; WYOMING — Bart Koehler and Keith Becker. Ken Lay, Orrie Amnos and Hermann Bruns helped us with roadless areas in British Columbia contiguous to those in Washington and Montana.

Our mates, Nancy Morton and Marilyn Olsen, encouraged us in this seemingly unending task and put up with bushels of maps and government documents cluttering our homes. We appreciate their support and patience. Kris Sommerville and Nancy Zierenberg in the *Earth First! Journal* office in Tucson made it possible for Dave Foreman to devote enough time to this project to finally finish it. They are two unsung heroines of the battle to protect wilderness.

John Davis, Editor of *The Earth First! Journal,* applied his peerless wordsmithing skill to help us hammer a mass of data into a readable book. We particularly appreciate John's tireless and enthusiastic work on this project. Dale Turner, Associate Editor of *The Earth First! Journal*, reviewed the text and offered valuable editorial suggestions. He, Nancy Morton, Jim Eaton and Kris Sommerville helped Dave Foreman through numerous befuddlements in using the computer and laser printer to lay out and typeset the text. Helen Wilson applied her fine cartographic talent to draft the final maps for the book from base maps produced by the authors. Thanks, Helen, the hours you put in are much appreciated. Kelly Cranston helped Helen in the final rush to get the maps ready to be sent to press. George Wuerthner and Kevin Proescholdt provided photos for areas the authors did not have pho-

tographs of. Dark Room Images in Tucson did a special job of trans-
forming color slides to black and white prints. Charles Withuhn, of Signs
and Graphic Designs, in Chico, California, created the cover and the
chapter headings in the inventory section. Ed Caldwell and his staff at
Ed's Printing in Chico, California, did the dirty work with ink and printing
presses to print the book.

We sincerely thank all of these friends for their assistance in pro-
ducing **The Big Outside.** They have contributed greatly to the accuracy and comprehensiveness of the book.[*]   This is not to imply that any
of these people necessarily agree with our comments or recommendations, or that they bear any responsibility for oversights, mistakes,
omissions or other errors. That responsibility rests entirely with the
authors.

The Big Outside is an ongoing project. We hope to produce a
Second Edition within two years based on what we hope will be an out-
pouring of additional information on large roadless areas in the United
States from readers of this book. New or corrected information on areas
in this book, updates on the status of areas, and information about
qualifying areas not in this book, should be sent to Dave Foreman, Ned
Ludd Books, POB 5141, Tucson, AZ 85703.

Maps

Maps of various sorts were a crucial part of our research. We each
spent countless hours pouring over them, drawing lines, counting
square miles and doing our damnedest to determine what was roadless.
The primary maps we used were Class A National Forest maps
(generally half inch to the mile scale); NF Wilderness Area maps; Forest
Plan roadless inventory maps; 1:100,000 scale BLM surface management status or 1:100,000 USGS topographic maps; various Forest Service, BLM, Park Service and Fish & Wildlife Service maps illustrating
their Wilderness Review programs and management units; and standard
USGS topo maps of 1:24,000 or 1:62,500 scale.

Government Documents

We consulted a large number of government documents, including
National Park Service Wilderness Study Reports, Environmental Impact
Statements, and Master Plans; US Fish & Wildlife Service Wilderness
Study Reports, Environmental Impact Statements and Master Plans;
US Forest Service RARE I and RARE II (& RARE III!) reports, individual
Unit and Forest Plans, Environmental Impact Statements, and Primitive
Area Study reports; BLM documents covering all phases of their Wilder-
ness Review program, as well as Land Use Plans and EISs; manage-
ment plans for military ranges; State of Michigan, New York and Califor-

---

[*] Due to the length of time this project has taken, we've probably
neglected to mention a few folks who helped. For that we apologize.

nia maps & documents on their state wilderness systems; and brochures, pamphlets, maps and reports from a variety of agencies on specific Wilderness Areas, other management units, Endangered and Threatened Species, and Biological Diversity.

Conservation Group Materials

We extracted information from numerous brochures, fliers, reports, testimonies, proposals, maps, newsletters and magazines from the Sierra Club and its state chapters, The Wilderness Society, National Audubon Society, Nature Conservancy, American Rivers, Arizona Wilderness Coalition, California Wilderness Coalition, Friends of the River, California Desert Protection League, Colorado Environmental Coalition, Idaho Conservation League, Committee for Idaho's High Desert, Friends of the Boundary Waters Wilderness, Montana Wilderness Association, Friends of Nevada Wilderness, Nevada Outdoor Recreation Association, New Mexico BLM Coalition, New Mexico Wilderness Study Committee, Oregon Natural Resources Council, Southern Utah Wilderness Alliance, Utah Wilderness Association, Utah Wilderness Coalition, the Western Canada Wilderness Committee, Wyoming Wilderness Association and others. We also utilized information from local Earth First! groups across the country. Of particular value were Earth First! statewide or bioregional wilderness proposals (these are about the only all-inclusive proposals that have been produced to date).

Listing of any group here does not constitute their endorsement of this project or our viewpoint.

Field Guides and Other Sources

We consulted a variety of standard field guides for birds, mammals, trees, etc. to double check species listings from other sources.

Wilderness books on Idaho, Montana, Wyoming, Oregon, New York, etc. published by American Geographic Publishing (many by George Wuerthner) and **Utah Wildlands** by Stewart Aitchison were consulted, as was information from Jasper Carlton of the Earth First! Biodiversity Task Force.

HELP!

The Big Outside is an ongoing project. We hope to publish a revised, updated Second Edition by 1991. Please send information on additional areas, as well as corrections, revisions, additional information and updates on status of areas included in this edition. We would like to include roadless areas of 50,000 acres and larger in Hawaii in the Second Edition also. Any assistance would be appreciated. Send all material to Dave Foreman, Ned Ludd Books, POB 5141, Tucson, AZ 85703. Thank you!

ABOUT THE AUTHORS

Dave Foreman has spent the last eighteen years of his life as a professional conservationist. During the 1970s he worked for The Wilderness Society as their Southwest Regional Representative and later as their lobbying coordinator in Washington, DC, but left in 1980 to co-found a more militant preservation group -- Earth First!. From 1981 to 1988 he was editor and publisher of *The Earth First! Journal*. He has worked on administrative programs like the Forest Service's RARE I and RARE II, and on legislation like the Endangered American Wilderness Act and New Mexico Wilderness Act. He is the co-editor and publisher of **Ecodefense: A Field Guide to Monkeywrenching.** Foreman was born in New Mexico in 1946 of pioneer stock and is a former professional horseshoer and mule packer. He currently owns and operates Ned Ludd Books, and also has a busy speaking schedule on college campuses and at conservation conventions. He is married to a cardiac care nurse and university instructor, Nancy Morton. They have no children, and spend their time in the wilderness river running, canoeing, backpacking, birdwatching, cross-country skiing, flyfishing and snorkeling.

Howie Wolke is a professional wilderness guide, writer, bow-hunter, cross-country skier, and longtime wilderness proponent. He is widely recognized as one of the top wilderness/public lands experts in the country, and since the mid-1970s has worked as a lobbyist, organizer, spokesman and board member for various conservation groups, including Friends of the Earth and the Wyoming Wilderness Association. He is a cofounder of Earth First!, and, in 1986, he spent six months in jail after pleading "guilty" to the "crime" of de-surveying a destructive road that was later bulldozed into Wyoming's Grayback Ridge roadless area.

Although Wolke was a leader in the Wyoming conservation community during the Forest Service's disastrous RARE II process during the late '70s, he later renounced the compromises made by environmental leaders during that period. Wolke is author of *Save Our National Forests: A Citizens' Primer to Stop US Forest Service Destruction* and has recently completed **Wilderness on the Rocks**, a book-length critique of the wilder-